CORRUPTION, GREED AND CRIME MONEY:

SLEAZE AND SHADY ECONOMY

IN EUROPE AND BEYOND

CORRUPTION, GREED AND CRIME MONEY:

SLEAZE AND SHADY ECONOMY

IN EUROPE AND BEYOND

Petrus C. van Duyne
Jackie Harvey
Georgios A. Antonopoulos
Klaus von Lampe
Almir Maljević
Anna Markovska
(eds.)

Corruption, greed and crime-money. Sleaze and shady economy in Europe and beyond

Petrus C. van Duyne, Jackie Harvey, Georgios A. Antonopoulos, Klaus von Lampe, Almir Maljević, Anna Markovska (eds.)

ISBN: 978-94-6240-128-0

This volume contains a selection of peer reviewed papers based on the presentations of the authors at the fourteenth Crossborder Crime Colloquium, hosted 12-14 May 2013 by Anglia Ruskin University, Cambridge.

This project was supported by Tilburg University (the Netherlands)

The Cross-Border Crime Colloquium is an annual event since 1999. It brings together experts on international organised (economic) crime to discuss the latest developments in empirical research, legislation and law enforcement, with a special geographical focus on Western, Central, and Eastern Europe.

The Colloquia aim at building bridges in three respects: between East and West Europe, between scholars and practitioners, and between old and young. The Cross-border Crime Colloquium, so far, has been organised fourteen times:

2013 Cambridge, UK
2012 Manchester, UK
2011 Tilburg, the Netherlands
2009 Gent, Belgium
2008 Belgrade, Serbia
2007 Prague, Czech Republic
2006 Tallinn, Estonia
2005 Sarajevo, Bosnia and Herzegovina
2004 Berlin, Germany
2003 Ainring, Germany
2002 Ljubljana, Slovenia
2001 Bratislava, Slovakia
2000 Budapest, Hungary
1999 Prague, Czech Republic

Copies can be ordered at:

Wolf Legal Publishers (WLP)
P.O. Box 313
5060 AH Oisterwijk
The Netherlands
www.wolfpublishers.com
E-Mail: sales@wolfpublishers.nl

Table of contents

List of authors

Georgios A. Antonopoulos
Teesside University, UK

John Bae
John Jay College of Criminal Justice, New York, USA

Nicholas Dorn
Formerly of Erasmus School of Law, The Netherlands

Petrus C. van Duyne
Tilburg University, The Netherlands and Manchester University, UK (emeritus)

Steve Hall
Teesside University, UK

Jackie Harvey
Northumbria University, UK

Michael Hutchinson
Northumbria University, UK

Daniela Irrera
University of Catania, Italy

Matjaž Jager
Institute of Criminology at the Faculty of Law, University of Ljubljana, Slovenia

Ciril Keršmanc
Institute of Criminology at the Faculty of Law, University of Ljubljana, Slovenia

François H.G. Kristen
Utrecht University, The Netherlands

Marin Kurti
Rutgers School of Criminal Justice, Newark, New Jersey, USA

Klaus von Lampe
John Jay College of Criminal Justice, New York, USA

Anita Lavorgna
University of Trento, Italy

Anna Markovska
Anglia Ruskin University, Cambridge, UK

Radu Nicolae
Centre for Legal Resources, Romania

Adam Peacock
Northumbria University, UK

Anna Di Ronco
Department of Penal Law and Criminology, Ghent University, Belgium

Mihaela Sandulescu
USI-University of Lugano, Switzerland

Miroslav Scheinost
Institute of Criminology and Social Prevention, Czech Republic

Alexey Serdyuk
National University of Internal Affairs, Kharkiv, Ukraine

Anna Sergi
University of Essex, UK

Jon Spencer
Criminological Research Unit, University of Manchester, UK

Katja Šugman Stubbs
Faculty of Law, University of Ljubljana, Slovenia

Wouter de Zanger
Utrecht University, The Netherlands

Marija Zurnić
Nottingham University, UK

Greed: the deadly sin as red thread
An introduction

Petrus C. van Duyne

Greed: a brute drive

According to Catholic dogma there are seven deadly sins. The sixth one on the list is *greed*: the desire for material wealth or gain, ignoring the realm of the spiritual. The last sentence part can be considered as an aggravating condition. Such a serious sin deserved an appropriate punishment, if not during the earthly existence, then certainly in hell: being boiled in oil. It is not just a 'self-centred' sin, but one with serious social implications, because according to Thomas Aquinas "it is a sin directly against one's neighbour, since one man cannot over-abound in external riches, without another man lacking them." This places greed in a harmful relationship with the social surrounding. Greed causes harm because being covetous of wealth may be at the expense of the fellow man.

This sounds all very edifying. However, even if greed is a sin, bad enough to be cooked in oil in the afterlife, it is not a crime. As a matter of fact it is an elementary driving force. In Freud's conceptual framework it is a 'lust', though subordinate to the sexual lust as the most elementary driving force of life. It is interesting to speculate about their similarities, differences and interdependent relationship. Sexual lust has its enjoying and disappointing variations: it can peak, decline, flame up and eventually wither, often together with the relationship in which it usually functions. Its uncertainty in fulfilment, disappointment, attraction and rejection is an inexhaustible source of drama, art as well as a sustainable income of sex-workers, therapists and illegal Viagra sellers, to name just a few benefiting service providers.

How different is the lust of greed. It has no glowing romance and is depicted in art as a low, mean trait. If it is the subject of drama, it is one of betrayal and (self or mutual) destruction as in the *Nibelungen-song* or *The Good, the Bad and the Ugly*, just to name two greed centred dramas two millennia apart. Greed has no 'friends' and is not served by a (surrogate) satisfaction service industry. Apart from the speculation that it can function as a compensation for the unfulfilled sex drive, and apart from all morality, it is a self-centred drive without the vicissitudes in the life history of sexuality and the uncertainties of potency. There is no 'greed Viagra' in case of 'failing greed' and there is no warm, understanding therapist helping you through "difficult greed phases". Greed is a cold self-propelling 'growth-drive', increasing life-long with every new acquisition and rarely has a tragic heroic end. On the contrary: the greedy can die rich and respected (for his wealth) in his bed. The only punitive and tragic event is the inevitable cauldron with boiling oil in the afterlife, but that is a surprise for non-believers only.

Greed as a drive, is a given without excuse, with no 'friends' but only 'followers' as no-one is exempt from it, except an odd self-extincting pillarist or a saint in the desert. Even if one is not clearly aware of the drive to possess and hoard ever more valuables, there is the general admiration or envy of the lesser ones: the failed greedy. This is an important accompanying condition: while greed is essentially a self-centred trait, it needs a social embedding: even if Robison Crusoe would have been greedier than anybody else, being alone on the island made indulging in accumulated richness pointless. With this social necessary condition we return to Thomas Aquinas, since "one man cannot over-abound in external riches, without another man lacking them". Indeed, greed does not target goods which are in abundance, but those which are valuable because of their relative scarcity. Surrounding the successful greedy there is always a needy crowd.

With this observation we enter the field of economics, morals and crime. The a-moral brute drive becomes a sin, not because it ignores the "realm of the spiritual", but because unboundedly indulging in it can lead to inroads on social justice. And depending on the way societal values are protected the satisfaction of greed may be accomplished by criminal means, or may remain just on the borderline, "illegal but not criminal". Before we enter the field of law breaking, we should point at the licit greed satisfaction. Despite sermons of Church Fathers or moralist reformers, there is no other stimulus but greed to maintain a thriving capitalist economy. When after the Second World War Russia imposed its hapless socialist economic principles on Eastern Europe, particularly concerning 'fair pay' (rather the lack thereof), production plummeted (Applebaum, 2013). Conversely, when after the death of Mao the new Chinese leadership aspired to achieve economic expansion, it declared "get rich" (but not 'free'). The (legal) greed function in the financial system of the industrial world hardly needs further clarification after the credit crisis of 2008: stepping up the greed satisfaction by a system of ever higher bonuses contributed, among other circumstances, to the housing bubble and credit crisis. According to various authors this unbounded social system of greed led to a neglect of responsible risk management, if not to abuse and deception (Dorn, 2010; Dorn and Levi, 2011; Keršman and Ahtik, 2013; Levi, 2013). Despite that, the bonus is back again.

Recognising the potentially criminal satisfaction of greed and its social imbedding, an important corollary is loss of integrity and corruption: the agreed mutual smearing by exchanging coveted assets or favours. This must be compared with the ways society reacts against such ways of greed induced law breaking.

Smearing greed– and fighting it?

Why do we cross over to corruption and not to other forms of profit motivated crime, such as property crime, drug trafficking or fraud? The reason is the nature of corruption and offenders: it is not about the 'usual suspect' we meet in trafficking, theft or fraud, but about a consensual and hidden transaction satisfying at least two desires by bending or violating a legal decision rule. This implies one party having a formal decision power and another party with something desirable in the offing. It is a 'soft' criminal transaction, albeit with hard consequences for citizens, the economy as well as for the integrity and stability of a country. Essential is the decay of the decision making discretion, which may occur at all the levels of an organisation where functionaries must have some latitude, from street cop to the head of state. Though this means a whole organisation can be riddled by corruption, it is nevertheless mainly a *leadership* disease: if the management is characterised by a lack of integrity, the fish of the organisation starts to rot from the head (Van Duyne, 2001).

While most of the attention in literature and research is traditionally devoted to corruption in the administration (often referred to as 'abuse of power') corruption in the private sector has been less put to the fore, until recently. This has changed, internationally under pressure of the US, feeling outcompeted by corrupting wily foreign companies (Gelemerova, 2010). Also within the business sector corporations became aware that even as a corporate profiting co-offender (if not caught), one can become a victim of the own corruption because of the all permeating decay of integrity grows into a state of normality. In her chapter on *multi-national anti-corruption self regulation in the pharmaceutical secto*r Anna Di Ronco describes the awareness of this "normalisation of corruptive acts" in this sector and the measures taken to reverse this ingrained conduct. This is not an easy task, as basically the share value at the stock exchange is not determined by the ethics of the corporations but by their annual dividends. The principle of 'profits first, ethics second' may therefore result in all sorts of wishy-washy internal regulations. Compliance offices are established and anti-corruption policies are drawn up, which is prudent to have 'on the shelves' in case questions are asked, either as a consequence of the discovery of a major corruption case or when outside pressure is exerted, for example from the European Commission. This pressure is not only motivated by morality concerns, but by the public health budgets: health is big money, for the public and pharmaceutical sector alike. It is a clash of affordability and profitability: low prices and stiff competition versus high prices and rigged ('fair') competition. In this tension the salesmen representing their corporations at hospitals and doctors must keep up their weekly rates to get their bonuses. The author describes how companies have introduced a gratification calculation system in which also 'ethics compliance points' are integrated. However, at the same time this stimulates cheating not to lose 'ethic points'. If bankers cheat their million-plus bonuses upwards, so do the humble sale reps for a more basic wage.

While the first chapter shows how difficult it is to balance commercial 'rational' greed against ethics, such a balancing does not seem to be relevant in the public administration. Instead of profit expectations, readiness to serve is the official aim and motivation. While in trade and industry an anti-corruption policy has to gain ground against the basic greed drive for profit, a similar policy initiative should theoretically not find this kind of opposition. Therefore, does this make the implementation of an anti-corruption policy in public administration easier? The answer to this answer appears to be negative, particularly in countries where the public service is riddled with corruption. Research findings in Bosnia-Herzegovina (Maljević, Datzer *et al*, 2008) and Serbia (Van Duyne and Stocco, 2012) demonstrate that such policies amidst a general indifference, from the political elite down to the policeman on the beat, leads to many 'legislative Potemkin Villages', ineffective institutions and half-hearted provisions never intended to function fully. From our greed perspective, the greedy elite cherishes its spoils while neutralising outside pressures for reform by a lame implementation of the required measures. The chapter by *Radu Nicolae* on the *ethics policy of the Romanian public administration* describes a corresponding situation in his country.

Yes, Romania has a formal anti-corruption ethics policy and many important measures are implemented, for example the institution of the ethics officer in the municipalities and counties. However, according to the author, the system is fragmented, being different for the private and public sector and within the latter again differentiated according to the kind of public office. In addition, the ethics officers are poorly trained and mainly perform this function next to other tasks. Ethical dilemmas? Two third of interviewed ethics officers did not know they could have one. Reporting on the integrity policy? 80% of the administrative units did not report and whatever reports submitted were of poor quality. The question whether this reflects a real concern of the leading policy makers and the political elite is indeed a rhetorical one. It is more realistic to assume that the elite's real concern is to keep a grip on the spoils of the country and to implement only 'safe' reform to show they did something. Is this a rash conclusion?

The answer to that question is negative if we compare the findings in Romania and the Balkan states with those of the most 'western' of the previous socialist countries, namely the Czech Republic, as described by *Miroslav Scheinost* in his chapter *Shadows of corruption and bribery in the Czech Republic.* He compares the corruption situation in the country before and after the transition from socialism. During the socialist era the country was full of corruption, which was manifested in two ways. To the normal citizen corruption was more or less a kind of self-help barter to get coveted scarce goods. Within the party *nomenclatura* corruption took the form of extending their clientele: the more followers one could buy with favours the better. And these were not followers in the Twitter meaning of the word, but a kind of personal power basis. The situation changed when the country opened up after the fall of the communism. 'Self-help corrupt barter' disappeared to be replaced by a corrupt scramble for the rich spoils in the liberalisation of the plan economy. The author describes a corrupt interaction of new businessmen and office holders at all levels of society, from below in the village up to the central government squandering the public funds for own gain. Interestingly, the prevalence of petty corruption subsided.

This did not escape the attention of the public which considers the politicians and office holders responsible for the corrupt state of the country, to which should be remarked that citizens are equally active in initiating a corrupt act to their own advantage. This could have spurred the competent authorities to an active preventive policy and an intensification of law enforcement. However, neither happened. The criminal statistics, reflecting law enforcement efforts remain dismally low (as is the case in Romania and Serbia). Though during election times the 'fight against corruption' was usually high on the agenda, the after-election policies proved generally disappointing: since 1998 five government anti-corruption strategies have been adopted, followed by five failures. This lends support to my observation concerning the political elite in Romania: the political elite's real concern is to keep the spoils in their hands to satisfy its greed. To that end it is prepared to design any anti-corruption programme – as long as it does not work to its disadvantage. This is anything but a rash conclusion.

I think we can conclude that the combination of greed and power is considerably resistant to calls for change. This is not surprising: possession of mere power can be a greed satisfier in its own right, reinforced by wealth to be obtained or safeguarded. However, there is always the danger that a major scandal about serious breaches of integrity, be it corruption or embezzlement by the political elite, undermines this comfortable position. However, in the chapter *Political scandal and anti-corruption debates in Serbia,* the author *Maria Zurnić* makes clear that even major scandals appear to have only a temporary impact. Once the publicity storm calms down, the waves of the troubled water flatten again.

After the fall of Milošević a massive amount of money appeared to have been illegally channelled to Cyprus. How could that happen and where was the evidence? To answer these questions a Commission for the Investigation of Malfeasance was established, but failed dismally amidst accusation against the chairman who resigned after two months in office. The allegedly embezzled € 11,5 billion were not found and therefore no money was repatriated. Taxing the wealth of the Milošević era profiteers instead, failed also: of the expected € 800 million not more than € 60 million was collected. This created various streams in the angry political debate. The mainstream discourse denied the legitimacy of the Milošević regime and condemned the greed with which the regime misused public funds. But some of these critics could hardly be taken seriously as they abandoned the investigation of the massive embezzlement. Their opponents took a defensive stand and did not make much impact. In between another discourse identified the responsibility of the business elite. However, these streams of awareness raising did little to bring about an effective institutional change, despite the fact that Serbia ratified all conventions and international agreements (Trivunović, 2007). But that was due to outside pressure of the Council of Europe and the EU. All own initiatives to secure a lasting institutional change petered out: no career was really damaged by the Cyprus scandal while the political elite is still enjoying its spoils. And the Anti Corruption Agency? After 11 months its director was dismissed because of lack of integrity.

It seems that on the one hand, a political and business elite of 'crooks and thieves' are 'bedevilled' by the public and the media while on the other hand, this state of affairs is born with equanimity. To a large extent this is an outcome of media presentation itself: after all, the media are the public ears and eyes (at present extended with social media). This is researched as far as Ukraine is concerned by *Anna Markovska* and *Alexey Serdyuk* in their chapter on *media representation of corruption in Ukraine*. As research focuses they took two events: the football event *Euro 2012* and the *Shell* or *shale gas agreement negotiation 2013* and investigated whether and to what extent the topics of corruption and racism were represented. For the Shale gas agreement the authors also studied the foreign press releases.

What was the outcome of this comparison? The British media represented the *Euro 2012* in the lights of racism, human rights abuse, totalitarian state and selective justice. Corruption featured much less. In the Ukrainian press the football event was naturally presented as a major success, with corruption during the tendering process and construction ranking second. In contrast, the *Shale agreement* was represented in the British press positively with little attention to corruption and environmental hazards, while in the Ukrainian press there was ample mentioning of corrupt deals, apart from ecological problems and expected damage. While normally the western media in general are lavish in criticising the Ukrainian authorities of corruption and abuse of office, they looked away in the case of a major breakthrough in the exploitation of Ukrainian mineral wealth. Corruption is 'in the eye of the beholder' and in this case the western beholding greedy eye was coveting Ukrainian gas. The media reports on corruption was received by the authorities with as much indifference as can be observed in Serbia. However, thinking it could persevere in this arrogant indifference proved to be a miscalculation when the Ukrainians revolted against the President's rejection of the EU offers and chose for Russia instead. That ignited the slumbering emotions against corruption, exposing the greed of the elite, the President's family in the first place, and the intertwinement of government and crime.

Organised crime, corruption and terror

In much of the literature it seems to be taken for granted that organised crime goes hand in hand with corruption. This proposition is nuanced by *Anita Lavorgna* and *Anna Sergi* in their chapter on *different manifestations of organised crime and corruption in Italy*. Taking the broad concept of organised crime the authors show that in Italian legal thinking corruption is fundamentally implied in the former concept, that is, if it overlaps with the *mafia* or *mafia type organisations*. These are covered by two main sections in the Criminal Code and concern the 'ordinary' organised crime, a kind of 'mafia light' and a mafia heavily involved in corruption and political penetration, inclusive meddling in the election of representatives. In short, the kind of organised crime Berlusconi appeared to be receptive to (Stille, 2006). That is well known though this does not cover the whole spectrum of organised crime: the authors differentiate two other forms of organised crime in Italy, much less involved in corruption. These are the *mixed criminal networks*, the usual kind of organised crime in Europe. To carry out their crime business, such groups are not averse of corruption, but that is a matter of opportunity and connected to their criminal logistics. The other variety, more Italian specific, constitutes the *migrated* groups of organised criminals, wandering branches of mafia groups who settled in Northern Italy. These are not 'colonists': a kind of off-spring of the Sicilian mafia or 'Ndrangheta, but rather a kind of criminal 'gastarbeiter', sending their ill-gotten profits home. They are much less fluid than networks and have to establish good corruptive contacts with the surrounding business community they are interacting with. But this is still 'operational corruption', connected to 'doing crime business'. The endemic corruption of the 'home' mafia's is different and characterised by a "tacit understanding of corruptive practices assumed without interventions or specific initiative." From the mayor to street cop, all swim in the same warm pool of corruptive relationship, which often leads to the dismissal of the staff of the whole municipality: the ultimate democratisation of greed and corruption.

According to many policy makers and some scholars, organised crime is not only connected to the phenomenon of corruption, but also to 'terrorism' (Clutterbuck, 1995). This connection is often manifested in a particular military conflict, such as in Bosnia 1993-1995, much to the advantage of outcome of the conflict (Mincheva and Gurr, 2010). Indeed, a multi-interpretable connection. This is researched by *Daniela Irrera* in her chapter on *the multilateral response in tackling the crime –terror nexus*. Though we are scant of empirical evidence, the idea of such a threat has haunted the international security policy making community long before the terrorist attack on the Twin Towers of 11 September 2001. Of course, this nexus is something the international security community relishes, certainly if reinforced with the attributes 'transnational', 'cross-border' or 'global'. This has contributed to the formulation of multilateral security policy as a response to the allegedly blurring dividing line between organised crime and terrorism. In this policy development the US played a major role: it 'exported', rather imposed, its concepts, whether it concerned (transnational) organised crime or money laundering by using the UN as forum for making its opinions known and accepted (Van Duyne and Nelemans, 2011). Naturally, the EU did not want to lag behind and also designed an internal security strategy covering all sorts of crime, however, with the subject of corruption lacking. That is strange, because having to deal with corrupt political leaders, such as Berlusconi (always left untouched by the EU), the whole Greek government or Yanukovich (with whom a nice shale gas agreement was concluded), is a primary risk in any security strategy. Is this serious policy making?

Money laundering and (crime-)money catching

Naturally, saying that money is the source of a lot of conflict, is a platitude. However, this platitude has manifold implications and ramifications few customers and policy makers are aware of. Does the 'colour' of the money aggravate such problems? No, in principle not. If the money is not of a white origin and the owner wants to use it, he must parade that money as 'white': the essence of laundering. Does that money and the connected launderers harm, in particular the financial system? The official answer is 'yes', but without substantiating facts (Reuter, 2013). My answer is 'no', if only because of its lack of logic: which launderer will cut the (financial) branch on which he is sitting?

Reputational damage is repeatedly presented as the other major harm a financial institution can sustain. However, reputational with whom? Not with the numerous (otherwise law abiding) 'black' savers of fiscally undeclared wealth who are facing problems with the coming abolishment of the bank secrecy of Switzerland, Luxembourg and Austria. They must either confess their fiscal sins or move their hidden wealth to other 'disreputable' banks, in the hope these are as efficient and honest as the banks of the mentioned jurisdictions which will soon disclose their savings. 'Black savers' could rush to the Vatican Bank if the Pope promises to absolve their sins and maintain strict bank secrecy. However, the present Pope has decided differently: to clean out the dark corners of his bank, without absolution to murky financiers. Though the reputation dogma is kept up, bankers know that there is only one reputational damage which counts in real financial life: the failure to pay back savers' deposits. And to maintain that capacity the bank must make money with other people's money, which is a basic foundation for strict honesty and trust.

This sounds like a simple rule of morality for making money. However, that is of old-time: next to the plain banker as 'money maker' the anti-money laundering regime has posited the figure of *compliance officer* who has to guard that abstract risk of 'wrong' money entering the financial institutions. This looks like an additional morality, not oriented to honestly making money (with socially acceptable moderate greed), but a moral screening 'at the gate'. The tension, inherent in this juxtaposed (if not opposed) moral positions is known, but only a handful of researchers investigated this tension empirically (Verhage, 2009, 2011).

One of them is *Mihaela Sandulescu* in her chapter on *Reconciling the anti-money laundering compliance duties and the commercial objectives of the bank.* She analysed the responses to her questionnaire from bank officers from three Swiss cantons. The questions concerned the relationship between the relation managers (the real money makers for the bank) and the compliance officers: the money laundering risk guardians/preventers. The findings confirmed that the employees at both sides of the morality axes, 'money making' and 'money purity', find themselves in an inherently conflict situation. Even if compliance officers genuinely try to help the relation manager, they realise that "*it is very difficult that a true friendship will develop between a CO and a RM*". So there is little love lost between the two which does not impede a loyal cooperation for their common organisation.

This loyalty is furthered if not exacted by the keen awareness that their institution is under constant threat: not of wily launderers, but of a whole hierarchy of institutional supervision which hangs as flock of birds of prey over the whole regulated sector, ready to peck down if lack of compliance is observed: this 'supervisory flock' consists of national supervisors, the politically responsible ministers and ultimately the FATF: the unofficial global organisation wielding a worldwide power, but accountable to nobody. Indeed, a strange power construction. The interesting thing is that while all think to know what it is good for, no-one is capable to specify this in empirical terms. So, in the end nobody knows what it is actually good for. The chapter *AML and the political power weight*, contributed by *Jackie Harvey, Michael Hutchinson* and *Adam Peacock* provides us an astonishing insight into the socio-politics of supervisory agnostics which serves the continuation of control power.

The first 'known unknown' in this policy agnostics is the extent and seriousness of the laundering problem. That is critically elaborated in most serious research literature, though without having any impact on the stand of the FATF and all parallel institutions (UNODC, World Bank, IMF) or underlying political, supervisory and executive layers. There are some old crude estimates (Tanzi, 1998) which have grown into the canonized 'IMF consensus range' of between 2-5% of global GDP (UNODC, 2011). As this consensus functions as a *belief* (Credo quia absurdum, Tertullian, ca 160-230 AD), there is little debate with dissident researchers: they are not part of the 'FATF congregation'.

While this knowledge question remains unresolved, we are still left with the unanswered question what this whole AML regime is good for. Is it for crime prevention? The authors make clear that there is no causal connection with the underlying prevalence of crime-for-profit and AML (Harvey, 2008). As a matter of fact, the most important crime market, prohibited drugs, does not flinch: prices are still going down and the availability of contraband is still high. Hence, applying the ultimate effect measure of crime reduction does not answer the question: "What is it all good for?"

This does not bring the FATF to sing another tune. On the contrary, it can brow-beat countries as 'non-compliant' (small countries only and verdict without appeal) with severe financial consequences (till 2006 a blacklist was used). This is not the only form of exerting what is often called 'soft' power (with hard consequences). Mutual evaluation or peer review is another way of keeping everybody in line. This works with the basic social principles of a congregation: nobody questions the assessment criteria and otherwise *no questions* are asked. What are these criteria? Sufficient legislation, organisation and the state of the FIU are criteria reasonably to asses. But comparing *effectiveness* – a fundamental yardstick – is a decisive matter: complying to all requirements is nice, but not able to tell whether this is also effective actually annuls all the previous lofty efforts. Here the shoe of AML assessment pinches and it does so from the beginning. So observe the strange spectacle: a parade of well-intentioned member states wearing the same wrong shoes; they all walk a bit cripple, but nobody whimpers and duly comply. Now just reflect for a moment on the huge power of the FATF and judge the congregational discipline: collectively enduring the pain and continuing with their mutual evaluation benchmark reports without a real benchmark. Ironically that is called 'benchmarking' nevertheless. For want of a real benchmark, the members of the FATF grasped for some proxy: the totals of the produced Suspicious Activity Reports (SAR). Methodologically fully unfit, but despite that accepted without any methodological reflection. What does just counting SARs tell us? Does the sum of SARs in country A mean the same as in country B; are we sure SARs are collected and counted in the same way? What is the relationship between the modern 'risk based approach' and just counting SARs? From the risk based perspective it looks like a step back, but endorsed nevertheless. Hence, no questions being asked, the FATF (or the congregation of member states) embarked again on the misbegotten 'benchmarking' and SARs counting, as described by the authors. Thus the Mutual Evaluation Reports are produced without real questions raised: for example, what about the Delaware or Nevada corporations; the Russian oligarch finances in the London City? Do the latter not have the capacity of undermining the financial system?

I must pause a moment for reflection. Throughout my discussions I kept the red thread of greed and money to arrive here at what looks like the summit of 'soft' power: the ability to make (globally) accepted something which is plainly flawed and without opposition of any significance. I know only three historical examples in which the same was accomplished: the Catholic Church (at least till the Reformation, but still a global operator), the Bolshevik party which after seven decades failed dismally, and the Chinese Communist Party, still in power as an empty shell for the greedy elite families. Should we not speak of a 'control greed' or a desire to retain the political power and wealth that has been conquered? No surprise that an open critical debate never developed.

Jackie Harvey and co-authors mention in their concluding section that "the only real method to judge efficacy of the system would be through a drop in underlying crime (see above) and the subsequent prosecution and asset recovery data". *Asset recovery* is the topic of the next chapter by *Petrus C. van Duyne, Wouter S. de Zanger* and *François H.G. Kristen.* After having investigated the first phase of SAR-reporting (Van Duyne and De Miranda, 1999), the confiscation of real estate (Van Duyne *et al.*, 2009) and monetary assets (Van Duyne and Soudijn, 2010), the authors thought it proper to investigate also the final phase of the fight against crime-money and laundering: the actually estimated ill-gotten profits and how much is eventually collected from the convicted criminals. While preparing the project, the researchers were somewhat out run by the Minister of Justice who not only repeated his policy that asset recovery is a financial instrument benefitting the public funds, but on top of that he announced a substantial expansion of the number of financial investigators: 250 fte's. But there are strings attached: they must earn back their salary from successful recovery *three times* over. In plain language: the Minister wanted to see money, very much money! Asset recovery serving the principle of restoring justice becomes subordinate to replenishing the state coffer. The minister does not stand alone in this greed for crime-money: in the 1990s, the US experienced an even more outspoken form of criminal asset hunting under the general assumption of the enormous amount of money being hoarded by criminals (Blumenson and Nilsen, 2001; Rasmussen and Benson, 1994).

How does this compare with the ultimately determined wealth of convicted criminals and with their capacity to fulfil recovery orders? The analysis of the more than 10.000[1] cases of the recovery database of the Dutch Central Recovery Agency reconfirmed in the first place that the income distribution among criminals is very skewed: "few move much and many move only few" (Van Duyne and De Miranda, 1999; 257). All empirical research findings demonstrate a huge inverted J-like distribution with most of the criminal income under € 10.000 while only a tiny minority of the distribution is in the category of "one million plus" (Euros). Apart from that expected, but to policy makers still new and sobering finding, getting money from reluctant criminal debtors is an arduous task, costing much time and money. The execution time of recovery cases is 2,6 years (median 1,5 year), which is of course also unequally divided: small recovery cases (under € 5.000) lasted 2,3 years; "rich" cases (> € 1 million +) 3,5 years.

Naturally, the state is not powerless to make the criminal debtors pay: there are various measures of coercion (apart from selling (expropriating) the confiscated possessions), the most severe being putting the unwilling debtor in jail for a maximum term of three years. That is a kind of sword of Damocles hung up above the head of the *unwilling* debtor. Execution of this coercive measure occurs only by court order but rattling with the sword can sometimes be enough. In general such coercion cases lasted more than 6 years. In between the debtor can submit a request to the court to reduce his debt because of inability to pay. Putting someone in jail for not paying is expensive which induces the state to seek a settlement: this produced 57% of the money due.

The authors also carried out a file analysis of a sample of 35 cases, ranging from 'one million +' criminals to those at the low end of the criminal income ladder to address the question whether the non-paying criminals were hiding and smartly laundering their loot. However, there were only a few criminals who had made an attempt to launder, but technically mainly shallow. All to no avail because the recovery order is 'laundering neutral': one has to pay irrespective whether the recovery order is to be paid from criminal or 'licit' sources such as granny's heritage

1 All numbers in this volume are in normal *European* annotation: the comma is for the decimals and the dot for the thousands

(whether real or invented). Compared to an effective asset recovery policy money laundering should be rated of a secondary priority.

Meanwhile, if the reader would think our qualification of the minister's conduct as greedy a bit over-stretching its meaning, at the time of writing the minister has put forward a bill intending to charge prisoners for their stay behind bars: € 16 per day. Criminal law philosophy? Nothing but an expected € 60 million to be contributed per year to the state coffer. States can be greedy too.

Common crime business & crisis

By morally locating the trait of greed "at the other side of good and evil" ("jenseits von gut und böse"), we get a more neutral picture of its functioning in market relationships, irrespective of their legality. If need be, we can always slip in morality retrospectively. The cigarette market is a good example for our purpose. It is a tax and price difference driven market: the commodity is cheap but the superimposed imposed taxes create high prices and given the state's tax sovereignty there can be interesting price differences due to different tax policies. And it would be a miracle if traders would not take advantage of these artificial price difference, given a stable demand on the one hand, and stable supply of product on the other hand. Of course, this is only the baseline of the illegal cigarette market story which is further shaped by special local or regional characteristics as 'windows of opportunity'. A concentration of demand in deprived inner city areas is such an opportunity. Special regulations for 'tax pockets' provide other opportunities in addition to an abundant legal production part of which can be channelled to the illegal market. In the chapter *Land of opportunities: the illicit trade in cigarettes in the United States* the authors *Klaus von Lampe, Marin Kurti* and *John Bae* provide an elaborate account of the illegal cigarette market situation in the US.

Concerning the 'tax window of opportunity', the US is as much a state patchwork of different tax levels as Europe. In addition, local governments can impose extra excises as is the case in New York City. One does not need to travel far for a handsome tax difference though such an inter-state smuggle is a criminal offence punishable by up to five years in prison. A specific role in this market is played by the Native American Reservations who enjoy a fiscal autonomy. Consequently by imposing lower tobacco excises than is the case in the surrounding state Reservations can give rise to thriving underground markets, as has been the case in New York. One tiny Reservation on Long Island accounted for a turnover of almost 12 billion sticks in ten years. If consumed themselves, such hard smoking would have wiped out the Reservation's population. The wholesale delivery of cigarettes to the

Reservations was provided by the licit tobacco industry, a third important 'window of opportunity'. Of course, the industry knew it sold to outlets directly connected to the illegal market, but as long as it was not illegal (which it became in 2011), why should it not profit from such an opportunity? Every market has a zone of moral ambiguity: greedy but legal.

Every criminal market has also a zone of political ambiguity, *e.g.* concerning a cluster of social, political and health problems. Then the institutional question arises: who should own the problem and thereby bring it under the institution's banner? Basically it is a question of who has the best story, or narrative, to claim ownership. If one overviews the story of various important political portfolios (drugs, organised crime, money laundering), it is difficult to deny the factor of greed (institutional as well as personal) as a driving force in the chase of a coveted problem. *Jon Spencer* describes in his chapter on *human trafficking policy making and the politics of international criminal justice* how this has evolved in this specific field in the UK. Human trafficking, a sub-phenomenon of migration which is itself again a sub-phenomenon of the on-going global mobility for 'greener meadows', has been brought into the perimeter of crime, namely *organised* crime. Politically and institutionally this is a major amplifier: what is organised is serious and consequently contributes to the seriousness of the narrative. Loaded with so much seriousness as well as OC connections, human trafficking for sexual exploitation was also embraced by the Palermo Convention and subsequently by UNODC. The UK did not lag behind and a new institution was established: the UK Human Trafficking Centre (UKHTC), which became a part of the Serious Organised Crime Agency (SOCA), a huge organisation that was later renamed National Crime Agency, usually not a sign of smashing success. Was that commensurate to the size of the problem? As a matter of fact: despite huge (gu)estimates, the prosecution and convictions numbers remain stably low. And though the press always has an emotive trafficking story ready, sometimes the convictions do not even concern trafficking; a change of outcome which after the first heated broadcasts, often goes unnoticed.

It is interesting to observe the same institutional conduct as we observed with the FATF: stressing the importance of the field by producing huge estimates based on a shamelessly flawed methodology; disregard of proper effectiveness analysis; evoking public and political emotions. But with the right narrative as public and political tear-jerker and concerned NGOs, of which there are many, such methodological flaws remain unnoticed or are brushed aside: "hands off my portfolio". The stakeholders can do so as long as people love this narration while there are no competing narratives. And like the greedy miser in Molière's comedy *Avare* who counted his hoarded coins, the UKHTC and NGOs count their budgets.

While these are 'political emo-narratives' satisfying a hard greed for power and control, one may long for a real-life narrative of the 'common man' struggling between law abiding and crime, between insolvency and fraud, between morality and survival. Such a narration is sketched by *Georgios A. Antonopoulos* and *Steve Hall* in their chapter "*The death of the legitimate merchant? Small to medium-size enterprises and shady decisions in Greece during the financial crisis.*" The socio-economic history of Greece is assumed to be known: a clientelistic corrupt economy living far beyond its means which was disguised by fraudulent statistics (seconded by Goldman Sachs; Keršmanc and Ahtik, 2013). When the fraud was disclosed, the economy quickly spiralled downwards especially concerning the middle and small entrepreneurs. The authors interviewed 13 small and middle-size entrepreneurs to find out first-hand how they managed to keep their head above water. The entrepreneurs, none of them having a criminal record, first tried to keep their enterprises afloat: economising and dismissing trusted staff. A chocolate maker was at the end of his tether. With no more options to economise he could get hold via friends of cheap 'dark' raw material, the origin of which he surmised, but otherwise did not want to know. It was a kind of 'survivor's fencing' of stolen material, which entailed some disguising management.

An internet café entrepreneur and his father ran a successful business, expanded, hired extra staff, till the financial austerity began to bite. For days on a stretch no customer entered the premise. As they had already the computers for gaming, it was easy to convert them into gambling machines, which was illegal, having no license to run a gambling business. Though the Greeks are great gamblers, the dabbling in crime did not work out. The other interviewees likewise slid into the crime-market, or made a deliberate cross-over. Were they only victims of greed and corruption in the Greek economy? Or was the crossing over to crime-markets by taking advantage of those legal sectors also an act of greed? If 'yes' it still was a moderate one.

Contradictions in economic crime

With the chapter written by *Matjaž Jager* and *Katja Šugman Stubbs* on the *inner contradictions of economic crime control* we enter a realm of dialectic philosophy: from opposing perspectives something good must develop. That sounds very deep, but the reference to Hegel and Marx raises suspicion. Are we going through some historical pattern of opposing views? Well, Hegel is too metaphysical for the dirty reality of economic crime, while Marx has been refuted definitely. Apart from that, the authors rightly point at the contradiction in economic crime law enforcement: it is intended to stem the social consequences of the greed of the economic powerful while leaving them intact. The reader may remember Thomas Aquinas quoted in the first section: hoarding wealth at the expense of one's fellow man. That is quite modern: indulging in greed satisfaction can be against a socio-economic policy that protects also the interest of the lower paid classes. But on the other hand, we cannot run a profit making economy without it. That contradiction can lead to internal inconsistencies. The authors describe two Slovenian cases which illustrate this. One case concerned the establishment of an illegal construction cartel for building per kilometre the most expensive highway in Europe, with the connivance of the authorities. The second case was a social insurance swindle: 3.000 firms stopped paying their social security and pension obligations in order to keep labour costs down. The Prosecution Service at first refused to initiate a prosecution until the public protest became so loud, that it had to turn 180 degrees from 'understanding' the sorry plight of the entrepreneurs to the protection of the duped employers.

Of course, all these economic 'white-collar' perpetrators are respectable citizens and *proportionally* their greed may not be bigger than that of a common lower class offender, the difference being only their income baseline. Should that proportionality be a 'yard stick' for punishing economic offenders when the state seeks to apply a more severe penal policy? The authors struggle with the contradiction between dissuasiveness (severity) and proportionality: is the latter not a kind of barrier for more severe sentencing? While the authors do not succeed in solving this problem, practitioners of law enforcement – the prosecution services in the US and other jurisdictions – simply upgraded their idea of proportionality related to swindling banks: in the Libor-scam one of the main culprits, the Dutch Rabo bank, had to settle for € 774 million. If the authorities get greedy, they want to have their full pound of flesh.

In the chapter on economic crime in Slovenia, *Bestiarum vocabulum of economic crime*, the author *Ciril Keršmanc* looks at economic crime from a kind of medieval collectioneurs perspective to find 'exemplary beasts' of Slovenian economic crime. At first sight, the pattern of the economic crime statistics do not deviate from what is found globally: more recorded common crime with on average low damage, less recorded economic crime, but with a higher average damage. Within the set of economic crime the author differentiates between business fraud and abuse of position or trust. The average damage is for the period 1999-2011 is for common and economic crime respectively € 12.939 and € 221.079; a sizeable difference.

These are only rough outcomes, for which reason the researcher performed an in-depth analysis of 1255 cases, almost equally divided between business fraud and abuse of trust cases. The case analysis confirmed the general picture: business fraud was prosecuted more often and lasted less long than can be observed with abuse cases, often of a technically more complicated nature. Looking at the content of the two categories, the authors looked at what people were really doing: the simple business fraud cases concerned defaulters who speculated that if they did not pay their bill, the civil procedure of debt collecting might appear too unwieldy and expensive to their creditor to pursue his case. In reaction to this abuse of civil law, the creditors turned to the more stringent method of charging and pressing for prosecution of the defaulters. One can say that both sides abuse the system of justice; de debtor speculating on the ineffective civil law and the creditor using the heavy gun of penal law for civil law debt collection assuming that other criminal law conditions are fulfilled, such as intent. For the prosecution service this means large case inflow, but given the relatively simplicity of the cases, a moderate workload and higher turnover statistics. One can say: this category represents a bit of greed with a moderately positive turnover outcome, but still due to their big numbers a threat to the system which should reserve more capacity for the more serious abuse cases.

In addition, the author selected from his small album of "criminal beasts" a few cases which reveal the innovative imagination of internal abuse of trust and position: financial rewards for phony company 'innovations'; insurance abuse (company pays the premium and the CEO becomes the beneficiary); treating a patient for a third breast and manipulating and tinkering with the roulette and the tools in the control room. According to the author the latter case has some metaphoric meaning for the functioning of the capitalism running towards its demise in 2008. The greedy operator having also the keys of the electronic control room as is a metaphor for the functioning of the financial markets.

To what extent is the case-metaphor correct for the 2008 crisis? A greedy operator tinkering with the managerial safety procedures compared with the financial market? Yes, but then enlarged to all the financial layers and centres: the floor of the stock exchange and the control rooms were staffed by socio-economic *equals* which allowed the tinkering to continue until the system imploded. Had that a sanitizing effect of washing away the sick parts of the system? No, the operators and their institutions were not discarded, but kept alive with public funds. "Too big to fail" was the adage and to which may be added as sub-adage: "Too high for jail". This strange mechanism is the subject of the last chapter by *Nicholas Dorn*. He analyses aspects of the financial market from the perspective of an economic and a sociological thinker: *Boom and bust in financial and housing markets: re-readings through Schumpeter and Bourdieu.* Abstracting from Dorn's subtle theorising, the basic idea is simple. Most capitalist and financial innovations are greed satisfiers (nothing wrong with that) going through a cycle of success, growing, bulging, more bulging, bubble and bust. Then, from the ashes arise new innovations, which is 'creative destruction'. This is simple capitalism denuded of moralising: the essentials of the pre-war economist Schumpeter in 35 words. If capitalists would leave it at that, we would have a simple outcome of 'rise and fall'. But now a complicating factor enters the scene: the 'greedies' do not want to be hit by their own basic capitalist rule and, though failing, want to be bailed out. That is what higher-level greedies do: 'let other people toil and bleed' (actually, this was the name of a Dutch phantom-firm LAWIS). That should be taken literally, for while the risk-takers were saved from the consequences of their folly the principles of capitalist rigour were perversely to be applied to the public sector suffering serious cuts. Indeed, capitalism's *creative destruction be applied to others*. Let others bleed.

An aspect which to which the author pays special attention and which should be researched more extensively (comparing numerous countries) is the sociological and cultural dimension. Discussing the Bourdieu's analysis he points at the "ascendency of economic over cultural capital", and the way "the market forms that were encouraged by policy elites eventually took charge of their thinking", overwhelming critical reflection. Is this a kind of political elite group think?

Stock taking the measures taken in the UK and EU, the author conveys not much optimism, given the shallowness of thinking, primarily with the usual socio-economic intellectual dimension dominating. That points already in a cheerless direction: whatever has to be changed and how, we still find the same sort of greedy ones. We find the failed banker moving as consultant to the government and the former dozy supervisor or senior policy maker entering the board of a bank. Among each other, they use see to it that none of the club ends in destitution as long as their sin of greed remains wrapped in financial technicalities and they succeed to avoid Madoff-like proportions.

And Aquinas' observation of their "external riches", and the fellow man lacking them? That inequality will never be settled in this earthly world. Maybe the afterlife cauldron with boiling oil for the greedy will be the final retribution – for the right believers only.

References

Applebaum, A., Iron curtain. The crushing of Eastern Europe. London, Penguin Books, 2012

Clutterbuck, R., *Drugs, crime and corruption. Thinking the unthinkable.* Macmillan, United Kingdom, 1995

Datzer, D, A. Maljević, M. Budimlić, E. Muratbegović, Police corruption through eyes of bribers. The ambivalence of sinners. In P.C. van Duyne, J. Harvey, A. Maljević, K. von Lampe and M. Scheinost (eds.), *European crime-markets at cross-*

roads. Extended and extending criminal Europe. Nijmegen, Wolf Legal Publishers, 2008

Dorn, N., The governance of securities: Ponzi finance, regulatory convergence, credit crunch', *British Journal of Criminology*, 2010, *50*(1): 23-45

Dorn, N. and M. Levi, Theorising the Security and Exchange Commission's 2010 settlement with Goldman Sachs. In G.A. Antonopoulos *et al.*(eds.), Usual and unusual organising criminals in Europe and beyond. Antwerpen, Maklu, 2011

Duyne, P.C. van, Will 'Caligula go transparent?' Corruption in acts and attitude. *Forum on Crime and Society*, 2001, vol. 1, *nr. 2*, 73-9

Duyne, P.C. van and E. Stocco, *Corruption in Serbia. From black box to transparent policy making.* Nijmegen, Wolf Legal Publishers, 2012

Duyne, P.C. van and M.R. Soudijn, Crime-money in the financial system: what we fear and what we know. In: M. Herzog-Evans (ed.), *Transnational Criminology Manual, Volume 2*, Nijmegen, Wolf Legal Publishers, 2010

Duyne, P.C. van, M.R. Soudijn and T. Kint, Bricks don't talk. Searching for crime money in real estate. In: P.C. van Duyne, S. Donati, J. Harvey, A. Maljevic and K. von Lampe (eds.), *Crime, money and criminal mobility in Europe.* Nijmegen, Wolf Legal Publishers, 2009

Duyne, P.C. van and H. De Miranda, The emperor's cloths of disclosure: hot money and suspect disclosures. *Crime, Law and Social Change*, 1999, *no. 3*, 245-271

Gelemerova, L., Fighting foreign bribery: the stick or the carrot? In: P.C. van Duyne *et al.* (eds.), *Cross-border crime inroads on integrity in Europe.* Nijmegen, Wolf Legal Publishers, 2010

Harvey, J., Just how effective is money laundering legislation? *Security Journal*, 2008, vol. 21, *no 3*, 189 – 211

Keršmanc, C. and M. Ahtik, Learning the ABC's of deceptive practices in banking. In: n: P.C. van Duyne *et al.* (eds.), *Human dimensions in organised crime, money laundering and corruption.* Nijmegen, Wolf Legal Publishers, 2013

Levi, M., Financial crimes and the global financial system. In: P.C. van Duyne *et al.* (eds.), *Human dimensions in organised crime, money laundering and corruption.* Nijmegen, Wolf Legal Publishers, 2013

Mincheva, L.G. and T.R. Gurr, Unholy alliances: evidence on linkages between trans-state terrorism and crime networks: the case of Bosnia. In W. Benedek et al., Transnational terrorism, organised crime and peace-building. Basingstoke, Palgrave, 2010

Rasmussen, D.W. and B. Benson, *The economic anatomy of a drug war. Criminal justice in the Commons.* Lanham, Rowman and Littlefield, 1994

Reuter, P., Are estimates of the volume of money laundering either feasible or useful?. In B. Unger and D. van der Linden (eds.), *Research handbook on money laundering*. Cheltenham, Edward Elgar, 2013

Stille, A., *The sack of Rome. Media + money + celebrity = power = Silvio Berlusconi*. London, Penguin Books, 2007

Tanzi, V., Money laundering and the International financial system. IMF Working Paper, Washington, 1996

Trivunović, M., V. Devine and H. Mathisen, *Corruption in Serbia 2007. Overview of problems and status of reforms*. Bergen, Chr. Michelsen Institute, 2007

UNODC, *Estimating illicit financial flows resulting from drug trafficking and other transnational organised crimes*. Vienna: United Nations, 2011

Verhage, A., *The anti money laundering complex and the compliance industry*. London, Routledge, 2011

Verhage, A., Between the hammer and the anvil. The anti-money laundering-complex and its interactions with the compliance industry. *Crime Law and Social Change*, 2009, *no. 1*, 52, 9-32

Multinational anti-corruption self-regulation in the pharmaceutical sector: evidence of (in)effectiveness

Anna Di Ronco[1]

Applying criminological perspectives to organisational corruption

By contending that business is inherently criminogenic, Clarke (1990: 8) argued that "*the key to understanding* [crime and misconduct in business] *lies in recognising the structure that the business environment gives to misconduct, both in terms of opportunities and in terms of how misconduct is managed*" (in Newburn, 2007: 386). Relevant literature on corporate deviance maintains that some aspects of organisational culture facilitate workplace crime and corruption while other aspects impede it. The former facilitating aspects relate to the question whether there are clear messages about what it is acceptable, and depend on factors such as the attitudes of colleagues (Hollinger and Clark, 1983), the example set by the top management (Hollinger and Clark, 1983; Stead *et al.*, 1990; Challinger, 1997.), and on other workplace practices (Cooke, 1991). Many scholars have linked the opportunities for corruption with a permissible ethical climate at the organisational level(s), which places particular emphasis on economic and financial goals and accomplishments (Gorta, 1998). As argued by Ashforth and Anand (2003), the pursuit of the major organisational goals (which are mainly associated with resource procurement and financial success) is often tied up with a plethora of economic-driven values (such as free enterprise, individualism, competitive achievement, profitability, efficiency, pragmatism and so forth). The pursuance of such economic values, therefore, may lead individuals to disregard basic moral concerns.

According to the rational choice perspective in criminology (Cornish and Clarke, 1986), individuals are thought to engage in a rational assessment when deciding on

[1] The author is a Ph.D. Student at IRCP (Institute for International Research on Criminal Policy), Department of Penal Law and Criminology, Ghent University. E-mail: Anna.DiRonco@UGent.be

whether to commit a crime. In this calculation, costs and benefits of the (criminal or, more generally, deviant) choice are carefully weighed. The balance tilts in favour of the commission of the crime insofar as the benefits that the individual would likely obtain from it exceed the costs (*e.g.*, risk of being caught, prosecuted, sentenced etc.).

The engagement in unethical conduct may even be reinforced by the presence of corporate dynamics (or corporate deviant subcultures) which neutralise the shame or negative value attached to the commission of corrupt activities, leading to their institutionalisation. To reverse the trend and instigate a process of structural (ethical) change in corporations, some emphasis has been placed on the implementation of self-regulation. Progressively in the last decade, Multinational Companies (MNCs) operating across all private sectors have implemented compliance systems and adopted ethical codes, as a result of the collective action pursued by international, European and pan-European organisations, as well as by pressure groups and civil of society organisations. Despite their intuitive value as meaningful tools in the prevention of corruption, it remains unclear whether compliance systems, as currently implemented by corporations, are effective in managing corruption risks and in developing a corporate ethical culture that is incompatible with the perpetration of corrupt acts (Pope, 2000).

This chapter shall first cast a glance on the factors that in the last decade have triggered the development of compliance systems and of Anti-Corruption Programmes (ACPs) across all private sectors. Second, it shall focus on the risk of corruption presented by the pharmaceutical sector, by focusing particularly on the area of drug promotion. Third, it shall provide some indication of the (in)effectiveness of ACPs as a means to prevent corruption. To this end, the outcome of recent interviews carried out with Compliance Officers (COs) of Belgian branches of pharmaceutical giants will be described. Such interviews have been conducted in the context of an exploratory study, aimed to gain knowledge about the vulnerabilities to corruption (and/or competition distortion) deriving from the practice of gift-giving in (private-to-public and private-to-private) business relations in the pharmaceutical sector.

Rationalism and rule setting

A rationalist perspective in criminology may well contribute to explaining why people in business organisations decide to engage in corrupt activities. In corporations, in fact, as emphasis is placed on the accomplishment of economic and financial goals, preference may easily be given to the decision to get involved in corrupt conduct, at least when it coincides with the fulfilment of corporate and/or of private interests. Given a permissive ethical climate with a focus on financial accomplishments and an opportunity to act amorally, the decision to engage in corrupt activities may represent the most rational response of the individual to situational opportunities. As pointed out by Ashforth and Anand (2003: 3), when a permissive ethical climate permeates the organisation, corruption can then become normalised (or institutionalised). Such a normalisation implies that corruption becomes "*embedded in organisational structures and processes, internalized by organisational members as permissible and even desirable behaviour, and passed on to successive generations of members.*" Through socialisation dynamics, ultimately a situation is created in which corruption is justified and regularly practiced. Here, the sub-cultural theory also plays a role, in that it might explain how corporate crime might be encouraged and justified (i.e., normalised) by workplace subcultures (Sutherland, 1949; Geis, 1993).

As a consequence, organisational assumptions, values and beliefs (which draw on the business values mentioned above), evolve to rationalise corrupt practices in ways that neutralise the stigma attached to them (Sykes and Matza, 1957). Deviant subcultures, moreover, may lead the individual to develop a specific social identity tailored to the social domains, groups and roles occupied, resulting in its insulation from the wider social culture and its dominant beliefs. New identities as such may then be internalised at the micro level through the dynamics of socialisation, and even passed on to the newcomers. As a result, because many of the corrupt practices are institutionalised and rationalised, employees may not believe that their behaviour is corrupt and often have strong incentives to continue their (deviant) malpractices.

To reverse the process of systemic normalisation of corruptive acts, it is necessary to devise systematic responses, which often require a significant structural organisational change (Ashforth and Anand, 2003). In other words, to halt the emergence of deviant subcultures, or of neutralising techniques aimed to justify the perpetration of corrupt acts, the organisation should bolster the development of a strong ethical culture which firmly prohibits corruption and which spells out clear ethical standards with which employees should comply. Setting clear rules is the first step of this organisational drift (Hollinger and Clark, 1983). As argued by Clarke (1992: 20):

> "*one important stand of situational crime prevention (. . .) is the introduction of new rules or procedures (and the improvement of those that are already in place). These are intended to remove any ambiguity between acceptable and unacceptable conduct. They make it harder for offenders to make excuses to themselves or, in Matza's (1964) language, to make use of 'techniques of neutralisation' such as 'I am only borrowing it' and 'Everybody else does it'*".

On Homel and Clarke's (1997) account, rule setting is a fundamental step to prevent potential offenders from denying the wrong of their actions, in a view to induce shame or the feeling of guilt (see also Wortley, 1996). Spelling out clear rules of conduct may play a meaningful role also when it comes to ethical 'grey areas', as employees' misconducts may be incentivised by the absence of a clear understanding of what is allowed and forbidden in the corporate self-regulation (Stevens, 2007). As Gordon and Myake put it (2001: 162):

> "*it is not easy to define exactly what constitutes bribery and other corrupt practices. Clear-cut cases do exist, but greyer areas arise in connection with facilitation payments, gifts and hospitality, conflicts of interest and use of intermediaries. The assessment of what constitutes acceptable practice may also be coloured by local circumstances; but cultural diversity and varying local conditions can also be used as excuses for inappropriate business conduct.*"

Literature on organisational change (Treviño *et al.*, 1999; Parker, 2002), suggests that via an ethical codification, associated with regular training, guidance, and a system of compliance monitoring, ethical values and norms are inculcated and institutionalised at the different (individual, subunit, organisation, industry) levels and incorporated into everyday business decision and action. To invert the unethical spiral, corporations should also set up an anonymous and confidential mechanism to encourage whistle blowing (*e.g.*, hot lines, ethics boards, inquisitive boards of directors etc.) (Pope, 2000). In addition, compliance with ethical norms and standards should be ensured through the establishment of system of enforcement that imposes real sanctions to punish employees' misbehaviours (Cleveland *et al.,* 2009).

By contrast, hazy self-regulatory rules, coupled with the absence of precise guidelines and trainings insufficiently clarifying the meaning of corporate standards, and of an ineffective system of controls, may facilitate employees' engagement in corrupt deals. Therefore, self-regulation alone, however, especially when its implementation is left to the 'good will' of corporations, may not be effective in preventing corruption (as well as other corporate and organisational crimes).

In introducing his theory of enforced self-regulation, Braithwaite (1982) argued that corporations are more capable than governments in regulating their business activities and preventing the occurrence of crime. As opposed to corporate legislation, in fact, corporate own rules can be tailored to match the characteristics of the company and its way of doing business, quickly adjust to changing business environments, and likely to be accepted and embedded in the corporate culture. Compliance units moreover, which are normally well-aware of the criminogenic circumstances present within the organisation, are better suited than external governmental agencies to monitor employees and to enforce their compliance with the rules. However, even if companies are more capable to regulate themselves and to exert oversight over their employees, they are not necessarily more willing to do that, or only by way of lip service. This is the fundamental weakness of self-regulation: good norms on paper may not be accompanied by an effective system of compliance aimed to enforce those rules.

To avoid the risk of companies implementing a compliance system that is a mere 'window dressing' deprived of any enforcing substrate, Ayres and Braithwaite (1992) developed a model of public enforcement of corporate self-regulation, aimed to grant legal benefits to firms that prove to have invested the time, resources and personnel needed to make a programme of self-regulation effective. In the short term, the introduction of a system of legal incentives that attaches to the presence of an effective compliance model may encourage individual corporations to enhance their self-regulatory efforts. In the long run, furthermore, the implementation of an effective compliance system may also succeed in altering the rational calculus of cost and benefits associated with the commission of corrupt acts, ultimately making it more convenient for the (rational) individual and the organisation not to engage in corrupt practices. However, despite the emphasis placed by some scholar on systems of publicly enforced private self-regulation as a means to prevent corruption (Ruhnka and Boerstler, 1998; Gobert and Punch, 2003; Hess, 2009), a meagre number of EU Member States have so far adopted such systems (Martín, 2012; Asser Institute, 2012).

Recent developments of Anti-Corruption Programmes

Broadly speaking, ACPs are implemented as a part of the so-called 'compliance system' (or Ethics and Compliance Programme, ECP) which is established within the corporate group, both at the global and divisional levels. The term compliance system usually refers to an organisational structure designed to monitor employees' compliance with external and internal standards and rules (Carson *et al.*, 2008). Multinationals have established this organisational structure through the setting up of centralised bodies operating worldwide within the group (*e.g.*: the corporate compliance committee) and of single authorities present in every business unit (notably, the divisional compliance offices, the legal – or equivalent – departments, etc.). At the level of the corporate individual unit, the compliance department is in charge of:

i. conducting risk assessment evaluations aimed to track down the areas that are most exposed to the risk of corruption;
ii. organising training sessions in view to communicating and disseminating legal and ethical standards to employees;
iii. providing guidance to employees facing ethical dilemmas (who raise issues directly to the compliance officer or indirectly through 'hot lines' frequently administered by external vendors);

iv. investigating cases of alleged misconduct reported to it and conducting proactive inspections; and
v. enforcing the rules by initiating disciplinary procedures as to verify reports of alleged misconduct (Wulf, 2012).

In corporate ethics literature different reasons have been provided in the attempt to explain the rise in popularity and progressive diffusion of ACPs among corporations operating in different commercial sectors. Among them, a prominent role has been given to the presence of a (tougher) legal framework on corporate liability (Gordon and Miyake, 2001), and to the collective action of pressure groups, civil society organisations, NGOs, international and regional organisations etc. increasingly concerned with making companies behave as socially responsible citizens (Rama *et al.*, 2008; Lambooy, 2010).

A (hard-law) tougher response on corporate liability

According to the aforementioned literature, ACPs have progressively been adopted by Multinational Companies (MNCs) for a twofold motive. First, their enactment has been driven by the need to comply with enhanced legal standards enshrined in European, pan-European and international legal acts. At the European level, for example, particularly relevant to this ambit is the Second Protocol to the 1997 Convention for the Protection of the Communities' Financial Interests (the so-called PIF Convention) which at article 3 par. 1 requires Member States to ensure that legal persons are to be held liable for the offences of fraud, active corruption and money laundering committed for their benefit by any person having a leading position, an authority to take decisions on behalf of the company or to exercise control within it, as well as for involvement as accessories or investigators in such crimes. Moreover, pursuant to art. 3 par. 2, Member States are also required to adopt the necessary measures to hold the legal person liable where the lack of supervision or control has enabled the commission of the aforesaid offences for the benefit of that legal person by a subject under its authority. Partially[2] overlapping with the provisions included in the Second Protocol are the ones included in the 1999 Criminal Law Convention Against Corruption, adopted by Member States in the context of the Council of Europe.

---

2 The normative overlap is just partial since the 1999 CoE Criminal Law Convention Against Corruption extends liability of corporations also to cases of passive corruption, thus not limiting corporate liability to active corruption as in the Second Protocol to the PIF Convention.

At the international level, the 1997 OECD Convention on Combating Bribery of Foreign Public Officials solicits states parties to adopt any measure that may be necessary to establish the liability of legal persons for the bribery of foreign public officials (article 2). Finally and in addition, the 2003 UN Convention Against Corruption (UNCAC) at article 21 exhorts state parties to consider introducing in their domestic legal systems provisions that hold a legal person liable for the offences of active and passive bribery. On top of that, the UNCAC is the first multilateral agreement urging state parties to take action in order to prevent corruption in the private sector. As article 12 par. 2(b) stipulates, in fact, states parties are encouraged to achieve this end "*by promoting the development of standards and procedures designed to safeguard the integrity of relevant private entities, including codes of conduct for the correct, honourable and proper performance of the activities of business and all relevant professions and the prevention of conflict of interest, and for the promotion of the use of good commercial practices among businesses and in the contractual relations of businesses with the State*".

As a consequence of the entering into force of these (hard-law) legal acts, an overall tendency towards the introduction of criminal liability for legal persons can be witnessed among EU countries (Vermeulen *et al.*, 2012).[3] Consequently, in some Member States, such as Italy, Austria, the UK and recently in Spain, initiatives have been taken in order to spur the development of corporate compliance schemes and to praise companies boasting (effective) compliance systems (*e.g.*, through the application of favourable sentencing regimes by courts) (Martín, 2012). However, in contrast to this, little to no effort has so far been made by EU countries to encourage corruption prevention in the private sector (Asser Institute, 2012)[4].

Soft-law approach: Corporate Social Responsibility (CSR)

A second reason that can explain the progressive adoption of ACPs on the part of MNCs can be associated with the increasing pressures exercised over private sectors' organisations and industry associations by NGOs, pressure groups, civil society associations, and other key stakeholders, concerned with making companies behave

---

3 This notwithstanding, a recent study (Vermeulen *et al.*, 2012) underscores that, albeit the general tendency of Member States to introduce criminal liability for corporations, several differences still continue to exist in the actual approach adopted to corporate liability in the domestic laws of EU Member States.

4 In this report, the Asser Institute maintains that in the majority of the EU states investigated, no specific measures have been taken in order to promote the development of standards and procedures designed to safeguard the integrity of relevant private entities, including anti-corruption codes of conduct and compliance mechanisms.

in a socially responsible (and environmentally sustainable) way. As argued by Lambooy (2010: 10):

> "*[t]he role of business has become vital in integrating the sustainable development perspective into the process of economic globalisation, because business decisions have a direct impact on all levels of society: economic, social, environmental and cultural. The private actors have thus been encouraged to conduct their business in a 'socially responsible way' and to pursue best practices that enhance value in three dimensions: 'Planet, People, Profit'. The expectations for the business sector to contribute at all levels will continue to grow.*"

To fulfil their specific obligations of the Corporate Social Responsibility (CSR), enterprises are required to have in place processes which integrate social, environmental, ethical, human rights and consumer concerns into their business operations. Authoritative guidance to CSR is provided to companies by internationally recognised principles and guidelines, such as the recently amended OECD Guidelines for Multinational Enterprises, the ten principles of the UN Global Compact, the ISO 26000 Guidance Standard on Social Responsibility, the ILO Tri-partite declaration of principles concerning Multinational Enterprises and Social Policy, and the UN Guiding Principles on Business and Human Rights.[5]

CSR was first defined by the EU Commission as "*a concept whereby companies integrate social and environmental concerns in their business operations and in their interactions with their stakeholders on a voluntary basis*" (European Commission, 2001). In a recent communication on a renewed EU strategy for CSR, the Commission defines it as the "*responsibility of enterprises for their impacts on society*" (European Commission, 2011: 6). In the latter document, the Commission encourages Member States to step up their efforts in the promotion of CSR among corporations and urges them to create a peer review mechanism for the national review of CSR policies. Additionally, it also declares its intention to set up mechanisms aimed to monitor the commitments made by EU companies to comply with internationally recognised CSR principles.

The EU Commission, furthermore, has recently adopted a proposal for a directive on the disclosure of non-financial and diversity information by large companies and groups, aimed to enhance the transparency of enterprises'

5 Along with the other existing EU policy documents on CSR (e.g., the 2001 Green Paper (COM(2001)366)) and initiatives (e.g., the European Multi-stakeholder Forum, the European Alliance for CSR etc.). More recently, the EU Parliament has adopted two resolutions acknowledging the importance of companies' transparency in social and economic matters ("Corporate Social Responsibility: accountable, transparent, and responsible business behaviour and sustainable growth" and "Corporate Social Responsibility: promoting society's interests and a route to sustainable and inclusive recovery").

communications on social and environmental matters and to harmonise the domestic regulation in the area (European Commission, 2013). If adopted, this directive would require the concerned companies and groups to annually disclose information regarding policies, risks and results on matters related to environmental issues, social and employee-related concerns, respect for human rights, anti-corruption and bribery issues, and diversity of the board of directors.[6]

Through the adoption of such plethora of (soft-law) initiatives and policy documents, international and regional organisations have called on industry associations to guide companies in the formulation of ACPs. Among the most active, one could enlist the Confederation of Danish Industry, the CSR Netherlands (Maatschappelijk Verantwoord Ondernemen or MVO Nederland) and so forth (Asser Institute, 2012).

Corruption in the pharmaceutical sector

(High) exposure to corruption risks

The pharmaceutical sector is crucial for contributing to the economic growth, as well as to public health and societal wellbeing. However, a number of different factors inherently present in the sector render it particularly exposed to the risk of corruption (Clinard and Yager, 1980; Transparency International, 2006; Cohen *et al.,* 2007). Therefore, when these (corruption-inducing) factors are not well managed, detrimental (and even harmful) consequences can be brought about and (potentially) affect not just the soundness of the economic system (in terms of, for instance, increased costs of medicines, competition distortion practices etc.), but also the health conditions of millions of people (in terms of limited access to drugs and treatments, poor quality of medicines etc.).

According to Cohen *et al.* (2007), the vulnerability of the pharmaceutical market to corruption can be explained in light of the high level of governmental involvement in a number of 'core decision points' throughout the lifecycle of a

6 Currently, a fragmented regulatory scenario can be witnessed among EU countries. While some EU Member States have privileged the approach 'report or explain', according to which companies can choose between reporting or disclosing the reasons why not to do so, some others have established an outright legal obligation to disclose particular information. Additionally, some EU countries target large companies, whereas some others focus on certain listed or government-owned companies only (Asser Inst., 2013; EU Commission, 2013)

medicinal product. A governmental approval, in fact, is usually requested before a clinical trial test can begin, and, after the trial phase, to allow the drug to circulate in the market. In addition, registration, price setting, procurement, distribution, and pharmaceutical prescribing and dispensing all imply a large interface between the industry and the government (Transparency International, 2006). Corruption in the sector can spread throughout these core decision points and can manifest itself in a variety of forms. As argued by Vander Beken (2007), it finds expression mainly in pharmaceutical companies offering gifts and lavish consulting fees (through their representatives) to doctors to get their medicines prescribed to patients. A bribe can also take the form of a payment made to medical journals (and to their journalists) to write favourable articles on their products. Moreover, it can also take the form of financial support provided to university pharmacological research institutions or of stock options given to scientists in companies benefitting from the research (Vander Beken, 2007). Even when the practices adopted by relevant actors in the sector are not (yet) considered corrupt, they can distort fair market competition and easily border on corruption or at least undermine integrity.

A recent sector inquiry of the European Commission conducted during the period stretching from 2000 to 2007 suggests that the sector has recently undergone some structural changes which have led to an intensified consolidation (European Commission, 2008). Originator companies, in fact, have undertaken various acquisitions of both manufacturing and generic companies, and, at the same time, have lost patent protection of their best-selling drugs. According to the report, in order to maintain the revenue associated to their (patent) blockbusters medicines, pharmaceutical companies have adopted practices aimed to block or delay the generic competition and the development of competing originator products, which affect fair competition and negatively impact on public health expenditure. As pointed out by the EU Commission, in fact, "*competition, in particular competition provided by generic medicines, is essential to keep public budgets under control and to maintain widespread access to medicines to the benefit of consumers/patients*". This seems to be particularly important in current times of economic austerity in which budget cuts have substantially restricted access to health care (Karanikolos *et al.*, 2013).

Competition distortion practices, however, far from occurring only in the form of cartels between a small group of powerful pharma-corporations, can also take the (more subtle) form of gifts given to public or private business counterparts. The US Security and Exchange Agency, for example, filed in 2012 ten enforcement actions for violation of the Foreign Corrupt Practices Act (FCPA), which in half of the instances involved a pharmaceutical or a medical devices company.[7] Corporations were accused of having given, directly or through third parties, improper payments to subsidiaries, distributors, vendors, consultants and agents abroad (especially in Europe) to win business *advantages*, and notably to obtain regulatory and formulary approvals, sales and prescriptions. To conceal (or misrepresent the true nature of) the bribes, payments were improperly recorded as legitimate expenses for promotional activities (*e.g.*, marketing expenses, advertising in scientific journals, professional training etc.), or otherwise illegally channelled into off-shore bank accounts (thanks to over- or fictitious invoicing which allowed the corporation to conceal the true nature of the payment). Funds for payments through false invoices were generated also through collusive vendors (*e.g.*, travel agents or restaurants), or via charitable donations and educational support. According to the SEC enforcement action, for example, Pfizer was accused to have put 'point programmes' in place, aimed to reward government doctors who had accumulated points on the number of prescriptions they issued. As Kara Brockmeyer, Chief of the SEC Enforcement Division's Foreign Corrupt Practices Act Unit put it:

> "*Pfizer in several countries has bribery so entwined in their sales culture that they offered points and bonus programmes to improperly reward foreign officials who proved to be their best customers.*"[8]

The points accumulated were rewarded with various gifts ranging from medical books to cell phones, cash, international travel or free products. Although just the more lavish and expensive items given to clients or business associates would count as corruption, also inexpensive gifts may have a considerable impact on the recipients' behaviour. For example, a large body of evidence stemming from the social sciences has profusely demonstrated the effects yielded by gifts of nominal value on the prescription attitudes of physicians (McFadden *et al.*, 2006; Katz et al., 2010; Moskop *et al.*, 2011 etc.).

A specific risky area for corruption: drug promotion

Across private sectors, an area that is laden with prominent corruption risks is the sale and marketing of the product (Argandoña, 2003; Transparency International, 2009).

---

7 To have a complete overview of the SEC enforcement actions, see http://www.sec.gov/spotlight/fcpa/fcpa-cases.shtml

8 The SEC charges against Pfizer for immediate release are available at http://www.sec.gov/News/PressRelease/Detail/PressRelease/1365171483696#.UlkrWRCPh8F

The typical case of corruption occurring in this area is that of a company manager or sale representative who gives, or promises to give, money, presents or other rewards or advantages to the purchasing manager or buyer of a public or private counterpart in order to win an order. Since the pharmaceutical sector heavily invests in the promotion of its medicines, this has been regarded as especially vulnerable to the risk of corruption (Clinard and Yeager, 1980; Braithwaite, 1984; Vander Beken, 2007). According to the PM Group, for instance, European pharmaceutical promotion expenses increased in 2010 by 0,5% in the top five developed markets of France, Germany, Italy, Spain and the UK and 2,2% in the rest of Europe.[9] Substantial expenditure supporting the products' marketing in this sector is justified in light of the large investment costs in research and testing that pharmaceutical companies face before a product reaches the market. Since the time to wait before a drug is licensed and approved for sale is relatively long, pharmaceutical firms may be willing to accelerate the return on the company's investment by encouraging sale representatives to adopt unethical marketing strategies to have their medicines purchased by clients and/or prescribed by doctors (Braithwaite, 1984). Elliott (2006), in an article published in *Atlantic Monthly* titled 'The drug pushers', illustrates how the monumental profits of pharmaceutical manufacturers in recent years depend on the promotional activities of their sale representatives. Relying on interviews with former 'sales reps', the author describes a system in which representatives influence physicians' prescribing patterns and induce customers to buy the company's products.

If sale reps can be prodded by companies to offer a wide variety of enticements to public and private business counterparts, however, they also bear a personal interest in having the firm's product prescribed or purchased. Sale reps, in fact, usually work for a performance bonus which adjusts their monthly income to the amount of products they manage to sell or the number of contracts they are able to conclude. Therefore, in order to earn more money from their jobs, sale reps need to rake in as many orders or win as many lucrative contracts as they can. As rent-seekers, they may be tempted to use all means available (also the offering of lavish gifts) to have the company's product prescribed by doctors or allocated in pharmacies or private practices (Fisher, 2007).

As outlined in the literature (McFadden et al., 2007; Katz et al., 2010), a wide variety of gifts may be offered to business counterparts, and particularly to physicians, stretching from inexpensive 'reminder' items such as pens, notepads, and coffee mugs bearing the trade name of particular drug products, moderately priced gift such as

---

9 PM group, Trends in promotion available at http://www.pmlive.com/pharma_news/trends_in_promotion_273187,accessed 12/9/2013

reference tools, books and meals, along with expensive gifts such as tickets, trips, and large 'honoraria' for participation in pharmaceutical-sponsored activities. If some of these gratuities may be authorised by the company and recorded in the firm's official logs, others can be concealed from the company and lavished personally by the sale rep to the public/private business partner, insofar as the compensation offsets the loss (Cohen *et al.*, 2007). Circumventing an effective system of compliance monitoring that prevents employees' misconduct, sale reps may use the practice of gift-giving as a silent alternative form of corruption. Generally speaking, in fact, cases of (unlawful or inappropriate) gift-giving may be difficult to identify by the compliance department. Unless sale reps seek the company's official authorisation supporting the gift's bestowal, the chance that Compliance Officers (COs) become aware of their transgressions is relatively low (Abraham, 1995). Sale reps, in fact, interact with physicians and costumers 'behind close doors' and engage in relationships that imply mutual advantages.

Gifts may also be unofficially authorised by the company and financed with money resulting from the laundering of proceeds of crime and stemming from 'slush funds' to be drawn on by the company whenever needed (Chaikin, 2008).

Ethics and Compliance Programmes: an exploratory study from three pharma-companies

As mentioned in the preceding sections, progressively in the last decade international, European and pan-European organisations, as well as pressure groups, civil society organisations and NGOs have called on MNCs and industrial organisations to devise self-regulatory schemes aimed at the prevention of corruption. In response to such pressures, MNCs have increasingly implemented compliance systems and enacted ethical codifications spelling out the external (legal) and internal (corporate) standards and precepts of 'good' business behaviour that ought to influence employees' commercial conduct. However, albeit self-regulatory schemes may systematically be present in corporations across all private sectors, they may not be effective in preventing the risk of corruption being perpetrated by firms' employees.

One example of such ineffectiveness is provided by a report issued in 2008 by PricewaterhouseCoopers, a private company that offers industry-focused consultancy and auditing. In this report, PwC examined the efforts made by private companies to internally manage the risk of corruption on the basis of a broad survey of 390 senior executives and on in-depth interviews of chief executives and anti-corruption experts from 14 different countries. According to the report, albeit 80% of the surveyed companies had a programme in place to prevent and detect corruption episodes, they were not effective in identifying and mitigating corruption risks for they lacked in clear communication, enforcement, rigorous risk assessment, and monitoring.

To get a better grasp on how the compliance component has been developed in the pharmaceutical industry in view to managing and preventing the specific corruption risks presented by the sale and marketing of the product, three interviews with Compliance Officers (COs) of pharma MNCs have been recently held. This activity constituted a part of the methodology of an exploratory study carried out during the time span stretching from September 2012 to April 2013. It aimed to assess whether individual corporate self-regulation in the pharmaceutical sector sufficiently prevents corruption deriving from the practice of gift-giving in business relations.

In order to interview compliance officers (*i.e.*, legal counsels or equivalents) and sale reps operating in the industry, four Belgian Branches of pharmaceutical giants have been contacted via a phone call. The four pharmaceutical companies have been selected from the top-scoring MNCs included in a report issued in July 2012 by Transparency International. In this report multinational corporations were ranked according to the level of transparency provided about their anti-corruption strategies: the highest ranks given to the most transparent. In three out of four cases it was possible to talk by telephone with the compliance officer, whereas in one instance the request to pass the call to the officer concerned was subjected to the condition that the full name of the employee was mentioned. Providing that we did not flag any name, and that such names are difficult to find through the Internet, we did not manage in the short time span to talk with the compliance officer of this fourth pharmaceutical company. Conversely, in the former three cases the phone call was followed up by the forwarding of an e-mail containing the list of main themes and topics to be discussed during the interview.

All the three compliance officers reacted on the e-mail and accepted to have an informal and off-the-records conversation, under the condition that either a confidentiality agreement was signed or that the highest level of anonymity and confidentiality was otherwise fully granted.[10] In one instance, the confidential and informal nature of the conversation was justified in light of the official 'no-go' issued

10 In all three instances, semi-structured interviews were conducted with the aid of a checklist containing the main topics to be discussed with the respondent during the interview. This interviewing technique allows for a quite flexible and fluid interaction with the respondent, as it allows the interviewer to ask probes and follow-ups questions after every answer. It also permits to gain a more profound overview of the respondent's experiences and habits in sensitive matters (Dexter, 2006). All the individual interviews took place in the offices of the MNCs involved.

by the Regional Ethics Board, which formally denied permission to the firm's compliance officer and sale reps to hold any interview with the team of researchers from Ghent University (Belgium). In order not to disclose their identity, these firms will be differently regarded as company A, B and C, on the basis of the chronological order of the interviews.

In the following sub-sections, the outcomes of the three interviews will be briefly outlined. To facilitate this activity, six different components of Ethics and Compliance Programmes (ECPs) have been identified, namely risk assessment, rule setting, training, guidance, reporting, and monitoring. The state of the art of corporate self-regulation in the three pharma MNCs will be discussed in relation to these six indicators or components. At the end of the section, a reference to corporate best practices will also be made.

Risk assessment

Risk assessment procedures are usually followed by MNCs to track down the areas that are most exposed to the risk of corporate misconduct, and more specifically corruption. With the exception of company C, risk assessment is generally conducted on the basis of the general guidelines provided annually by the company's headquarters. There (*i.e.*, in companies A and B), risk assessment is also not tailored to the specific characteristics (and sets of risks) presented by each separate business unit. In company C, by contrast, the evaluation of risks is independently conducted by the Legal Department in strict cooperation with the Financial Department of every single corporate division. To develop a tailor-made monitoring plan, the level of exposure of the separate business unit to a particular misconduct (*i.e.*, the likelihood of its occurrence) is weighed against the seriousness of the consequences that such transgression would likely bring about in case a corruption accident would arise (and, thus, would be submitted to public scrutiny). According to the CO of company C, just the set of risks that are more likely to occur and that will determine the gravest consequences for the company are managed and mitigated through the development of a monitoring plan. All the actions that are taken under this plan are documented thoroughly, as to allow the company to demonstrate that all possible actions have been taken in order to lessen the opportunities of corrupt misconduct. Mostly, as pointed out by the CO, the promotional practices of sale reps fall within this area of intervention.

Rule setting

Albeit all companies claimed the existence of detailed internal regulations spelling out the specific standards of conduct of employees' behaviour (also related to the so-called ethical grey areas), none of them agreed to make such documents available to the research. The CO of company A, for example, refused to provide any information on the actual standards of conduct that apply to employees (beyond those included in the global code of conduct available on the company's website) on the consideration that the ACP constitutes a 'proprietary know-how' the firm does not want to share with competitors. More detailed information was provided by the CO of company C, who asserted that courtesy gifts (*i.e.* small inexpensive (and, in some cultures, socially acceptable) presents given at culturally recognised occasions (weddings, funerals) or special times of the year (Christmas, New Year), albeit allowed by the global corporate code of ethics, are considered as prohibited at the level of the local business unit. In this company, moreover, as well as in company B, low value items such as pens, notepads, coffee mugs bearing the company name are allowed insofar as they are accounted for in an internal database.[11] Gifts whose money value is up to 50 euro, on the contrary, may be given to customers as long as they are useful for the Health Care Professional's (HCP's) daily practice, and have a scientific purpose (*e.g.*, medicine books, stethoscopes, etc.). Such items, moreover, need to be approved and purchased by the company at the central level, upon request of the sale rep filed via a web-tool. In both companies B and C, the total value of gifts given annually to each HCP should not exceed a certain threshold (*e.g.*, which ranges between 125 and 150 euro). Since the relevant information regarding the types, characteristics, worth and even motives upholding the offering of a gift are stored in a software which all employees can access, sale reps can (potentially) keep track of the total value of gifts offered to physicians in a year and avoid offering enticements whose worth would surmount it.

Training

According to the CO of company A, training seminars are delivered once a year in a standard form to the whole workforce which are not tailored to the specific characteristics of the group of employees at risk of engaging in corrupt practices. As opposed to company A, where the training component seem to be particularly underdeveloped, in the other two companies education and training seem to have been better formulated. In company B, for example, training sessions are organised regularly, addressing both the entire workforce and particular categories of employees (*e.g.*, sale reps, purchasing agents, financial units etc.). In this firm, moreover, training seminars are delivered both directly (via face-to-face oral presentations) and via

---

11 The same procedure applies for samples, which can be provided as long as they are listed in the company's records.

interactive web-tools and platforms, whose completion is left to the supervision of the CO.

In company C standards of conduct are disseminated in different ways. First, a series of e-learning directed at the whole workforce are imposed globally and administered (on average) four times a year. The divisional CO oversees that such trainings are effectively taken and completed by employees. Second, overarching training curricula are followed by new employees, along with face-to-face seminars delivered by the local business unit. Third, the so-called 'cycle meetings' are organised at the local level every four months targeting specifically sale and purchasing agents. The aim of these meetings is to update them on the use of promotional strategies, on the existing regulation on the interactions with HCPs and to discuss with them the most problematic and frequent ethical dilemmas.

Guidance

As mentioned above, CO are usually in charge for providing guidance to employees facing difficult ethical dilemmas. One would think that given the abstract nature of the applicable (self-regulatory) provisions, a conspicuous number of requests for clearance and approval are filed to the compliance department before a gift might be offered to a business counterpart. On the contrary, according to the interviewee of company A, COs are just rarely addressed with such requests, which normally result in the issuance of a recommendation which can be easily disregarded by employees.

Nor do COs seem to be able to provide consistent guidance to the workforce. In fact, when asked to resolve an hypothetical ethical dilemma often encountered by employees when private and professional spheres overlap, the respondent A issued contradictory statements. In fact, in the event of advising a sale rep on whether to offer a gift on a personal basis to a vendor for the occasion of a birthday or a wedding, the officer would consent the giving of the gift just in the latter mentioned circumstance. The criterion adopted by the CO to resolve the ethical concern is the frequency of the event at issue. For example, the celebration of the wedding of a vendor or physician is argued to occur, if not once in his/her life, certainly on an infrequent basis (unlike the birthday, for instance). Then the giving of gifts is considered permissible and unlikely to embarrass the company if the episode will be submitted to public scrutiny (the so-called "newspaper test", see Transparency International, 2009). This argument does not fully convince, since the circumstance that the giving of gifts is allowed may induce sale reps to bestow lavish gifts that may nonetheless be perceived as an improper influence on the recipient and objectionable by the public. In companies B and C, in contrast, gifts that are offered by sale reps to business partners on personal basis do not need to be first examined and approved by the COs. Therefore, in the latter two companies if sale reps want to bestow a gift to a business counterpart claiming a personal bond and drawing on their own money, they do not need to seek a prior authorisation or advice by the companies' management. However, this can be rather problematic since a (claimed) personal relationship may often conceal an unethical commercial intent.

What is more is that also the existing ethical climate in a particular firm may not encourage employees to raise ethical issues they might be dealing with. The CO of company B, for instance, facing the request to help solving an ethical issue, reacted as following: "*If after so many trainings, sale reps are still doubting on how to cope with a certain ethical situation, I would just turn the same question to them (what would you think is the appropriate way of dealing with the situation?) as to understand if they did not get the message yet.*" This statement underscores an over-confidence in the clearness of the corporate rules, as well as in the ethical commitment of employees, thus neglecting the existence of ethical grey areas in which the line between what is permissible and what is not may be blurring.

Reporting (whistle-blowing)

Although all three companies have set up at the global level a 'hot-line' to collect all the reports of alleged misconducts filed by employees, none of them has promoted at the local level the existence of such means to channel complaints. In company B, for instance, the presence of a corporate hot-line is not promoted during the training seminars as it would raise (not explained, and incomprehensible to us) 'privacy concerns'. In practical terms, this means that whenever an employee witnesses a violation of corporate policies and of standards of conduct and intends to report it, he/she has to refer to his/her front-line superior, who is in charge for making a *prima facie* assessment of the case and (if substantiated) for subsequently channelling the complaint to the compliance (or equivalent) department. However, such systems guarantee a lower degree of anonymity and confidentiality to the employee, who much more likely may be victim of the retaliation of the colleagues.

Monitoring

From the interviews with the three COs, it emerged that the monitoring system is a major weakness of the compliance scheme. However, while companies A and B had implemented no monitoring systems to oversee the promotional activities of sale reps, company C could indicate that some sort of oversight is in place to track sale reps' marketing strategies towards HCPs and private costumers. According to the CO, in fact, sale reps of company C are required to report daily to their regional sales manager the number of visits they made to physicians and costumers via a web-reporting tool available on their I-phones. Moreover, they are also required to provide a number of data regarding the professional (and/or private firm or organisation) who has been visited, the name of the product that has been promoted, the marketing strategies employed therein etc. Since all these data are stored on a web-based application, which is accessible by the (regional and divisional) managers as well as by other sale reps, the latter can easily keep track of the promotional activities pursued by their colleagues. As stated by the CO, information as such becomes especially relevant when a sale rep retires or resigns, and his/her workload needs to be taken over by another employee. As underscored by the CO, knowing which products have already been promoted, which marketing strategies have been adopted, and the professionals' (or private costumer's) general attitude towards the company's products, are all pivotal information for a sale rep who deals with a client for the first time.

According to the CO, the regional sale manager not just monitors sale reps by regularly checking the web-tool in which information related to their daily visits are stored, but also does so by carrying out 'field inspections'. Once a month, in fact, the sale manager accompanies the sale rep in his/her visits to doctors or private businesses. During these inspections, the manager assesses the employee on the basis of his/her compliance with given (external and internal) standards and rules, his/her integrity, the correctness of the information provided, the promotional approach and tactics utilised, and the overall effectiveness in accomplishing his/her commercial goals.

Best practices: ethical performance indicators

Noteworthy are some ethical best practices in use in company C. First, in this firm, managers are encouraged to include ethical targets in their multi-annual plans, in order to allow the company's top management to screen the 'integrity track record' of the manager before deciding over his/her promotion to a higher leadership position. Second, managers are required to calculate the annual bonus of the employees working in their teams on the basis of both commercial and integrity indicators. In practical terms, this means that the successful fulfilment of (expected) business targets on the part of the individual employee is weighed against the level of compliance with certain ethical values and standards that has been shown by him while doing his job.

> By taking into due care these two indicators, departmental managers are required to annually evaluate employees and to grade their (commercial and ethical) performance. The grading scale stretches from 1 to 3. While 1 qualifies a performance that is below the expectations and 2 a level of (economic and ethical) accomplishment that meets the expectations; 3 corresponds to a degree of

commitment that stands above the corporate expectations. At the end of the yearly exercise, approximately 80% of employees obtains a 2 as a score, whereas a minority of them are expected to be under- or over-performing. The (economic) bonus is then calculated by multiplying the grade received by a certain multiplier, which is higher as the commercial and ethical performance increases (for 1 the multiplier varies from a minimum of 60 to a maximum of 90%; for 2 from 90 to 100%; and for 3 from 130 to 150%).

Since managers are evaluated according to the performances of their teams, they have a clear stake in having their employees positively evaluated. To prevent managers from overstating their workforce's performance, all the given grades are re-discussed by the leadership of the business unit in the so-called 'calibration meetings'.

Discussion

The overall results of the interviews held with the three COs provide an indication of the fact that the compliance component may be poorly developed in private sector corporations and a mere window dressing. Risk assessment, for instance, is not frequently carried out by the individual business unit according to the specific (country- and culturally-based) set of risks which are associated with the company's way of doing business. Rules of conduct are not carefully spelled out in corporate's and individual units' policy documents, and explained via regular training delivered both to the whole workforce and to the specific categories of employees more exposed to the risk of corruption. Employees, moreover, are not always encouraged to seek guidance from their front-line managers and/or their divisional COs.

Anonymous and confidential systems for filing reports of (alleged) misconduct are often not properly promoted at the level of the local business unit. Very often, therefore, the only means at the disposal of an employee willing to report a rule violation of his/her colleagues is to contact directly the company's managers and/or the CO. However, such system does not fully guarantee individuals' anonymity and the confidentiality of the information, ultimately exposing employees' to the retaliation of their colleagues.

Finally, corporations may not always have specific mechanisms or procedures in place to monitor the commercial behaviour of sale reps. By contrast, companies may have developed systems of incentives which may (directly or indirectly) reward individual unethical and corruption-leading performance. For example, as already mentioned, sale reps are usually paid on the basis of the so-called 'bonus system': and thus the more drugs they succeed to sell, the higher their income. By contrast, poorly performing sale reps may see their revenues decreased and even jeopardised. Usually, in fact, to up the minimum wage established in their employment contracts, sale reps need to pursue a number of daily visits to doctors and private costumers (which, in the case of company C is 5,5 visits per day). Cheating on the number of daily visits is a frequent trend in sale reps, who can easily fail to accomplish their targets, for example, due to the long waiting lines attending at doctors' private practices. Although the sanction envisaged for such misbehaviour is normally the termination of the employment contract, sale reps may be very much encouraged to provide false statements on their business performance (as their monthly income is at stake). A system that attaches economic benefits to the financial performance of employees is prone to unethical practices, which are conducive to competition distortion, or worse, to corruption.

Conclusion

This chapter aimed to provide an indication of the ineffectiveness of compliance systems in managing corruption risks stemming from the area of drug promotion. Evidence from the exploratory study suggests that faults lines are present in all the analysed six components of the compliance system, namely risk assessment, rule setting, training, guidance, (complaints) reporting and monitoring. Such evidence clashes with the main findings of the academic literature on organisation change, which suggest that it is via the setting up of a thorough ethical codification, of regular training, of enforcement and whistle-blowing mechanisms that ethical values are disseminated throughout the corporation and inculcated in the workforce. More specifically according to the rational choice perspective, the systematic enforcement of ethical values, accompanied by the development of a system of corporate incentives fostering individual ethical behaviour, may significantly alter the rational calculus involved in the decision to seize corrupt agreements: the (perceived) costs are increased, while the benefits associated with the engagement in corrupt acts are decreased. Furthermore, by developing a system of incentives that rewards employees' compliance with (enhanced) ethical standards, corporations may render it more convenient for the (rational) individual to refrain from participating in corrupt deals. Ultimately, the process of institutional normalisation of corrupt practices can as well be halted, as corporations engage with promoting a climate which does no longer tolerate and facilitate corrupt activities.

However ineffective companies may be in implementing corporate self-regulations, the development (or enhancement) of corporate self-regulatory schemes should not be abandoned or regarded as unsuitable to thwart corruption in the private sector. On the contrary, to the extent that it actively contributes to restoring and disseminating a corporate ethical climate, the implementation of effective self-regulatory schemes should be firmly upheld. However, compliance mechanisms may only be effective if all the compliance components are well developed. To reverse the deviant spiral instigated by corporate subcultures and alter the system of incentives that leads to corruption, risk assessments should be individually conducted by every business unit, in view to design a monitoring plan that mitigates the specific set of risks that it presents.

Clear rules should be spelled out not just at the global or group level, but also at the level of the single division, which tailors them to the specific risks and relevant domestic (cultural) variables underpinning business relationships in the country. Training should be delivered to employees on a regular basis, both in a standard and in a tailor-made format, also considering the specific risks born by certain business areas and activities.

Whistle-blowing should be encouraged through the setting up of systems of anonymous and confidential reporting, which should be consistently promoted among the personnel. Employees dealing with difficult ethical issues, moreover, should be prodded to submit the matter to front-line managers and COs, who should be concerned with leading the example, setting the ethical tone and fostering a 'speak-up' culture.

The actions of employees, in general, and of sale reps, in particular, should be constantly monitored by the firm, in order to avoid the thriving of unethical and corruption leading practices. In addition, emphasis should be placed on the ethical as well as on the commercial performance of employees. In the business area, which is dominated by profit-laden values, commitment to ethical mores may not appeal on individuals (especially when their salary depends on their specific commercial accomplishments): that lesson is brought home to us from all entrepreneurial sectors, whether from the pharmaceutical or the financial services industry.

The opposite conclusion may be drawn for the cases in which compliance with ethical standards is rewarded with economic benefits. If, at the outset, the prospect of having economic incentives recognised by the company may lead (rational) individuals to engage in ethical thinking while adopting business decisions, in the long run the ethical dictate may be internalised by the individual. Effective compliance schemes, in fact, may succeed to establish a deeply-rooted culture of integrity in which corporate values can become embedded among companies and employees, leading them to develop a corporate conscience, and accept that as corporate citizens they have an obligation to act in a socially responsible way.

References

Abraham, J., *Science politics and the pharmaceutical industry. Controversy and bias in drug regulation.* London, UCL/St Martins Press, 1995

Alvesalo, A., S. Tombs, E. Virta and D. Whyte, Re-imagining crime prevention: Controlling corporate crime? *Crime, Law and Social Change,* 2006, *no. 45*(1), 1-25

Argandoña, A., Private-to-private corruption. *Journal of Business Ethics*, 2003, *no. 47* (3), 253-267.

Arunthanes, W., P. Tansuhai and D.J. Lemak, Cross-cultural business gift-giving: A new conceptualization and theoretical framework. *International Marketing Review,* 1994, no. 11(4), 44-55

Ashforth, B.E. and V. Anand, The normalization of corruption in organizations. *Research in organizational behavior*, 2003, *no. 25*, 1-52

Asser Institute, *Prevention of fraud, corruption and bribery committed through legal entities for the purpose of financial and economic gain. Comparative overview.* The Hague: The Asser Institute, 2012

Ayres, I., and J. Braithwaite, *Responsive regulation: Transcending the deregulation debate.* New York, Oxford University Press, 1992

Blount, E.C., *Occupational crime: deterrence, investigation, and reporting in compliance with federal guidelines.* New York, CRC Press, 2003

Braithwaite, J., *Corporate crime in the pharmaceutical industry.* London, Routledge & Kegan Paul Books, 1984

Braithwaite, J., Enforced self-regulation: A new strategy for corporate crime control. *Michigan Law Review*, 1982, *no. 80* (7), 1466-1507

Carson, A. S., M. Baetz and S. McGill, *Codes of conduct in the private sector. A review of the academic literature from 1987 to 2007.* Ontario, University of Laurier, 2008

Chaikin, D., Commercial corruption and money laundering: A preliminary analysis, *Journal of Financial Crime,* 2008, *no. 15* (3), 269 – 281

Challinger, D., Will crime prevention ever be a business priority? In: M. Felson, and R. V. G. Clarke, *Business and crime prevention.* New York, Criminal Justice Press, 1997

Clarke, M., *Business crime: Its nature and control.* Cambridge, Polity Press, 1990

Clarke, R. V., Introduction. In: R.V. Clarke (ed.), *Situational crime prevention: Successful case studies.* (pp. 3-36). New York, Harrow and Heston, 1992

Cleveland, M., C.M. Favo, T.J. Frecka and C. L. Owens, Trends in the international fight against bribery and corruption. *Journal of Business Ethics,* 2009, *no. 90*(2), 199-244

Clinard, M.B. and P.C. Yeager, *Corporate crime.* New York, The Free Press, 1980

Clinard, M.B., *Corporate ethics and crime.* Beverly Hills, Sage Publications, 1983

Cohen, J.C., M. Mrazek and L. Hawkins, Tackling corruption in the pharmaceutical system with courage and conviction. *Clinical Pharmacology and Therapeutics,* 2007, *no. 81*(3), 445-449

Cooke, R.A., Danger signs of unethical behavior: How to determine if your firm is at ethical risk. *Journal of Business Ethics*, 1991, *no. 10* (4), 249-253

Cornish, D.B., and R.V. Clarke, *The reasoning criminal: Rational choice perspectives on offending.* New York, Springer-Verlag, 1986

Dexter, L. A. *Elite and specialized interviewing.* Vol. 13. Essex, Ecpr Press, 2006

Driscoll, D., E. Hoffman and J. Murphy, Business ethics and compliance: What management is doing and why. *Management Review,* 1998, *no. 10* (4), 823–836

Elliott, C., The drug pushers. *Atlantic Monthly*. 2006, *no. 297* (3), 82

European Commission, *Communication from the Commission. Executive Summary of the Pharmaceutical Sector Inquiry Report.* Brussels, European Commission, 2008

European Commission, *Green Paper, Promoting a European framework for Corporate Social Responsibility. COM(2001) 366 final.* Brussels, European Commission, 2001

European Commission, *Proposal for a directive of the European Parliament and of the Council amending Council Directives 78/660/EEC and 83/349/EEC as regards disclosure of non-financial and diversity information by certain large companies and groups. COM(2013) 207 final.* Brussels, European Commission, 2013

Fisher, J., Business marketing and the ethics of gift giving. *Industrial Marketing Management,* 2007, no. 36 (1), 99-108

Geis, G., *White-collar crime.* London, Sage Periodicals Press, 1993

Gobert, J., and M. Punch, *Rethinking corporate crime.* London, Butterworths, 2003

Gobert, J., *Controlling corporate criminality: Penal sanctions and beyond. Web JCI.* 1998, XVII

Gordon, K. and M. Myake, Business approaches to combating bribery: A study of codes of conduct. *Journal of Business Ethics,* 2001, *no. 34* (3-4), 161-173

Gorta, A., Minimising Corruption: Applying lessons from the crime prevention literature. *Crime, Law and Social Change,* 1998, *no. 30,* 67-87

Grande, D., Limiting the influence of pharmaceutical industry gifts on physicians: Self-regulation or governmental intervention? *Journal of General Internal Medicine,* 2009, *no.* 25 (1), 79-83

Hess, D., and C. Ford, Corporate corruption and reform undertakings: A new approach to an old problem, *Cornell International Law Journal,* 2008, *no. 41* (2), 307–346

Hess, D., Catalysing corporate commitment to combating corruption. *Journal of Business Ethics,* 2009, *no. 88* (4), 781-790

Hollinger, R.C., and J.P. Clark, *Theft by employees.* Lexington, LexingtonBooks, 1983

Homel, R, and R. Clarke, A revised classification of situational crime prevention techniques. In: S.P Lab (ed.), *Crime Prevention at a Crossroads*. (17-27). Cincinnati, Anderson Publishing, 1997

Kaptein, M., Business codes of multinational firms: What do they say? *Journal of Business Ethics,* 2004, 50(1), 13-31

Karanikolos, M. *et al.*, Financial crisis, austerity, and health in Europe. *The Lancet,* 2013, *no. 381*, 1323-31

Katz, D., A.L. Caplan and J. F. Merz, All gifts large and small: Toward an understanding of the ethics of pharmaceutical industry gift-giving. *The American Journal of Bioethics,* 2010, *no. 10* (10), 11-17

Klitgaard, R., Introduction: subverting corruption. *Global Crime,* 2006, *no.* 7 (3-4), 299-307

Lambooy, T.E., *Corporate social responsibility: legal and semi-legal frameworks supporting corporate social responsibility*. Deventer, Kluwer, 2010

Martín, A.N., Cosmetic use and lack of precision in compliance programs: any solution? *EUCRIM, The Criminal Law Associations' Forum,* 2012, *no. 3*, 124-127

McFadden, D.W., E. Calvario and C. Graves, The devil is in the details. The pharmaceutical industry's use of gifts to physicians as a marketing strategy. *Journal of Surgical Research,* 2007, *no. 140* (1), 1-5

Moskop, J.C., K.V. Iserson, A.L. Aswegan, G.L. Larkin and R. M. Schears, Gifts to physicians from industry: the debate evolves. *Annals of Emergency Medicine*, 2012, *no. 59* (2), 89-97

Newburn, T, *Criminology*. Cullompton. Devon, Willan Publishing, 2007

Parker, C., *The open corporation: effective self-regulation and democracy*. Cambridge, Cambridge University Press, 2002

Pope, J., *The TI source book 2000. Confronting corruption: The elements of a national integrity system*. Berlin, Transparency International, 2000

PricewaterhouseCoopers, *Confronting corruption. The business case for an effective anti-corruption programme*. London: PricewaterhouseCoopers, 2008

Punch, M., *Dirty business: Exploring corporate misconduct: Analysis and cases*. London: Sage, 1996

Rabl, T. and T.M. Kühlmann, Understanding corruption in organisations – Development of an empirical assessment of an action model. *Journal of Business Ethics,* 2008, *no. 82* (2), 477-495

Rama, D., B.J. Milano, S. Salas and C.H. Liu, CSR implementation: developing the capacity for collective action. *Journal of business ethics*, 2009, *no. 85* (2), 463-477

Ruhnka, J.C. and H. Boerstler, Governmental incentives for corporate self-regulation. *Journal of Business Ethics,* 1998, *no. 17* (3), 309-326

Scholtens, B. and L. Dam, Cultural values and international differences in business ethics. *Journal of Business Ethics,* 2007, *no. 75* (3), 273-284

Simpson, S., and C. Gibbs, *Corporate crime.* Aldershot, Ashgate Publishing, 2007

Stead, W.E., D.L. Worrell and J.G. Stead, An integrative model for understanding and managing ethical behavior in business organizations. *Journal of Business Ethics*, 1990, *no. 9* (3), 233-242

Stevens, B., Corporate ethical codes: Effective instruments for influencing behavior. *Journal of Business Ethics*, 2007, *no. 78* (4), 601-609

Sutherland, E.H., *White collar crime.* New York, Dryden Press, 1949

Sykes, G.M. and D. Matza, Techniques of neutralization: A theory of delinquency. *American sociological review*, 1957, *no.* 22 (6), 664-670

Transparency International, *Corruption and Health.* Berlin: Transparency International, 2006

Transparency International, *TI Global Corruption Report 2009. Corruption and the Private Sector.* Berlin, Transparency International, 2009

Transparency International, *Transparency in corporate reporting. Assessing the world's largest companies.*_Berlin, Transparency International, 2012

Treviño, L.K., D.G. Gibson, G.R., Weaver and B.L. Toffler, Managing ethics and legal compliance: What works and what hurts. *California Management Review*, 1999, *no. 41* (2), 131-151

Tully, S., *Research handbook on corporate legal responsibility.* Cheltenham, Edward Elgar, 2005

Vander Beken, T., *The European pharmaceutical sector and crime vulnerabilities.* Antwerpen-Apeldoorn, Maklu Publishers, 2007

Vermeulen, G., W. De Bondt and C. Ryckman. *Liability of legal persons for offences in the EU.* Vol. 44. Antwerpen, Maklu, 2012

Wortley, R., Guilt, shame and situational crime prevention. *The politics and practice of situational crime prevention*, 1996, *no. 5*, 115-132.

Wulf, K., *Ethics and compliance programs in multinational organisations.* PhD dissertation. Wiesbaden, Springer Gabler, 2011

Ethics and systemic corruption: assessing ethics policy of the Romanian public administration

Radu Nicolae[1]

Introduction and research questions

During the last 10 years, the Romanian justice system (prosecution and courts) has seriously been engaged in fighting high-level corruption. High level officials have been prosecuted and convicted for corruption, including a prime-minster[2], ministers[3], members of Parliament, magistrates and mayors of major cities. Nevertheless the perception of corruption has not significantly diminished. The fight against corruption is concentrated at high levels of power, with significant impact on the political game but without visible impact on administrative/organisational behaviour or capacity, in terms of quality of service.

Maybe it is a matter of 'integrity balance'. Langseth, Stapenhurst and Pope (2003) argue that eight interwoven fundamental elements[4] may be considered to sustain national integrity and these elements have to be equally strong and reformed so that integrity can be maintained in equilibrium, rather than collapsing. In practice not all integrity elements are equally developed in Romania and the measures implemented in the framework of the national strategies against corruption seem to have no impact on the perception of corruption. Romania has pursued an anti-corruption agenda that focused on passing new legislation and establishing new enforcement agencies, but without being able to ensure the actual enforcement of that new legislation or the independence and effectiveness of the newly-established agencies. One fundamental

---

1 Radu Nicolae is the anticorruption program manager at the Centre for Legal Resources, a Romanian independent foundation. He holds a PhD in political science and teaches an anticorruption academic course at SNSPA University in Bucharest.

2 Former prime-minister Adrian Nastase, 2001-2004 mandate;

3 Former ministries of defense (Victor Babiuc), of agriculture (Avram Mureşan, Decebal Remeş), of transport (Relu Fenechiu), of economy and commerce (Codrut Sereş), of communication and information tehnologies (Zsolt Nagy).

4 Political will, administrative reform, monitoring agencies, Parliament, justice, civil society, media, and private sector.

element of an integrity system, namely the administrative reform, was mainly pursuit by enacting legislation, in a context of poor administrative capacity in terms of infrastructure (information systems), management, training and human resources. Thus, within this 'poor context' new corruption prevention legislation was adopted in 2004 regarding whistle-blowers protection, code of conduct/ethics, declaration of gifts etc. This chapter examines the limitations of the approach of enacting legislation focusing on the administrative reform element of the national integrity system, more specifically on conduct and ethics policies.[5]

Romania has developed ethics policies in public administration with effect from 2004[6] in an effort to meet the accession criteria for membership of the European Union[7]. Despite these efforts, corruption continues to be rampant in Romania as reported by Transparency International (TI), the World Bank (WB) and the World Justice Project (WJP).[8] The European Commission also reported that "*Despite this progress since July 2010, consistency and results in a number of areas remain a challenge. Progress in the fight against corruption still needs to be pursued.*"[9]

Giving the prevalent perception of corruption, we face the question of efficacy of an ethics policy in public administration. Do ethics really matters when corruption is widespread? What is the ethics policy in relation to the criminal anti-corruption policy? To address these questions, this study compared the number of disciplinary files with the number of criminal corruption files to find that people do not use administrative proceedings to complain about abuses or wrongdoings. Instead they complain to the prosecutors. What can be achieved in the long run? Romanian

---

5 In order to have a broader view of integrity in Romania, each fundamental element of the national integrity system has to take into consideration but this is not the scope of this paper. In other instances (see Petrus C. van Duyne, Jackie Harvey, Georgios A. Antonopoulos, Klaus von Lampe, Almir Maljević, Jon Spencer, 2013), I have given a detailed account of other elements of the Romanian national integrity system, namely monitoring agencies.

6 Law no. 7/2004 on the Code of Conduct for the Public Servants

7 Romania closed accession negotiations with E.U. on 14 December 2004 but agreed on several specific requirements. After accession, a Cooperation and Verification Mechanism (CVM) to address specific benchmarks in the areas of judicial reform and the fight against corruption was established between Romania and European Commission.

8 Romania scores 3,6 in TI Corruption Perception Index 2011 and 0,6 at Absence of Corruption Factor in WJP Rule of Law Index 2011. World Bank's Trends in Corruption and Regulatory Burden in Eastern Europe and Central Asia reports corruption in Romania to be a third major problem in doing business.

9 Report from the Commission to the European Parliament and the Council on progress in Romania under the Co-operation and Verification Mechanism, p. 3

experience with this issue may have practical importance for those engaging in the anti-corruption work.

Ethics may be approached differently. Lewis and Gilman (2005) make a distinction between compliance, integrity and a 'fusion approach'. They see compliance as merely oversight and control whilst integrity is a basic value: it relies on moral character and it is a matter of individual responsibility, with no external inducements or penalties. Fusion means "*moving on both fronts at once [. . .] at a slow pace*".[10]

Giusta (2006) discerns between ethics, law and deontology (duty dogma) from the perspective of their source, their scope and their enforceability. While laws and deontology are established by a source external to the moral agent, the ethics rely on individual's conscience: it must come from 'within'.

Table 1
Distinction between ethics, law and deontology

	Ethics	Law	Deontology/Conduct
Source	Individual's conscience	Legislator, an external authority	Official body of the profession
Scope	whole sphere of human action	Social life (individuals and organisations)	Professional life
Enforceability	Not enforceable	Judicial sanctions	Disciplinary sanctions

Source: Giusta, 2006

Following Lewis and Gilman (2005) and Giusta (2006), this chapter makes a distinction between ethics and deontology/conduct. Ethics can be defined as a matter of moral behaviour, personal choices and virtues that rests on an individual's conscience. Ethics also covers actions that are known only by the moral agent or that can impact merely on the moral agent, in this sense not being enforceable by external agencies.

DeMars (1998: 84-85) highlights three chief characteristics of the ethical organisation[11]:

10 Carol W. Lewis and Stuart C. Gilman, *The Ethics Challenge in Public Service: a Problem-Solving Guide*, 2nd ed., San Francisco: Jossey-Bass, 2005, pp.17-18

11 Nan DeMars, *You want me to do WHAT?: when, where, and how to draw the line at work.* Simon & Schuster, 1998, pp. 84-85: 'a metaphor for any place or space where people work together'

1. a corporate conscience, which is a shared understanding and agreement of what the standards are for acceptable and unacceptable behaviour;
2. a commitment to hold yourself and each other personally responsible and accountable for upholding those standards, and
3. an ongoing discussion or system of honest communication about ethical issues that promotes trust and fairness.

The shared standards are embodied in an organisational code of conduct. Nevertheless, a code of conduct is not enough. Without internal commitment and ongoing discussions the code of conduct turns out to become a dead letter: "*This communication creates an expectation of conformity to this code of conduct, thus making it routine to discuss ethical dilemmas and resolve them in a way that is aligned with the code of conduct.*"

These elements are important benchmarks during an implementation of a code of conduct policy. That is why this research report to what extent the Romanian ethics policy reflects these requirements. What is the impact of the ethics policy in Romania? How the policy has been implemented and what did it produce? The chapter will elaborate the ethics policy and compare it with some of the available data.

Ethics policy in Romania

Giving the brief theoretical approaches outlined, the Romanian ethics policy is merely a code of conduct legislation. It comprises two general laws and an implementation order. [12] Due to the characteristics of Romanian public administration, public employees may have a public servant statute or they may work on a standard labour contract. Giving this formal difference in statute, each type of public employee has a different ethics regulation or code of conduct. Thus, two general laws are applicable: one for public servants and one for contractual employees. Apart from these general regulations, Romania also passed several codes of conduct for specific professionals: magistrates, auditors, police officers, customs

12 Law no. 7/2004 on the Code of Conduct for the Civil Servants, Law no. 477/2004 on the Code of conduct of contractual personnel in public institutions and authorities and Order of the President of National Agency of Public Servants no. 4500/2008 for establishing a common framework of methods of colleting and transmitting data and information relating to compliance with the conduct of conduct and implementation of disciplinary procedures.

officials etc.[13] Each code has a different implementation mechanism, hindering the monitoring process and aggregated data collection. Acknowledging this lack of proper monitoring, the National Anti-Corruption Strategy 2012-2015[14] prescribes biannual self-evaluation reports by each public organisation. For the purpose of this chapter, the general framework, namely the laws no. 7/2004 and no. 477/2004, will be examined.

Both regulations explain the mandatory professional behaviour enforceable by disciplinary sanctions. For public servants, special disciplinary commissions are entrusted with investigative powers when informed about a breach of the code. The commissions may recommend a specific sanction but the final decision about the sanction is left to the leader/manager of the organisation.[15] For regular employees, the general labour code is applicable, the employer having the right to find whether disciplinary violations occurred and to impose sanctions under the collective labour agreement and internal regulations.[16]

Both regulations similarly define the terms 'public interest' 'personal interest', and 'conflicts of interests'. Acting in public interest means "*observance by public institutions and authorities of the rights, freedoms and legitimate interests of citizens, recognised by the Constitution, domestic legislation and international treaties to which Romania is part*", while the personal interest implies "*any material benefit or otherwise, sought or obtained, directly or indirectly, for himself or for others, by public servants using reputation, influence, facilities, relationships, information they have access, because of the exercise of public function.*" [17] Conflict of interests occurs when the private interest contradicts the public interest, affecting the independence and impartiality in decision-making or the fulfilment of the public office's duties.

Both regulations define a set of 15 norms of behaviour regarding the quality of public service, the observance of the Constitution, laws and regulations, the loyalty towards public organisations, ways of expressing opinions, public activity, political activity, using own image, relationships during public office exercise, behaviour in international context, acceptance of gifts, services or advantages, involvement in

---

13 Superior Council of Magistracy Decision no. 328/2005 approving the Code of Ethics for judges and prosecutors, Order no. 252/2004 for the approval of the auditor's ethical conduct, Code of conduct of the servant of the customs authority, Code of conduct of police officers.

14 National Anti-Corruption Strategy 2012-2015 <sna.just.ro>

15 Article 1 and article 23 of the Law. no. 7/2004 and article 50 of the Government Decision no. 1344/2007 on the rules of organisation and functioning of the disciplinary commissions

16 Article 40 of the Labour Code

17 Article 4 of Law no. 7/2004 and Law no. 477/2004.

decision-making, evaluation, exercise of public power, public resources usage, participation in procurement, concessions and hiring.

Both regulations benefit form enforcement and monitoring systems but the systems are different. In the case of public servants, the National Agency of Public Servants (NAPS) is entitled to coordinate, monitor and control the implementation of the Code but without having the right to interfere with the disciplinary proceedings. In the case of regular employees, the monitoring, coordination and control powers are given to the Ministry of Internal Affairs with the same interdiction to interfere with the disciplinary proceedings.

The enforcement and monitoring system for the public servants is organised around an innovative concept for Romania: the 'ethics officer' or 'ethics adviser'. This concept has been developed into legislation beginning since 2007. Under the law, each leader/manager of a public organisation has to appoint an ethics officer. The ethics officer has to be a public servant and it is recommended to be selected from the human resources department. The ethics officers have three broad responsibilities[18]:

1. to provide advice and assistance to public servants from the respective public organisation on compliance with the code of conduct;
2. to monitor the implementation of the Code of Conduct in the respective organisation; and
3. to prepare quarterly reports on compliance with the rules of conduct by the public servants and biannual reports on disciplinary proceedings.

The reports have to be approved by the managers of the public organisations and they have to be submitted online to NAPS. The NAPS has to deliver a national statistics on ethics in their annual report and biannual specific reports on ethics.

The enforcement and monitoring system for the contractual employees is a classic one. Any legal or natural person may complain to the Ministry of Internal Affairs, Ministry of Foreign Affairs and/or to the public organisation involved regarding inappropriate conduct of contractual personnel or undue pressure on such a person. The Ministry of Internal Affairs or Ministry of Foreign Affairs has the right to investigate the complaint and may submit a report with recommendations for the public organisation involved. The public organisation has to reply in 30 days on the implementation of the measures recommended. An annual report labelled "Standard of Conduct for contractual personnel" has to be submitted to the Government by the Ministry of Internal Affairs and by Ministry of Foreign Affairs highlighting the

[18] Article no. 21 of Law no. 7/2004 and article 2 form Annex 1 of Order no. 4500/2008.

number and subject of complaints regarding infringements of rules of professional conduct, the categories and the number of contractual employees who have violated rules of professional conduct and ethics, the causes and consequences of non-compliance with this Code of Conduct, the number of cases where contractual staff was asked to act under pressure from political sides, the proposed recommendations and the public organisations which did not meet recommendations.[19]

The main task is to assess whether this ethics framework really works to prevent corruption when high-level corruption is reported. However, the corruption literature tends to consider this policy merely irrelevant in such contexts.

Ethics and good governance

Huther and Shah (2000) put forward an evaluation framework of the anti-corruption programs: "*successful anti-corruption programs will lower the expected gains and raise the expected penalties of corrupt behaviour*" (p. 2). The anti-corruption programs may alter the factors influencing each element of a public official's cost-benefit analysis. Thus, the anti-corruption programs may reduce the expected gross benefits from corruption, may reduce the number of corrupt transactions, may increase the probability of being punished for corrupt behaviour or they may increase the magnitude of penalties. Huther and Shah (2000) understand the 'ethics office' policy as a way to increase the probability of punishment for corruption. Based on OECD evaluation criteria, the authors discuss the rating factors for anti-corruption programs. For instance, an anti-corruption policy or program may prove worthwhile depending on the country's quality of governance. Following their ideas, the 'ethics office' policy is not relevant when the quality of governance is weak or it has low relevance when the quality of governance is already fair: a "*positive influence (of ethics office policy) may be limited to societies with good governance*" (p.9).

Several studies indicate Romania has such a 'lower quality of government'.[20] Thus, the 'ethics office' policy is believed to be not relevant for Romania. To test

---

19 Article 20-23 of the Law no. 477/2004

20 Gothenburg Quality of Government Institute, *Quality of government in EU region,* 2011 World Bank, *Diagnosis Surveys of Corruption in Romania*, 2000, p. 43: "indicators of the quality of public administration are individually highly negatively correlated with the average level of corruption".
Kaufmann, Daniel, Kraay, Aart and Mastruzzi, Massimo, Governance Matters VII: Aggregate and Individual Governance Indicators, 1996-2007 (World Bank, Policy Research Working Paper No. 4654, 2008)

this hypothesis, I will review the results of the ethics policy as found by an independent study[21] and several official reports.[22]

Policy Outcomes

The analysis has two steps: (a) assessment of the uniformity in policy implementation and (b) the quantitative and qualitative policy results. We deal with the policy regarding *public servants* only as data on contractual personnel does not exist. The Ministry of Foreign Affairs reported that it did not receive any complaint and Ministry of Internal Affairs reported that it did not compile any report on this matter.[23]

The data from both the independent study and the official reports confirm that the ethics policy for public servants is implemented unevenly. In many public organisations the ethics officers are not even appointed and the mandatory reports are not submitted to the NAPS.

Table 2

Mandatory reports on ethics submitted to NAPS 2009-2012[24]

Year	Quarter	No. of public organisations reporting	% of pub. organisations reporting from the total no. of pub. organisations	No. of pub. servants in the organisations reporting	% of pub. servants in the organisations reporting from the total no. of pub. servants
2009	1st Quarter	1.018	21,7	71.566	63,3
	2nd Quarter	1.248	26,6	85.974	76,1
	3rd Quarter	1.225	26,1	81.953	72,5

21 Centre for Legal Resources, *Implementation of ethics officers' regulation*, 2009

22 National Agency for Public Servants' bi-annual compliance reports on the conduct of public officials, ethical standards and disciplinary procedures

23 Responses to public information requests

24 The data were compile form the NAPS' bi-annual compliance reports on the conduct of public officials, ethical standards and disciplinary procedures: report on first half of 2009, report on second half of 2009, report on the first half of 2010, report on second half of 2010, report on first half of 2011, report on second half of 2011, report on first half of 2012, report on second half of 2012. Total number of public servants in Romania in 2009 and 2010 is 112,944 persons. Total number of public servants in Romania for 2011 is 120,684.

	4th Quarter	1.105	23,5	73.065	64,6
2010	1st Quarter	989	21,1	72.543	64,2
	2nd Quarter	956	20,4	71.794	63,5
	3rd Quarter	973	20,7	71.052	62,9
	4th Quarter	984	20,0	72.362	64,0
2011	1st Quarter	773	16,5	67.406	55,8
	2nd Quarter	826	17,6	69.502	57,5
	3rd Quarter	822	17,5	69.165	57,3
	4th Quarter	764	16,3	66.621	55,2
2012	1st Quarter	678	14,4	52.486	41,6
	2nd Quarter	716	15,3	NA	NA
	3rd Quarter	632	13,5	42.528	32,1
	4th Quarter	536	11,4	NA	NA

Two years after the 'ethics officer' concept have been converted into legislation, from 500 public organisations included in the 2009 independent study[25], 409 organisations (81,8%) confirmed that ethics officers are appointed, 69 organisations (13,8%) responded that ethics officers are not appointed and 22 public organisations (4,4%) did not responded to this question at all.[26] Discriminating by the type of public organisation, the mayor's offices had the lowest percentage of appointments. Ethics officers were appointed in 113 townships from a total 161 included in the study (70,2%). The Mayor's office is the most common public organisation in Romania, there being almost 3000 such bodies across the country. The only type of public organisation that had 100% appointment was the county level employment agency.

According to the law, each public organisation has to submit quarterly reports to NAPS but the average level of submission is below 19% and there is a decreasing trend. Although the vast majority of public organisations failed to report (more than 80%), those that are reporting tend to be large organisations in terms of number of

25 National Agency for Public Servants (NAPS), First half of 2010 compliance report on the conduct of public officials, ethical standards and disciplinary procedures, p. 4: 'in Romania there is a total number of 4695 public organisations'

26 Centre for Legal Resources, op. cit. p. 19

public servants employed. All data regarding reports submission are compiled in Table 2 above.

Another policy implementation problem arises from the practical experience and vocational training of the ethics officers. They are not properly trained to perform the advising and assistance duties.

Few officers have practical ethics experience in their day to day job due to the recommendation that ethics officers are selected from the human resources department. Human resources departments in public organisations in Romania have to deal mostly with reporting and cumbersome procedures regarding the conclusion, modification, suspension and termination of employment contracts, preparing and managing the professional files of civil servants, verifying and approving timesheets, or calculating salaries. As the ethics function has just been added to a pre-existing job description, most of the ethics officers (43,3%) have a daily task that is not connected in any way with ethics and only 13,2% of the ethics officers have a daily job connected with ethics. The table below gives account of the primary job description of these ethics officers.

Table 3
Primary job description of the ethics officers[27]

Pre-existing job description (daily responsibilities)	% of ethics officers having the job description
managing labour contracts and keeping labour records	15,1
communication, secretariat and Public Relations	14
calculating budgets, salaries and financial rights	9,3
keeping retirement records or performing internal audit	4,9
staff recruitment	11,6
conducting professional performance evaluation	9,8
implementing integrity and transparency standards	7,3
legal advising	5,9
other	22,1

27 Centre for Legal Resources, op. cit., p. 32

Only 30% of the ethics officers attended vocational training. The 2009 independent study report that "*from the total of 149 ethics officers who participated in training only 28 persons (18,8%) participated in training on ethics assistance and 49 of them (32,9%) in courses that are only partially related to the implementation of the rules of conduct for public servants and ethics counselling.*"[28]

Another concern is the amount of time available to ethics officers for completing their duties as this kind of person would have, on average, responsibilities in 4,7 major areas of work.[29]

Also, the reports submitted by the ethics officers are poorly drafted and do not provide information on the causes and consequences of breaches of conduct.[30]

The data reflects a poor administrative capacity for policy implementation. Although the ethics policy was intended to boost integrity and prevent corruption, thus improving the quality of government, it seems to fail because of poor implementation capacity. Despite the implementation shortcomings, we need to examine the results obtained by those able to implement the policy.

The first discernible impact can be measured on the awareness side. In four years 3.833 public servants requested ethics assistance from the officers and 8.486 public servants received such assistance (around 12% from the total population of public servants). The difference between the demand and the supply side can be explained by the pro-active approach of the officers that organised information meetings with public servants. The discussion topics, during this kind of meetings, were conflicts of interests and ethical dilemmas, (in)appropriate behaviour during interactions with the citizens, the rights and obligations of the public servants, the job description[31], assets and interests declarations, the conditions under which a public servant may refuse an assignment, rules of promotion, rights related to wage[32]. The data are presented in Table 4.

---

28 *Ibid,* p. 28

29 Centre for Legal Resources, op. cit., p. 34

30 National Agency for Public Servants, Second half of 2010 compliance report on the conduct of public officials, ethical standards and disciplinary procedures p. 8-13

31 *Ibid* , p. 7

32 National Agency for Public Servants, First half on 2011 compliance report on the conduct of public officials, ethical standards and disciplinary procedures, p. 5

Table 4
Number of public servants that requested and received ethics advice and assistance[33]

Year	Quarter	No. of pub. servants that requested ethics advice	In % no. of pub. servants in the reporting organisations	No. of pub. servants that received ethics advice	In %. of pub. servants in the organisations reporting	No. pub. servants in the reporting organisations
2009	1st Quarter	116	0,2	157	0,2	71.566
	2nd Quarter	354	0,4	813	1,0	85.974
	3rd Quarter	193	0,2	376	0,4	81.953
	4th Quarter	212	0,2	306	0,4	73.065
2010	1st Quarter	147	0,2	213	0,2	72.543
	2nd Quarter	333	0,4	1.025	1,4	71.794
	3rd Quarter	315	0,4	964	1,3	71.052
	4th Quarter	611	0,8	1.285	1,7	72.362
2011	1st Quarter	315	0,4	492	0,7	67.406
	2nd Quarter	339	0,4	1.550	2,2	69.502
	3rd Quarter	347	0,5	515	0,7	69.165
	4th Quarter	370	0,5	533	0,8	66.621
2012	1st Quarter	33	0,06	62	0,1	52.486
	2nd Quarter	51	NA	60	NA	NA
	3rd Quarter	47	0,1	78	0,1	42.528
	4th Quarter	50	NA	57	NA	NA

Source: National Agency for Public Servants

33 *Ibid*

The second impact of the ethics policy can be measured in relation with the disciplinary proceedings. The number of public servants under disciplinary proceedings has tended to be stable in the last four years, representing less than 1% of the total number of public servants. The downtrend in disciplinary proceedings can be explained by the downtrend of reports as fewer and fewer public organisations submit their numbers to NAPS. Thus, the ethics policy does not seem to have a significant impact on decreasing the number of public servants under disciplinary proceedings although there is a slow decreasing trend in the number of complaints. Almost half of the complaints are investigated and dismissed every year. The other complaints turned out to be valid and disciplinary sanctions are proposed. Nevertheless, around 50% of the sanctions consist of a written reprimand. Table 5 shows the disciplinary statistics in details.

Table 5
Disciplinary sanctions[34]

Disciplinary statistics	2009	2010	2011	2012
No. of public servants under disciplinary proceedings	1.122	901	869	674
% of public servants under disciplinary proceedings from the total no. of public servants	*1,0*	*0,8*	*0,7*	*0,6*
No. of disciplinary complaints	1.077	740	755	673
No. of reports issued by disciplinary commissions = 100%	1.072	916	826	573
No. of complaints investigated and dismissed	586	356	453	280
% of complaints dismissed	*54,6*	*38,8*	*54,8*	*48,8*
No of complaints where disciplinary sanctions were proposed by the disciplinary commissions	486	560	373	293
% of complaints where disciplinary sanctions were proposed	*45,3*	*61,1*	*45,1*	*51,1*
No. of disciplinary sanctions applied	571	370	312	256
of which written reprimand	307	232	139	119
% written reprimand	*53,7*	*62,7*	*44,5*	*46,4*
of which severe sanctions	264	138	173	137
% severe sanctions	*46,2*	*37,3*	*55,4*	*53,5*
No. of cases referred to the prosecutors' office for criminal investigation	50	22	32	20
total no. of public servants	112.944	112.944	120.684	120.684

Source: National Agency for Public Servants

The number of whistleblowers is irregular and few public servants (under 0,01%) put themselves under the protection of whistleblowers law.[35] An independent analysis

[34] The data were compile forms of the NAPS' bi-annual compliance reports on the conduct of public officials, ethical standards and disciplinary procedures: report on first half of 2009, report on second half of 2009, report in the first half on 2010, report on second half of 2010, report in first half on 2011.

confirms the NAPS statistics: "since 2005 the number of whistleblowers who visited the *Advocacy and Legal Advice* Centre [of Transparency International Romania] and were willing to continue the procedures, by offering evidence in support of their petitions, has increased (29 in 2005, 11 in 2006 and 18 in 2007), compared to 2 in 2003 and 3 in 2004) to return again to its old position in 2011" (Figure 1). The majority of the petitions submitted to the Centre are from people who have suffered directly from the abuse or disrespect of the laws or rules of conduct. "*They are forced to choose between their fear of retaliation and the need to solve a pressing personal problem.*"[36] However, Alistar and Nastase (2008: 11) concluded that "*the high hopes generated by this very promising start were not confirmed during policy implementation. Today whistleblower protection measures are virtually unknown to potential beneficiaries as well as receptors of public disclosures.*"

Figure 1
Number of whistleblowers

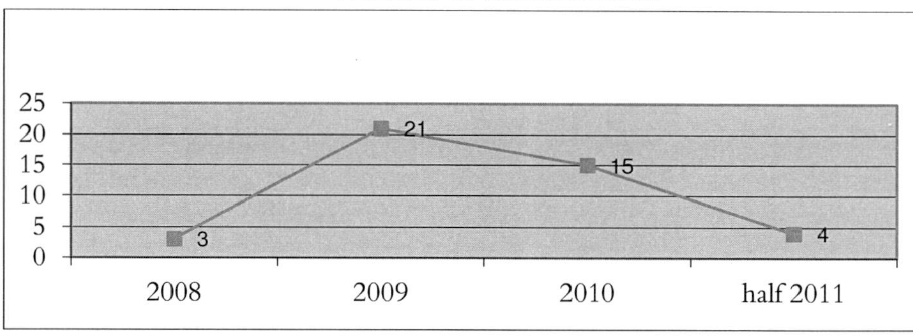

Source: National Agency for Public Servants

The disciplinary complaints are submitted mostly from within the public organisations, by managers (65% of the complaints) or peers (22% of the complaints). The beneficiaries of the public services are responsible for only 12 % of complaints[37].

Taking into account the widespread corruption indications, the number of severe disciplinary sanctions seems low: 0,23% of public servants severely sanctioned in 2009 and 0,11% in 2012. Also, the number of criminal complaints pursued by public

---

35 Law no. 571/2004 on the protection of public officials complaining about violations of the law

36 Victor Alistar and Andreea Nastase, The protection of whistleblowers in Romania, NISPAcee Conference paper, 2008, p. 10

37 The data were compiled from the NAPS bi-annual compliance reports on the conduct of public officials, ethical standards and disciplinary procedures: report on first half of 2009, report on second half of 2009, report in the first half on 2010, report on second half of 2010, report in first half on 2011.

organisations against their public servants is low: 38 complaints in 2008, 50 in 2009, 22 in 2010, 32 in 2011 and 20 complaints in 2012.[38]

These numbers continue to trouble us if we compare them with the criminal corruption investigations. The National Anticorruption Directorate (DNA), the specialised prosecution office, had 7.406 corruption files under investigation in 2012. The DNA concluded 3.578 files. In only 234 files (3,2%) did the DNA file corruption indictments and prosecute 828 defendants. The rest of the files (2.202) were investigated but dismissed.[39] Still, the total number of persons proposed for disciplinary sanctions in the public servants' system is less than the number of people prosecuted for corruption by the DNA. However, during the ethics policy implementation, the number of people investigated and sentenced for corruption increased as reported in Figure 2 and 3.

Figure 2
Corruption criminal cases

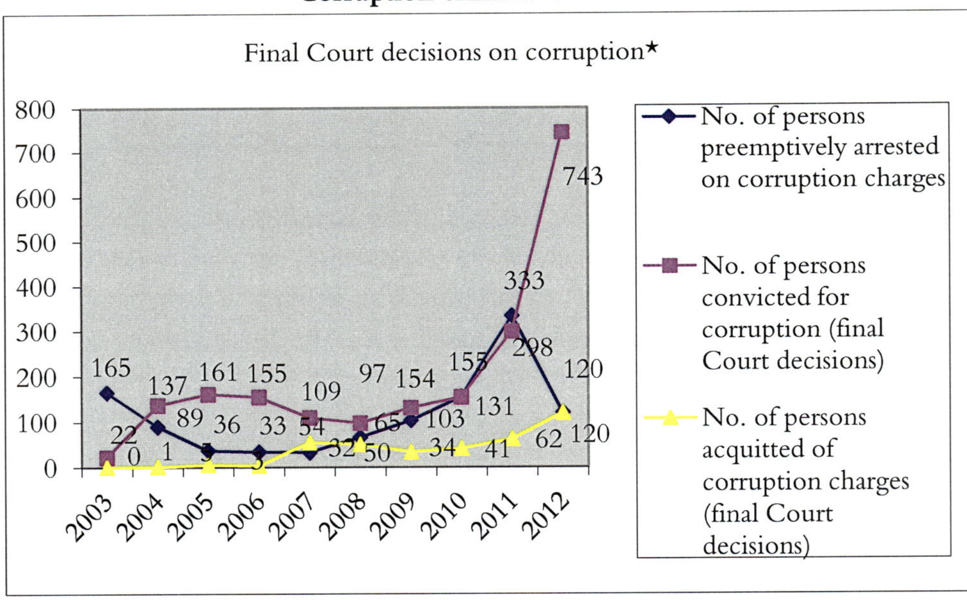

(Source: National Anti-Corruption Directorate)

38 *Idem*

39 The data were compiled from 2012 National Anticorruption Directorate report on National Anticorruption Directorate activity, 2012

Figure 3
No of persons prosecuted for corruption 2003 – 2012

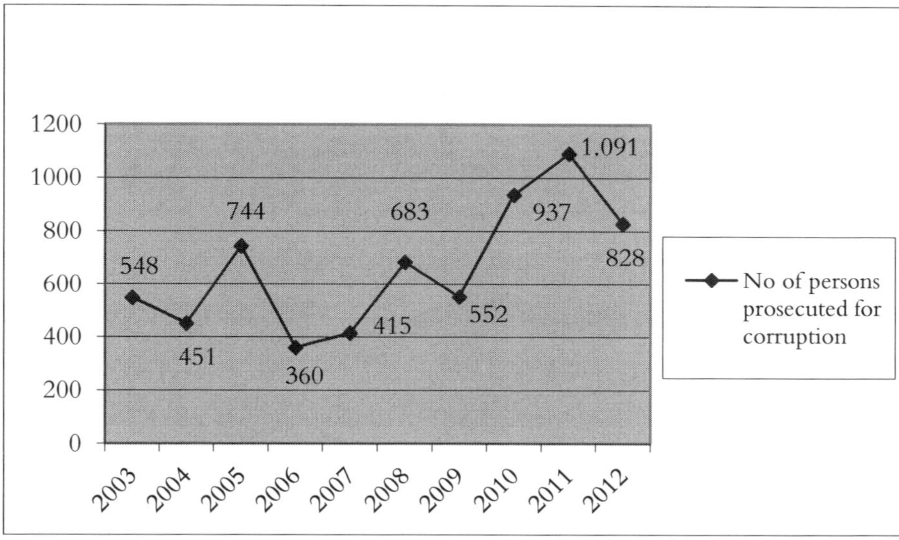

Source: National Anti-Corruption Directorate

Usually a corruption file takes several years from prosecution to final court decision as Romania has three levels of jurisdiction. This explains why the number of persons prosecuted is higher each year than the number of persons convicted or acquitted by final decisions. In the last years (2011-2012) the number of corruption files that reached the third level of jurisdiction increased and thus the number of final decisions increased. Another reason for this increase in final convictions may be attributed to a better management of Romanian High Court of Cassation and Justice. This is also reflected in the European Commission report on Romania progress under the CVM:

> "*The High Court's approach towards high-level corruption cases has continued to be characterised by a welcome degree of proactive case management. The HCCJ reported significant progress in the handling of high level corruption cases with a decrease from 28 to 10 open cases, as well as a rise in the number of cases solved in first instance. [. . .] The HCCJ has continued to make progress with setting standards and guidelines for lower courts.*"[40]

The unexpected circumstance described above that the total number of persons proposed for disciplinary sanctions in the public servants' system is less than the

40 COM(2013) 47 - Final report from the Commission to the European Parliament and the Council on progress in Romania under the co-operation and verification mechanism, 30.01.2013, p. 9

number of people prosecuted for corruption, may be explained by infrequent use of the disciplinary mechanisms. Thousands of individuals have been investigated by the DNA to find that, in fact, they did not commit any criminal corruption offence. But despite that, they may have committed several disciplinary abuses that remained unpunished. In terms of media attention the law enforcement attracts greater media attention than the disciplinary commissions. Hence, both media and citizens tend to complain to the law enforcement agencies instead of to the disciplinary commissions. This vicious circle may explain why the people are frustrated with corruption in Romania. The large number of criminal corruption cases being dismissed by the Prosecution feeds the public perception of injustice, rewarding cynicism and discouraging citizens to become involved in public life.

The results of both awareness and disciplinary proceedings are insufficient. The ethics policy does not seem to significantly prevent corruption. A grass-root study will be analysed to see how the ethics policy is perceived by the public servants, citizens and private organisation.

Grass-root study: ethics in a mayor's office

Another side of the story is what the public servants and the beneficiaries of public services think about ethics and code of conduct themselves. The data for the grass-root study was compiled from an independent report[41] on ethics in a mayor's office in *Mures County*. The report used three surveys:

a. of public servants within the mayor's office (N = 40);
b. of private suppliers of the mayor's office (N = 40) and
c. of citizens that applied to mayor's office for public services (N = 40).

More than two third of the public servants analysed from the mayor's office (70%) reported not having ethical dilemmas; such dilemmas were reported by 22,5% of the public servants. Most of those confronted with ethical dilemmas in exercising their duties (55,6%) did not talk about their dilemmas with anyone and did what they considered to be correct. 33,3% said they consulted with the supervisor, while 11,1% had consulted with colleagues. It is striking that no one consulted with the ethics officer although, when asked about who should advise the public sector employees

41 Centre for Legal Resources, *Piloting working tools for ethics officers in Mures County*, 2010. Report developed within the project RO 0010 CD 03 'Ethics officer: balance and integrity in public administration', implemented by in partnership with Pro Democracy Association and supported by Iceland, Liechtenstein and Norway under the European Economic Area Agreement (EEA) Financial Mechanism.

when they have ethical dilemmas, 22,5% mentioned the ethics officer. Anyway, 67,5% of the public servants think advice should be asked from supervisors. Another point worth mentioning from the independent report is that *none* of the respondents could provide any examples of an ethical dilemma.

Regarding the awareness of the rules of conduct, less than a fifth of respondents (17,5%) believe that public servants from mayor's office understood the code of conduct. The remaining respondents (82,5%) think that officials of the institution are either unaware of the Code of Conduct, or not very familiar with it.

The public servants surveyed indicated almost unanimously (97,5%) that they need additional information on ethical standards. Some of them have indicated several areas where additional information is deemed necessary: "*How to proceed and who can help me when I have ethical dilemmas*", "*which are the rules of conduct that apply to me*", "*which are the sanctions for breach of standards of conduct.*"

When public servants responses are compared with the views of beneficiaries (citizens) and suppliers, a gap in perception can be noticed. Mayor's office employees have more favourable perceptions than the citizens or the suppliers about the public servants' attitude to 'temptations', represented by gifts, services, favours or any advantage.

Thus, 72,5% of public servants surveyed are of the opinion that officials in the mayor's office, in exercising their duties, neither *seek* gifts, services, favours, invitations nor any other advantage, compared to 30% of citizens and 70% of companies. Contrasted with this, 52,5% of the public servants surveyed believed that officials in the mayor's office, in exercising their duties, neither *accept* gifts, services, favours, invitations nor any other advantage, compared to only 2,5% of citizens and 12,5% of companies.

A gap is also noticeable about the expected attitude towards unlawful deeds. 12,5% of the mayor's office public servants consider that it is ethically correct for a public official to say nothing when his/her superior acts in a way that gives rise to conflicts of interests because it is *not his/her business*, while only 2,5 % of citizens and suppliers gave a similar reply.

This grassroots perspective complements the aggregate data. Together they justify the conclusion that the awareness raising process is growing slowly, with little impact on actual behaviour.

Reform alternatives

The ethics policy implementation as well as the results obtained are not encouraging. Only around 20% of the public organisations are engaged in implementing the policy and that activity remain mostly formal. NAPS have been working in the last three years to improve the legal framework of ethics officers and to increase the budget available for training but their reform proposal is not yet completed.[42] Three alternative solutions are discussed by NAPS with the stakeholders from civil society:

1. *Improved legal framework* by widening the powers of the ethics officers
   Several legislative measures are envisaged: (a) regulating the obligation of ethics officers to develop corruption vulnerability analyses at the organisational level, (b) giving them the powers to monitor the wealth and interest declarations of the staff and acting as contact point for the National Agency of Integrity, (c) appointment of the ethics officer by election within the organisation;
2. *Strengthening organisational culture*
   This alternative favours publishing extended guidelines for ethics counselling and the development of specialised training for ethics officers.
3. *Technical improvements*
   The third approach favours targeted measures able to foster better implementation: reducing the number of mandatory reports from four to two and ensuring of a unitary terminology in the laws.

Other stakeholders[43] advocated for a multi-layered change of the ethics system: broadening the scope and the instruments of ethics officers to advise the public servants as well as the contractual personnel and dignitaries/elected officials. Such a reform will require the ethics function to become a fulltime job so that the ethics officer have enough time to dedicate to the process of ongoing communication about ethical issues. This far-reaching proposal aims to build an ethics framework, a comprehensive ethics management system for the public administration, including procedures, instruments, resources, monitoring and independent audit.

A key issue in this is also ensuring *independence* and *protection* against retaliation for the ethics officer in order to build confidence and professionalism. Another key issue is ensuring legitimacy of the ethics officer within the organisation by allowing an open recruitment procedure for the nomination of the ethics officer for a certain mandate. The ethics officer should work with the manager of the public institution to identify risks, vulnerabilities as well as internal prevention measures and virtues in public office exercise.

---

42 National Agency for Public Servants, Dezvoltarea standardelor etice în administraţia publică – Propunere de politică publică. Bucureşti, 2011.

43 Primarily the nongovernmental organisations Centre for Legal Resources and Agenda 21.

An ethics officer, from this perspective, should have an appropriate intrinsic motivation and skills (formal logic, legal argumentation, mediation, communication). An ethics officer should have a broad range of instruments and internal procedures available: questionnaires, case studies, matrices, checklists, manuals of procedures and techniques, as well as access to resources (internal information and reports, participation to external events, appropriate space for internal meetings and discussions. In order to properly use the instruments, the ethics officers should attend an initial training programme and regular external professional training.

Regarding the personal characteristics, an ethics officer should be a person with very good reputation. The ethics officers should be part of regional and national networks in order to allow consultation and communication, exchange of good practices and stakeholders' involvement (such networks should be managed by NAPS).

Finally, the monitoring and evaluation system of the ethics officer should include a well-defined set of indicators, targets and annual external audit. The ethics officers should be evaluated also in terms of the number of integrity incidents uncovered by the enforcement agencies and *external* perception about the integrity within the organisation. NAPS should administer the monitoring and evaluation process and be able to request the dismissal or sanctioning of the ethics officer.

All the solutions require appropriate budget allocations but such a policy is hardly a priority at national level. All the proposed solutions have their limitations. First, all the proposals mentioned above avoid the underlying issues of poor administrative capacity and the general perception of corruption in the public sector. Secondly, when talking about integrity in an organisation, the 'tone' is set by the top management. The ethics officer will be unable to function properly in an organisation administrated by corrupt or abusive elected/political appointed officials. Thirdly, in order to create a culture of integrity, external environment of the public administration is also a key factor. The efforts of the ethics officer should be complemented by a continuous pressure for integrity from regular citizens, local companies, media or civil society stakeholders.

Sadly, as reported above, there is a lack of 'demand' for integrity as the beneficiaries of the public services are responsible for only 10-12 % of total disciplinary complaints.[44] In order to circumvent these limits, such a reform of ethics policy in the public administration should be a part of a more comprehensive package of measures able to reinforce the administrative reform element of the Romanian

44 National Integrity Agency, *2007 - 2009 Activity report*, p. 41: at the National Integrity Agency, the level of complaining is 10,2 % - "*from 1948 files, 1750 files were ex-officio investigations and 198 files were based on complaints*".

national integrity system. This policy package could include simplification of procedures, *ex-ante* impact assessments, mandatory evaluation of public policies, improving salary schemes in the public sector, redesigning organisational schemes, better evaluation procedures, better budgeting and public consultation, to name a few.

Conclusions

At the beginning of the chapter this study sought to discern whether ethics policy in Romania really matters when corruption is widespread, whether ethics policy is able to boost integrity in public office and reduce corruption, or whether it generated ethical organisations. Following Huther and Shah (2000), the hypothesis was that the 'ethics office' policy is not relevant for Romania's anticorruption framework. The arguments discussed above indicate indeed that the ethics policy of the Romanian public administration is not relevant from an anti-corruption point of view.

First, the ethics framework is fragmented: there is a system for public servants, a different one for contractual employees, several ones for other public jobs like magistrates, auditors, police officers, customs officials, each with different implementation and monitoring rules, with different oversight bodies that do not communicate with each other.

Second, almost 80% of the public organisations do not report on the implementation of the ethics standards and the reports submitted are poorly drafted.

Third, ethics officers are not properly trained to perform the advising and assistance duties: they lack practical experience with ethics, as only 13,2% have a daily job connected with the integrity and transparency subjects, and therefore lack time to dedicate to their part-time ethics job.

Fourth, disciplinary proceedings do not have dissuasive effects as 50% of the sanctions consist of written reprimand. There are more people prosecuted or sentenced for corruption than staff recommended for disciplinary sanctions in the public servants' system.

Fifth, there is little awareness about ethics and ethical dilemmas among public servants but also among beneficiaries of public services. The public servants from a mayor's office in Mures County indicated almost unanimously (97,5%) that they needed additional information on ethical standards, two thirds of them saying they do not have ethical dilemmas, and *none* being able to provide any example of an ethical dilemma. This indicates that public and civil servants share the same low level of awareness. At the same time, there is little external demand for the disciplinary systems as the beneficiaries of the public services are responsible for only 10-12 % of total complaints.

Huther and Shah (2000) proved to be correct in that ethics officers work better in a system with a well-established appreciation of the ethical code and good governance. The results show that the ethics policy cannot be easily 'transplanted' to Romania, at least for the time being, and that the ethics officer's role in the fight against corruption is overestimated.

Factors like poor administrative capacity, political patronage, corruption, and red tape hinder the policy development and challenge any alternative solution proposed. Reform proposals vary from few technical improvements to multi-layered changes and fuel a continuing debate among policy makers and stakeholders.

Unfortunately, in the last 20 years several administrative reforms has been implemented in Romania and created a 'reform fatigue' in the public sector. Sometimes the reforms were adopted as a response to external demand (mostly from the European Union) and they were uncoordinated and poorly carried out. Thus, they evoked resistance within the public sector, furthering formalistic and half-hearted implementations. Such situations exist also in other countries that recently joined the European Union or that are preparing to do so. In Serbia, for instance, Van Duyne and Stocco (2010) reported lack of data, lack of transparency and uncoordinated anticorruption efforts as criminal justice institutions operated at random. The subject of corruption is declared to be a priority in Serbia by solemn official proclamations, but few public organisations seems to care about it and citizens feel powerless and disappointed: "Many do it and few care". This reflects the major obstacle of the past decade: indifference, displayed either openly or behind the stage settings of law and institutions (Van Duyne, 2013: 330). Romania as well as Serbia has to find internal motivation for reform in order to avoid the Potemkin village impression. This means creating a critical mass of citizens, public sector organisations, public servants and decision-makers that have something to gain by making the administrative system transparent, fair and responsive. Such critical mass may benefit from Romania's joining the EU and the opportunities such as structural funds and access to the free market.

References

Alistar, V. and A. Nastase, *The protection of whistleblowers in Romania*, NISPAcee Conference paper, 2008

Centre for Legal Resources, *Implementation of ethics officers' regulation,* 2009,

<www.crj.ro/Raportul-privind-aplicarea-legislatiei-referitoare-la-consilierii-de-etica-317>

Centre for Legal Resources, *Piloting working tools for ethics officers in Mureş County*, 2010

DeMars, N., *You want me to do WHAT? when, where, and how to draw the line at work*, Simon & Schuster, 1998

Duyne P.C. van, J. Harvey, G.A. Antonopoulos, K. von Lampe, A. Maljević, J. Spencer, (eds.), *Human dimensions in organised crime, money laundering and corruption.* Wolf Legal Publishers, 2013

Duyne. P.C. van and E. Stocco, *Corruption in Serbia. From black box to transparent policy making*, Nijmegen, Wolf Legal Publishers, 2012

European Commission, *Final report from the Commission to the European Parliament and the Council on progress in Romania under the co-operation and verification mechanism*, COM (2013) 47, 2013

European Commission, *Report from the Commission to the European Parliament and the Council on progress in Romania under the Co-operation and Verification Mechanism*, COM (2011) 460 final, 2011

Giusta, P., *Ethics Matters: Practical Micro-Ethics for Civil Servants of the European Union.* (Luxembourg: Office for Official Publications of the European Communities, 2006)

Gothenburg Quality of Government Institute, *Quality of government in EU region*, 2011 <http://ec.europa.eu/regional_policy/newsroom/pdf/20110504_shortnote_governance.pdf>

Huther, J. and A. Shah, *Anticorruption Policies and Programs: a framework for evaluation.* (Policy Research Working Paper No. 2501, The World Bank, 2000)

Kaufmann, D., A. Kraay and M. Mastruzzi, *Governance Matters VII: Aggregate and Individual Governance Indicators, 1996-2007.* (Policy Research Working Paper No. 4654, World Bank, 2008)

Kolthoff, E., L. Huberts and H. van den Heuvel, The ethics of new public management: is integrity at stake? *Public Administration Quarterly*, 2007

Langseth, P.; R. Stapenhurst; J. Pope, *The role of a national integrity system in fighting corruption.* EDI working papers, 1997, Washington, DC: World Bank.

Lewis, C.W. and S.C. Gilman, *The ethics challenge in public service: a problem-solving guide*, 2nd ed. (San Francisco: Jossey-Bass, 2005)

National Agency for Public Servants, *First half of 2009 compliance report on the conduct of public officials, ethical standards and disciplinary procedures.* <www.anfp.gov.ro/PaginaContinut.aspx?Id=237>

National Agency for Public Servants, *Second half of 2009 compliance report on the conduct of public officials, ethical standards and disciplinary procedures.* <www.anfp.gov.ro/PaginaContinut.aspx?Id=237>

National Agency for Public Servants, *First half on 2010 compliance report on the conduct of public officials, ethical standards and disciplinary procedures.* <www.anfp.gov.ro/PaginaContinut.aspx?Id=237>

National Agency for Public Servants, *Second half of 2010 compliance report on the conduct of public officials, ethical standards and disciplinary procedures.* <www.anfp.gov.ro/PaginaContinut.aspx?Id=237>

National Agency for Public Servants, *First half on 2011 compliance report on the conduct of public officials, ethical standards and disciplinary procedures.* <www.anfp.gov.ro/PaginaContinut.aspx?Id=237>

National Agency for Public Servants, *Dezvoltarea standardelor etice în administratia publica – Propunere de politica publica.* Bucuresti, 2011.

National Anticorruption Directorate, *2010 report on National Anticorruption Directorate activity*, 2011

National Integrity Agency, *2007 - 2009 Activity report*, 2009

Nicolae, R., *Corupţia şi politicile anticorupţie*, Polirom, Iaşi, 2010

Nicolae, R., Corupţie şi management public. In: M. Păunescu, *Management public în Romania*, Polirom, Iasi, 2008

Transparency International, *Corruption Perceptions Index 2011*, Berlin, 2011

World Bank, Trends in Corruption and Regulatory Burden in Eastern Europe and Central Asia, 2011, <http://siteresources.worldbank.org/ECAEXT/Resources/2011_report_fullreport.pdf>

World Bank, *Diagnosis Surveys of Corruption in Romania* (2000), <www1.worldbank.org/publicsector/anticorrupt/romenglish.pdf>

World Justice Project, *Rule of Law Index* (Washington, D.C. 2011)

Shadows of corruption and bribery in the Czech Republic
Can we see through them?

Miroslav Scheinost[1]

Introduction: awareness and focus

During the last years the word corruption became a very frequently used term in the public parlance in the Czech Republic. Speaking of the public it does not only mean that corruption became a most frequent subject of conversations among citizens, but also that corruption reached the top positions on the list of burdensome problems in society as perceived by people. It has become also the focus of media attention. Of course one may wonder whether and to what extent the public perception of the importance of the problem of corruption is influenced the heightened media attention or whether the growing attention of media was rather a reaction to the feelings of citizens. Of course, many studies show the substantial impact of media on the consciousness, knowledge and attitudes of people (see e.g. Scheinost, 2011, Van Duyne, 2004). Nevertheless, in the growing attention for corruption public perception and media coverage went hand in hand.

As a result of media pressure and criticism from the public, the phrase of corruption has become subsequently one of the most used words of the parlance of politicians themselves, even to such an extent that the government, respectively the governmental coalition of political parties that ruled since 2010 to 2013, has made the combat against corruption one of the central pillars of its program. We can, however, guess whether the politicians really wanted to acknowledge and reflect the extent and depth of this phenomenon in society, or whether it was only one of the means "*captatio benevolentiae*" of the discontent and critical public. However, the real effect of this "priority section" of the governmental programme remained rather weak while this government ended its functional period under the burden of several corruption scandals.

---

1 The author is director of Institute of Criminology and Social Prevention, Prague.

Of course, the term corruption is quite vague, in common use and the more so in the political language: it includes many different connotations, meanings and references. This is the case not only of common and political language, even official documents offer different definitions of this phenomenon or they do not offer any, as does United Nations Convention against Corruption which in its article 2. *Use of terms* does not introduce any definition of corruption (see also Jager, 2004).

The problem of insufficient precision is determined by the nature of corruption. Corruption is a many-facetted phenomenon. Bribes can be money (from a few to hundreds of million Euros), performance in kind, favours or provided social benefits. The number of involved persons may vary from two to several dozens. Also the complexity of these activities vary – a bribe can be easily passed from hand to hand, but it can also have a form of complicated cash flows, and such conduct does not need to be once-only as corrupt dealings also includes organised long-term activities. Sometimes corruption has been understood only in the limited meaning in the relationship with the public administration whereas sometimes it also includes the corruption in the private sector (Van Duyne, 2001).

This broad spectrum of forms and manifestations significantly hamper the effectiveness of the fight against corruption and limits the unintentional or focused orientation of anti-corruption efforts to only its most obvious manifestations (Transparency International, 2012). It means that the phenomenon of corruption can be approached from different points of view and angles. We may study its character, phenomenology, forms, impact on the state administration or economy, on social relations, moral consciousness, behaviour of people, values etc. etc. What is probably most complicated is the evaluation of the real extent of corruption in certain areas because of the usual reluctance of both briber and bribe-taker to report their acts of bribery or even to give evidence. Corruption is a consensual crime.

Instead of valid data what we usually have at our disposal are rather the opinions of the public, of experts and of professionals in certain fields on the state, intensity and influence of corruption. These opinions do not provide us the hard data on the state of corruption but we may learn from them more about the meaning of this phenomenon (it is by way the method of construction of Corruption Perception Index produced regularly by Transparency International). It means that though we have not an exact indicator on the state of corruption we have an indicator of the *social climate*: critical, favourable or unfavourable to corruption. And the state of social climate with regard to corruption is very powerful factor affecting the real behaviour of people in relation to corruption.

Therefore in this article we especially focus on the 'picture' of corruption as seen in the 'eyes of public' in the CR. It is general truth that the public do not need an exact definition and conceptualisation of corruption as it tends to understand the phenomenon of corruption rather intuitively; more by feeling than by strict specification of concept. From this social angle the changes in the views of public on corruption (how is corruption perceived and what kinds of corruption are in the eyes of the public most alarming and sensitive) may serve as an indicator of the development in the society. Therefore, we must take this changing opinion into account. Once formed, regardless of the definition and the source of information, as it becomes a social fact *sui generis* that acts as an indispensable and powerful factor of the aggregate corruptive climate in the society and the behaviour of people.

This is the question that is addressed in this chapter in which we follow the social view and meaning on corruption since the communist period across the period of transformation till today. While the substance of corruptive behaviour may have little changed, its manifestations as well as the way they are perceived may have been adapted to new conditions.

Corruption in time of communist regime and after

The communist period

If we try to compare the manifestation of corruption during the communist regime with the current situation, we find significant differences. The life under the communist regime was characterised by an apparent permanent 'minor' corruption at the level of everyday life. The prevalent form of that kind of corruption can be labelled as 'networks of mutual favours'. This form of corruption arose and developed in the society and economy that was characterised by a chronic shortage of not only luxury goods but also by lack of ordinary goods and services, when the demand of many of these goods and services permanently exceeded the supply or rather, the possibility to cover the needs.

It is plausible statement that corruption which developed under socialist conditions consisted only partly of direct financial exchange (bribes) being rather characterised by mutual exchange of coveted goods and services among people that were able to dispose of them. It means that corruption manifested itself in the form of networks of mutual favours that ensured for participants the provision and procurement of scarce goods and services (e.g. between mason and auto-mechanician or between butcher and shop assistant). However, these networks functioning on the basis of an informal market, disqualified those who had nothing to offer.

Another characteristic feature was that it still maintained a form of 'minor corruption of everyday life' which did not transit into a huge black market and an extensive shadow economy as it occurred for example in the former Soviet Union.

At the mid-level value of assets and services (for example a flat in the situation of permanent lack of dwelling or presumed higher quality of medical care) the financial bribes occurred more often but they were still often accompanied by the offer of practical services as a complementary barter.

Corruption at a higher level could be rather denoted as *clientelism*. The primary motive for corruption behaviour at this level was an effort to obtain, maintain and secure the good position in the political power system. For people at influential and decisive positions in the communist party, governmental and state administration hierarchy it was of vital importance to have at lower positions 'friends' or people (clients) who were in some way obliged to them, ready to support them or at least not to intrigue against them. For people on lower positions inside this power system it was important to have a 'protector' at higher ranked position. The primary intention which resulted from the then political-economic arrangements was: reach and keep the position on the ladder of political power and not reap economic profits in the first place.

It is not surprising that in this period there were no opinion surveys about corruption in the socialist society. One can say that the corrupt conduct at daily level was not understood as 'corruption' but as the normal adaptation to the realities of life (maybe it could be interpreted as a compensation of non-existing market of goods and services at the individual level). Only at the mid-level of the socio-political life did people speak of corruption but this kind of conduct was commonly known as a 'public secret': officialy admitted as a reality, let alone a social problem. It was understood as behaviour that is incorrect but in fact not reprehensible. And anyhow, the clientelism inside the political power system was for ordinary people 'far and high' and, of course, officially did not exist at all.

The post-communist period

The transformation of policy, economy and society in the post-communist period has also brought a transformation of forms of corruption. 'Small' corruption at the level of everyday life has subsided to some degree, as both common and luxury goods and services are now available without much difficulty, the amount of the customer's money being the only limit. The 'natural' exchange of goods and services was no longer necessary because of their availability for payment. The importance of this type of corruption has also decreased in the eyes of the public. The persistent manifestations of these 'minor' corruption are rather tolerated as shown by the survey findings, probably due to the decline of its importance and maybe also due to the fact that people got used it as a part of everyday life in the past. It holds also for the corruption at mid-level economy that existed during the communist period.

What changed significantly is the corruption at higher level of social and especially economic life. Corruption began to be motivated first and foremost by economic benefits. In the initial phase of the transformation the access to public resources was the main thing that mattered; this meant the access to the privatised property and to the information in order to gain advantage at the expense of potential competitors. Bribery was associated also with possibilities of obtaining credits, without which it was hardly conceivable to start a business in the newly opened and the only created market in a situation of absolute lack of dispensable private capital. The ways how to obtain credits from banks (and in many cases not to repay them) has been sometimes called '*the banking socialism*'. Corrupt conduct was undoubtedly strengthened by a policy-driven effort to speed up the transition process disregarding the deficiencies and gaps in its statutory regulation.

This situation holds for the first phase of transformation during which the major part of the privatisation process took place. Corruption was mostly connected with efforts to obtain advantageous positions and resources with regard to privatisation of state property.

In the next phase, after the privatisation process was more or less accomplished and new strong players in the business and financial market established their areas of interest, the effort to gain privatised state property was replaced by struggle for state and public contracts.

At present, in a situation when the possibility to privatise some lucrative state property is strongly limited by its residual extent (i.e. there is little left to privatise; some spare attractive objects of state property could represent a political problem if they should be privatised, as e.g. Prague airport), state and public contracts still represent a huge source of possible revenues and profit. Another possible source of profit – and incentive of corrupt behaviour – came after entering EU in the form of European funds.

Thus in contrast to the situation under the communist regime, corrupt behaviour at a higher level became to be primarily motivated by a desire to achieve increased economic profits. The effort has been focused on circumventing mandatory rules and procedures instead of trying to achieve and maintain a position in formal power systems. The real influential players on the market operating on the edge of the law, called in the political and journalistic jargon 'godfathers', have not tried to gain official political positions. They rather prefer to influence the politicians and state officials 'from behind' using different means, of course mainly corruption (Scheinost, 2013). The object of corruptive pressures are not only government officials but also politicians from local through regional to central level.

Direct engagement of rich entrepreneurs in the polical arena has been untill now remained exceptional. Only at the last parliamentary elections in October 2013 the situation changed. Two new political parties (rather movements than classical parties) were established, initiated and lead by well-known and rich entrepreneurs. But what is important is that both of them are not associated by the public and media to some suspicious economic and financial activities. They represent rather a 'populistic' undercurrent and very effectively quarry favour of people from the dissatisfaction of public with traditional political parties.

Thus, generally spoken, the character of corruption changed hand in hand with the changes that run in the society and economy within the period of transformation and after it. Unlike the period of communist regime we now have the surveys of public opinion dealing with corruption. Therefore we may have a look how has been corruption perceived by public.

State of corruption in the eyes of the public

As remarked before, people do not need the exact definition of corruption to have an opinion on this matter. Regardless of the question of the definition the Czech general public use to be quite sceptical in terms of the state of the corruption in their society and believe that the incidence of corruption is significant. It is hard to estimate in which extent this opinion is influenced by the frequency of this topic in the media which has different forms. Research on the source of information of the public about organised crime showed a clear influence of mass media: television, followed by newspapers and internet – this especially with regard to younger people (Scheinost, 2011:212). We may suppose similar results with regard to corruption and we may also suppose the relationship between the frequency of occurrence of such a topic in the media and the opinion about the assumed extent of its manifestations in the society. Indeed, the reporting of corrupt causes and the problem of corruption in general became highly frequent topic within last five years in the Czech media and public area.

However, if we compare this general opinion about the extent of corruption in society with the real number of persons prosecuted and indicted for corruption and bribery we find substantial difference although we can note that the Czech criminal law is quite strict against the corruption. An offence of bribery has a maximum prison sentence of up to six years, with the maximum limit relating to acts committed with the intention to procure for himself or another person a substantial benefit or committed against a public official. For accepting a bribe an offender may be in these cases even imprisoned for up to twelve years. The Criminal Code also recognizes the offence of indirect bribery, consisting in requesting or accepting a bribe for influencing an official. Such an offence is punishable with the imprisonment of up to three years whereas giving or offering a bribe in this case can be punished with the imprisonment of up to two years (Czech criminal code, 2009).

But if we would only base our judgments on the number of prosecuted offenders, we would have to conclude that the extent of corruption is almost negligible. As an illustration we present the following table with the number of persons prosecuted for the bribery.

Table 1
Number of persons prosecuted for bribery

Crime	2005	2006	2007	2008	2009	2010
Bribe-taking	91	40	37	42	31	31
Bribe-giving	82	96	65	78	68	82

Source: Judicial statistics of the Czech Ministry of Justice

The 'voice of the public', nevertheless, is absolutely different. The results of various surveys of public opinion on corruption and the corruption situation demonstrates that the public holds a very deviating opinion about the state of corruption.

In the first place we may mention the well-known Corruption Perception Index CPI, regularly produced by Transparency International and based on the views on corruption by the inhabitants of respective countries. In 2010 the Czech Republic was classified by the index 4,6 (on a scale from 0 to 10, where 10 indicates a country with almost no corruption and 0 means a high level of corruption) and ranked the 53rd position in the chart covering 178 countries (Transparency International, 2010). In 2011, the Czech Republic was classified by the index of 4,4 and ranked the 57-59th position together with Namibia and Saudi Arabia. In 2012 it was 4,9 and 54-57th position. These results are not satisfying, especially not only in comparison with developed countries but even with regard to other post-communist countries. For example, Poland and Hungary are better in this ranking (Od korupce k integritě, 2013).

In 2010, the Institut of Criminology and Social Prevention conducted a research project on a representative sample of 977 respondents, which focused on the views and experiences of people regarding the corruption in relation to the public administration. The concept of corruption was defined in this project as: a relationship between a corrupting person and a corrupt person when a corrupting person offers, and usually provides some form of remuneration for being granted an undue advantage; a corrupt person provides or promises such an advantage and expects or requires a reward for this.

The findings of the research showed that about one third of respondents say they know someone who was forced to give a bribe to an official. This argument, however, has to be confronted with only 13% of respondents saying that during the last three years they themselves got into a situation when someone directly or indirectly required a bribe from them (18% of respondents have had no dealings with the authorities during the last three years). The opinion of the respondents as to who is the initiator of corruption is of interest:

- 24% of respondents said that the initiative comes mostly from an official;
- 29% considers the level of activity of citizens and officials in corrupt conduct roughly the same;
- 18% believe that the activity is mostly on the part of citizens;
- 29% do not know.

Moreover 46% of respondents believe that the official usually accepts an offered bribe.

Thus, the public opinion on corruption, respectively the corruption resistance of state officials is not very favourable. In this situation, a rather positive finding is the statement that 40% of the respondents claim that they never offered a bribe and never gave any, although this statement is to be taken critically.

Table 2

Weights given to reasons for giving bribes: scale 1 - 5

They consider it a **courtesy** to the official	2,85
An official directly **requires** this from them	2,57
They want **to thank the** official for taking care of it	2,48
The official **indicated** this to them	2,25
They believe **there is no other way**	2,25
Someone has **indirectly** said them they should give a bribe	2,16
They want **to force** an official to act in their interest	2.11
They want to **influence the** official to act in their interest	1.96

Source: ICSP survey 2010

A variety of reasons why people give bribes to officials seems to be less positive at least if we try to evaluate the level of tolerance of corrupt behaviour in the society. The results from this survey show the order of these reasons by weight attributed to them by respondents: the weights are as follows (the weight was indicated at the five-point scale, where the 1 was the lowest weight attributed by respondent, 5 the highest: see table above).

These statements indicate a rather considerable degree of tolerance towards corruption, or its acceptance as the view that a bribe to an official is an expression of grace, gratitude and necessity, prevails. This corresponds to a statement as to what would a citizen do upon encountering a corruption. Only 26% would complain about the institution where this behaviour took place or would notify the police and only 3% within these 26% would be willing to testify in court (Cejp, 2011).

Since 1998, the proportion of respondents who consider corruption as immoral has been decreasing and the number of those who consider it as a natural part of life has been increasing. In 1998, 85% of respondents considered corruption immoral compared to only 74% respondents in 2010 (GfK, 2010).

A similar study has also brought interesting findings on the general corruption atmosphere in the country. For example, comparing the years 2006 and 2009, according to their own statements 12% more people gave a bribe (increase from 36% to 48%). In 2009 50% of respondents agreed with the opinion that if there is no other option, one should not be afraid to give a bribe. Roughly two thirds (65%) of people agreed with the statement that no company is able to get a state or municipal contract without giving a bribe (Mravec, 2012).

The personal and institutional level of corruption

These results give a Janus' double-faced shape of corruption in the eyes of public. On the one side significant tolerance and exculpation of bribery, on the other side quite critical and sceptical attitude to the state of corruption in general. At least a partial explanation could consist of a differentiation between on the one hand, corruption at the level of 'personal conduct' or 'personal relationship' to the officials and on the other hand, 'entrepreneurial conduct' in relation to public resources. We may also formulate a hypothesis that the higher tolerance toward corruption at the 'personal level' is related to the way of daily behaviour under the communist regime showing much continuity.

The belief of the public that corruption in the public administration is especially problematic in the management of public resources (i.e. at institutional level), such as public procurement, is confirmed by a survey on corruption among businessmen, which in the beginning of 2010 was carried out by the Association of Small and Medium-Sized Enterprises and Tradesmen (AMSP, 2010).

The question "Do you think it's possible to get a public contract in the Czech Republic without a commission or bribe?" was answered as follows:

- "definitely not" – 29,4% respondents,
- "somewhat not" – 29,9% respondents.

Thus, almost 60% of the entrepreneurs believe that without a bribe no public contract can be obtained. Only 7,1% of respondents "strongly" believe that public procurement can be obtained free of corruption, and 23,3% "somewhat" believe that it is possible.

An important aspect depicting the state of corruption in the country as is seen by entrepreneurs is also the willingness of managers to resort to the corruption or to accept it. According to a recent study by Ernst & Young Consulting Company 41% of the managers stated that, in order to obtain the contract extra expenses for the 'representation' can be justified (the European average is 17%). A third of respondents would be willing to consider a bribe in order to obtain a contract (the European average is again only 17%). According to this survey, in comparison with the European average (66%), there are significantly fewer Czech respondents (37%), who believe that a good reputation is a business asset for a company (EY, 2011).

Another area that is seen as gravely burdened by corruption is the public administration. In the survey conducted in 2009, respondents identified the public sectors most hit by corruption as follows:

Table 3

Respondents: % considering public administration entities as corrupt

Institutions	**Respondents %**
political parties	22
state offices	17
ministries	14
government	10

Source: Mravec, 2012

Respondents associated corruption the least with the education system, customs officers, the 'voluntary sector', churches and banking and also the media (Mravec, 2012).

These findings are supported by the results of the research carried out in 2011 (Buriánek, 2011). According to them, corruption has taken a first place among the problems that disturb the public and overtook both crime that has been long in the first place, and unemployment. Also, more and more people are starting to consider corruption as organised (almost 50%), or even systemic (over 20%). Ever less people consider it to be just occasional, or frequent yet an elemental activity.

However, a low willingness to report corruption cases has also been confirmed: almost half of the respondents believe that it does not make any sense. Roughly one third would be certainly willing to report corruption, but to the anonymous hotline and only 20% would be willing to report it to the police. Research showed the correlation between the understanding of corruption as a systemic and organised phenomenon and the critical attitude to the current political system (Buriánek, 2011).

The fact that people consider political institutions as the most corrupt can be attributed to some extent to high levels of general disgust towards the state of politics and the conduct of politicians. This is also underlined by a representative periodic study of competitiveness published by the World Economic Forum. The study assesses the country according to many different criteria. While within the overall competitiveness ranking the Czech Republic was classified relatively well for the 2010-2011 period (36th place in the world out of 139 surveyed countries), it scored a 72nd position in terms of the quality of government institutions. It is worth noting the sub-criterion of '*public trust in politicians*', where the Czech Republic ranked 121 (out of 139!) (Schwab, 2011).

Contradictions and explanation

The above research findings point at an explanation of the apparent contradiction between the generally shared views on a corruption-ridden country and the relatively limited amount of persons who really got in contact with corruption (as providers or recipients of bribes). According to the research "Actor 2011" approximately 60% of people is not involved in corruption neither as providers nor recipients (Buriánek, 2011).

The explanation may be that the occurrence of such kind of corruption that is peceived as real and serious problem in the Czech Republic is at least in eyes of public concentrated in the distribution of public funds, in the chaotic intertwining of the interests of political parties, government and business. The main societal problem is not primarily felt as the individual (own) corruption commited in order to provide various (sub-)services, but the systemic corruptive manipulation of public resources. This is an area that is "out of the perimeter of the ordinary citizen" and that is how the corruption is particularly critically perceived. Citizens consider the big, politically conditioned corruption substantial and more serious, while areas dominated by the so-called minor, administrative corruption related to personal matters at the personal level are not so much sensitive and are not considered as serious (Bureš, 2012).

However, if there would be indications that the political representation is willing to fight corruption seriously, the pessimism of citizens would decrease accordingly. The GfK survey showed that citizens were waiting for a positive signal from the government: if it were only ready to face the corruption. In the autumn 2009, when there was the growing scepticism about the anti-corruption commitment of politicians, 47% respondents believed that corruption would continue to grow, and only 4% of respondents felt that the situation would improve. Compared to 2006, the respondents' pessimism was about 11% higher (GfK 2010).[2] It points out the close interconnection between the perception of corruption and the notion of the political situation.

In 2010, the election to the Chamber of Deputies as well as to the Senate and local elections turned the theme of corruption and combating corruption into a major political and election issue. One of political parties (Věci veřejné/Public Matters) built its whole program and campaign on the theme of the fight against corruption. Citizens responded to this election program very positively and with high expectations. The survey in July 2010 (i.e. very shortly after the election when this new political party became a participant in the governmental coalition) reported a sharp rise in optimism. On the whole, 46% of respondents believed that political representation is interested in fighting corruption, and 33% believed that the government can implement effective anti-corruption measures and to reduce corruption (GfK, 2010).

Unfortunately, expectations were disappointingly not met. The ensuing sharp decline in trust in government, parliament, and the politics in general indicated by the polls in the spring and summer of 2011 (the decline made nearly 20%), pointed at an even greater disappointment and disillusionment than in 2009 (CVVM, 2009).

Again, the social frustration has been growing especially due to the reluctance (or inability) of the representatives in Parliament to effectively deal with cases of political corruption and to neutralise politicians, who were under a serious suspicion of corruption (Bureš, 2012). We can only mention the fact that since 1998 at least five government programmes and strategies to combat corruption have been adopted, the last of which was approved by the government decision in January 2012 under the title "From corruption to integrity". These strategies often included well-intentioned measures such as the regulation of lobbying, the law on public service, and arrangements of the financing of political parties or specialisation of law enforcement bodies. But their effect has failed to satisfy and a number of these measures were either lost, not applied or did not actually work.

It should be added that the Czech Republic never considered the involvement in the international anti-corruption efforts as a priority. This is reflected in the fact that the Czech Republic has belatedly ratified the UN Convention against Corruption at the end of 2013.

---

2 In 2006 pursuant to the results of the general election to the Chamber of Deputies of the Parliament of the Czech Republic the left-center coalition was replaced by the right-center coalition.

The development of corruption and the present state

It is possible to make observations about the stages in the development of corruption and the way it was perceived in the Czech Republic:

1. At the 1990s the issue of corruption as a problem was not thematised: it was not a part of the 'discourse' and no anti-corruption policy existed. But at the same time the mass privatization associated with redistribution of huge public funds and state property was under way. At that time a great criminogenic potential for corrupt behaviour was created and was gradually realised.
2. In the beginning of the 21th century there were intensive legislative changes associated with the accession to the European Union and the effort to strengthen 'good governance' and the rule of law. From 1999, the anti-corruption policy of the government did exist, which brought some fruits, despite all half-heartedness and criticised aspects.
3. After 2007, a distinct worsening of the situation could be observed. The continuous sheer formalism, the failure to fulfil the governmental anti-corruption strategies and incapability to respond to the expectations of citizens are to be the most striking observations (Bureš, 2012). The growing scepticism of the public can be also related to increasingly frequent information on possible corrupt activities associated with the top echelons of the politics, to which no adequate response came.

The mentioned research projects and analyses support the conclusion that the core problem of corruption in the Czech Republic as it is perceived by public lies in the corruptive contagion inside political parties and in the functioning of state institutions. At least most of people consider that to be the most serious problem of corruption. The public administration as a place where public funds are (mis)managed seems to be the primary target of massive corruption interests. In this playing field the sphere seems largely affected by corruption while at the same time it seems to be the weakest point of the anti-corruption efforts.

On the other hand, according to the opinions expressed in the public opinion surveys, other parts of the public sector providing public services have been mainly free of corruption: the sectors of education, as well as health care and police are assessed relatively positively. With regard to these sectors it is even possible to say that their evaluation by the public from the point of view of their burden by corruption has got better. At this point the Czech Republic differs from countries with high levels of corruption, such as Ukraine, Russia, Bosnia-Herzegovina (Maljević, 2007) and Serbia (Van Duyne and Stocco, 2012).

This again confirms the conclusion that the problem of the Czech Republic consists of a systemic corruption, in the organised abuse of public resources, with links to the political structure rather than in a 'petty corruption'. And the public has been perceived it as such. In this sense corresponding to the view that the corruption in the political sphere and at higher state administration levels is massive some authors identify the state of corruption in the Czech Republic as the situation that literature refers to as 'state capture' (Bureš, 2012).[3]

Studies also show the contradiction between the general concern about the high levels of corruption and self-determination to change things. This confirms that despite all individual and group initiatives it is at the first place the 'State': its political representatives and the government that are expected by citizens to initiate real action against the corruption and to convince the citizens about seriousness of its will.

At the same time the State must also convince citizens that the prosecution and conviction of some – even high positioned politicians – that have occurred in recent years, after all, is not just a reflection of internal political power struggles, but the result of actual efforts to combat the 'big' corruption.

The best-known recent case is the case of the arrest and prosecution of an important politician, high-ranked member of a great political party, a former minister of public health, former governor of one of the regions and since some time a deputy of Parliament that was accused of demanding and accepting bribes to the amount of millions of crowns in public procurement. The prosecution took more than one year until now. This politician was released from custody after more than one year awaiting trial which still has to begin. From the point of view of its impact on the political and public life the result of this high level case will be most important.

Also several other MPs, though not so prominent, were convicted for requesting and accepting bribes for matters at local and regional level. These scandals contributed to the decline of trust of people in the government. The last coup before the fall of government in 2013 and untimely elections was the prosecution of three members of Parliament accused of 'political corruption' consisting in the 'barter' when they agreed to abdicate to their mandates in exchange for well-paid positions in the

---

3 'State capture' is a term used by the World Bank, which is defined as "activities of individuals, groups and companies, both in the public and private spheres aimed at influencing the creation of laws, regulations, decisions and other governmental procedures for their own benefit as a result of illegal and non-transparent provisions of the private nature to public authorities officers . . . thanks to informal, non-transparent and preferential channels. This also takes place through unclear alliances between political and business interests of public officials . . ." (see Dančák, Hloušek, Šimíček, 2006)

management of state companies. Nevertheless, according to the decision of Supreme court their action has been covered by parliamentary immunity . . . and the prosecution had to be terminated.

For a long period there have been discussions about the establishment of a specialised unit of state prosecution, which would deal with a serious economic crime and corruption. The draft of the respective law was passed in the amendment procedure but after the fall of government and the dissolution of the Parliament this process came to a halt.

Conclusion and discussion

The anti-corruption policy remains clouded in ambiguity. On the one hand, we observe some efforts of the government to adopt at least partial measures against corruption. It also tries to direct the attention of the public to value of this efforts although the original programme of the government at the beginning promised much more than it could make true. On the other hand, these efforts were continually undermined by corruption affairs of prominent politicians and by conspicuous wasting of the public funds which was by the opinion of media and public very closely associated or not directly caused by corruption. Therefore the perceived importace of all the steps of the government against corruption, even if more or less genuinely intended, was in the eyes of the public significantly reduced. The result of the elections in October 2013 confirmed the general mistrust of people to the politicians and to the traditional political parties.

Two of three political parties that created the last governmental coalition scored badly and were sent to the opposition banks (altogether under 20% of votes) while the third party of this coalition was totally wiped off the political scene. It may be of course understood as a "bill" drawn by the voters for the years of their unpopular governance. But the outcome should also be interpreted as the result of corrupt scandals of members of these parties and dissapointment in relation to the results of their anti-corruptive proclamations followed by miserable results.

But what is even more interesting is that the party that was for eight years in opposition and four months before the elections scored in the polls indicated more than 30% of votes finally received only 20,45%! This was due to the fact that a half year before the elections two quite new political movements entered the political scene. They presented themselves as not being burdened by the past and attracted the sympathy of voters disappointed by the 'old' political parties. The above mentioned party albeit being in opposition in Parliament, however, still was a part of the traditional political establishment which fact prevailed in the voters' eyes. As a result these new movements received more than 25%.

This is not unique. Similar processes took place in other countries as well, e.g. Italy, Greece, Austria etc. And the populist style of these 'newcomers' on the political scene has been characteristic nearly for all of them including the Czech ones.

In the Czech Republic as in other countries it was of course not only the conviction of the state of corruption of political parties that led to this election result. Other social and economic factors played a role as well. But the belief of citizens that the political parties and the state administration represent the most rotten sectors of the society was without any doubt one of the decisive reasons for the 'wash-out' of established political parties that dominated the Czech political scene since 1989. The power of public opinion proved to be a very strong weight in the voting. This opinion boosted significantly new movements/parties and helped them to be elected as trustworthy – only because they have been the new ones and were represented by candidates not tainted by corrupt scandals from the past. Substantial number of votes gained in the elections went to these 'newcomers', irrespective of the unpredictability of further real behaviour in the next parliamentary term.

Van Duyne in his study on the situation in Serbia stated that "any genuine policy of change must find its roots in the daily life and feelings of common people . . . The internal motivation must come from the people: they can either resign themselves to corruption, be part of it or make their dissatisfaction known, for example during elections . . ." He states also that opinion surveys in Serbia show that 77% of the respondents consider the political parties corrupt and this lack of trust is a stable given over the past decade (van Duyne, 2013: 326).

Comparing the situation in the Czech Republic one may state that "there is nothing new under the sun". But what is after all significant and characteristic for the public opinion in the Czech Republic is the belief of people that corruption on the level of everyday life is only 'small': in many sectors of public life corruption is not rated as serious and is often considered as just the expression of thanks or courtesy. Opposed to this there a strong belief that serious corruption is engrained in the higher echelons of policy and state administration to such an extent that the 'common citizen' feels himself powerless. This feeling gives justification to the resigned attitude of "waiting for Godot", i.e. the opinion that the initiative must come from the state while admitting that this may be waiting in vain. It means that in everyday life there is not a feeling of urgency to change the usual behaviour with regard to corruption, because it does not represent any essential problem either moral and social in daily life. The essential problem of corruption is believed to be inherent in the conduct of political parties and of upper echelons of state administration and this belief, irrespective whether this is well-founded or not. This belief also serves at the same time as an exculpation of 'the own 'everyday behaviour and as a rationalisation why the initiative must come from 'above'. The only possibility how to express this attitude has been found in the elections in the form of relatively broad rejection of political parties that have taken part in the political establishment for years even though the newcomers represent actually only a very fuzzy and dubious promise for the future.

We cannot simply say that the analysis of the public opinion on corruption based on results of surveys and partly on results of last elections brings a true picture of the state of its phenomenon. But in connection with at least partial evaluation of experience and knowledge that stems from social, economic and political development since the communist period, this analysis seems to be an important source of information. It is namely possible to describe a double-end process: manifestations and forms of corruption as reflected, albeit not completely, in the public's image of corruption. And irrespective of its precision, this image again substantially influences the behaviour of people in corruptive situations and towards corruption in general.

References

AMSP, 2010. http://www.amsp.cz/uploads/soubory/pruzkum4_web_final.pdf

Bureš, R., Korupce v České republice [Corruption in the Czech Republic]. *Kriminalistika* 2/2012, pp.105-121

Buriánek, J., Aktér 2011 [Actor 2011], European Social Survey, Round Czech criminal code, No. 40/2009 Coll.

Corruption Perception Index. http://www.transparency.org/policy_research/surveys_indices/cpi/2010/results

Cejp, M., Od obecného pojetí k některým dílčím poznatkům z výzkumu veřejného mínění o korupci ve státní správě [From general concept to some partial findings from public opinion survey on corruption in state administration]. *Trestněprávní revue* 9/2011, pp. 256-260

CVVM, 2009. http://www.cvvm.cas.cz/upl/zpravy/101164s_pi110627.pdf

Dančák, B., V. Hloušek, V. *Šimíček, Korupce. Projevy a potírání v České republice a v Evropské unii* [Corruption. Its manifestations and combat against in the CR and EU]. Brno 2006, pp. 13 -15

Duyne, P.C. van, Will Caligula go transparent? Corruption in acts and attitude. *Forum on Crime and Society*, 2001, vol.1, no. 2, 73-98

Duyne, P.C. van, The creation of a threat image. In: P.C. Duyne, M. Jager, K. von Lampe and J.L. Newell (eds.), *Threats and phantoms of organized crime, corruption and terrorism*. Wolf Legal Publishers, Nijmegen 2004

Duyne, P.C. van, E. Stocco, Searching for contours of anti-corruption policy in Serbia. In: P.C. van Duyne *et al.* (eds.), *Cross-border crime inroads on integrity in Europe*. Wolf Legal Publishers, Nijmegen 2010

Duyne, P.C. van, Serbian anti-corruption policy: Welcome to Potemkin village? In: P.C. van Duyne *et al.* (eds.), *Human dimensions in organized crime, money laundering and corruption*. Wolf Legal Publishers, Oisterwijk 2013

Ernst&Young. http://www.ey.com/CZ/cs/Newsroom/Newreleases/2011_Europeanfraudsurvey_CZ

GfKhttp://www.gfk.cz/imperia/md/content/gfkpraha/press/2010/100322_vyvoj_korupcniho_prostredi.pdf

Jager, M., In the quest for essence: the principal-agent-client model of corruption. In: P.C. van Duyne, M. Jager,M., K. von Lampe and J.L. Newell (eds.), *Threats and phantoms of organised crime, corruption and terrorism*. Wolf Legal Publishers, Nijmegen 2004.

Mravec, M., Korupční klima v ČR 2012 [Corruptive climate in the CR]. http://www.transparency.cz/doc/projekty/NIS/Konference/Martin_Mravec_GfK_Korupcni_klima_v Ceske_republice.pdf

Od korupce k integritě [From corruption to integrity]. The strategy of the government for combating corruption for the period 2013 and 2014. The decision of the government of the Czech Republic No. 39/2013

Overview of ratifications. http://www.unodc.org/unodc/en/treaties/CAC/signatories.htm.l.

Scheinost, M., Organised crime, the media and the sentiments of the public. In: Antonopoulos,G. et al. (eds.), *Usual and unusual organising criminals in Europe and beyond*. Apeldoorn, Maklu 2011

Scheinost, M., Organised crime in the country of transition after twenty years. In: P.C. van Duyne *et al.*, (eds.), *Human dimension in organised crime, money laundering and corruption*. Wolf Legal Publishers, Oisterwijk, 2013

Schwab, K., The Global Competitiveness Report 2011-2012. World Economic Forum, Geneva, 2011 http://www3.weforum.org/docs/WEF_GlobalCompetitivenessReport_2010-11.pdf

Transparency International, 2012. http://www.transparency.cz/ohlednuti-konferenci-vime-nevime-korupci/

UN arrangement against the corruption. In M. Scheinost: *Dokumenty OSN ke korupci a organizovanému zločinu [UN Documents on corruption and organised crime],* Institut pro kriminologii a sociální prevenci, Praha, 2008 http://www.ok.cz/iksp/docs/341.pdf .

UN Convention against corruption. New York, 2004. http://www.unodc.org/documents/treaties/UNCAC/Publications/Convention/08-50026_E.pdf

Political scandal and Anti-corruption debates in Serbia

Marija Zurnić[1]

Introduction: an awkward scandal

One of the most reported scandals in Serbia, the Money in Cyprus Scandal, is related to the repatriation of public funds, which had been informally transferred abroad during Milošević's regime in the 1990s. The state-run investigation of this case started in 2000 when the Democratic Opposition of Serbia coalition (DOS) came into power. The story obtained the character of a scandal when the investigation was abruptly cancelled in 2001. The reason for the cancellation of the investigation was not communicated to the public by the state authorities. Those responsible for the cancellation of the investigation have not been investigated or prosecuted.

The media archive *Politika*, Serbia's leading daily broadsheet newspaper, which was consulted in this research, offers a rich source of material in relation to the scandal. However, interviews with civil servants in the judiciary, as well as interviews conducted with journalists and academics, have not revealed new information concerning the case. The interviewees either avoided talking about the scandals or merely echoed the public debates already reported in the media. Several politicians and civil servants, whose insider view would have shed new light on the cases, have died during the past decade, including Borka Vučić, manager of the state owned bank involved in the transfers, and Vuk Obradović, president of the Commission for the Investigation of Malfeasance from 1989 to 2000. However, the fact that the stories about the Money in Cyprus Scandal are still present in the public debates suggests that the public considers them an important part of post-Milošević political life.

This research understands public debates about corruption scandals as a form of political communication and aims at explaining whether these debates influenced the anti-corruption policy. The exploratory part of the research aims at answering the following questions:

---

1 The author is researcher/PhD student at the University of Nottingham.

- What practices were perceived as being corrupt in the Money in Cyprus Scandal?
- Who are the main actors in anti-corruption debates concerning the scandal?

As the questions suggest, this part of the case study focuses on the process of concept formation in the public discourse. The data, necessary for answering the questions, were collected from the media reporting on political scandals and from in-depth interviews with high ranking people in state institutions. The data collected from the media reports were analysed within the theoretical framework of Discursive Institutionalism (DI) and the theoretical approaches to concept formation of Mark Philp (2007, 2008, 2009), William Connolly (1983) and Peter Bratsis (2003).

This chapter is also focused on developing a causal relationship between the two phenomena – corruption scandals and anti-corruption institutions. This explanatory part is aimed at testing the following hypothesis: The Money in Cyprus Scandal is likely to have acted as the catalyst for political action in the area of anti-corruption. This aspect of the case study is intended to determine whether such corruption scandals have had direct impact on institutional change in the field of anti-corruption.

First, the chapter will outline the main assumptions of the theory of Discursive Institutionalism and its application in corruption studies. Second, the chapter will offer an overview of political developments in the early 2000s when the informal financial transfers with Cyprus were investigated. Last, the scandal will be discussed from the perspective of Discursive Institutionalism as a potential cause for change in public policy.

Discursive Institutionalism and Corruption Studies

Discursive Institutionalism (DI) focuses on the impact of public debates on policy change and institutional reform. DI starts with the assumption that ideas, formalised in discourses, are the main factor of institutional change. Discourse is conceptualised as both the content, that is ideas, and as a process of communicating those ideas. On the other hand, an institution is understood as fixed and contingent at the same time. In sum, ideas, and the members of institutions associated with those ideas, are constitutive elements of the institution and, at the same time, they represent the main force in the process of institutional change (Schmidt, 2002, 2006, 2008, 2011). According to DI, an institution is a flexible discursive structure, open to change, fixed and contingent at the same time. DI considers the formal institutions important, still secondary to public debates. The focus of this theory is not on institutions searching for new ideas in order to create policy change. Instead, as Peters (2012) metaphorically explained, DI focuses on ideas which are constantly in search of structure and the power of these ideas lies in the ways in which they are communicated by the actors in the debates.

In this research, the theoretical framework of Discursive Institutionalism is complemented by three theoretical approaches to concept formation. Firstly is William Connolly's approach to discourse from the perspective of linguistic philosophy. In his study *The Terms of Political Discourse* (1983), Connolly focuses on interconnectedness of language and political practice. Secondly, Mark Philp's view that the formation of political concepts is closely related to the socio-political context in which the concept is used (Philp 2009, 2008, 2005). Third is Peter Bratsis' (2003) explanation of concept formation from a historical perspective. These authors share the view that concepts of political discourse are not neutral terms, which describe political reality (Connolly 1983: 10; Bratsis, 2003: 17; Philp 1997). Instead, actors in political debates contribute a normative dimension to the concept, by characterising political reality from a particular point of view.

Bratsis (2003) argues that the concepts themselves are not appropriate or moral; concepts only become so in a certain context and within specific sets of rules. Philp (2008) suggests that transitional or post-conflict societies represent a specific context in which political concepts, such as corruption or accountability, tend to be understood by political actors differently, than in stable political systems. This, according to Philp, should be taken into account when anti-corruption policies are to be implemented. Connolly suggests that discursively engaging with the terms of discourse is not just a way to approach politics, but this engagement is "*a dimension of politics itself*" (Connolly 1983: 3).

Moreover, Connolly argues that concepts, connected to a wide network of meanings, constitute the language of politics. Concepts in political discourse, according to Connolly, are composed of several elements and each element contributes to the meaning of the composed concept. Therefore, public debates may seem caused by disagreements concerning the composed concept, but the conflict originates, according to Connolly, in the disagreement concerning its basic elements. It is considered that a concept is accepted in a community if none of the concept's elements are being contested. However, as Connolly points out, even the accepted concepts in political language have no fixed meaning. According to Connolly, certain concepts are constantly open to debate regarding their meaning, elements or their point. Even if a community reaches a consensus about what is understood by a certain term, the meaning is only temporarily fixed, as revisions and changes can take place later.

The three authors stress that the change of political concepts reflects and contributes to a change in political practice. Connolly identifies several ways in which the revision of a concept can take place. One involves changing of the criteria of the concept and keeping the concept's point unchanged; another is to change the point of the concept in order to preserve its criteria; lastly, the approach of revision can be "*to leave the criteria, the point, and the theory within which the concept is embedded intact, but then treat the whole complex as an anachronistic system irrelevant to the modern age*" (Connolly 1983: 31-32).

Mark Philp emphasises the influence of the socio-political context on the way that the concept of responsibility is understood. States in transition and societies, which are deeply divided after armed conflicts, struggle with the articulation of public interest, and have weak and ineffective institutions, and slow economic development. Moreover, the expectations from public office in such environments may vary, as there are numerous interpretations of the concept of accountability and power. Therefore, the concept of political misconduct, according to Philp, can be understood differently than in stable systems, either because misconduct is justified as necessary to ensure the existence of the community, or because of the lack of fixed norms and values against which the act of misconduct can be evaluated (Philp 2008: 321).

Mark Philp (2009) distinguishes two forms of accountability. On the one hand, formal accountability, as he suggests, "*concerns the requirement that public officials act within the formal responsibilities of their office. Formal accountability is linked to systems of regulation and reporting*" (Philp 2009: 38). On the other hand, "*[p]olitical accountability concerns the answerability of those in public office to partisan elements within the political system. The issue is not whether someone acted within his or her legitimate and allocated powers, but whether they exercised those powers in ways their political constituencies are willing to endorse or approve*" (Philp 2009: 38). Political misconduct, when it is related to formal accountability, is subject to investigation and prosecution by relevant judicial authorities; lack of political accountability is judged by the electorate which can refuse to give political actors legitimacy at elections.

As this paper is concerned primarily with corruption scandal, it is important to gain insight into the wider literature on corruption. The literature suggests a striking lack of agreement among the scholars concerning the concept of corruption. The debates are still open regarding the definition of corruption (Philp 1997; Heidenheimer 1970) and a comprehensive explanation of the causes of corruption (Rose-Ackerman 1999; Tanzi 1998). Moreover, there is a lack of consensus on how the extent of corruption should be measured (Andersson and Heywood 2009; Langseth 2006; Philp 2006; Lambsdorff 2006; Miller 2006) and what are the appropriate ways to curb it (Bjorvatn and Søreide 2003; Rose-Ackerman 1999; Tanzi 1998; Ades and di Tella 1997; Shleifer and Vishny 1993). However, what is shared by academics across the disciplines is that corruption is a negative phenomenon, which can significantly affect political processes, hamper economic growth and decrease the level of social capital.

The generic definition of corruption involves the abuse of power for the purpose for illicit gain. In order to understand what the concept of corruption entails, researchers have developed a wide range of typologies (Johnston 2005; Alatas 1990; Heidenheimer 1970). These typologies suggest that there are three spheres within which corrupt practices emerge. Firstly, corruption emerges at the interface between public and private sectors, where informal financing of political parties influences the decision-making process of public officials. Secondly, corrupt exchanges can emerge in the market sphere as rent-seeking behaviour or the informal exchange of goods and cash. Lastly, incidences of corruption occur in the sphere of public administration, receiving and offering bribes becomes a part of the everyday interaction between public officials and citizens.

Corruption in these spheres may vary significantly across countries (Johnston 2005). In developed countries, incidences of corruption are mainly related to party financing, while in developing countries, due to the weak institutions and lack of relevant legislation, both administrative and political corruption are spread. Moreover, transitional countries are characterised by a specific form of political corruption, state capture (Hellman *et al.* 2000), which, as defined by the World Bank, "*tends to subvert, or even replace, legitimate and transparent channels of political influence and interest intermediation, reducing the access of competing groups and interests to state officials*" (World Bank 2000: 3).

The topic of corruption became prominent in public debates in Serbia after the political changes of October 2000. This new prominence can be linked to the new understanding of corruption, which includes a clearer division of the public and private spheres. This understanding of the term corruption appeared in North-western Europe with the arrival of the bourgeois revolution and the intensive development of state and capitalism in the eighteenth and nineteenth Centuries (Bratsis, 2003: 14). Due to the different historical context, these processes took place in Serbia in the early 2000s.

It is important to point out that the surfacing of the Money in Cyprus Scandal was the moment when the meaning of corruption in the public discourse significantly changed. In the 1990s, public discourse implied that politicians were responsible for the protection of the nation. Therefore, irrespectively of the formal definition, a betrayal of national interests or failure to protect state sovereignty was perceived as corruption, rather than the use of public money for private gain or the lack of a transparent political decision-making. The new concept, which was introduced after the change of government in 2000, was based on the clear public/private distinction and implied that the responsibility of politicians in power was to protect and promote the economic and political rights of individual citizens. The modern definition of corruption was applied to the events in the 1990s which successfully de-legitimised Milošević's regime. The new understanding of corruption was introduced exclusively at the level of discourse, without being acknowledged in the existing legal or institutional frameworks.

However, two events enabled this discursive change. The first event was the fact that the new democratic government identified, as their priority, the protection of individual economic rights, instead of the protection of national interests and the State's sovereignty as it was in the previous regime. Secondly, the modern understanding of corruption in Serbia was influenced by the global discourse concerning good governance, which emerged in the early 2000s. These developments jointly influenced a change of the theory within which the concept of corruption had been previously conceptualised in Serbia (Connolly, 1983).

Exploring discourse through process-tracing

According to Discursive Institutionalism, change is most likely to happen when there is *"a clash of ideas"* (Peters 2012: 89) concerning different understandings of a concept which is fundamentally important to the society. The starting assumption in the analysis is the general hypothesis of Discursive Institutionalism that ideas and the actors associated with these ideas are the most important elements in the causal mechanism of institutional change. As Peters pointed out: "*Given that these ideas and values are created through discussion, that is discourse, among the members then institutional change much also reflect that change in that discourse*" (Peters 2012: 155).

The causal link between ideas and institutional change related to the Money in Cyprus Scandal is explored in this chapter through the process-tracing method which is defined as "*the examination of 'diagnostic' pieces of evidence within a case that contribute to supporting or overturning alternative hypotheses. A central concern [of process-tracing] is with sequences and mechanisms in the unfolding of hypothesised causal processes*" (Bennett, 2010: 208). According to Beach and Pedersen (2013), there are several approaches within the process-tracing method, such as the *case-centred approach* and the *theory-centred* method. In this research, the case-centred process-tracing approach is applied in its inductive form, which Beach and Pedersen (2013: 20) define as "*a bottom-up type of analysis, using empirical material as the basis for building a plausible explanation of causal mechanisms whereby X (or multiple Xs) produced the outcome*". As there is no quantifiable threshold, which would guarantee that a minimally sufficient explanation is achieved, the authors suggest that a satisfactory explanation is one which explains all the relevant elements of the case study (Beach and Pedersen, 2013: 20).

In this research, the process-tracing method was applied to a set of ideas in public discourse, concerning the conceptualisation of corruption and anti-corruption, in order to explain policy change in the area of anti-corruption. Thechapter, firstly, explores what practices are identified in public debates as corruption and what ideas are put forward as appropriate anti-corruption policy. Subsequently, the main discourses were identified and associated with specific political actors; in Berman's words, "*ideas do not have any impact by themselves, as disembodied entities floating around in a polity*" (Berman, 1998: 21). According to DI, the position of power in formal institutions is not necessary for the actors in order to bring change successfully. Instead, it is the strength of their arguments and the convincing communication of their ideas that empower the actors (Schmidt, 2011b: 59; Peters 2012).

Therefore, the identified discourses were assessed with respect to coherency and consistency of their ideas, and the strength of their cognitive and normative arguments. The relevance of the ideas was explored, as well as the timing and viability of policy solutions. The ideas were also assessed regarding their appropriateness in terms of national values, tradition and culture (Schmidt, 2008a; Metha, 2011). Then, the analysis explores whether the discourses reached consensus on relevant issues, as this can increase their transformative potential (Peters, 2012: 158). The focus was on discursive strategies, such as advocacy coalition (Sabatier and Jenkis-Smith, 1993) and so forth, which actors in debates employed with the aim of creating a common ground.

After the ideas and their communication are examined, the focus shifts to anti-corruption institutions, which had been established after a scandal had emerged. The research explored whether those institutional changes addressed the practices identified in the debates as corruption. If the newly-established institutions reflected the policy solutions put forward in the scandal, there were reasons to believe that the discourse(s) contributed to institutional change. When the newly-established institutions could not be explained as a result of public discourse, an alternative explanation was identified.

In order to clarify what evidence constitutes as support for the hypothesis, it is necessary to define two concepts: (a) influence of scandals and (b) institutional change.

Firstly, it was expected that the scandal under investigation would exert a *direct effect* on institutional setting.

Secondly, institutional change is expected to be: 1) a long-term measure, at the state level, 2) sanctioning the practice perceived as corruption, 3) in the sector where the scandal emerged.

The hypothesis was considered refuted if no institutional change can be explained as a direct consequence of the impact of the Money in Cyprus Scandal in the period between October 2000 and May 2012.

It must be noted that Discursive Institutionalism needs further improvement regarding the explanation of causality in institutional change: how change occurs exactly, under what circumstances and when the outcome can be expected. Sheri Berman points out that all ideational theories face the same obstacle when it comes to their testing against the real-world environment: it is the difficulty to conceptualise ideas in such a way that they can be observed as "purely" independent variables, separate from other influences in a given context and that their impact on political behaviour can be measured (Berman 1998: 15). According to Berman, these methodological challenges are due to the nature of ideas which are "*vague, amorphous and constantly evolving [. . .] and never surrendered easily to empirical study or quantification*" (1998: 16). Therefore, according to Berman, an ideational theorist should aim at examining "*how different conditions enable certain ideas to take on a life of their own, influencing political behavior over an extended period of time. If this can be done [. . .] then the fact that its development was influenced by other factors is an analytically distinct subject that is only indirectly related to the ultimate outcomes being explained*" (Berman 1998: 18).

The Money in Cyprus Scandal

After the change of government in October 2000, the Democratic Opposition of Serbia (DOS) came to power. The new, first democratic government symbolically started its mandate by promising an uncompromised fight against corruption.[2] On the first day of its mandate, the government announced ten steps which would be taken in order to address the relevant issues regarding corruption in Serbia and the Federal Republic of Yugoslavia.[3] The DOS' goals for their first hundred days in power

---

2 The Program of the Democratic Opposition of Serbia(2000) is available at: www.g17plus.org.yu/srpski/files/aktiv/program/1.htm [Accessed 20 April 2013].

3 The ten steps included: an urgent change of the Constitution; the termination of the political and economic blockade of Montenegro; the development of an appropriate approach to relations with the UN Security Council, in order to secure territorial integrity and sovereignty of Serbia regarding its southern province of Kosovo; reducing the number of ministries; adopting a Law on Conflicts of Interest; opening secret police files containing information about citizens; checking property of high-ranking state officials; abolishing laws which had a negative impact on civil society, such as the Law on Public Information; establishing an independent audit institution; and forming an independent expert commission to investigate the responsibility of

included the adoption of laws relating to the economy, anti-corruption, public information, higher education, local government, the army and police, the judiciary, the prosecutor's office, the Penal Code and electoral law. Moreover, the DOS planned to implement radical economic reforms through a fast privatisation process and large investments in infrastructure (Sekelj, 2001). Lastly, an important goal of the new political elite was to reintegrate Serbia into international institutions.

In August 2001, the DSS (Democratic Party of Serbia) left the Government due to conflicts with the DS (Democratic Party) concerning the extradition of Slobodan Milošević to the International Criminal Tribunal for the former Yugoslavia (ICTY). The DS leader, Zoran Djindjić, continued leading the Government. His assassination, in March 2003, increased the political instability and, in November 2003, the government lost support of some of the other coalition members. In the same year, the government was disbanded and new elections were called for 28 December 2003.

Concerning public debates during this period, the main topics for discussion included the consolidation of democracy, economic development and the State's sovereignty regarding Kosovo and Montenegro. The topic of corruption was frequently mentioned during the electoral campaign in September 2000. At the beginning of the DOS mandate, the concept of corruption in public debates had blurred boundaries and these references were usually applied to a large number of non-democratic practices which took place during the previous Milošević government.

Open debates about corruption were still a novelty in the public life of post-Milošević Serbia and corruption was often conceptualised in the context of the violation of human rights during the wars in the Balkan region, or linked to the activities of organised criminal groups and money-laundering during the previous regime. At the end of the mandate of the first democratic government, the term corruption was increasingly used to describe the lack of the rule of law and the violation of universal rights during the mandate of the DOS coalition.

One of the first scandals which occurred after the political changes in 2000 was related to illegal financial transfers from Serbia to Cyprus during the Milošević regime. Due to the international sanctions imposed on the FRY, the formal channels of money transfer were replaced by informal and illegal ones. The National Bank of Yugoslavia and the ruling Socialist Party of Serbia established contacts with banks in Cyprus, Switzerland, Russia and other countries, and opened branches of state-

---

state officials who participated in domestic and foreign policy from 1987 to 2000 (Sekelj 2001).

owned banks and off-shore companies in those counties. Allegedly, the money was carried out of Serbia in cash, deposited in banks abroad and from there legally transferred to bank accounts in over 50 countries. The money originated from confiscated citizens' savings and from the illegal trade in oil, cigarettes and so forth, which was largely supported by the authorities in FRY during the 1990s.

The exact amount of money has never been reported, but it has been estimated in the media that $11,5 billion were illegally transferred from the FRY to the Republic of Cyprus between 1992 and 2000. Part of these funds was used for military expenditure, which was investigated by the ICTY as a part of the indictment against Slobodan Milošević. On the other hand, part of the money was used for international trade and buying food and medications for the citizens of FRY, while the country was under international sanctions.

Investigation of the Money in Cyprus

In January 2001, the Serbian government established the Commission for the Investigation of Malfeasance with a mandate to investigate illegal financial transactions from 1989 to 2001. The head of the Commission was Vuk Obradović, the Deputy Prime Minister and the leader of the Social Democracy Party. Two months after assuming his mandate, Obradović was forced to resign due to allegations in the media of sexual harassment. This particular scandal happened immediately before the adoption of the *Law on Extra-Profit* and coincided with Obradović drafting a highly-confidential document – a list of businessmen in Serbia who illegally acquired their wealth during the 1990s.

Another important member of the Commission was the Governor of the National Bank of Serbia, Mladjan Dinkić, who was in charge of providing the government with the evidence and documentation necessary for the recovery of the money deposited in Cyprus. The Governor Dinkić and his team visited Cyprus, and met with the local politicians and bankers who offered to help on the case (Cyprus 05-06-2006). Several months later the Governor halted the investigation and ceased to inform the Serbian public about the case. Among the most intriguing explanations in the media was that the Governor had benefitted in some way from the cancellation of the investigation. These suspicions arose from the fact that the Governor did not regularly inform the Serbian authorities about the progress of his investigation (Cyprus 10-06-2004, 20-04-20006, 22-04-2006, *Insajder* 2007).

Besides the state-run investigation, there have been several more attempts to recover the money transferred illegally from Serbia. For instance, a Serbian businessman based in Cyprus, Predrag Djordjević, conducted private research into the matter and gathered relevant information about illegal financial transfers. He was critical towards the investigation conducted by the state authorities and he filed a complaint against the Governor and his co-workers for abuse of office.[4] The businessman argued that several off-shore companies in Cyprus, involved in the money laundering of Serbian funds, remained active after the Governor identified them, which may indicate that the Governor himself had an interest in not blocking them. According to Djordjević, the Governor had enough evidence to inform the authorities in Serbia about the illegal financial scheme that he had discovered but which he did not do so.

Another party in the investigation was the London-based company, Forensic Investigative Associates (FIA), who the National Bank of Yugoslavia hired in February 2001 to help with the investigation. Half a year later, the contract was terminated because the National Bank of Serbia was not satisfied with the progress of FIA on the case. Moreover, the political leader of the party, New Serbia, and a member of the ruling coalition, Velimir Ilić, also offered to help in the investigation. In April 2001, Ilić travelled to Cyprus and tried to recover the money through his personal contacts. The attempt was unsuccessful. In parallel with this, the then Minister of Justice, Vladan Batić, contacted the banks in Switzerland in order to trace the money transfers. His efforts were also unsuccessful.[5] The last time when the problem of the money in Cyprus was officially addressed by state officials was in March 2006, during the official visit of the Serbian President Tadić to his Cypriot counterpart, Papadopoulos. The Presidents exchanged their views on the case and agreed that, despite all efforts, the illegal banking transfers could not be traced. The media on both sides critically reported about the meeting: "*Papadopoulos' statements were false and Tadić's nebulous*" (Cyprus 31/3/06).

As the investigation of the money in Cyprus was losing its momentum, public debates about the scandal were increasingly less frequent and enthusiastic. After several unsuccessful attempts to recover the money in 2001, the Serbian authorities changed their approach to the problem. They introduced a tax on illegally-acquired

---

4 Djordjević's complaint is available in Serbian at: www.srpskapolitika.com/Tekstovi/Komentari/2006/075.html [Accessed 25 April 2013].

5 Vladan Batić, Minister of Justice (2001-2004), was allegedly offered the dossier on this case by Carla del Ponte, Chief Prosecutor for War Crimes at the ICTY. From the dossier, the Minister learnt about six bank accounts in Switzerland belonging to Milošević's relatives and friends. However, the Serbian Prosecutor's Office did not provide the Swiss bank with the relevant documentation and did not initiate an investigation within three months as is stipulated by Swiss legislation. Therefore, the bank accounts were unblocked and the money legally withdrawn by the owners.

capital during the 1990s as stipulated by the *Law on Extra-Profit* (2001). The Law was criticised in the media for its revolutionary-political character and for the huge discretionary powers given to the authorities to ensure its implementation. Moreover, the Law was described as retroactive – as it covered the previous 12 years – and therefore it clashed with other laws.[6] According to the media, it was not uncommon that the implementation of the Law was informally negotiated between the political and business elites. The opposition claimed that the inconsistent implementation of the Law contributed to the creation of informal connections between the richest businessmen in Serbia and the political parties in power. According to the economic expert, Prokopijević, "*[t]he results of enforcement of the extra-profit law are disastrous to its authors – till August 2002 just $ 60 million has been collected, although $ 800 million was expected*" (Prokopijević, 2002: 50). In June 2002, the Law was abolished and the Secretary of the Commission for the Investigation of Malfeasance, Slobodan Lalović, resigned due to the inefficiency of the Commission.

Despite the fact that the investigation of informal financial transfers was cancelled and the money was not recovered from Cyprus, in 2006, the Serbian judiciary investigated several high-ranking civil servants who were allegedly involved in the transferring of the money during the 1990s. One of those prosecuted was the long-term director of the Federal Customs Bureau, Mihalj Kertes, and Borka Vučić, who was the manager of the Serbian bank, *Beogradska banka*, allegedly involved in transferring state funds during the 1990s.[7] Both Kertes and Vučić denied the accusations of being involved in illegal activities. They argued that the transfers of money with Cyprus were the only legal way of doing international trade when the UN sanctions were imposed on FRY. No charges were brought against Borka Vučić, as she obtained legal immunity after becoming Member of Parliament for the SPS in January 2007. In 2009, she died in a car accident. As for Mihalj Kertes, the Belgrade Special Court rejected charges against him, in February 2014. Kertes was acquitted, since the statute of limitations in the case has expired.

---

6 The *Law on One-Occasion Taxation of Extra Revenue and Extra Property Acquired by Using Special Privileges in Period January 1, 1989 - June 1, 2001* was adopted in June 2001 and abolished in June 2002. Critical comments on the law are from Prokopijević (2002).

7 Mihalj Kertes was a director of Federal Customs Bureau of FRY from 1993 to 2000 and as a person of Milošević's trust he provided logistic and financial support for various undercover operations of Serbian regime. Borka Vučić was head of the state-owned *Beogradska banka* and was considered important in the maintenance of that regime. She was referred to by the media as *Milošević's personal banker*. She was a member of the SPS and when elected to Parliament in 2007, served as the acting President of the National Assembly of the Republic of Serbia.

Public debate concerning the money in Cyprus scandal

The analysis of the media reports concerning the investigation of the money in Cyprus suggests that three views regarding this event surfaced in the public discourse over the past decade. In this section, they will be briefly outlined and named as (a) the Mainstream Discourse, (b) the Sub-Discourse and (c) the Counter Discourse. The three groups of actors can be differentiated according to the following characteristics. First, the actors in each discourse conceptualise corruption differently. Second, the actors are active in different types of institutions and organisations. Third, the actors have access to the policy-making process concerning the fight against corruption in different ways and to the different extent; they are policy-makers, state advisory bodies or non-governmental institutions. Last, the groups of actors communicate their ideas in various ways and by using different type of media communications.

The Mainstream Discourse

The actors in the Mainstream Discourse are representatives of the institutions at the state level, such as the government, the Prime Minister or the President's cabinet: they are often veto players in decision making processes concerning the corruption scandals, and their views are largely present in the digital and printed media. The Mainstream Discourse was developed by the pro-European elites, who won the elections in 2000. They presented the investigation of the money in Cyprus as an event of high importance. According to this view, the investigation was expected to bring justice to society and to punish those who "betrayed citizens" trust and took advantage of their life savings."[8] Moreover, the extensive amount of money, if had been recovered, would have helped the devastated Serbian economy and enable a smoother transitional process. In one of his first public speeches, held on 6 October 2000, the newly-elected President of Yugoslavia, Vojislav Koštunica, clearly stated that the investigation of the financial transfers to Cyprus was the priority of the new government.[9] Besides the moral and financial reasons, the investigation of this case was an opportunity for the new political elite to prove their readiness to fight

---

8 Interview with governor Dinkić (*Insajder* 2007).

9 In the speech directed to his supporters, Vojislav Koštunica announced radical changes: "[. . .] When the new Serbia comes [. . .] the stealing will end, there will be no poverty, no theft, the law will rule, not the thieves, money of the people won't be taken out of the country, it will stay here and more of it will come from our compatriots in Diaspora" (Cyprus 6-10-2000).

corruption and organised crime, which would distinguish them markedly from the previous regime.

The concept of corruption, as understood by the actors of the Mainstream Discourse, was based on two elements. Firstly, corruption was identified as an abuse of power by the Milošević regime, which enabled the illegal transfer and embezzlement of state funds. This form of corruption harmed citizens' individual rights and threatened their economic security. As the actors of the Mainstream Discourse argued, the return of the money from Cyprus was a way to restore justice in economic and symbolic terms. The trial of Mihalj Kertes, who was in charge of the Customs Bureau during the 1990s, confirmed the arguments put forward by the actors of the Mainstream Discourse. The second argument supporting the accusations of corruption in the Mainstream Discourse is related to the political accountability of the members of the previous regime. The money from Cyprus was used, according to this view, for financing the politics of nationalism during the 1990s and to support the armed conflicts in the region. The members of the previous regime, who were often named in the Mainstream Discourse as fake patriots, allegedly used patriotic rhetoric as a screen for corrupt practices and connections with organised criminal groups.

Lastly, the Mainstream Discourse argued that Milošević's regime did not enjoy legitimacy during the most part of its mandate. This authoritarian rule was, according to the Mainstream Discourse, perpetuated through non-transparent decision-making and frequent election-rigging, which was also identified in this Discourse as a form of corruption. Therefore, the Mainstream Discourse implied that the change of Milošević's regime, which was achieved in the Fifth of October Revolution, together with the prosecution of those responsible for the financial transfers to Cyprus would eradicate corruption in Serbia.

However, the Mainstream Discourse could not explain the failure of the investigation and repatriation of the funds from Cyprus. In March 2001, the Governor optimistically commented that during his visits to Cyprus the investigation progressed significantly (*Insajder* 2007). In the following months, the media stopped reporting about developments concerning the investigation and the Governor did not give a comprehensive and coherent explanation to the public as to why the investigation was cancelled or why the organisers of the money laundering scheme were not brought to justice. In the following years, several explanations for the cancellation of the investigation were reported by the media. The official position of the Serbian authorities became even less clear to the public when some state officials stated, during their visits to Cyprus, that the investigation of the money in Cyprus was not the State's priority.[10]

Later, in 2007, the Governor said that he stopped the investigation for personal reasons.[11] Afterwards, he explained that the investigation revealed a very complex case of international organised crime and that he lacked reliable sources and technical support to fight it.[12] In the early 2001, when the investigation started, there were indications that high-ranking members of the Milošević regime had destroyed relevant documentation between 5 and 6 October 2000, immediately before the government was changed. According to media reports, the investigation of the new state authorities was based mainly on the information available from the ICTY and Cypriot officials. However, neither of the sources could offer relevant evidence.

For instance, among the crucially important people in the money laundering scheme was the Cypriot lawyer and politician, Tassos Papadopoulos, who became President of Cyprus in 2003. According to the Mainstream Discourse, this circumstance made the investigation more difficult, as the Cypriot authorities were not motivated to cooperate fully.[13] On the other hand, the concluding remarks in the report of the ICTY investigator, Morten Torkildsen, confirmed the complexity of the case: "*In my career, I have never encountered or heard of an offshore finance structure this large and intricate. I consider that to conduct an overall and comprehensive analysis of what happened to all of the funds that were deposited or transferred into the bank accounts of the eight*

10 The Minister of Justice, Vladan Batić, said: "We are focused now on the future; we're not interested in Milošević's money anymore." *Financial Mirror*, 16 October 2001. Another politician, Velimir Ilić, stated: "We focus now on developing the country; the issue [of the money in Cyprus] is not on our agenda anymore" *Cyprus Mail* 22 February 2002.

11 Governor: "At the end of 2001 I literally stopped trying to do any serious investigation. My enthusiasm lasted about a year, but afterwards I realised, I said to myself – you can't do it."
Journalist: "Did you have the right to give up? It wasn't your private investigation after all."
Governor: "I didn't give up . . . I gave up as . . . I admitted to myself that I couldn't do it. There are moments when you say to yourself – you can't do it, nobody can. The issue was beyond my capacities, beyond my ability" *Insajder* 2007.

12 In the interview to *Insajder* TV programme, in 2007, the Governor said: "It is unrealistic to expect that any government after Milošević would be capable of solving this issue without getting help from outside. We were offered some help at the beginning but only in words; there were several meetings as well but practically we didn't get any help."

13 According to the Serbian Governor, Cypriot authorities were not genuinely interested in cooperation when he visited them in 2001: "[. . .] they obviously let us search for something that wasn't there anymore and they knew it wasn't there. They let us search for a needle in a haystack, so to speak, but the needle wasn't there, it was in some other haystacks in some other country" *Insajder* (2007).

Cypriot companies would almost be impossible and would be an extremely resource intensive exercise" (Torkildsen, 2002).

The Mainstream Discourse concerning the investigation of the money in Cyprus made significant impact on the overall anti-corruption discourse in Serbia as it (a) introduced the concept of corruption based on the principle of good governance and (b) underlined the negative impact of corruption on democracy. The Mainstream Discourse also contributed to the de-legitimization of the previous regime by explaining the nationalist foreign policy of Milošević as a tool for illicit enrichment of the political elite in power.

However, this Discourse was less successful in explaining the sudden change in political action of the first democratic government concerning the repatriation of the funds from Cyprus. The statements of the Governor, who led the investigation, imply that the lack of evidence and the reluctance of the international authorities to cooperate in the investigation significantly influenced his decision to abandon the investigation. These accounts have been strongly questioned in the public debates over the past decade.

Moreover, the Mainstream Discourse showed several weaknesses. Firstly, the responsibility of state officials and high-ranking civil servants for the financial transfers was not differentiated from the responsibility of the business elite, which was close to the previous leadership. As a result, the allegations of corruption were interpreted by some actors as 'politically motivated'. Moreover, this tendency ensured that the financial resources of the businessmen, who supported Milošević's regime and who benefitted from the informal money transfers to Cyprus, as well as their mechanisms of influence on political decision-making, remained intact.

Secondly, the fact that the advocates of the Mainstream Discourse abandoned the investigation of the money in Cyprus, suggested that their anti-corruption discourse and their actions were unconnected. Vivian Schmidt (2010) identifies this as a weak point in communicating and coordinating the discourse. Schmidt argues that the *being* of the actors becomes strongly questioned in public debates if the actors' *doing* is missing in their discourse.

Thirdly, the Mainstream Discourse failed to explain, coherently and convincingly, the reasons for the cancellation of the investigation of money transfers to Cyprus. This inconsistency was followed by another change in the valuation of the money transfers, as Serbian state officials argued that the investigation was abandoned as it was not among the state's priorities. This time, the approach of the state towards the act of corruption was, in Connolly's (1983: 31) words: "*To leave the criteria, the point, and the theory within which the concept is embedded intact, but then to treat the whole complex as an anachronistic system irrelevant to the modern age.*" The inability to communicate the failure of the investigation to the public, as well as the inconsistent approach to what was considered as corruption, significantly limited the transformative power of the Mainstream Discourse.

Lastly, the Mainstream Discourse was weakened by the lack of coordination between the members of the DOS coalition, who took part in the investigation. Alternative approaches to the enquiry did not appear to be coordinated with the state-run investigation and their results were not discussed by the coalition partners. Moreover, media coverage consulted in this research suggests that the actors, which were involved in the independent investigations, communicated their results mainly during the electoral campaign. This suggests that the actors were possibly more interested in raising their political profile, than with addressing the scandal as an issue of public interest.

The Sub-Discourse

The second view on the scandal concerning the money transfers to Cyprus can be identified as the Sub-Discourse. It surfaced after the investigation was abandoned, in late 2001, and it is still present in public debates today. The Sub-Discourse has been represented by a wide range of actors, including the businessmen Djordjević, the politician Ilić and the former Minister of Justice, Batić, who each conducted separate investigations. The Sub-Discourse was also formalised through the activities of the State Anti-Corruption Council, who became actively involved in this debate after the lawyer, Verica Barać, was appointed its President in 2003. The common assumption of this discourse is that the attempt of the state authorities to investigate the money in Cyprus was not genuine and that Governor Dinkić politically benefitted from sabotaging the investigation.

The actors of the Sub-Discourse identified several aspects of the investigation as cases of corruption. Firstly, the lack of transparency in conducting the inquiry is highlighted, as, reportedly, Governor Dinkić did not regularly inform the government about his progress in the investigation. Secondly, the fact that the enquiry was cancelled in secret and without being debated in public was considered by the actors of the Sub-Discourse as a form of corruption itself. The new government was criticised for the lack of responsiveness and efficiency in conducting the investigation and for abandoning the issue of common interest for political gain. Thirdly, the assumption that the decision to abandon the investigation was made under the influence of the business elite is viewed within the Sub-Discourse as a form of political corruption.

Lastly, the Sub-Discourse argued that the authorities replaced the investigation of the transfers to Cyprus by the Law on Extra-Profit, in order to avoid conflicts with the financial elite and the criminal groups close to the previous government. The Law on Extra-Profit provoked a heated debate about the understanding of illegality.

The actors of the Sub-Discourse argued that the Law enabled rich businessmen to buy out their freedom by paying a one-off tax. On the other hand, some members of the Mainstream Discourse argued that the Law was a genuine attempt to bring justice to the society and to compensate the impoverished citizens for their financial losses during the 1990s.[14] Moreover, they argued that the businessmen subject to the law should not be treated as criminals buying out their freedom, since Serbian legislation in the 1990s did not directly regulate business-state relations. The actors of the Sub-Discourse, who were mainly experts in anti-corruption, argued that the state anti-corruption policy must not be based on taxation. They insisted, instead, on the investigation of the origin of the capital and on confiscation of the illegally-acquired assets.[15] However, this change in policy has not occurred.

The following words of Verica Barać, who served as the President of the State Anti-Corruption Council from 2003 till 2012, summarise the main arguments of the Sub-Discourse: "*[. . .] as for Dinkić abandoning that business [the investigation of the money in Cyprus], I see it as the crucial moment for his later successful career.[. . .] If he had uncovered the case, probably, he would never have become either governor or minister. He realised it himself, for sure, and decided to take the side of the stronger. He gave up, so to speak. Our authorities abandoned all the promises they made in 2000 anyway. [. . .] [T]hey considered it more profitable to join them than to undertake complicated and difficult reforms which can endanger their position in power [. . .]*" (Trivić, 2011).

From the perspective of Connolly's understanding of concept formation, the Sub-Discourse did not question the criteria of the concept of corruption or its point. Instead, it accused the new democratic government of applying a modern definition of corruption on the developments in the 1990s, but not on their own political conduct. The approach to corruption, which was advocated by the Sub-Discourse, had a character similar to what Bratsis (2003: 17) defined as "*an a-historical and a-critical understanding of political phenomena that takes the integrity of the public/private split at face value, as a quality immanent in all societies, as the normal.*" The Sub-Discourse had great transformative potential, as the discourse's arguments, focused on the strengthening of

14 From interviews with Josip Bogić, employee of the Anti-Organised Crime Units (UBPOK) of the Ministry of the Interior and Governor Dinkić in *Insajder* (2007); also, the interview with Governor Dinkić conducted by Sanda Savić on 24/4/2001 is available at www.b92.net [Accessed 20 July 2013].

15 The most prominent advocates of this idea include the academic Čedomir Čupić, who was a member of the Anti-Corruption Council at that time, and Verica Barać, the President of the Council from 2003 till 2012. More information is available in the interview conducted by Branka Trivić on 19-04-2011, available at www.slobodnaevropa.org/content/Barać_sminkanje_Miloševićevog_rezima/9497627.html [Accessed 25 April 2013].

the new democratic institutions and supporting the modern understanding of corruption, were in line with the wider discourse of democratisation. However, the actors of the Sub-Discourse, including the State Anti-Corruption Council and a part of the media, had insufficient political clout in the policy-making process. For example, some activities conducted by the Anti-Corruption Council were disregarded by governments irrespective of the governments' composition (Van Duyne and Stocco, 2012).

The Counter-Discourse

The *Counter-Discourse* is the third voice in the debates concerning the financial transfers to Cyprus. This Counter-Discourse has become more visible in public debates since 2006 when the judiciary started the investigation and prosecution of state officials from the Milošević regime. The most relevant actors of the Counter-Discourse were the members of Milošević's SPS, including the aforementioned Mihalj Kertes and Borka Vučić. They denied the accusations of corruption and argued that the financial transfers to Cyprus were conducted according to the law. They denied that the money was stolen from the citizens and that the process of decision-making was not transparent, stating that records of all banking activities were accurately kept during this time (Cyprus 22-03-2001, 26-02-2005). On several occasions Borka Vučić explicitly stated that the new administration lacked a professional attitude and formal accountability. This implied that the new democratic government was responsible for the missing evidence, not the former regime. Moreover, the actors of the Counter-Discourse hinted that someone might have benefitted from the financial transfers but those who could have benefitted were not the state employees in the National Bank and the Customs Service.

Moreover, the actors of the Counter-Discourse interpreted the financial transfers as a patriotic act (Cyprus 22-03-2001, 06-09-2007) since the money transferred back to Serbia was, according to them, used to secure food and other necessities during the years of isolation and sanctions. Moreover, the Counter-Discourse criticised the post-2000 elites for interpreting corruption in relation to national identity and national interests. They argued that this misinterpretation was a form of corruption as the same interpretation was used by the pro-European political elites, also often named as traitors in this discourse, for the legitimisation of the influence by Western powers on their political decisions.

Mihalj Kertes criticised the Mainstream Discourse for the alleged misrepresentation of the previous regime as corrupt nationalists, who were defeated by their own greed and ambitions. The actors of the Counter-Discourse denied that nationalism and discrimination on the basis of ethnic origin were the leading ideology during their mandate. The state interests reflected, as Kertes implied, the interests of all Yugoslavs, regardless of their ethnic origin. The following statement of Mihalj Kertes in court summarises the main arguments of the Counter-Discourse: "*I'm not guilty and I do not admit the crime that I am accused of. I was only implementing the policy that kept the state of Serbia functioning. [. . .] This trial is politically motivated. [. . .] My trial is at the same time a trial to the dead Milošević. [. . .] People loved me; they adored me because I was bringing them money. As a matter of fact, it wasn't me who they loved, it was the money*" (Cyprus 06-09-2007).

However, this understanding of state interests, based on the interests of people in Yugoslavia as demos, not ethnos, was not persuasive enough in post-2000 Serbia. The process of investigation and prosecution for war crimes, which was being conducted by the Hague tribunal and by the Serbian judiciary, strongly confirmed the opposing argument that the political leadership in Serbia during the 1990s had a nationalist-oriented agenda. Mihalj Kertes was prosecuted for abuse of office and embezzlement relating to the money transfers to Cyprus and he was acquitted in February 2014 as the statute of limitations in the case had expired in October 2010.

Institutional change in the Cyprus scandal

The anti-corruption debates, which developed during the investigation of the financial transfers to Cyprus and after the cancellation of the investigation, contributed towards several institutional changes. At the beginning of the investigation, in early 2001, new institutions were established in order to support the investigation. A team of experts was tasked by the National Bank of Serbia with collecting information about the transfers, locating the money and informing the government about the progress of the investigation. Also in 2001, the Commission for the Investigation of Malfeasance was established with a mandate to investigate the wider political context in which, during the previous decade, these financial transfers to Cyprus took place.

Regarding the institutional changes relating to the scandal of the Money in Cyprus, two important institutions were formed. Firstly, the Commission for the Investigation of Malfeasance was established in January 2001 with a mandate to investigate the illegal financial and political activities of the previous government. It is highly likely that the establishment of the Commission was primarily aimed at addressing the problem of repatriation of the money in Cyprus. The Commission's work was disrupted twice: when its director, Vuk Obradović, stepped down, two months after he assumed the mandate, due to a sexual harassment scandal; and in June 2002, when the secretary of the Commission, Slobodan Lalović, resigned due to the inefficiency of the Commission. The second important institutional change was the adoption of the *Law on One-Occasion Taxation of Extra Revenue and Extra Property Acquired by Using Special Privileges in Period January 1, 1989 - June 1, 2001*. The Law was adopted in June 2001 and abolished in June 2002 achieving only modest results.

The scandal concerning the money in Cyprus caused several other *ad hoc* and short-term institutional changes, such as the forming of a team of experts by the National Bank of Serbia (2001) who were tasked with the investigation of financial transfers to Cyprus. What is characteristic for the institutional changes relating to this scandal is that they were initiated by the national political elite. These institutions reflected the political will of the new DOS government to addressing concrete problems with corruption in this local context, that is the informal money transfers with Cyprus. However, the work of these institutions proved to be inefficient and ill-coordinated. Moreover, these institutions did not become permanent structures, as they were formally abolished or seized to exist *de facto* soon after they were established.

When the Governor ceased to inform the public about the progress of the investigation in March 2001, more institutional changes took place. Firstly, the President of the Commission for the Investigation of Malfeasance resigned due to a scandal concerning his involvement in sexual harassment. Secondly, the *Law on Extra-Profit* was adopted in order to tax businessmen who allegedly acquired their wealth through connections with the Milošević regime. This institutional formation suggests that the ambitions of the authorities to investigate money laundering in Cyprus were reduced to a taxation policy, whose implementation did not involve foreign actors. However, the *Law on Extra-Profit* did not yield the expected results, as the wealth owned by Serbian businessmen was mainly registered abroad and therefore not subject to taxation by Serbian legislation.

An important institutional change in the field of anti-corruption was the establishment of the Anti-Corruption Council in October 2001. The Council was established as an advisory body to the government with a mandate to suggest anti-corruption measures and monitor their implementation. According to interviews conducted with a former member of the Council, this particular institution was not established as the result of a particular corruption scandal, but the initiative came from the then Prime Minister, Zoran Djindjić (Brkić, 2013:19). Later presidents avoided any communication with the ACC, responding to none of the letters and documents sent by the institution (Van Duyne and Stocco, 2012).

Based on analysis of the institutional framework in Serbia, it can be argued that the institutional changes in the area of anti-corruption were not originated by the Money in Cyprus Scandal. The primary drivers for the anti-corruption institutional reform have been the recommendations of the Group of States Against Corruption (GRECO), since Serbia joined this initiative within the Council of Europe in 2003.

Moreover, Serbia signed the Stabilisation and Accession Agreement (SAA) with the EU in 2005, which enhanced the externally driven changes. For example, one of the most important institutional changes was the adoption of the *Law on the Anti-Corruption Agency* in 2008 and the establishing of the Anti-Corruption Agency in 2010. This change was recommended by the GRECO and required by the EU Plan for visa liberalisation.

The scandal concerning the money in Cyprus did not make a significant impact on the activities and structure of the political parties involved in the scandal. The SPS, once led by Milošević and directly involved in the financial transfers to Cyprus, remained active in political life. In 2004, the SPS supported the minority government of Vojislav Koštunica; in 2008, the party was a part of the ruling coalition; in 2009, the SPS joined the Socialist International as a reformed party of social-democratic orientation. In the parliamentary elections in May 2012, the Socialists won 14,5% of votes and their leader, Ivica Dačić, is currently in the position of Prime Minister and Minister of the Interior. Hence, the scandal on the money in Cyprus has had no significant impact on the SPS, neither morally or electorally.

The scandal also did not have a significant impact on the future political careers of the involved actors. The current coalition government, which assumed its mandate in July 2012, is led by the national-conservative Serbian Progressive Party (SPP) whose members were highly-positioned in the government during the Milošević regime. Mladjan Dinkić, who conducted the investigation of the Cyprus scandal as the Governor of the National Bank of Serbia, served as Minister of Finance (2004-2006), as Minister of Economy and Regional Development (2007-2011) and Deputy Prime Minister (2008-2011). Mladjan Dinkić now serves as Minister of Finance. Furthermore, Ivan Mrkić, who was a high-ranking Yugoslav diplomat in Cyprus from 1993 until 1999, serves as Minister of Foreign Affairs in the present government.

Considering these appointments and their political backgrounds, it is interesting to consider that, at the beginning of their mandate in July 2012, the current government announced thorough political reforms using the following words: "*We will start the reforms that citizens have been waiting for long time. SPP [Serbian Progressive Party] will make the Sixth of October happen again*" (Isailović, 2012: 6).

Discussion and conclusion on the Cyprus scandal

During the Money in Cyprus Scandal, it was the political elite in power which, through the Mainstream Discourse, pioneered the conceptual change in the anti-corruption discourse. The allegations of corruption against the previous governments were related to the formal accountability (Philp 2007) of the civil servants, who were allegedly involved in embezzlement and abuse of office, in order to make the contested money transfers. Moreover, some allegations of corruption referred to the political accountability (Philp, 2007) of the state officials in the previous governments. Their nationalist foreign policies as well as the violation of human rights and economic destruction during the 1990s were also identified as corruption. The Mainstream Discourse changed the previous understanding of corruption by introducing new criteria to the concept while keeping its negative normative point (Connolly, 1983: 31). The fact that this definition of corruption was applied to events in the past granted the Mainstream Discourse a great transformative potential.

The Counter-Discourse put forward a conceptualisation of corruption that was opposing to the one promoted by the Mainstream Discourse. The Counter-Discourse denied the accusations of corruption due to the fact that there was a lack of evidence of embezzlement and money laundering. The conflict between the Mainstream and the Counter-Discourse arises from the fact that the evidence, which would confirm the illegality of the money transfers to Cyprus, was missing. The actors in the two discourses accused each other of having vested interests in destroying the evidence. From the perspective of an analysis of discourse, the lack of a reliable evidence of corruption is crucial for the nature of the scandal. As Connolly (1983: 7) argues, the sphere of politics is delimited in a way that "*[. . .] neither the resort to force nor to evidence constitutes what is distinctive to this dimension of social life.*" If reliable evidence about the money transfers was available or responsibility for the destruction of this evidence was established, the Money in Cyprus Scandal would be transformed into a legal case which would significantly reduce the number of debates about it, after a final court decision was made.

Moreover, the actors of the Counter-Discourse rejected the accusations of nationalism, by offering a different interpretation of the concept of state and national interests. The Counter-Discourse argued that, during the armed conflict in the Balkans, ensuring the State's sovereignty and the physical safety of the citizens was prioritised over the protection of the individual economic interests of citizens. According to this view, the modern understanding of corruption, which implies that individual rights are priority, is not applicable to the situations which are characterised by a conflict of the units of sovereignty. This type of fundamental conflict is identified by Philp (2007) as the case when "*politics is centrally concerned with the maintenance of sovereignty within a territory and/or over a nation-state, and the practice of politics is irretrievably connected to negotiating and sustaining that sovereignty in the face of competition from other groups or states. War is [in such circumstances] always potentially a component of political rule*" (Philp, 2007: 64-65).

The fact that only one person was charged – and eventually acquitted – for the informal transfers to Cyprus, and that the members of the previous regime, who were accused in the media of money laundering in Cyprus, remained active in politics until today, can be partly explained by the well-developed communicative and coordinative aspects of the Counter-Discourse. The arguments of the Counter-Discourse were mainly present in those media outlets critical of the then government. Moreover, the actors of the Counter-Discourse used the opportunity to communicate their views effectively in court, as witnesses or defendants. This, among other things, enabled advocates of the Counter-Discourse, mainly members of the political elite and the high-ranking civil servants in Milošević's era, to remain active in politics.

The weakness of the Counter-Discourse arises from the fact that its actors did not offer a convincing account for the devastating consequences of their governance during the 1990s. The argument that the informal transfers to Cyprus were used to protect citizens' safety and basic needs, such as food and medications, during the years of isolation, was overshadowed by the prosecution of the Serbian leadership for war crimes and genocide at the Hague Tribunal. Moreover, the Counter-Discourse argued that the financial transfers to Cyprus were conducted on legal grounds and with legitimacy. However, the Counter-Discourse failed to articulate the idea, and to communicate it effectively, that the individual businessmen and politicians, who benefited from the money transfers to Cyprus, should be investigated. The failure to establish a discourse-coalition (Jobert, 2001), with the Mainstream Discourse concerning responsibility for the financial transfers, significantly diminished the potential of the Counter-Discourse to influence the anti-corruption policy.

The analysis of the Money in Cyprus scandal indicates that the anti-corruption discourse in Serbia in the early 2000s had a low capacity for reform. Formal and informal institutional structures in Serbia and abroad proved to be an obstacle to the political action and discourse aimed at the repatriation of the money from Cyprus. No long-term institutional changes at the state level have been identified as a direct outcome of the public debates about the Money in Cyprus scandal. Therefore, the hypothesis set at the beginning of the research was not confirmed.

To conclude this chapter, the research and analysis focused on the anti-corruption discourse in Serbia in relation to one of the major political scandals which surfaced in the early 2000s – the Money in Cyprus scandal. The research has a two-fold aim. Firstly, the research explores the concept of corruption in public debates and aims to identify the practices which were perceived as corruption. Secondly, the research explores whether the high-profile corruption scandal caused political action in the area of anti-corruption. The findings suggest that the public debates involved at least three different concepts of corruption, which were mainly based on the different understanding of national and state interests. Moreover, no long-term institutional change at the state level was identified as a result of the scandal.

References

Ades, A. and R. Di Tella, The new economics of corruption: a survey and some new results. *Political Studies*, 1997, 45: 496-515

Alatas, H., *Corruption: its nature, causes, and functions*, Aldershot: Brookfield, 1990

Andersson, S. and P.M. Heywood, The politics of perception: Use and abuse of transparency international's approach to measuring corruption. *Political Studies*, 2009, 57: 746-767

Beach, D. and R.B. Pedersen, *Process-tracing methods. Foundations and guidelines*. Ann Arbor: University of Michigan Press, 2013

Bennett, A., Process tracing and causal inference. In H.E. Brady and D. Collier (eds.) *Rethinking social inquiry: Diverse tools, shared standards*. Lanham, MD: Rowman and Littlefield, pp. 207-20, 2010

Berman, S., *The social democratic moment: Ideas and politics in the making of interwar Europe*, USA: Harvard University Press, 1998

Bjorvatn, K., and T. Søreide, Corruption and market reform, *CMI Working Paper, WP* 2003:07, Bergen: Chr. Michelsen Institute, 2003

Bratsis, P., The construction of corruption or rules of separation and illusions of purity in bourgeois societies. *Social Text* 77, 2003, 21(4): 10-33

Connolly, W.E., *The terms of political discourse*. Oxford: M. Robertson, 1983

Dimitrijević, N., Paradoksi ustavnog kontinuiteta u kontekstu osporene državnosti. In I. Spasić and M. Subotić (eds.) *R/evolucija i poredak. O dinamici promena u Srbiji*. Beograd: Institut za filozofiju i društvenu teoriju, pp. 273-280, 2001

Duyne, P.C. van and E. Stocco, *Corruption in Serbia. From black box to transparent policy making*. Nijmegen, Wolf Legal Publishers, 2012

Heidenheimer, A.J., *Political corruption: Readings in comparative analysis*. New York; London: Holt Rinehart and Winston, 1970

Hellman, J.S., G. Jones and D. Kaufmann, "Seize the state, seize the day". State capture, corruption and influence in transition. *Policy Working Research Paper, no.* 2444, The World Bank Institute, 2000

Johnston, M., *Syndromes of corruption. Wealth, power and democracy*. Cambridge: Cambridge University Press, 2005

Lambsdorff, J,G., Measuring corruption – validity and precision of subjective indicators (CPI). In C. Sampford *et al.* (eds.), *Measuring corruption*, Abington: Ashgate, pp. 81-100, 2006

Langseth, P., Measuring Corruption. In C. Sampford *et al.* (eds.), *Measuring Corruption*, Abingdon: Ashgate, pp. 7-44, 2006

Mehta J., The varied roles of ideas in politics. From 'whether' to 'how'. In D. Béland and R.H. Cox (eds.), *Ideas and Politics in Social Science Research*. Oxford: Oxford University Press, pp. 47-64, 2010

Miller, W.L., Perception, experience and lies: What measures corruption and what do corruption measures measure? In C. Sampford *et al.* (eds.), *Measuring corruption*. Abington: Ashgate, pp. 163-188, 2006

Rose-Ackerman, S., *Corruption and Government: Causes, Consequences, and Reform*, Cambridge: Cambridge University Press, pp. 163-188, 1999

Shleifer, A. and R. Vishny., Corruption, *Quarterly Journal of Economics*, 1993, 108(3): 599-617.

Peters, G.B., *Institutional theory in political science. The new institutionalism*. 3rd edition. New York: Continuum, 2012

Philp, M., Defining political corruption. *Political Studies,* 1997, 45: 436-462

Philp, M., Peace building and corruption. *International Peacekeeping,* 2008, 15(3): 310-327

Philp, M., *Political conduct*. Cambridge, Mass. London: Harvard University Press, 2007

Philp, M., Delimiting democratic accountability. *Political Studies,* 2009, 57: 28-53

Prokopijević, M. (ed.), *Two years of Reform in Serbia: a Wasted Opportunity*. Available 2002 at: http://pdc.ceu.hu (accessed on 27 January 2013)

Sabatier, P.A. and H.C. Jenkins-Smith, *Policy change and learning: An advocacy coalition approach*. Boulder, CO: Westview Press, 1993

Schmidt, V., *The futures of European capitalism*. Oxford: Oxford University Press, 2002

Schmidt, V., *Democracy in Europe: the EU and national polities*. Oxford: Oxford University Press, 2006

Schmidt, V., Discursive institutionalism: The explanatory power of ideas and discourse. *Annual Review of Political Science*, 2008, 11: 303-326

Schmidt, V., The problems of identity and legitimacy in the European Union. In S. Lucarelli, F. Cerutti and V. Schmidt (eds.) *Debating political identity and legitimacy in the European Union*. London: Routledge, pp. 16-37, 2011

Sekelj, L., Prinudna demokratizacija kriminalizovane drzave. In Spasić I and Subotić M (eds.) *R/evolucija i poredak. O dinamici promena u Srbiji*. Beograd: Institut za filozofiju i društvenu teoriju, pp. 93-105, 2001

Tanzi, V., Corruption and the budget: problems and solutions. In K. Jain Arvind (ed.) *Economics of corruption*, Mass: Kluwer Academic Publisher, pp. 111-127, 1998

Torkildsen, M., *Amended expert report of Morten Torkildsen.* Case No. IT-02-54-T 7, 3 June 2002, available 2002, at http://hague.bard.edu/icty_info.html (accessed on 20 July 2013)

Trivić, B., *Make up for Milosevic's regime,* available 2011 at: www.antikorupcija-savet.gov.rs/radio-televizija-i-stampa/cid1037-1404/barac-sminkanje-milosevicevog-rezima (accessed on 20 July 2013).

World Bank, *Anti-corruption in transition. A contribution to the policy debate.* Washington D.C, 2000

Archive material

[The archive of *Politika* does not offer full reference for all media news]

Cyprus 6/10/2000: Kostunica se obratio Beogradjanima da se okupe, jer Milošević ne priznaje rezultate izbora, author n/a, *Politika,* p. 1.

Cyprus 10/06/04: Nikoga ne stedimo, author n/a, *Novosti,* page n/a.

Cyprus 31/3/06: Kipar zataskava istragu o pljacki Srbije, author n/a, *Glas javnosti,* page n/a.

Cyprus 20/04/06: Banke za pranje para, author n/a,*Politika,* page n/a.

Cyprus 22/04/06: Batic: Dinkic I dvojica tajkuna uzeli pare, N. G. *Glas javnosti,* page n/a.

Cyprus 05/06/2006: Spasić: Izneto 11 milijardi maraka, G. J. *Glas javnosti,* page n/a.

Insajder 2007: Državna pljačka države, TV B92, available at www.b92.net [Accessed 20/04/2013]

Interviews

Anonymous source, Civil Servant, Ministry of Justice, 27 October 2012.

Anonymous source, Civil Servant, Ministry of Justice, 12 August 2012.

Anonymous source, Journalist, 20 October 2012.

Begović, Boris - Professor, Faculty of Law, University of Belgrade; Founder and director of the NGO Centre for Liberal Democratic Studies, 20 August 2012.

Analysing media representation of corruption in Ukraine: who is panicking?

Anna Markovska and *Alexey Serdyuk*[1]

Introduction

While the smoke of the battle on the Maidan Square was clearing, this chapter was finalised discussing another interesting year, that of 2012: for some it was a year of pride because the country hosted its first major sporting event, while for others, the year was marked by fierce debate on human rights, political imprisonment and the high level state corruption. In May 2012, the reported advice on travel to the country were very different, ranging from "*stay at home, watch it on TV. Don't even risk [going] because you could end up coming back in a coffin*" (BBC, 2012), to the un-famous speech of the President of Ukraine who aimed to invite more people to visit the country during the spring time of 2012, as "*the trees are in blossom and women are getting undressed for the summer*" (Youtube, 2012). Once the FA Cup 2012 started, British football supporters summarised their experience in Ukraine as: "*beer is cold, girls are hot*" (BBC, 2012).

Before and during the football event of the spring 2012, European leaders were united in reporting the abuse of human rights in Ukraine, describing the state of "bandits and crooks", and as such creating the short span of media interest and even moral blaming about the 'bad state', Ukraine. However, few traces of this were to be found by January 2013. Then one of the dominant news about Ukraine reported by Euronews and other European sources concerned its government signing a major gas exploitation deal worth a potential 7,5 billion Euro (BBC, 2012), an important development for the country in transition. It seems nothing is more fleeting and short-lived than media attention. So, does that matter?

Yes, it does matter: the media are the eyes and ears of the general public of all that people cannot observe themselves, and that is almost the whole world outside their

---

1 Dr. Anna Markovska is a senior lecturer in criminology at the Department of Humanities and Social Sciences, Anglia Ruskin University; Dr. Alexey Serdyuk is a head of the Scientific Research Laboratory of the Distance Education, Kharkiv National University of Internal Affairs.

own premises. Media broadcasts can make and unmake heroes and folk-devils: in 2004 The Scotsman reported on the knighthood of Fred Goodwin, quoting the chairman of RBS Group who said that the honour is richly deserved. Only a few years later Mr Goodwin was publicly shamed for his role in the collapse of RBS, was named as "a man who sank the bank", and who was stripped of his knighthood (Robinson, 2012). This media makability has its limits: the downfall from public favour is usually irreversible. A media folk devil is unlikely to return as a hero. In England Guy Fawkes remained a folk devil (though in New South Wales a national park carries his name). This applies to individuals, institutions as well as whole nations.

Media sources portray events in order to inform, to establish interest, to blame or to set up conditions for *moral panic*. Young (2011) describes three criteria in determining the presence of moral panic:

1. understanding "*whether social reaction is significantly disproportionate to the problem, as it presents itself at the present moment*" (Young, 2011: 251);
2. understanding the character of representations, as such, the *irrational character* of the reaction is a second criterion of moral panic;
3. a third criterion "*involves negative stereotype of a deviant, a reaffirmation of normality and the denigration of the transgressive other, a person or a place where one definitely doesn't want to be*" (*Ibid.* : 254).

Mass media actively participate in constructing "*the reality and particular configurations of social relations*" (Ericson, 1991: 222). Of course, there is an interaction with the 'receiver' of the news: one cannot sell every folk-devil to every audience, as the introductory example above makes clear: the football fans did not buy the devilled depiction of Ukraine and discovered to their delight that beer and girls were both acceptable. So, though fleeting and transient media are, they do matter, even if sometimes difficult to predict.

Our second and related starting point in this chapter is to consider Levi's (2009) elaboration on conditions conducive to devilling and to moral panic and non-devilling and to no moral panics in relation to white-collar crimes. While Levi (2009) discusses a very specific representation of identity theft and investment fraud, we propose to extend his arguments and analyse corruption using non-devilling and devilling paradigms. We then aim to briefly analyse the media representation of crime in Ukraine in general, and concentrate on the analysis of media representation of two recent events in the country: *Euro 2012*, the football tournament hosted by Ukraine and Poland, and the *Shell Agreement* about the exploration of the shale gas signed by Ukraine in 2013. We consider the examples from national Ukrainian and international media sources in order to explore varied ways in which the presentation of events are in different ways susceptible to the application of the *devilisation techniques* in media reporting. The targeted subjects are *corruption* and *racism* in Ukraine.

To devil or not to devil?

Law breaking and becoming 'folk-devilled' is not an automatic outcome. And if one is depicted as folk-devil, it does not necessarily follow that one is considered an evil threat to society. Levi (2009: 49-50) analysed 'moral panic' in relation to financial crimes and argued as follows. First,

> "*most corporate fraudsters are, for most of the time, only 'folk-devils-in waiting' because their actions do offend some sectors of public morality, those actions (even when of dubious legality) are not seen as being dramatically different from the routine functioning of capitalism. Nonetheless, some social groups and elite individuals who commit frauds are 'folk-devilled' as outsiders because their background or the individual nature of their offences enables their portrayal as 'organised criminals' or as 'rogue traders' who have clearly transgressed both official and moral values. They are not seen as seriously threatening the economic and/or moral fabric of society.*"

Does this uncertain outcome also apply to elite-law breakers in Ukraine? In this chapter the authors look at the representation of the Ukrainian political elite in two contrasting situations, before and during the Euro 2012 and during the Shell agreement negotiation 2013, arguing that one background was more conducive to the devilling than the other.

Levi's second point is that "*most questionable corporate practices and personnel are able to maintain a subterranean existence characterised by low visibility to outsiders. In this, they are aided by the 'softly, softly' approach of the enforcement agencies, media averse to the genuine risk of libel suits, and governments and public almost superstitiously afraid of meddling with the market, at least until September 2008*" (2009: 49). This observation is country specific. In contrast, the present authors will identify a difference in the representation of the Shell gas agreement within the national Ukrainian media and by western media: devilling is "in the eye of the (media) beholder" and the 'West beholder' may differ from the 'East beholder'.

With white collar crime it can happen that moral 'cracks' or the moral panic that society is on the verge of moral collapse is experienced "*when corporate crimes become embodied in visible and known persons*" (*Ibid.*: 50). What is noticeable in Ukraine is that the idea of 'moral collapse' and low morality has been widely accepted by the general population in the sense that it feels that morals have already collapsed. People discuss systemic corruption, in general trust is very low and the criminal justice system is seen as serving the needs of the rich and powerful (Boiko, 2012). In such situation, a burst of moral outrage is very difficult to initiate. It is difficult, but not impossible as the events of November 2013 in Ukraine suggest. If there is a moral outrage about the level of corruption in a country where corruption is systemic, how and who should satisfy 'the public taste for retribution'? The country's folklore has some wisdom in saying, "*those who in [in prison] should be let out, those who are out should go in [in prison]*". Levi (2009) points, "*the white-collar offender is only folk-devilled when he frightens the horses*". In other words, politicians and law enforcement practitioners should feel that without reacting to the issue of white-collar criminality they can endanger their own positions, and the public can turn against them. And so it happened in Ukraine that the political leaders did not understand this: the absence of the will of the political elite to tackle corruption in Ukraine or even to mention it, led to the violent protest of January-February 2014. The east of Ukraine had a slogan "stop them stealing" in Russian, and the west of the country say the same thing but in the Ukrainian language.

The question is where do you find the sources that can 'frightened the horses'? Are they to be found outside, as representatives of international media and international pressure groups? Can we trust the local civil society to deal with this, and the local media to support the cause? Provided there is a media interest that leads to moral blaming, will moral panic begin? Can we predict its outcomes? Levi argues that it is difficult to predict the longer term outcomes of these panics. In some situations, it is also difficult to establish the moral panic about corruption and white-collar criminality.

Levi (2009: 62) elaborates on the examples of identity theft and investment fraud to suggest conditions conducive to devilling and moral panics in relation to (other) white-collar crime (for example, "*powerful political devillers or totalitarian state, low defamation risk for journalism*") and conditions that are conducive to *non*-devilling and to *no* moral panics in relation to (some) white-collar crime (for example, conditions such as "*restrictive libel laws, journalist intimidation, plus fear of protective laws*", lack of motivation to alarm the public).

Given this uncertainty, for us it is interesting to observe the relationship between folk devilry, moral panic and corruption in Ukraine. Following Christie (1986) and Levi (2009), it may be argued that the creation of folk devils should work very well in Ukraine because there is "a simple juxtaposition of good victims and evil perpetrators", hard working members of the general public opposite to hard working but corrupt officials and politicians.

Media and Crime

Media reporting crimes has been a focus of attention for a number of years. Chibnall (1977:. 23) discusses "*eight professional imperatives which act as implicit guides to the construction of news stories*". Naturally, news must be "news", "*it is about what has just happened*" (*ibid.*), but there must be something more which transcends this tautology. Apart from 'informativeness' there must be an emotional arousal of curiosity, that will be dependent on the dramatisation, personalisation, sensationalisation and titillation imperatives in construction the news stories (*ibid.*). Any newsman knows there are only a limited number of arousals for the markable product, sex and fear being the most prominent. An element of the fear is *moral panic.* Young (2011) discusses how moral panic *then* and *now* differs. He writes: "*The moral panics coalesced around the feeling of resentment with regard to an older generation against youth cultures which carried with them harbingers of the future. The present period this side of 9/11, the recession and restructuring of the economy is accompanied by the breakdown of community and the rise of an unparalleled hyper-diversity of ethnic and sub-cultural formations*" (*ibid*: 256). According to Young, it is no longer about the intergenerational conflict, but it is about "ontological disturbance and widespread economic insecurity" (*ibid.*). In the diverse world the focus of attention shifted to the bad other, or as Young (2010) defines them, 'transgressive other': it can be a country or a group of people within a country.

To become a 'transgressive other' a number of forces should be in place, forces that are described by labelling and sub-cultural theories as the "*actors and reactors, deviants and controllers*" (*ibid*: 247) who operate in a certain cultural context. The label of 'transgressive other' can be applied to the individuals, groups or the country as a whole. For example in Ukraine, 'transgressive others' are politicians and businessmen, and for the rest of the world, Ukraine is considered as transgressive other because of the absence of the rule of law. In January 2014 David Cameron mentioned Poles living in the UK while discussing EU citizens working in the UK and claiming child benefits for children living abroad, hence creating a label of 'transgressive others' and applying it to the specific group of population (BBC, 2014). The label of 'transgressive other' is a very powerful one, as given it strikes the right accord: it has a potential to lead to the moral panic.

Public fear fuels moral panic and sustains political interests around the transgressive others. Critcher (2011: 259) argues that fear can be symbolically constructed, and as such, it can distort and misrecognise social realities, it can generate the hostility to outsiders. The authors look at the fear created by different actors in the representation of the same events.

Media, crime and (corrupt) politics in Ukraine

Different labels were given to describe the stage in the development of the post-Soviet countries. The term '*anomie*' can be applied to define the new cultural goals for many, but the financial success of only a selected few. In Soviet times, the aspirations of financial success were limited to the selected few (either the underground businessmen or the corrupt elite), while the rest of the country was busy building communism employing their own imagination and networks. 'Dirty togetherness' was originally introduced by Podgorecki (1987) as a feature of the shortage economy and in reference to "*cliquishness and close-knit networks in the context of scarcity and distrust of the state*" (in Wedel, 2005, 102-103). The law-abiding majority of the country was very much aware of the "*symbiosis among politics, law and criminality*" (*ibid.*: 103) but resigned to this state of their society. This symbiosis of the Soviet era imposed restricted physical and moral boundaries: the boundaries being clearly defined by the communist party in terms of the means of production and the state ownership.

With the collapse of the Soviet Union, this very severe imposition or restriction collapsed as well, and meanwhile transformed politicians into business people, criminals into politicians, and provided more prominence to legal professionals, who can now help to move people and money. Twenty-three years of transformation later, and Ukraine is still an example of an endemically corrupt country. "*I think he is not struggling for Ukraine under his rule, but Ukraine under his personal property*", said Zamyatin, Ukrainian political analyst (Ayres, 2014). Corruption is not a new problem for Ukraine, but the present government centralised corruption. For example, in 2012, the President signed a law eliminating the need for state enterprises to issue public tenders for contracts, meaning "*there is now no transparency over billions of dollars in government contracts,*" (Akymenko, as quoted in Ayres, 2014).

The 2013 Global Corruption Barometer survey of ordinary people showed that "*69 per cent of Ukrainians think that corruption has increased in the past two years and 80 per cent believe that the government's actions to fight corruption are ineffective*" (Transparency International, 2014). The report shows that Ukrainians view the judiciary, public sector and law enforcement as the most corrupt sectors in the country (*ibid.*). If crime control is an industry captured by the state (Christie, 2001), the problem in Ukraine is in the fact that the state has been captured beforehand by a section of the criminals it is supposed to control. Politicians and state officials become agents who "*subvert their own role or suborn others to influence legislation in ways which directly or indirectly benefit them personally*" (Philp, 2001: 1-8). A theatre of absurdity in its own right.

Discussing politics and power in Ukraine Hale (2010: 84) writes "*the 2010 elections disappointed by amply revealing the stomach-churning nature of Ukraine's democracy, so unruly and corrupt that most Ukrainians question whether it is really a democracy at all*". Hale suggests that Ukraine is not a democratic failure either, "*in fact, it is partly the dirtiness of Ukraine's democracy that sustains it and in fact augurs well for long-term success*" (*ibid.*). For the Ukrainians the dirtiness is the most repugnant and at the Maidan Square the protesters showed their determinedness the clean that up.

As a post-Soviet state Ukraine inherited a number of problems, including and often originating from high levels of corruption and the absence of the rule of law. It has been argued previously that Ukraine can be considered an example of the captured state (Hellman and Kaufmann, 2001; Markovska and Serduyk, 2012). Soviet legacy has also encouraged (already existing) clientelism, discussed by Hale as "*specific punishments and rewards meted out to specific individuals*" (*ibid*: 85). The mechanism that sustains democracy in Ukraine, according to Hale (2010: 95-96), is better understood as an example of a rare combination of competitive clientelism that is rooted in a division of executive power, and that is capable of creating an opening for public opinion to matter directly. The division of power prevents "*any one side from utilising corruption opportunities to dominate politics*" (*ibid.*: 96).

Analysing the relationships between media and politics during the 2010 presidential election, Hale (2010: 88) pointed out:

> "*the chief editor of Telekritika, a journal devoted to monitoring media practices in Ukraine, reported that both campaigns concluded actual contracts with editors to buy positive reports as election day approached. Some such material would be marked explicitly as advertising, but much would not, being presented instead as news stories without any indication that they were paid for . . . one indication that much of the media was for sale is that sometimes similarly positive articles about rival candidates would appear in the very same issue of the same publication.*"

Media manipulation is a subject for debate within the Western and established democracies, with many politicians being accused of creating very strong ties with media corporations, such as the erstwhile Prime Minister Berlusconi. Media for sale is not an anomaly that puts Ukraine in a different camp of countries. What puts Ukraine in a different camp is the fact that there is too many sale assistance, too much corruption, and very few channels to follow the exposure of the press.

The monitoring of the quality of news reported by nine main TV stations in Ukraine (Telekritika, 2013) provides an interesting insight in the realities of the news reporting and the priorities of the news of the day. Reporting on the information provided from May-September 2013, Telekritika (2013) reports that not a single TV station reported on the facts or issues that would be considered unprofitable for the officials. Devilling and non-devilling media parameters in Ukraine work as a powerful tool in the hands of the government and elite. It leaves journalists to concentrate on reporting road traffic accidents and violent crimes, providing only a selection of pre-confirmed news on freedom of speech, white collar and economic crimes (Telekritika, 2013).

Case study

In order to analyse devilling and non-devilling aspects of the media representation of serious crimes we looked at two events: Euro 2012, the football tournament hosted by Ukraine and Poland, and the Shell Agreement about the exploration of the shale gas signed by Ukraine in 2013. The authors conducted a content analysis of the selected Ukrainian media (in Ukrainian and Russian) and selected English speaking sources, with the aim to contrast the views and representations of both groups of sources published in English within the UK.

In Ukraine six sources were selected, four newspapers and two magazines. These sources have been identified on the basis of the results of the study conducted by TNS marketing, as the most popular. The National Internet search engine was used to select the articles in Ukraine. Table 1 shows the sources and the number of publications per source.

Table 1
The list of the sources and the number of the articles analyzed for Euro 2012 and Shale gas 2013

	«Euro 2012»	«Shale gas»
Ukraine		
Facts (Факты / Факты и комментарии http://fakty.ua)	24	4
Segodnya (Сегодня http://www.segodnya.ua)	38	23
Korrespondent (Корреспондент http://korrespondent.net)	74	44
Ukrainski tuzhden' (Український тиждень http://tyzhden.ua)	113	30
Kommersant (Коммерсантъ http://www.kommersant.ua)	54	11
Zerkalo nedeli (Зеркало недели http://zn.ua)	6	32
Total	**309**	**144**

The search was limited by the date of publications. In the case of Euro 2012, the selected time frame for publications was from May to July 2012 (one month before and one month after the games), 309 articles were selected for analysis. In the case of the shale gas agreement the time frame was from December 2012 to February 2013 (one month before the agreement was signed and one month after), resulting in 144 articles selected for analysis.

a. Euro 2012

In the case of Euro 2012 we have excluded all articles discussing football games as such, and selected 309 articles for our analysis. The three main content indicators studied were: (a) *racism and xenophobia,* (b) *corruption,* (c) *anti-social behaviour.* It was important to register not only the number of the relevant articles, but also, the problem indicators of the content of the story. Three indicators are identified: problematisation of the issue (the problems exist); rationalisation of the issue (the problem does not exist), and neutral representation (representation of the issue without clearly assigned label of 'bad' or 'good'). On the one side of the continuum there is problematisation with a negative connotation, on the other is rationalisation, absence of negative connotation, and in the middle there is a neutral representation that state the problem but does not push it to one or the other side of the extreme.

Table 2
Results of the content analysis of the Euro 2012 representation in the Ukrainian media (N=309)

	Representation			
Content indicators	*Problematisation of the issue*	*Rationalisation: the problem does not exist*	*Neutral representation of the issue*	Total = 100%
Racism	2 (0,6%)	46 (14,9%)	261 (84,5%)	309
Corruption	29 (9,4%)	8 (2,6%)	272 (88%)	309
Antisocial behaviour	17 (5,5%)	18 (5,8%)	274 (84.5%	309

Table 2 shows that the majority of the articles present the issues identified in the neutral and judgement free way without a clearly assigned label. For the purpose of our analysis it is interesting to look at the two columns where the judgement is that comments are offered. *Racism* has been discussed more than any other theme. 15,5% of publications discussed racism, however, the publications deny the existence of racism as a problem: only two articles out of 309 analysed state that racism is a problem in the Ukrainian society. The problem of *corruption* was discussed in 12% of the publications, and most articles confirmed it as a problem. The problem of *anti-social behaviour* was identified in 11,3% of the publications, and interestingly, the evaluative nature of these publications is rather ambiguous: the articles do not deny that there is a problem with anti-social conduct, but insists that the Ukrainian militia tackles this problem. The newspaper Segodnya reported that "*during the championship there were 293 crimes against foreign citizens . . . All the crimes were committed by the citizens of Ukraine and the majority of these crimes have been solved already by the militicia*" (Segodnya, 2012). Problem solved.

b. The shale gas agreement

For the representation of the shale gas we considered two main indicators: *corruption* and *environmental consequences*. Similar to the previous case, three separate groups have been established: problematisation of the issue (the presence of the indicator of corruption and the environmental harm); rationalisation of the issue (the problem does not exist), and neutral representation (representation of the issue without clearly assigned label of bad or good). The results are presented in Table3 below.

Table 3
Results of content analysis of the selected sources representing the shale gas agreement signed by Ukraine (N=144).

Content indicator	*Problematisation of the issue*	*Rationalisation, the problem does not exist*	*Neutral representation*	Total = 100%
Ecological harm	45 (31,3%)	10 (6,9%)	89 (61,8%)	**144**
Corruption	12 (8,3%)	1 (0, 7%)	131 (91%)	**144**

Table 3 repeats the pattern of representation shown in Table 2, and as such the majority of the articles state the issue of ecological harm and corruption in a judgement free manner. Critical discussion of the corruption in the agreement about the shale gas exploration features only in 9% of the national articles, and most of the articles in this subgroup are suggestive to the corrupt elements of the deal: as such they discuss it as a problematic context (12 articles, 8,3%). For example, *Korrespondent* (2012) reports,

> "*there are three flies in the ointment, two small and one large [the original text says: three spoons of tar in the barrel of honey]. The first one is that the Ukrainian media and the leaders of the opposition suspect that the agreement signed with Shell has direct interest of the family of the Ukrainian President, this is due to the fact that a small and not well known company called SPK-Geoservis features in the draft of the joint enterprise. The second is about those who oppose the exploration of the shale gas argue that it will lead to the ecological catastrophes. The third fly 'was placed' by the Gasprom, the Russian gas monopolist, who is extremely agitated and staged economic and informational attacks on Ukraine.*"

These 12 articles are very critical to the manner in which the agreement was reached at the local levels in the regions of Ukraine where the exploration will take place, arguing that the agreement was rushed through and that the legal procedures were not observed. Overall, from the Ukrainian side there is an involvement of corrupt politicians, from the side of the foreign investors, there are "*foreign executives, representatives of the clans of Rockefellers, the owners of the Royal Dutch Shell, who will, according to the agreement destroy our eco system in the next 50 years.*" There are three sources of fear: (1) the outsiders, (2) the activities of the western company and the Russian party; and (3) the insiders: the activities of corrupt government officials.

Problematisation of the ecological consequences is the most developed and charged area of concern, with 31,3% of the articles discussing negative consequences. Segodnya newspaper (2013) states that "*the foreign investors are coming to pollute our air and water*". The newspaper quotes Ecologist William Zagorodskij who says, "*the whole world is against the shale gas exploration, however in Ukraine the Cabinet of Ministers signed the decision to allow exploration*". The newspaper Tuzhden pointed to the fact that the leaders of the opposition promised to conduct an investigation into the details of the agreements signed by Shell and Nadra Yuzivska (the shale gas field). With one newspaper stating that "*our oligarchs wouldn't stop if there is a smell of money*". Corruption was negatively presented in 8,3 % of the articles.

There are some interesting contrasts to be observed when comparing the Ukrainian national press to the representation of the same issues in the UK. In the UK we used LexisNexis search to identify relevant publication (22 in total), analysing sources such as the *Times*, *The Independent*, the *Guardian*, *The Financial Times* as well as the BBC. Both events featured in the news: Euro 2012 was widely represented, providing not only sport comments, but also extensive comments on the background of the country. In contrast, the shale gas agreement Ukraine signed with Shell, was in the headlines almost exclusively to comment on the financial context of the agreement.

Naturally, events that happened or concern one country, in this case Ukraine, will be more represented in the national paper, rather than in the foreign media. The sample of the Ukrainian newspapers allowed us to quantify the data. The low frequency representation of the news about Ukraine in the UK allow only a more qualitative character.

Ukraine as one of the two hosts of the Euro 2012 had a rather negative reception in the British media. Most sources used the event to discuss the political, economic and social issues within the country. For example, *The Telegraph* in an article published on the 6th May 2012 discusses "*Ukraine's controversial Euro 2012*" and the imprisonment of the former Prime Minister Julia Timoshenko. In the reference to the president and the Ukrainian government the article uses phrases such as "*the only thing bandits care about is family and money. European countries need to freeze their foreign bank accounts*", "*they* [Ukrainian officials] *don't think about the criticism and the shame in front of the world because they are gangsters.*" *Sunday Telegraph*, June 3rd, 2012, discusses racism, corruption and human rights abuse in Ukraine as a background to the discussion of the Euro 2012. In anticipation of the event and during the event, the media used the opportunity to comment on the country's profile, specifically pointing to the issues of human rights, racism and corruption within the government. These issues provided the media with the space to discuss their concerns about the football supporters travelling to the country and their safety.

To the end of the tournament *The Independent* commented: "*After the final whistle-Ukraine's dark future of corruption*" June 30th, 2012, discusses "*a tournament that went a lot better than many expected in terms of organisation and fan experience*"; the article turns attention to allegations of corruption surrounding the president and his government. "*The government sees its power not as a service for the people but as a resource for profit for its members and their families.*" There is a reference to "*a shadowy entity based in Donetsk with a murky ownership structure, that nevertheless won more than half a million worth of government contracts for construction projects related to the Euros.*" Interestingly these accounts of corruption were more frequently to be reported by the Ukrainian regional papers.

Moving on to the newspapers reporting on the shale gas deal agreement signed by Ukraine, *The Financial Times* (2013) points to the "*potentially big step in reducing Ukraine's reliance on costly imports from Gasprom*", quoting experts who claim that the agreement is the "*paradigm shift for Ukraine, a major step towards energy independence.*" It is the dependency on the gas from Russia that dominated the representation of the news in Reuters and BBC. The overwhelming tone of the articles was about the positive impact of the signed agreement on Ukrainian economy, with many articles featuring the Ukrainian president shaking hands with the Shell official. "All the big boys were there" reports the New York Times (2012).

What is interesting to us here is how we can explain such an unfavourable evaluation of the football event by British media, and a positive response to the agreement signed by the president of the country, who, only six months before, was described by the same media sources as in charge of a 'crooked and bandit' government. It is possible that the answer lies in the devilling and non-devilling conditions described by Levi (2009)?

Conclusion: explaining the devilling or not-devilling dilemma

The representation of the two events inside and outside of Ukraine had different accents. For the ease of the comparison we will talk about the reaction of the East (Ukraine) and the West (British media sources).

So, the West presented:

1. Euro 2012 in the lights of racism, human rights abuse, totalitarian state, selective justice;
2. Shale gas exploration as a positive step for Ukraine, removing dependency on Russia.

The East presented:

1. Euro 2012 as a big success, with the local police working well, featuring corruption during the tender process and construction, but mainly attempting to concentrate on the positive sport image;
2. The shale gas agreement as a very problematic one. It features very detailed analysis of the ecological issues, discussion of corruption and corrupt schemes inside the agreement, looking at the agreement as a political show off in front of Russia.

The questions to be asked are: why discussion of corruption dominated the western representation of the Euro 2012, but not the shale gas agreement with Shell? In other words, why the media in Ukraine orchestrated the devilling of the shale gas deal and the West created the 'moral blaming' about the Euro 2012, but remained in a non-devilling mode about the other side of the shale gas agreement?

On the basis of the indicators suggested by Levi (2009) we can observe that in the case of the Western media and Euro 2012, powerful political leaders (Germany and the UK) were united in devilling the authority of the totalitarian state. The good and democratic West opposed the evil and totalitarian East. This case can be considered as an easy one for the journalists to portray and not be afraid of the defamation risks. Corrupt Ukrainian government officials were identified as a 'suspected offender population'; the opposition leader in prison worked as a message to help to separate good from bad. The Ukrainian population as well as those who decided to attend the games were presented as possible victims.

Why then, was the shale gas agreement not scrutinised as much by the Western media? Perhaps claims about the presidential family private interests in the deal created a message that is personalised, and different from claims of endemic and systemic corruption in the country. Personification (naming people as responsible) is much more difficult to deal with than generalisations. The claim 'Ukraine is corrupt' is much easier to publish than that the president of the country is corrupt. The presence of the big western player, makes it also difficult to report on corruption due to the libel laws in the West. As a general statement and on a general level, Ukraine may be corrupt and have corrupt government, but on a very specific matter, the representative of the Western world in the shape of the Shell company, is a different actor to take into the account.

When the East discussed the losses following the possible shale gas exploration it was about the ecological damage and corruption. When the West discussed the losses it was about politics and economy, the issues that are more appealing to the public. Moral issues were relevant within the Ukrainian media, and not within the western response. This is interesting as it is a reverse situation from the representation of the Euro-2012 games. Both sides generated fear and hostility by identifying the bad other.

The news production depends on participation of two groups: the deviant actors and the reactors, and it is by placing the two groups in the "structure and historic time" (Young, 2011) that could help us to understand the outcome. It is obvious that the West receives the information on the endemic nature of corruption in Ukraine, but finding the opportunity to act and react on these messages has been a very complicated business. The big sport event provided a good ground to expose many problems and to raise public awareness about the situation, personal messages could be hidden, and the momentum was there to portray the full picture. On the other hand, the agreement to explore the shale gas is personalised news item for the West, because it includes big Western players and the named political and economic representatives from both sides. In a reverse situation, the East found it easier to criticise the agreement using personalised claims of corruption. It may be the case that some sources that do expose corruption in Ukraine do it on a daily basis, and thus the element of distinct dramatisation is not always present in the stream of exposures. Interestingly, when the sources do mention corruption they mentioned it in the neutral, label free context. As discussed above, in the country where corruption has been centralised and spread endemically within the criminal justice agencies, exposing corruption does not necessarily lead to the investigations, and enforcement.

Levi (2006: 1054) argues that "*structural, cultural and personal factors interweave and interpenetrate to 'produce' news and documentaries . . . The publicity becomes the template for cultural conflict.*" Is that reflected in the contents of the written news broadcasting of the two events? In the case of the Euro-2012, the Western media appeared to have a structural and cultural interest in portraying Ukraine as less civilised, less disciplined. In contrast, the shale gas agreement was presented as a civilised way to build a strategy for future developments in Ukraine. The Ukrainian media presented both events in a rather different way using another template for conveying news items. One can observe the short term memory of the press from one side, and a message overload from the other side. The West presents and forgets, the East presents corruption and its many forms and shapes, but that not much changes. The representation of corruption in the media should be a very powerful element for the template of cultural conflict. The problem in Ukraine is that publicity of corruption cases very rarely leads to a reaction from the side of the authorities. This is not surprising given the scale of corruption in the country. 'Moral panic' that the West so often blames as an overrepresentation and overreaction from the side of the (western) authorities, to a certain extent is not discernible in Ukraine as a kind of 'emotional peak'. It almost does not matter what is published there, as the well-known chain-reaction of the 'moral panic' will not happen because the on-going rampant corruption smothered the ignition of that chain reaction of emotions. One can say that the underlying emotions in the Ukrainian society remained slumbering.

Slumbering, but not dead. From 22 November 2013 onwards a series of sharp negative *stimuli* brought these emotions to life and evoked the Maidan Square revolt.

References

Ayres, S., *Why are Ukraine's protesters so angry at President Yanukovych's 'Family'*? Available 2014 at: http://www.csmonitor.com/World/Europe/2014/0206/Why-are-Ukraine-s-protesters-so-angry-at-President-Yanukovych-s-Family-video

BBC, *Sol Campbell warns fans not to travel to Euro 2012.* Available 2012 at: http://www.bbc.co.uk/sport/0/football/18233822

BBC, *Cameron seeks to allay Polish benefit concerns.* [2014 available at: http://www.bbc.co.uk/news/uk-politics-25656429

Boiko, A., Systemic corruption in Ukraine. *Visnyk of the Lviv University.* Series Law, 2012, 56. P. 349–354

Chibnall, S., *Law and order news: an analysis of crime reporting in the British Press.* London: Tavistock Publications Ltd, 1977

Christie, N., *Crime control as industry.* 3rd ed, London: Routledge, 2001

Critcher, C., For a political economy of moral panics. *Crime, Media, Culture*, 2011 7, pp. 259-275

Cohen, S., *Folk devils and moral panic: the creation of the mods and rockers.* London: McGibbon & Kee, 1977

Erikson, R.V., Mass media, crime, law and justice: an institutional approach. *British Journal of Criminology*, 1991, 31, pp. 219-249

Hale, H.E., The uses of divided power. *Journal of Democracy*, 2010, *21*, pp.84-89

Hellman, J. and D. Kaufmann, *Confronting the Challenge of State Capture in Transition Economies*. [2001, on-line]. Available at: http://web.worldbank.org

Korresponden, *Point of view. The Ukrainian dream*, 2013 online, available at: http://korrespondent.net/world/worldabus/3204400-vzghliad-ukraynskaia-mechta

Levi, M., Suite revenge? The shaping of folk devils and moral panic about white-collar crime. *British Journal of Criminology*, 2009, 49, pp.48-67

Levi, M., The media construction of financial white-collar crimes. *British Journal of Criminology,* 2006, 46, pp.1037-1057

Levi , M., Social reaction to white-collar crimes and their relationship to economic crises in M. Deflem, (ed.) Economic Crisis and Crime, *Sociology of Crime, Law, and Deviance*, 2011, 16. pp.87-106

Philp, M., *Corruption and state capture: A theoretical framework*. 2001. Available at: http://siteresources.worldbank.org/

Philp, M., *Corruption and state capture: A theoretical framework*. University of Oxford. Department of Politics and International Relations. 2001, pp.1-8.

Robinson, N., *Former RBS boss Fred Goodwin stripped of knighthood*. Available 2012 at: http://www.bbc.co.uk/news/uk-politics-16821650

Segodnya, Druzhba narodov, 2012, online available 2013 at: http://sport.segodnya.ua

Segodnya, *Vo vremja Euro 2012 soversheno 30 krazh*. Available, 2012 at: http://www.segodnya.ua/ukraine/vo-vremja-evro-2012-bylo-coversheno-okolo-30-krazh.html

Segodnya, *Slancevui gas*. Available 2013 at: http://www.segodnya.ua/economics/enews/Ukraina-poluchit-slancevyy-gaz-pro-priemlimoy-cene-lish-cherez-5-let-ekspert.html
Telekritika, *Pro sho movchali SMI*, Available 2013 at: http://osvita.mediasapiens.ua/material/23691

Telekritika, *Pro sho movchali SMI*, 2013 http://osvita.mediasapiens.ua/material/23691

The Telegraph, *Euro 2012 should be investigated for corruption*, says Yulia Tymoshenko, 2012. Available at: http://www.telegraph.co.uk/news/worldnews/europe/ukraine/9248221

The Scotsman, *It's honours all round on Queen's list*, Available 2004 at:

http://www.scotsman.com/news/it-s-honours-all-round-on-queen-s-list-1-1019471

The Sunday Telegraph, *The welcome that awaits Ukraine*; racism, corruption, human rights abuse- could it be any worse for the co-host of Euro2012? Available 2012 at:
http://www.telegraph.co.uk/news/worldnews/europe/ukraine/9307372/The-Euro-2012-welcome-that-awaits-in-Ukraine.html

Transparency International, *Fighting corruption in Ukraine*. [On-line 2014]. Available at: http://www.transparency.org/news/feature/ukraine_standing_up_for_peoples_rights#sthash.Z3HtCcM3.dpuf

The Independent, *After the final whistle- Ukraine's dark future corruption*. Available 2012 at: http://www.independent.co.uk/news/world/europe/after-the-final-whistle--ukraines-dark-future-corruption-7899904.html

Young, J., Moral panics and the transgressive other. *Crime, Media, Culture,* 2011, 7, pp.245-258

Wedel, J.R., Flex organizing and the clan state: perspectives on crime and corruption in the New Russia. In W. Pridemore (ed.) *Ruling Russia, crime, law and justice and a changing society*. New York: Rowman and Littlefield Publishers, Inc., 2005, pp. 101-16

Different manifestations of organised crime and corruption in Italy: a socio-legal analysis

Anita Lavorgna and *Anna Sergi*[1]

Introduction

Organised crime is a curious phenomenon to research. While it was once considered a problem affecting only few countries – such as Italy and the US – since the late 1980s organised crime has become a major policy and research topic in many European countries (Rebscher and Vahlenkamp, 1988; Van Duyne *et al.*, 1990; Paoli, 2008). Nonetheless, because it is such an 'umbrella concept' (von Lampe, 2002: 191), it appears still insufficient to guarantee a common level of understanding in public and scientific debates and consequently its definition remains problematic (Wright, 2006; Van Duyne and Van Dijck, 2007). Indeed, organised crime is conceptualised around the world in different ways and many different types of criminal groups and activities are included within the label 'organised crime' depending on different countries and different academic areas (Albanese *et al.*, 2003; von Lampe *et al.*, 2006; Savona, 2010). After all, defining a criminal phenomenon as 'organised crime' suggests the existence of a whole set of characteristics (hierarchy, struggle for profit, tight ties, and so on) shared by a common mechanism in the commission of crimes. Its political representation is usual emotive and allows an 'emotional kick' that helps to get resources and powers (Levi, 1998: 336).

Despite divergences in identifying the core features of organised crime, *corruption* is conventionally considered in the academic debate as one of its constituting elements (Ruggiero, 1996; Arsovska, 2011), and specifically as an enabler or facilitating modus operandi to proceed with organised crime activities (Center for the Study of Democracy, 2010). Corruption has been widely depicted both in common sense and in institutional ways across national and international legislations. As a general concept,

1 Anita Lavorgna is a PhD Candidate (Doctoral School of International Studies, University of Trento), and Co-Editor of *The European Review of Organised Crime* for the ECPR Standing Group on Organised Crime. Anna Sergi is a PhD Candidate (Centre for Criminology, University of Essex), Co-Chair PG Committee of the British Society of Criminology and Newsletter Editor for the ECPR Standing Group on Organised Crime.

as defined by the Oxford Dictionary, corruption is dishonest or fraudulent conduct by those in power, typically involving bribery. Bodies such as Transparency International (2013) define corruption as the abuse of entrusted power for private gain, classifying it as grand, petty, and political, depending on the amounts of money and the sector involved. That is a broad description with an imprecise delineation. A stricter definition focuses on the decay of decision making characterised by illegal exchange of interests (Van Duyne, 2001). Such corrupt decision-making may occur at any level and not only at the level of the public administration.

The puzzle this contribution addresses concerns the role of corruption as an element of organised crime in the Italian scenario. To this end, the paper examines variations in corruptive behaviour associated with manifestations of organised crime in the country. More precisely, the paper shall investigate what function does corruption play in the organisation of crimes by cooperating criminals, which will be referred to in this chapter as 'organised crime groups'.[2]

To understand whether corruption is a constituting element of organised crime, this chapter suggests to look at the ways different organised crime groups operating in Italy make use of corruption. In order to do that, the chapter identifies four different manifestations of organised crime, and describes how they employ corruption in different ways, according to how they need to adapt to different social opportunity structures. This allows: (a) to give a more up-to-date picture of Italian organised crime, beyond the rhetoric of mafia, (b) to present the changing nature of corruption in relation to different manifestations of organised crime in the country, and (c) to discuss how well Italian criminal law addresses all four manifestations of organised crime. Given our research interest for corruption variation, *non*-corruptive organised crime has not been targeted as a research subject.

Methods and data

In order to see how different types of organised crime groups in Italy employ corruption, we necessarily had: (1) to distinguish among different types of organised crime groups that are currently present in the Italian criminal panorama and (2) to

2 This paper shall use 'organised crime', 'organised criminal groups', and 'organised crime groups' interchangeably, in line with international documents and policy papers (see, for instance, the UN Convention against Transnational Organized Crime, 15 October 2000, and the Conclusions of the Council of the EU on setting the EU's priorities for the fight against serious and organised crime between 2014 and 2017, 6-7 June 2013).

inspect empirical cases concerning organised crime groups where corruption may have been an element of the offending. To that end we used two main sources: (a) *law enforcement sources* (semi-structured interviews with law enforcement officers, official reports, judicial transcripts, and records from police investigations) and (b) secondary sources consisting of *media news articles*

With regard to the law enforcement sources, we carried out 23 semi-structured interviews with experienced Italian law enforcement officers and prosecutors form different agencies at the local, district (e.g., Direzione Distrettuale Antimafia), and national (e.g., Direzione Nazionale Antimafia) level. Because of the central role of prosecution in the Italian fight against mafias, the official reports published by the Anti-mafia agencies have been included in the analysis. Also primary documentary sources collected and analysed for the authors' PhD dissertations have certainly informed this study (Lavorgna and Sergi, 2013). In particular, 15 judicial transcripts and records from police investigations have been used.

As for the media sources, we did a keyword search on Italian newspaper online archives (*La Repubblica* and *Il Corriere della Sera*, which are the largest and most important newspapers in Italy). In order to be taken into consideration, the news had to deal with a specific corruptive behaviour involving organised crime [for details, including a list of the keyword used and the total of combinations obtained, see Annex A]. Indeed, many articles were dismissed because they were rather reporting generic information on corruption, the word corruption was mentioned only incidentally, or they were merely duplicates of other news. Trying not to miss potentially relevant documents, the keyword search was over-inclusive and followed by a careful reading of the news selected. Thus, the keyword search started with generalised search-phrases such as 'organised crime + corruption'. Being conscious of the possible overlapping in news media between the notions of mafia and organised crime, we extended the search towards more specific search parameters, such as 'trafficking + criminal + corruption'. In total, twelve keyword combinations were used. In respect to the same attempt of over-inclusiveness, broad temporal limits were set (March 2003–March 2013), and conjunctive (AND) rather than disjunctive (OR) queries sere utilised. The news has been sampled until thematic saturation was achieved – *i.e.*, when documents revealed no new significant insights (after 100 news per keyword search). A total of 747 cases were taken into consideration, divided as shown in Table 1 (below). The cases easily fit in the types this paper addresses for the purposes of the principal aim of the research, which is to assess the role of corruption in different Italian manifestations of organised crime.

Findings

In the course of our data collection and preparatory analysis we identified four types of organised crime groups. The four manifestations of organised crime in Italy have essentially emerged throughout the data collection and in particular they were supported by our primary law enforcement sources (for a closer examination of these four types of organised crime groups, see also Lavorgna and Sergi, 2013). Therefore, the collected data were sorted around those four manifestations which are summed up below and elaborated in a later section. The four types are:

a. ***'Simple' criminal organisation***
   Any criminal group formed by at least three persons that join together with the aim of committing an indefinite program of felonies if they have a permanent and structured internal organisation.
b. ***Mixed criminal networks***
   Criminal groups mainly involved in trafficking activities.
c. ***Migrated mafia groups***
   Mafia groups that moved away from their traditional territory.
d. ***Mafia-like organised crime***
   Criminal groups characterised by the use of mafia-method of intimidation, control of the territory, and infiltration in the public sphere.

The notion of organised crime and related corruption in Italy

We will first elaborate the notions of organised crime one finds in Italian parlance as well as (legal and academics) literature. This detour is required as in Italy the notion of 'organised crime' seems to be particularly problematic and sometimes misleading: indeed, the same phrase is used in both public and academic discourse to denote different groups, ranging from mafia groups to new illegal market players that often take the form of looser gangs (Lavorgna *et al.*, 2013). Nonetheless, a certain part of Italian scholarship seems to think about organised crime only in terms of the mafia (Santino, 2006; Bianchini and Sicurella, 2007) rather than considering traditional Italian mafia only as "a species of a broader *genus*, organised crime" (Varese, 2001: 4, italic in original; Paoli 2003, 2005). In this way, the presence of the *mafioso* method (Arlacchi, 2007) – a system of violence, corruption, and unscrupulousness – risks to be overstressed. Similarly, in common language the word 'mafia' has lost most of its value in denoting a specific criminal organisation (namely, Cosa Nostra) and has become a sort of umbrella term or rather brand name, covering sundry notions: not only mafia-like organisations (namely the 'ndrangheta, the Sacra Corona Unita, and the Camorra or at least the Casalesi clan, the most powerful group within the Camorra), but also smaller or looser organised criminal networks (Paoli, 2007, Lavorgna *et al.*, 2013). This situation does not contribute to clarity (von Lampe, 2008)

The criminal law is an important approach for investigating how the ambiguous notion is cast in a (legal) text or mould. If we look at the way in which organised crime is framed within Italian law in the Criminal Code (at articles 416 and 416-*bis*), we can observe that the focus of reference to organised crime is, most of all, the mafia, especially in its traditional mafia settings. While historically understandable, this has become obsolete and is no longer a sufficiently clear angle to describe the complexity of the phenomenon in its various manifestations.

Since the introduction of the Italian Criminal Code in 1930, the offence of *membership/belonging to a criminal organisation* (art.416) has criminalised 'organised crime' by requiring three elements: (a) an associative bond, (b) an organised structure, and (c) the aim of carrying out an indefinite program of felonies (*delitti*) in accordance to a specific and continuative criminal program.

After half a century of criminal development this legal provision proved no longer satisfying: indeed, by means of article 416 it was not able to capture the specificities of organised criminal groups operating systemically in certain parts of Southern Italy. Therefore, in 1982, article 416-*bis* – *membership of mafia-like criminal association* – was introduced to identify more precisely mafia-like groups, and this article soon became the centre of the Italian anti-mafia framework. In the terms of article 416-*bis*, a mafia-type association can be found when a criminal organisation operates according to a specific modus operandi and with a specific aim. In particular "when the participants take advantage of the intimidating power of the association and of the resulting conditions of submission and silence to commit criminal offences" with the aim "to manage or control, either directly or indirectly, economic activities, concessions, authorisations, public contracts and services, or to obtain unlawful profits or advantages for themselves or for others, or with a view to prevent or limit the freedom to vote, or to get votes for themselves or for others on the occasion of an election" (article 416-*bis* of the Italian Criminal Code, as translated in Council of Europe, 2004: 181). In essence, what differentiates article 416 and article 416-*bis* is the need, in the second case, to criminalise the mafia-method of intimidation, control of the territory, and infiltration in the public sphere. The difference between these two forms of organised crime groups is also made evident by article 416-*ter*, introduced in 1992 in completion of article 416-*bis* to explicitly criminalise the attempts of mafia-type groups in influencing the results of electoral competitions.

When it comes to the relationship between organised crime and corruptive behaviours, this difference is crucial. Criminal law differentiates among various forms of bribery and corruption (mainly *corruzione* and *concussione*). The way one or the other is linked to organised crime activities essentially depends on the presence of that same logic of power abuse and exchange of money with advantages, an interaction that characterises organised crime in the law (Aleo, 2009). According to the Criminal Code, *concussione* refers to a public official who, by abusing his/her power, induces a private citizen to pay or promises money or another benefit in order to perform his duty (art. 317 of the Criminal Code). *Corruzione* instead (arts. 318 and 319) refers to a public official who receives money or another benefit from a citizen who agrees with such behaviour in order to perform his/her duty, to not perform his/her duty, or perform an action in contrast with his/her duty. What is the connection to organised crime? That is the addition in art. 416-*bis*: control of the territory, and infiltration in the public sphere through control of elections and corruption. Thus, in legal thinking, corruption in Italy is fundamentally implied in the extended concept of organised crime both at the legal and at the social level as long as the concept of 'organised crime' overlaps with that of the 'mafia' (Davigo and Mannozzi, 2007).

To what extent is this built-in connection between organised crime and corruption a constant factor in Italy? In order to answer this question, in the following sub-sections we will describe more in details the four different types of organised crime manifestations and examine how they differently employ corruptive behaviour,

Different manifestations of organised crime types in Italy[3]

In the previous section we have seen how the Italian legal framework recognises two t ypes of organised crime: on the one hand, we have the '*simple*' *criminal organisation* (art.416), which describes any criminal group formed by at least three persons that join together with the aim of committing an indefinite program of felonies if they have a permanent and structured internal organisation. Next to that, we can find *mafia-like organised crime*. This offence of mafia membership (art.416-*bis*) is assumed and deducted from observable and proven *mafioso methods*: intimidation, violence and (political) control of territory as further specified by the jurisprudence (Antolisei, 2008).

In this latter case, the basis of mafia groups consists of the specific nature and

3 An earlier and extended version of this discussion can be found in Lavorgna and Sergi (2013).

intensity of their associative bond. Whereas article 416 requires a general agreement by two or more people to commit crimes over an extended period of time, article 416-bis further characterises mafia groups through the use of intimidation, subjugation and penetration of the upperworld, in addition to a criminal plan extending over time. In their territories of origin (roughly identified in the Southern regions) these groups are in competition with the State for the control of the territory (Sciarrone, 2009: 10), by affirming their presence and power through the mafia method as the basis of their associative bond. These criminal groups are not only engaged in criminal markets but they employ violence and intimidation to secure also a place in the legitimate economy (Paoli, 2003: 174).

From a closer observation of the criminal panorama in Italy, however, it emerges that these two types of organised crime identified by the law do not cover all manifestations of organising crime when they are compared against the current empirical findings. By looking at the variations of organised crime in Italy, the need emerged to identify two additional types of manifestations of criminal groups that currently seem not to be covered by the existing legal definitions. Indeed, from interviews conducted with national and district anti-mafia prosecutors and from constant monitoring of criminal activities within the Italian territory, either from newspapers or from legal case laws, it is possible to recognise at least two additional varieties of organised criminal groups or associations, which are not covered by existing substantive criminal law, namely *mixed criminal networks* and *migrated mafia groups*.

a. Mixed criminal networks

In *mixed criminal networks*, the actual profit driven crime is more prominent than the structure of the group itself. The criminal activities carried out by mixed criminal networks generally resemble so-called 'transit crimes', which are basically trafficking activities ("criminal groups . . . primarily involved in international illegal trade, using the same opportunity structure that facilitates legal economic activities" in the words of Kleemans, 2007: 176). Beyond Italy, transit crimes are considered the main activity of most organised crime groups (Kleemans, 2007). Even if sometimes in Italy mixed criminal networks are complex groups and they may also be in contact with local mafias (in the hope to establish themselves into the criminal underworld and to enjoy the guarantees of mafia protection), they certainly do not share the specific features of Italian mafias as concerns the characteristics of the associative bond in terms of strict internal cohesion. On the other hand, mixed criminal networks could not even meet the rigid organisational requirements of 'simple' criminal organisations (according to article 416), being often pragmatic, fluid and dynamic networks rather than what is observed with structured groups. As emerging from data, in fact, their mainly crime trade orientation is reflected in their relationship to corruption, which is rather a pragmatic tool for handling contraband than a structural element in their entrepreneurial conduct.

b. Migrated mafia groups

The last manifestation of organised crime that has been identified is that of *migrated mafia groups*. The movement of mafia groups has received increased attention in criminological research (Varese, 2006; Campana, 2011), especially concerning mafia transplantation – *i.e.*, when mafias (thus criminal groups meeting the definition of article 416-*bis*) transfer to a new territory outside their territories of origin and routine operations while replicating their structures and maintaining their ability to offer criminal protection over a sustained period of time (Varese, 2006: 4). In Italy, the presence of Southern Italian mafias has been largely documented throughout Italy and especially in the North-West (Varese, 2006; Direzione Nazionale Antimafia, 2011). However, while in certain areas – such as in some municipalities of the Milan and Turin hinterlands – real 'transplantations' have taken place and the 'colonising' attitude of mafia groups has been evident (Paoli, 1994; Varese, 2006; Chiavari, 2011; Savatteri, 2012), the situation seems different in other parts of Italy. In the North-East, for instance, it seems that the 'ndrangheta and some Camorra groups are not colonising –thus entering the political arena and investing money in the territory – but rather 'delocalising'[4] – *i.e.*, creating wealth in Northern Italy to converge in the South (Pennisi, 2012). This is why migrated mafia groups in some parts of Italy seem to be more interested in relationships with the professional and entrepreneurial world than with politics, and links to the latter exist to the point that they are functional to the achievement of other goals (Pennisi, 2012; Lavorgna *et al.*, 2013). As a consequence, the modus operandi and the aim of migrated mafias are different from those used in their territories of origin or the 'colonising settlements' which are considered as a mere offspring of the mother organisation.

Ideally, the four types identified could be placed side by side in a sort of continuum depending on their increasing degree of sophistication. 'Simple' criminal organisations are indeed the simplest ones, followed by mixed criminal networks, migrated mafia groups (which are mafia groups delocalised but not replicating the same structures of their territories of origin), and finally Mafia-like organised crime

---

4 'Delocalisation' in economics indicates the transfer of industries in new areas, which have competitive advantages compared to the main ones.

(which normally root in their territories of origin and at times successfully replicate their original structure elsewhere). A certain degree of overlap is present between the four types. However, the proposed distinction remains meaningful for analytical purposes, since different types of organised crime groups rely on different opportunity structures and have different aims and goals (Lavorgna and Sergi, 2013).

The four organised crime manifestations & corruption

So far, this chapter has described four different ways in which organised crime manifests itself in Italy. The way in which these various manifestations operate differs greatly, depending on the social opportunity structures they rely on and on the different goals they pursue. This sub-section focuses on the different ways in which the various manifestations of organised crime presented above employ corruptive behaviours. It will make clear that corruption is not always a characterising element for all types of organised crime in the country or not in the same way, and that it is used with different purposes.

a. 'Simple' criminal organisations

In cases that can be classified under article 416 of the Criminal Code – simple criminal organisations –corruption is a pragmatic technique, which is employed when and if it is needed for the execution of criminal plans. Without the mafia connotations, a criminal organisation can take different forms. In many of the cases considered, the criminal groups not always needed corruption. Actually corruption is a derivative of the execution of the planned criminal activities. For instance, where a criminal organisation is formed for the purposes of committing armed robberies or burglaries, corruption is not needed because both the preparatory acts and the ultimate carrying out of the criminal plan remain in the underworld. Where, instead, the criminal plan aims at more organisational extensive activities, infiltrating the upperworld, forms of corruption or bribery might be vital to secure the success of the operation. For example, following a robbery the groups may be in need of bribing a bank official for the purpose of laundering. Or, investing the loot in construction public officials need to be bribed to obtain construction permits. Generally speaking, these are one-off cases for use of corruption and do not involve structural corruptive connections. However, this does not exclude frequent high-profile cases, where corruption is employed to influence decision-making with the involvement of prominent political figures at the local, regional, or national level. Very recently (early

2013), for instance, a case pivoting around offences of a simple criminal association and corruption has involved a notorious politician (the former governor of a Northern Italy region).

b. Mixed criminal networks

As for simple criminal organisations, for mixed criminal networks corruption is a contingent, possible, but not characterising element. Kleemans (2007: 172) already underlined how groups involved in certain transit crimes such as smuggling and sex trafficking in the Netherlands try to avoid confrontation with law enforcement authorities: corruption, from this point of view, is used for specific needs, and in particular when the criminal network needs licences or other forged documents, when they want to evade surveillance, and when they need information on on-going investigations. Indeed, in a country such as the Netherlands where organised crime phenomena are usually of this type (Kleemans, 2007), studies on corruption have shown that this problem is limited and mostly connected to custom corruption (Fijnaut, 1993; Van Duyne, 1997; Fijnaut and Paoli, 2004; Huberts and Nelen, 2005; Transparency International, 2013). This is consistent with the cases emerging from Italian media news. First of all, only few cases were concerned with this type of organised crime; in all of them, however, corruption was directed towards public officers in gatekeeper positions, in the form of 'executive corruption' (van Duyne, 2013). Second, most of the news items mentioned the fact that custom officers were corrupted in cross-border trafficking flows – from precious antiquities in airports to cars travelling from Romania. Public officers were often corrupted (or attempts were made) with expensive travels and luxury goods rather than with money (as in a big case concerning trafficking in illegal waste). The same has been found concerning bribery, where also sex seems often to be used as a 'bribe' in cases of illegal smuggling.

c. Migrated mafia groups

For migrated mafia groups, corruption seems to play a vital role. In fact, corruptive behaviour has been used in cases of public contracts and sub-contracts concerning major public works on infrastructures, healthcare, the managing of the water system, and the construction of new malls, as well as in real estate speculation and illegal waste dumping (Sergi and Lavorgna, 2012). Corruption seems to be present also in 'new' businesses such as gambling – in particular to get the approval of new slot machines – and renewable energies (Sergi and Lavorgna, 2012). In all these cases, for mafia groups in territories far from the one of origin, corruption has been used to violate regulations with illegal activities for investing or laundering money. In some other cases, corruptive behaviour was used towards law enforcement officials to get inside information on law enforcement operations and to avoid controls on illegal slot machines. Furthermore, it was used towards the judiciary to get reduced sentences or to make the circumstances of the imprisonment less burdensome.

d. Mafia-like organised crime

In the territories of classic mafia-like formation the link between traditional mafia groups and corruption is implied in its description. Indeed, the main feature of this type of mafias is the attempt to control portions of legal sectors and to acquire social power in their territories. Corruption and bribery in this sense are not only practices implied in the social structures of the criminal clans, but are endemic to the way in which the clans infiltrate the public sphere and in different degrees every aspect of public (and sometimes private) life. When it comes to mafias in their territories of origin, the practice is that of endemic corruption: malpractices, sleaze, and bribery are not only widespread but also tolerated in many ways (up to the top political level, as the notorious cases regarding the former Prime Minister Berlusconi shown), similar to the acceptance of the mafia power. This essentially means that social elites are often complacent to the influence of criminal groups, and often social elites themselves and criminal groups overlap (Sergi, 2014).

With endemic corruption there is an assumption that certain activities can only be carried out and certain results can only be achieved through manipulation of legal boundaries: therefore, a tacit understanding of corruptive practices are assumed without interventions or specific initiative. Indeed, the more a criminal group is socio-economically established in such a territory, the more its members can enjoy an 'autonomous intimidating power' originating from the association itself (Turone, 2008:124).[5] This autonomous intimidating power is the warranty for success in practices of infiltration and corruption.

For corruption to be endemic it is necessary that interests are shared between entrepreneurs, public officials, mafiosi, and politicians. A clear example of this fact is the high number of dismissals of town councils in the South of Italy for mafia infiltration. Even though it is not a prerogative of these territories anymore, as also in other regions of Italy transplanted mafia groups have infiltrated public life, in the South of Italy the numbers are still quite high: at the end of 2012, 221 town councils

5 Endemic bribery or endemic corruption has been defined in Italian jurisprudence during the 1990s: it is a scenario were entrepreneurs and private citizens live with fear and respect of people in power at the point of granting and justifying illicit practices without being asked to do so.

in Italy had been the object of this procedure, 53 of which in Calabria (the reign of the 'ndrangheta) alone[6]; in 2012, out of 25 dismissals, 11 have been in Calabria 6 in Campania (the territory of the Camorra) and 5 in Sicily (land of Cosa Nostra) (Legautonomie Calabria, 2013). The recent dismissal of the municipality of Reggio Calabria has demonstrated that there is indeed a very thin line between the interests of the 'Ndrangheta and the ones of politics (Sergi, 2014). As previously noticed, the Criminal Code itself confirms by criminalising the endemic character of corruption in mafia territories: indeed, art. *416-ter* criminalises the exchange of money or favours for votes in political elections. This article fully represents the invasive power of mafias in corrupting public elections because of their influence and wealth.

The existing legal framework and the gaps in the law against organised crime

The Italian legal framework targeting organised crime has a complex history: it is characterised by several legal changes that reflect two main drives: first of all, the need to enhance the investigative capacities of law enforcement agencies towards evolving criminal phenomena. Secondly, political opportunism. Indeed, most of these changes were set as emergency responses to traumatic events for the country– such as the killing of anti-mafia judges Falcone and Borsellino in 1992 – and as answers to serious mafia infiltrations both in politics and in the social environment (Farrell, 1997).

In 1982, the introduction of article 416-*bis* with so-called 'La Torre Law' (Law 646/1982) was needed because, previously, law enforcement authorities were bound to prosecute mafia members only as long as they recognised them as parts of a criminal organisation under article 416. However, the offence of simple criminal organisation was inadequate in many instances: indeed, the illicit character of the associative bond was difficult to prove in cases with a high degree of *omertà* (code of silence, non-cooperation with authorities), which is common in mafia situations and in cases of endemic corruption. Article 416-*bis*, by requiring not only an associative bond but also the existence of conditions of intimidation, submission, *omertà* and ability to corrupt, *de facto* has allowed prosecutors to infer the existence of the mafia method in the manifestation of *omertà*. With article 416-bis, omertà alongside the

6 Since 1993, when the law allowing dismissals of town councils for mafia infiltrations was passed (Law 81/1993).

ability to corrupt became indicators of the existence of mafia-like activity. What emerges is that mafia-like crimes are more than just crimes: they are 'styles' in committing offences. Mafia crimes, in fact, are always characterised by intimidation or violence, the exercise of pressure coming from the social status most mafia members enjoy in their territories and corruption. Indeed, when article 416-*bis* was introduced, the offence already carried a certain expectation and its content referred specifically to the Sicilian Cosa Nostra, its structure, and its modus operandi (Farrell, 1997; Lupo, 2004). In this sense, targeting the structure of the group more than the actual crimes is the result of a wider and more flexible understanding of the phenomenon as social rather than just legal. An excerpt from the Supreme Court case law might help in understanding the mafia-style definition in the law.

> "The proof of the characterising elements of the criminal hypothesis at article 416-bis of the Criminal Code can be very well assumed inductively on the basis of the fact that the criminal group presents all, or at least some, of the revealing indicators of the mafia phenomenon, such as secrecy of membership, kinship relationships, respect for hierarchies, the fact that the group bears the costs of the justice systems, the diffused climate of 'omertà' as consequence and indicator of subjection to the criminal group."[7]

The necessity to introduce these specifications in article 416-*bis* has been dictated by the need to identify mafia conducts as activities beyond the mere criminal association. The penalty provided by article 416-*bis* is more severe than the one provided for criminal association in article 416, since this offence is considered a multi-threatening crime, a threat not only to the public order because of its corruptive undermining character. It is also a threat to the freedom of self-determination of people when the whole political and economic elite is corrupted and intimidated by *mafiosi* (Marini et al., 2002: 2027).

Apart from core articles 416 and 416-*bis*, in the Italian legal framework – both in the procedural and in the substantive law – there are many other references to organised crime and corruption (Vigna, 2006). The Italian legal system allows to deal with organised crime through a different criminal justice path (so-called 'double-track system', *sistema del doppio binario*), which is considered the winning card of the Italian anti-mafia (Jamieson, 2000; Vigna, 2006; Smedovska, 2010): in those cases where a link can be set with one of the two forms of organised crime offences recognised by law, the criminal procedure changes. These changes involve mainly investigation and prosecution powers and permissions: for instance, more time is allowed for

---

7 Cassazione Sezione III, 10/1/2000, n. 1612, imputato FERONE.

investigation and prosecution shifts from the general prosecution office to the specialist district anti-mafia prosecution office.

Furthermore, when a mafia-like situation is suspected, often inferred from corruptive behaviours, during a criminal investigation, intelligence gathering regulations and prosecutorial tools are further diversified. Article 51(3)-*bis* (as modified by Law on security measures no.92/2009) of the Criminal Procedure Code identifies a number of serious offences that are traditionally considered linked to mafia-like organised crime. When one of these offences is flagged, it is deferred for investigation and prosecution to specialised anti-mafia offices.[8] Moreover, in these cases additional investigative tools can be used, such as the use of more intrusive forms of surveillance and covert activities. Mafia-like cases have also the benefit of peculiar legal measures: for instance, the seizure and confiscation of property illegally acquired by the *mafiosi*, their relatives, and associates (*confisca dei beni*) is an essential tool in countering mafia-like organised crime.

The introduction of article 416-*bis,* and therefore the recognition of mafia as a criminal association *per se,* was the first and arguably more important of a number of legal changes whose impact has proven essential in targeting organised crime. Indeed, after 1982, more than 100 anti-organised crime laws have been enacted. Clear tendencies can be identified in the expansion of legislation addressing specifically mafia-like organised crime.

- First of all, by allowing law enforcement to prosecute as 'mafia' dangerous groups that were not initially considered as such, as in the case of the 'ndrangheta and foreign criminal organisations, included in the anti-mafia legislation only a few years ago (Law 125/2008 and Law 50/2010) (Lavorgna *et al.*, 2013).
- Secondly, by enhancing the investigative capacities of law enforcement agencies in cases attributable to mafia-like organised crime according to article 51(3)-*bis.*
- Finally, with the typification of the external support to mafia association (*concorso esterno in associazione mafiosa*) (Vigna, 2006) by the Italian Supreme Court in 1994 (Corte di Cassazione, Sentenza Demitry, 5 October 1994), which is achieved through the joint implementation of two different criminal law provisions.

This latter typification of external support to mafia associations covers those cases where a person (usually a politician or a person of social high status), free from any

8 According to art. 51(3)-*bis*, these offences are: membership in mafia-like associations; membership in associations aimed at unlawful drug trafficking; kidnapping for ransom; membership in criminal associations aimed at smuggling of foreign cigarettes and other tobacco products; enslavement or holding in slavery or servitude; human trafficking, purchase or sale of slaves; membership in criminal associations aimed at perpetrating any of the three aforementioned crimes.

formal subjection to the mafia organisation, effectively contributes to its activities by helping to implement its criminal plans, reinforcing the association itself, and gaining substantial profits. This new direction taken by the judiciary (that has not been converted into statutory laws yet) not only draws attention on a worrying gap in the law but it allows Italy, and Italy alone, to fight those cases that would normally remain in the so called 'grey zone' of mafia-like organised crime, the one in between the criminal and the legal worlds and that relies specifically on corruption and infiltration (Armao, 2003: 27; Sciarrone, 2009: 29). Though corruption and infiltration of the upperworld is anything but a novelty, the fact of bestowing these criminal aspects a special status is important. Indeed, this approach facilitated the prosecution of people working as support of the organisation and should be object of specific legislative aim.

Limitations

Despite the development of the Italian legal framework addressing organised crime manifestations and the links with corruption, gaps and loopholes can be found when this legal framework is projected against the current empirical reality as presented above, especially as concerns problems with evidence requirements in legal practice. Indeed, if we consider *mixed criminal networks* and *migrated mafia groups*, there seems to be confusion as to whether the criminal conduct of these groups can be subsumed under a legal description of organised crime.

Mixed criminal networks, even when the criminal offences committed are serious and/or profitable, could not meet the criteria of article 416 (simple criminal organisation). For instance, criminals might not be part of a permanent organisation but rather cooperate with criminal peers in a flexible way according to transient criminal opportunities. Furthermore, for sentencing purposes, article 416 distinguishes different levels of responsibility in terms of promoters, associates, members, constituents, bosses, and others if necessary. However, roles within the criminal network group may not be clear enough to be differentiated, and some loose networks of criminals might not reach the level of an organisation and sophistication required for the application of the article. Moreover, while in certain cases (such as in the case of drug trafficking) the specific transit crime they are carrying out could be covered by article 416 because it is considered a felony (*delitto*), in other instances this could not be the case. In fact, when the transit crime is considered only a misdemeanour (*reato contravvenzionale*, as in the case of trafficking in endangered species or art trafficking), the criminal activity is not covered by article 416. Similarly, mixed criminal networks cannot meet the requirements of article 416-*bis* (mafia-like criminal organisation). Indeed, because of their different aims (making profit rather than governing a territory) they do not need the mafia 'style' in committing their offences, since they do not need to invest in the territory, nor to control it. Consequently, anti-mafia instruments such as the possibility to use seizure and confiscation of the proceeds of crime as well investigative tools such as undercover operations or controlled delivery could not be used to counter these type of criminal networks, while currently they do not generally apply to the investigation of mixed criminal networks. Whether or not existing investigative procedures available for article 416-*bis* could be extended to these groups needs to be carefully weighed against the difficulty to blur distinctions among the criminal groups through such an extension.[9]

When it comes to *migrated mafia groups*, the problems are of a different order. In fact, when mafia groups migrate without a real transplantation in the territories of destination, it is usually difficult to cover their criminal activities with article 416-*bis*, since the modalities used and the targeted aims are different. While a mere expansion of the laws of article 416-*bis* to such cases might end to be disproportional, a difficulty remains in providing a proper coverage to serious criminal activities when a *mafioso* method does not exist. Indeed, as noticed by the majority of interviewees, specifically anti-mafia prosecutors whereas convictions and charges for mafia membership (416-*bis*) are very popular and successful in the South of Italy for traditional mafia groups and activities, the use of anti-mafia legislation seems difficult if applied outside those regions.

Therefore, the question arises what can be done when a criminal group does not meet the requirements of 416-*bis* but nonetheless the anti-mafia framework would provide the proper instruments to tackle it, in particular given the enhanced investigative capacities of law enforcement agencies in mafia cases.

The fact that mafia groups behave differently when they operate in new territories has already been recognised in the literature: Campana (2011), for instance, talks about 'functional diversification' to underline how the *modus operandi* of a Camorra clan changes across territories (namely their homeland in Campania, the Netherlands, and Scotland). However, Campana focuses on the different types of criminal activities that are carried out in these different territories, while here we want to introduce the difficulties that law enforcement encounters in investigating and prosecuting under article 416-*bis* members of a migrated mafia group when the presence of a mafia method is missing. However, in those cases of organised network criminality and migrated mafia groups, in which the perpetrators resort to corruption, it should be

9 Currently these tools are precluded for transit crimes, with the exception of those criminal activities that are included in the anti-mafia framework according to Law 146/2006 (for instance drug trafficking and human trafficking).

possible to allow law enforcement to prosecute as dangerous 'mafia' groups some that were not initially considered as such.

Conclusion

In this chapter we have first identified a total of four manifestations of organised crime and their corresponding corruptive practices in the Italian panorama and second, we have argued that the current legislative framework is not efficiently equipped to cover all these manifestations. The manifestations presented essentially stem from different social opportunity structures and have different aims: for instance, while the maximisation of profits is the ultimate purpose of mixed criminal networks, this is not always the main objective of mafia-like groups, especially in their homelands where other, social aims may be of greater importance (Paoli, 2005). While mafia-like groups often assume the role of underground political entities or directly challenge the social order by competing or cooperating with legal firms in legal markets, this is not the case for criminal networks engaged in illegal or illicit trades.

The reliance on different social opportunity structures is also the reason why, in some cases, corruption is a necessary ingredient of organised criminal offending, while in other cases it is rather a pragmatic technique, contingent on specific needs of the criminal group: organised crime responds to specific social opportunity structures, and as such each of its manifestations adapts differently to the social fabric of reference. Broadly speaking, whereas corruption appears to be endemic where the mafia presence is extensive, it is often occasional and opportunistic in areas where mixed criminal networks and simple organised crime are prevalent. In this sense, corruption can be either an enabler of certain crimes, a facilitating strategy for achieving certain goals (thus being occasional and opportunistic), or a set of practices which are taken for granted and largely accepted by a local community even though they are illegal or unethical (thus being endemic).

Considering the nature of organised crime in the form provided in article 416 (without the mafia connotation), the more the criminal activities are extensive in place and time, the more also a 'simple' criminal group will need to employ corruption. In the case of mixed criminal networks, corruption may be needed in order to execute a certain criminal activity. It has been noted that certain countries that are particularly affected by this organised crime manifestation do not face major corruption problems, which supports our claim that it is the existing opportunity structure – for instance, in the case of the Netherlands, good infrastructures (Kleemans, 2007) – that makes certain places vulnerable to different forms of organised crime and corruption. For mafia-like organised crime, corruption is a built-in feature needed to maintain or strengthen influence in the public/legal sector, while migrated mafia groups rely on corruptive behaviours as long as needed to smooth regulations and controls (Van Duyne, 1997).

A conceptual distinction between the four manifestations of organised crime identified – and between their use of corruption – has to be kept in mind in the fight against organised crime: if different organised crime groups rely on different opportunity structures to prosper, different responses might be necessary.

Before concluding, it is worth noting that even if the Italian anti-mafia framework lacks coverage for every criminal offending related to organised crime, it might nonetheless have the right framework to expand. This is in line with the Council of Europe Framework Decision *2008/841/JHA* on the fight against organised crime, as the need to criminalise participation in criminal organisations of different sort mirrors the European attempt to focus on *both* the activities and the structures of criminal groups. Such an approach could effectively complement Italian legislation, which generally focuses more on targeting the structure of the various organised crime groups, while the crimes are only of secondary interest from the perspective of the definition of organised crime (Jamieson and Violante, 2000; Tranfaglia, 1991; Sergi, 2013).

As far as the practical level is concerned, taking account of different manifestations of organised crime in assessing their modus operandi – for instance, their use of corruption – as well as their social, political and economic impact, could help researchers and practitioners to describe the problem to meet (and to identify solutions for) the real needs of a specific territory or society. Furthermore, the conceptual distinction among different manifestations can assist the dialogue among countries experiencing organised crime in different ways because of their various historical, social, and legal backgrounds.[10]

Further research on a broader set of primary documentary sources is needed to strengthen and generalise our findings. In particular, primary documentary sources on cases of corruption involving organised crime groups could certainly help refining the variations in corruptive behaviours we have sketched in this study.

10 This distinction has been used in Lavorgna and Sergi (2013) to assess the different attitudes of Italian criminal associations in the financial crisis and in the use of Internet technologies.

References

Albanese, J.S., D.K. Das and A. Verma (eds.), *Organized crime. World perspectives*. Upper Saddle River, Pearson Education, 2003

Aleo, S., *Sistema penale e criminalità organizzata. Le figure delittuose associative*, III ed. Milano, Giuffrè, 2009

Antolisei, F., *Manuale di Diritto Penale. Parte Speciale*. Milano, Giuffré, 2008

Arlacchi, P., *Mafia Business: Mafia ethic and the spirit of capitalism*. London, Verso, 1986

Armao, F., Why is organized crime so successful?, In: F. Allum and R. Siebert (eds.), *Organised Crime and the Challenge to Democracy*. Oxon, Routledge, 2003

Arsovska, J., Conceptualizing and studying organized crime in a global context. Possible? Indispensable? Superfluous?, In: C.J. Smith, S.X. Zhang and R. Barberet (eds.), *Routledge Handbook of International Criminology*. Abingdon, Routledge, 2011

Bianchini, E. and S. Sicurella, Il crimine organizzato in Italia: analisi evolutiva. *Rivista di Criminologia, Vittimologia e Sicurezza,* 2007, *no. 1* (3), 111-127.

Campana, P., Eavesdropping on the Mob: the functional diversification of Mafia activities across territories. *European Journal of Criminology*, 2011, *no. 8* (3), 213-228

Center for the Study of Democracy, *Examining the links between organised crime and corruption*. Sofia: CSD, 2010

Chiavari, M., *La quinta mafia. Come e perchè la mafia al Nord oggi è fatta anche da uomini del Nord*. Milano, Salani, 2011

Council of Europe, *Combating organised crime: Best-practice surveys of the Council of Europe*. Bruxelles, Council of Europe Publishing, 2004

Davigo, P., and G. Mannozzi, *La corruzione in Italia. Percezione sociale e controllo penale*. Roma, Laterza, 2007

DNA, *Relazione annuale sulle attività svolte dal Procuratore nazionale antimafia e dalla Direzione nazionale antimafia nonché sulle dinamiche e strategie della criminalitá organizzata di tipo mafioso nel periodo 1° luglio 2009 – 30 giugno 2010*. Roma, Direzione Nazionale Antimafia, 2011

Duyne, P.C. van, Organized crime, corruption and power. *Crime, Law and Social Change*, 1997, 26(3), 201-238.

Duyne, P.C. van, Will 'Caligula go transparent?' Corruption in acts and attitude. *Forum on Crime and Society*, 2001, vol. 1, *no. 2*, 73-98.

Duyne, P.C. van , Serbian anti-corruption policy. Welcome to Potemkin's Village? *Filozofija I Drustvo*, 2013, 14(1), 81-118.

Van Duyne, P.C. van, R. Kouwenberg en G. Romeijn, *Misdaadondernemingen. Ondernemende misdadigers in Nederland*. Arnhem, Gouda-Quint, 1990

Duyne, P.C. van, and M. van Dijck, Assessing organised crime: the sad state of an impossible art, In: F. Bovenkerk and M. Levi (eds.). *The organized crime community*.

Essays in honor of Alan A. Block. New York, Springer, 2007
Farrell, J., *Understanding the mafia*. Manchester, Manchester University Press, 1997
Fijnaut, C., *Politie corruptie in Nederland.* Arnhem, Gouda Quint, 1993
Fijnaut, C., and L. Paoli, *Organised crime in Europe: Concepts, patterns, and control policies in the European Union and beyond*. Dordrecht, Springer, 2004
Huberts, L.W.J.C. and J.M. Nelen, *Corruptie in bet Nederlandse openbaar bestuur: Omvang, aard en afdoening*. Utrecht, Uitgeverij Lemma BV, 2005.
Jamieson, A. *The Antimafia: Italy's fight against organized crime*. New York, St Martin's Press, 2000
Kleemans, E.R., Organized crime, transit crime and racketeering. *Crime & Justice,* 2007, no. 35, 163-215
Lavorgna, A., R. Lombardo and A. Sergi, Organized crime in three regions: Comparing the Veneto, Liverpool, and Chicago. *Trends in Organized Crime*, 2013
Lavorgna, A. and Sergi, A. Types of organised crime in Italy. The multifaceted spectrum of Italian criminal associations and their different attitudes in the financial crisis and in the use of Internet technologies. *International Journal of Law, Crime and Justice*, 2013 (online first).
Legautonomie Calabria, *Banca Dati Comuni Sciolti*, 2013. Retrieved from http://www.autonomie calabria.it/lac/comuni-sciolti/ (last accessed on April 15, 2013)
Levi, M., Perspectives on 'Organized crime': An overview. *The Howard Journal,* 1998, no. 37(4), 335-345
Lupo, S., *History of the mafia*. New York, Columbia University Press, 2011
Marini, G., M. La Monica and L. Mazza, *Commentario al Codice Penale*, III ed. Torino, Utet, 2002
Paoli, L., An underestimated criminal phenomenon: the Calabrian 'Ndrangheta. *European Journal of Crime, Criminal law and Criminal Justice,* 1994, no. 3, 212-238
Paoli, L., *Mafia brotherhoods. Organized crime, Italian style.* Oxford, Oxford University Press, 2003
Paoli, L., Italian organised crime: Mafia associations and criminal enterprises, In: M. Galeotti (ed.), *Global crime today. The changing face of organized crime*. Abington, Routledge, 2005
Paoli, L., Mafia and organized crime in Italy: The unacknowledged success of law enforcement. *West European politics,* 2007, no. 30(4), 854-880
Paoli. L., Organized crime: new label, new phenomenon or policy expedient? *International Annals of Criminology,* 2008, no. 1-2, 37-60
Pennisi, R., *Audizione del Sostituto Procuratore Nazionale Antimafia, Dottor Roberto Pennisi. 104a seduta Senato della Repubblica – Camera dei Deputati, XVI Legislatura. Resoconto stenografico n. 102 (edizione provvisoria). Commissione Parlamentare di inchiesta*

sul fenomeno della mafia e sulle altre associazioni criminali, anche straniere. Roma, 2012

Rebscher, E. and W. Vahlenkamp, *Organisierte Kriminalität in der Bundesrepublik Deutschland.* Wiesbaden: Bundeskriminalamt, 1988

Ruggiero, V., *Economie Sporche. L'impresa criminale in Europa.* Torino, Bollati Boringhieri, 1996

Santino, U., *Dalla mafia alle mafie. Scienze sociali e crimine organizzato.* Soveria Mannelli, Rubbettino, 2006

Savatteri, G. (ed.), *Il Contagio. Come la 'Ndrangheta ha infettato l'Italia.* Bari, Laterza, 2012

Savona, E.U., Infiltration of the public construction industry by Italian organised crime, In: K. Bullock, R.V. Clarke and N. Tilley (eds.), *Situational Prevention of Organised Crimes.* Devon, Willan Publishing, 2010

Sciarrone, R., *Mafie vecchie, mafie nuove. Radicamento ed espansione.* Roma, Donzelli Editore, 2009

Sergi, A., 'Ndrangheta and gangster politics: the local side of a global threat, *Crime Law and Social Change*, 2014 (forthcoming)

Sergi, A. Structure vs Activity: two models to fight organised crime and their criticisms, *Policing: A Journal for Policy and Practice*, 2013, doi: 10.1093/police/pat033

Sergi, A. and A. Lavorgna, Trade secrets. Italian mafia expands its illicit business. *Jane' Intelligence Review*, 2012, 44-47

Smedovska, R., *Specialized Institutions for the Combat of Organized Crime, Comparative Legal Studies.* Sofia, Risk Monitor Foundation, 2010

Tranfaglia, N., *La mafia come metodo nell'Italia contemporanea*, II ed. Roma, Laterza, 1991

Transparency International, *How do you define corruption*, 2013. Retrieved from http://www.transparency.org/whoweare/organisation/faqs_on_corruption#defineCorruption accessed on April 15, 2013)

Turone, G., *Il delitto di associazione mafiosa,* Milano, Giuffrè, 2008

Varese, F., *The Russian Mafia: Private protection in a new market economy*, Oxford: Oxford University Press, 2001

Varese, F., How Mafias migrate: The case of the 'Ndrangheta in Northern Italy. *Law and Society Review,* 2006, no. 40(2), 411-444

Vigna, P.L. Fighting organized crime, with particular reference to Mafia crimes in Italy. *Journal of International Criminal Justice, 2006, no. 4, 522-527*

Von Lampe, K., Afterword: Organized crime research in perspective, In: P.C. van Duyne, K. von Lampe, and N. Passas (eds.), *Upperworld and Underworld in Cross-border Crime.* Nijmegen, Wolf Legal Publishers, 2002

Von Lampe, K. Organized crime in Europe: Conceptions and realities. *Policing: A Journal of Policy and Practice*, 2008, no. 2(1), 7-17

Von Lampe, K., M. van Dijck, R. Hornsby, A. Markina, and K. Verpoest, Organised crime is . . . Findings from a cross-national review of literature. In: P.C. van Duyne,

A. Maljević, M. van Dijck, K. von Lampe, and J.L. Newell (eds.), *The Organisation of Crime for profit: Conduct, Law and Measurement*. Nijmegen, Wolf Legal Publishers, 2002

Wright, A., *Organised crime*. Cullompton, Willan Publishing, 2006

Appendix

Keywords	*Il Corriere della Sera*	*La Repubblica*	Results	
			Il Corriere	*La Repubblica*
crimine organizzato AND corruzione	41	137	1	9
416 AND corruzione	12	95	1	15
associazione a delinquere AND corruzione	579	2656	63	100+
associazione a delinquere semplice AND corruzione	21	3	10	3
associazione a delinquere AND corruzione AND organizzato	27	93	15	18
traffico AND criminale AND corruzione	24	97	6	16
criminalità straniera AND corruzione	3	5	1	2
associazione a delinquere AND corruzione AND traffico	26	125	5	28
416bis AND corruzione	2	38	1	15
mafia AND corruzione	503	2423	49	100+
camorra AND corruzione	133	838	37	100+
ndrangheta AND corruzione	239	493	52	100+

The multilateral response in tackling the crime – terror nexus The EU contribution

Daniela Irrera[1]

Introduction

The existence of organised crime on a global level and its potential capacity to perform within a transnational dimension, inside democratic as well as failed and weak states, and to link with other groups that violently oppose the state, that is, terrorist groups, are producing an increasing impact on the perception of security and stability of parts of the global political system. But what do we know for certain? The validity of analyses aiming at making empirically based evaluation of the phenomenon is inevitably affected by databases which may appear to be neither thorough nor systematic. This contributed to nurture some forms of scepticism among scholars and specialists[2], mainly focusing on law enforcement issues.

Irrespective of these methodologically based doubts, the Report issued by the EU Parliament in October 2012 – following public events – may re-open the debate and calls for further and deeper analysis, firstly on the different ways the nexus of (organised) crime and terrorism is perceived as a security threat and secondly how it is addressed within the security agenda. As already stated, the most crucial problem affecting such analysis is the nature of the empirical evidence and the subjectivity of the content of the available documents: the question of validity of content and concluding statements.

At the same time, the use of terror tactics by criminals for securing the environments in which they act and the exploitation of illicit markets by terrorist for funding remain the most visible manifestations of this nexus. The purpose of this

---

1 Daniela Irrera is Assistant Professor of Political Science and International Relations at the University of Catania, Italy. E-mail: dirrera@unict.it A version of this chapter has been published in *The ReShape Online Paper Series*, University of Catania, 04/2013. http://www.fscpo.unict.it/EUROPA/JMAP/repaper4.pdf

2 Among others, I refer to scholars like Alex Schmid and Phil Williams who have mainly underlined the different identities of criminals and terrorists.

chapter is to provide some more theoretical reflections in order to reconceptualise the nexus. The chapter will pay attention to more flexible and changing features so as to provide reasons why it requires a collective response.

Data provided by the above mentioned Report will be used since they can be considered as quite recent and will offer at least a possible official overview of the phenomenon.

If the report represents the responses to this nexus, the question arises within what framework they should be projected. This chapter proposes 'multilateralism' as a fruitful framework within which the set of responses can best be understood. Multilateral cooperation is here considered as a sophisticated form of interaction among states, international and regional organisations: it is founded on universal principles, equal participation of states in collective mechanisms, and no discrimination in putting principles into action (Attinà, 2010). This equality has not always been so self-evident. In this field, in fact, cooperation was essentially based on the attempts of Western powers to export and impose their domestic definitions, expressed in political, economic and moral terms to the rest of the world (Andreas and Nadelmann, 2006).

In the aftermath of the Cold War, this process developed towards the same rules which dominated the relations among political powers. This officially happened through the production of formal definitions, norms and documents. At the same time, this procedure is based on the governments' understanding of the dual threat of organised crime and terrorism, initially as two separate and distinct ones.

The different policies, produced by US and European states reflected their dissimilar perceptions of organised crime and terror, as well as dissimilar approaches to the related security questions. However, the shifting approaches to the security environment, together with the parallel transformation of the global system, have pushed the prominent states such as the US or Germany to change their attitudes to a more harmonious range and to strengthen multilateral cooperation for developing adequate responses to new threats.

The more substantial weight of the US contribution to multilateral cooperation in this field led at the end of the Cold War and, more importantly, after September 11, to a shifting process from an almost exclusive law enforcement approach to organised crime and terrorism to a more comprehensive strategy, essentially founded on the blurring boundary between internal and external security (White House, 2002).

This is the present trend towards which multilateral cooperation is moving, led by the US but with a different contribution from the EU security strategy.

Therefore, this chapter aims at addressing the following research questions:

- Does the crime-terror nexus represent a threat to the current global security agenda and if so, to which one?

- Based on the premise that challenges are posed to both individual states and the international system, how multilateral is the current state of response?
- Which actors are more relevant in shaping cooperation: Is the innovative approach proposed by the EU winning?

The chapter is divided into three parts. Firstly, the nexus will be analysed and reconceptualised in order to understand the level of implications which are posed both to the regional and global level. In the second one, the present set of strategies and approaches developed within the framework of multilateral cooperation will be explored. In the third part, the role of the integrated strategy developed by the European Union will be emphasised, stressing the potential of the deployment of civilian missions

The re-conceptualisation of the crime-terror nexus and global security

The implications organised crime and terrorism may produce on politics – at national, regional and global level – concern their own identity as 'non-state actors' – but declined in a criminal or subversive way. If civil society actors, lobbies and multinational are at the core of democratisation and developmental features of global politics, both organised crime and terrorist groups are perceived as subversive non-state actors. In that capacity their 'management' (repression, prevention, containment) requires a state response which should be properly expressed in terms of countermeasures (Rosenau, 1990). These are either deployed by those states which have a long standing experience and have developed several counter-attack means or those states which are indirectly affected by cross-border or long-term effects. The ways states reply to subversive actors depend on the 'strength' of the state in institutional and economic terms as well as its vulnerability. This implies that the states' response can produce different gradations of criminalisation and/or infiltration of those non-state organisations (Irrera, 2007).

The State can also retreat in the face of an illegal actor. The consequential inability of its institutions to fulfil their tasks on an illegal issue will then contribute to blur the separation between the public and criminal private spheres. Such blurring can be gradual. It begins from the lower level (*i.e.*, a public administrative officer illegally accepting money in doing or neglecting his/her job), passes to the middle level (*i.e.* a private company benefiting from public funds). It ends at the upper level: *i.e.*, politicians and party leaders involved in illicit affairs or criminals elected to high positions (Chiottolini, 1995).

Scholars sustain the statement that fragmented political and economic contexts, with neither cohesion nor autonomy, may represent the best ground in which subversive actors may seriously affect a state (Cornell, 2007; Hutchinson et al. 2007). They refer to these dimensions as ungovernability and conduciveness to terrorist or insurgent presence. That is to say, dimensions in which the presence of criminal networks opens the possibility of strategic alliances through which terrorists or insurgents and criminal groups can share logistical corridors, safe havens, and access to sources of funding and money-laundering arrangements (Rabasa *et al.*, 2007). This does not mean that the occurrence of these activities can only be observed in troubled contexts or that established democracies cannot offer those conditions which are essential to the subversive organisations to flourish. Cases like Afghanistan or Sierra Leone certainly constitute the most visible examples used by scholars and policy-makers to describe – and to some extent, to measure – the phenomenon, but corruption and state retreat may affect established democracies as well. These processes are rooted in the history of the country or the region. Thus the implications of the rise of such actors should be analysed over a long-term period and in a broader perspective, involving not only those states and territories which are most visibly affected, but also those ones which can suffer indirect detrimental effects. That is to say the regional levels and, depending on the nature of the clandestine goods and services, subsequently the whole international system. Thus, the analysis should be linked to the transformation occurring on the concept of global security (Migdal, 1988).

The traditional concept of security is associated to the state and to the military mobilisation of the potential for violence[3]. The technological improvements, the rising of non-state actors, the political innovations introduced during and after the Cold War contributed to change the perception of the nature of contemporary civil conflicts. These changes contributed to focus the attention towards a concept of security which was more based on human beings and on the civilian dimension of security itself. This notion reflected parallel transformations in the nature of conflicts, especially at the end of the Cold War, and represented an additional and fundamental dimension of security management, next to the military one.

In security studies the conceptualisation took various forms. Buzan introduced three levels of analysis (the individual, the state, and the international system), and different dimensions (the political, economic, and social one) in managing non-violently security issues in addition to the military (Buzan, 1991). The Copenhagen

---

3 This is the traditional state-centric approach to security, as developed by realist and neorealist school of International Relations.

School stresses the relevance of a comprehensive concept of security, bringing together a wide range of factors (military, environmental, economic, societal, and political), as well as different actors and forms of action. Also, these scholars draw the attention of the specialists to the importance of *securitisation*, a speech act that constructs *the other* as existential threat to the security of a particular group (Buzan, Waever and de Wilde, 1998). An issue becomes securitised when the majority of the group to whom the securitisation is addressed accepts it and urgent measures called for become to be seen as legitimate (Bonacker *et al.* 2011: 16-17). This may explain why, at the end of the Cold War and after the growth of a number of intra-state conflicts, humanitarian organisations became more engaged in conflict areas, in order to improve *securitization* (Morris, 2008). In the wake of state collapse, war becomes primarily a competition among various non-state actors over the use of scarce resources, including the residues of the state, the assets of the population and available inflows of materials, food and money (Kaldor, 1999: 90). The rising importance of non state actors and their developments contibute to shape the whole notion of security.

Concepts of *comprehensive security*, and *human security* "are being utilised to embrace the range of issues that are being placed on a revised security agenda of an emerging global polity" (Knight, 2001: 14). Human security is perceived as a multilevel dimension, both in a vertical sense (different threats shape the State by involving the individuals) and in a horizontal one (threats engage different sovereign States), blurring more and more the border between internal and external dimension of security itself. This premise can be functional to the understanding of the kind of threat the crime-terror nexus may represent.

It refers to the grouping of two different actors, with distinct identities, tools and methods but able to easily go over rigid distinctions for practical purposes. The first component of that nexus, organised crime, has been dealt with by the UN in which the US played a dominant role. According to the United Nations Convention Against Transnational Organised Crime, to be considered as organised crime, a group has to (a) consist of a collaboration of at least three people that are (b) gathered for a prolonged or indefinite period of time; (c) be suspected or convicted of committing serious criminal offences; and, (d) have as their objective the pursuit of profit and/or power.[4]

---

4 United Nations (2000), *United Nations Convention Against Transnational Organised Crime*, art. 3; Van Duyne and Nelemans. (2011), Transnational Organised Crime: Thinking in and Out of Plato's Cave in Allum F. and Gilmour S. (eds.) *Handbook Transnational Crime*, Routledge, London.

Terrorism is usually conceived as the conduct of premeditated violence or the threat of violence that is perpetrated by members of an organised group, in order to achieve a predetermined political objective, normally an attempt to influence political behaviour (EP Report, 2012: 10). This notion of terrorism differs from other forms of political violence, that is to say, from "paramilitary" which includes those groups that maintain some form of violent capacity and yet are not in any way part of the State, as well as private enterprises employed by the state for providing various services (Tupman, 2009). Some relevant example can be found during the Iraq war (*i.e.* the Halliburton which is still today very active in Basra) and at the time of writing in Afghanistan.

The different nature of both actors (entrepreneurial for criminals, more political for terrorists) is probably at the basis of the scepticism which has animated some scholarly debates. As Tamara Makarenko (2004; 2009) pointed out, the immediate post-Cold War environment – at least in many areas of the international system – provided both actors with more access to technological advancements and to financial and global market structures, which could be combined with the above mentioned increase in weak states and civil wars. They are traditionally separate phenomena, the increasing ability of organised crime to co-locate their activities in a more transnational dimension, in the 1990s, and the changing nature of terrorism, contributed to blur the distinction between political and criminal motivated violence and to reveal operational and organisational similarities (Makarenko, 2004; 2009). Such evanescence of traditional boundaries is, currently, the predominant character of the nexus and it deals with both the flexible set of interactions among criminals and terrorists and the set of implications which such interactions can produce on a regional and global (and not necessarily (trans)national) level, as will be explained.

As for the first one, Makarenko has efficaciously depicted the process through different phases or steps which can be put along a continuum (Makarenko, 2004). Nevertheless, the events which occurred after September 11 and the terrorist attacks in Europe – especially those ones in Madrid - have shown that intersections between terrorism and organised crime have diversified over the years. They easily dash from chronological or logical order and tend to be more and more flexible. Although the continuum is useful for understanding the escalating relationship between the two actors, the present analysis will focus on three large categories – coexistence, cooperation, convergence – which better describes such flexibility, in embracing various gradations of activity.

Coexistence is probably the most conceivable condition, in which criminals and terrorist groups operate in the same business and in the same geographical environment – local or regional – but explicitly tend to remain separate entities, unless it is rationally required that they do not. It may be facilitated by local conditions. Some of the features that build a situation conducive to organised crime also make it attractive to terrorist groups. They can be mostly furthered by the lack of border control and law enforcement and the eventual presence of certain types of infrastructure and services for operations. They can be more easily found in weak or fragile states, but can affect democratic states as well. The combined presence can amplify the threat to state structures of both weak or democratic states, even though they do not explicitly act together and produce cross-border effects.

Cooperation concerns established alliances between terrorist and criminal groups and is a more time-and-resources-consuming process. There are differences in motives, as already outlined and it is inherently risky to push to agree that real alliances between criminals and terrorist groups are unlikely to happen, especially in the long-term period. Short-term, occasional or *ad hoc* relationships may be frequent and outweigh these risks to terrorists and criminals of forming such alliances, especially if focused upon specific operational requirements. In some cases, as Hansen points out *customer-service provider relationships* have developed, as both criminals and terrorist groups often require similar expertise, support structures and services – including false papers, IT and communications specialists, and counter-surveillance technology (Hansen, 2012).

Convergence is apparently the most difficult to explain, but probably the most conceivable one. Organised criminal networks have long used terror tactics to safeguard business interests and protect their working environments, but conversely the use of criminal expertise by terrorist groups in order to meet operational requirements may increase. More frequently, for terrorist groups, the incentive to develop such capabilities deals with the need to provide a sizeable and reliable source of funding. The overlapping in motives and identities is the most difficult to imagine. Lucrative illicit activities may eventually transform politically motivated groups and override their political aspirations, and eventually it becomes difficult to clearly distinguish between collective or individual motivations, between ideology and greed. Therefore, if conceived in its broadest sense, convergence may be considered as the most relevant source of threats.

The term nexus still evokes the existence of alliances and the reciprocal use of tactics, which remain its main visible – and measurable – component. Nevertheless, it has evolved also into something more complex, as the three categories (coexistence, cooperation, convergence) may easily overlap or clash. Criminals and terrorist remain both able to separately exploit illegal markets and to influence policy-making but the fact that this may happen jointly make them potentially more dangerous.

According to empirical data which are provided in the Report – as specified at the beginning of this chapter – the use of criminal activities by terrorist groups is still relevant in the global security agenda and is, in some cases, increasing.

Figure 1 presents the number of terrorist groups extensively using (organised) criminal techniques, divided by region and including terrorist groups pursuing declared political goals and based in a specific country or territory. Al-Qaeda is not included as it is the only case which is formally considered as a global one, being not specifically linked to a country or region. While the *active* label refers to the gathering of information on recent actions by law enforcement, *inactive* may deal with different meanings. It includes remnant groups, disbanded or formally decommissioned ones, or those that are sporadic in operation. Drug trafficking and arms remain the major sources for funding, but there is a rising exploitation of local resources, that is to say: diamonds, oil and other locally available assets for which there is demand abroad. Traditional criminal methods, like extortion and smuggling are more diffused and more professionalised.

Figure 1
Number of terrorist groups using OC techniques

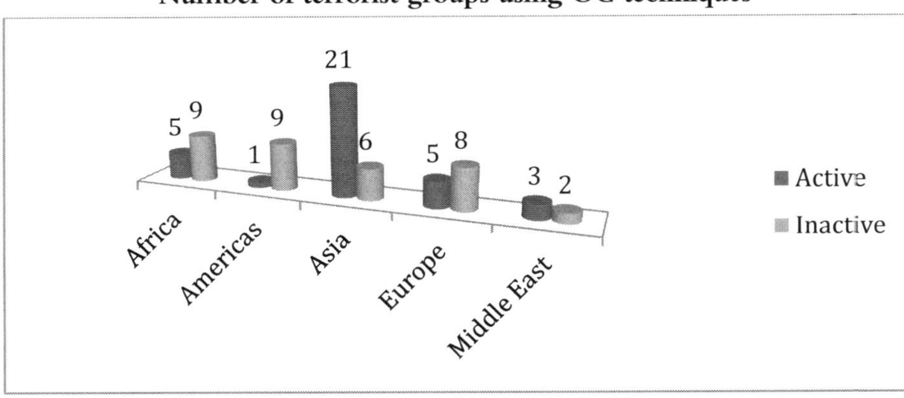

Source: EP Report, October 2012

Failed and weak states may represent a facilitator for connections but they are not their only privileged place. The report states that there is proof of the exploitation of illegal markets by terrorist groups in the Middle Eastern region and even a rising trend in Asia. In addition, those based in the UK, France, Spain, as well in the Balkans and neighbouring countries, like Turkey, directly challenge European internal and external borders, through the flows of illegal migrants and goods (EP, Report, 2012: 20-22).

Similar remarks may be formulated about the use or terror tactics by organised crime groups.

Figure 2
Terrorist tactics used by OC groups per region

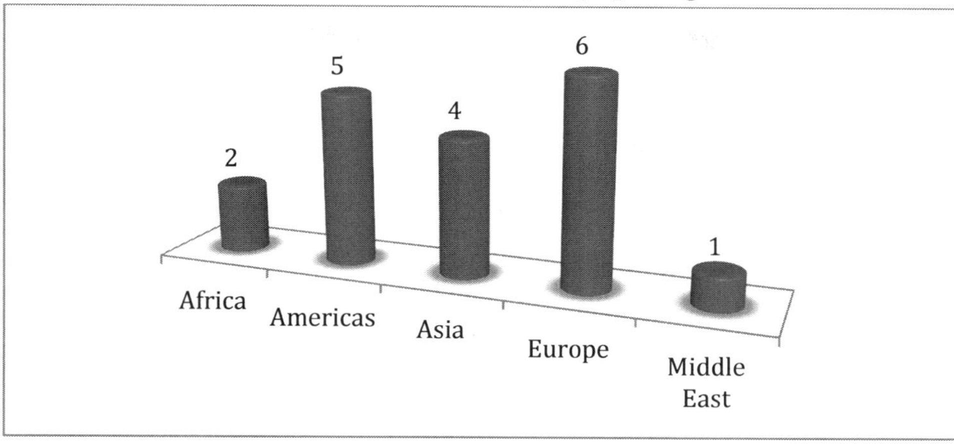

Source: EP Report, October 2012: 53-57

Figure 2 incorporates both occasional and more solid use of terrorist tactics practised by established group of criminals. They may vary, according to the local context, but usually deal with the use of violence for destabilising law enforcement control, or political power, if needed. From a quantitative point of view, the phenomenon may appear more limited, if compared to the previous figure, but it also presents more meaningful cases, which can be more difficult to categorise. Somali pirates, Tamil diaspora clans, Italian mafia and newly established forms or organised crime like Lebanese or Indian ones are undoubtedly to be categorised under the same 'criminal' label, but their purposes and rationale are completely different. Additionally, the interactions they have with other political or economic actors may hugely vary. The evaluation of such factors thus introduces some innovations in the re-conceptualisation of the nexus, in terms of how alliances may be conceived and how they work. Even this phenomenon affects all regions, with a significant impact on European countries, either as traditional bases of criminals and as one of the largest transit area.

It is true that the peculiar nature of the actors and activities dealing with the nexus complicates data collection and affects their reliability. According to the data used in this analysis, it appears that the set of flexible forms of interaction produce an impact and that it is rapidly and consistently evolving. Cooperation, in terms of definite alliances, is difficult to be proved and, probably, more expensive for criminals and terrorists themselves, while coexistence and convergence are more credible and consistent concern, since they are flexible and changeable.

The challenges the nexus – through its various forms – poses to states are definitively marked by the feature both figures have in common, that is to say, the global and regional widespread reach and can be placed on a double level. It constitutes a threat to the state capacity to provide security to its citizens and to the regional and international institutions' ability to manage cross-border flows.

Developing multilateral capabilities

The implications produced on both internal and external security and their cross-border dimension constitute the main factor for which the organised crime-terror nexus is listed among those issues of global concern which require a collective response. If the comprehensive security paradigm can be properly used for analysing the threats posed by the nexus towards the global system, multilateralism – in its more recent developments – then it can constitute the framework within which the set of responses can be understood.

Multilateralism has become, since its formal foundation through the United Nations, in 1945, the set of practices and principles, upon which the cooperation among states has tried to manage collective problem (Keohane, 1990; Ruggie, 1993). Scholars have extensively debated about the ways multilateralism has evolved, entangled more actors and diversified its outcomes. For the purposes of this research, two main features will be considered. Multilateralism is first of all a mode of action, a sophisticated form of cooperation which, over the decades, required specific qualities of international actors. The multi-layered dimension of security and the flexible nature of current global problems have imposed on states and international organisations, the need to develop and expand their capacity to contribute, by providing material and non-material resources and – more importantly – in legitimising common actions. Thus, the concept of 'multi-laterability', as scholars define such ability, has become increasingly important (Wouters *et al.* 2008; Telò, 2012). At the same time, the need to use more expertise and resources have pushed additional actors, like regional organisations, to assume more responsibility in managing global issues (Attinà, 2011).

This increasing set of incentives explain the second relevant feature, that is to say, the normative potential of multilateralism, in the sense of the conviction about how international cooperation should function to increase multilateral security (Caporaso, 1992).

By stressing the quality of negotiations and of actors which are involved, multilateralism can be perceived as a set of:

"*international practices that are founded on principles of conduct widely shared by states, the equal participation of states in the rules and mechanisms of the principles of implementation, and the non-discriminating application of the principles, rules and mechanisms*" (Attinà, 2010: 3).

Firstly, common rules and norms are generally created for solving problems. Secondly, *coordination*, instead of rivalry or simply juxtaposition, among relevant actors should be shaped. If the human security approach is considered as the most efficient to face global threats, then a greater coordination of policies in different fields, including external relations, trade, development and security is required (Keohane, 1990; Caporaso, 1993; Ruggie, 1993; Lake, 2006). These considerations bring some important political implications. The responses and the new partnerships created for replying to global threats and emergencies should be addressed, first of all, to solve a specific problem, and, at the same time, can serve as a catalyst for changing the existing political conditions to tackle other problems, for establishing new rules of conducts, and, in the long period, for enforcing the rules themselves.

Multilateral cooperation in tackling organised crime and terrorism is paradigmatic of such evolutionary process. Largely initiated and shaped by the US – as part of its hegemonic role – it involved later, most relevant and experienced European states and finally incorporated – and is still doing – some innovations introduced by the EU. The internationalisation of policing primarily reflects ambitious efforts by generations of western powers to export their own definitions of *crime* and *terror*, not just for political and economic gain but also in the attempt to export their own morals to other parts of the world (Andreas and Nadelman, 2006). According to these scholars, any internationalisation process of crime and terror definition and their subsequent control is the outcome of the export of domestic perceptions and definitions, which reflected the relations among political powers. Thus, it was essentially based on the attempts of Western powers to export and impose their domestic definitions, expressed in political, economic and moral terms to the rest of the world. This was accomplished by using the international forum of the UN (Van Duyne and Nelemans, 2011). In the aftermath of the Cold War, this process occurred according to the same rules which dominated the relations among political powers. This officially happened through the production of formal definitions, norms and documents. At the same time, this procedure is based on the governments' understanding of the threats, initially as two separate ones.

The different policies, produced by the US and the European states reflected their dissimilar perceptions of organised crime and terror, as well as dissimilar approaches to security. However, the shifting perceptions of the security environment, together with the parallel transformation of the global system, pushed these prominent regions to change their attitudes and to strengthen multilateral cooperation for developing adequate responses to new threats. Even before September 11, the transatlantic law enforcement infrastructure was actively working, through several joint initiatives against money laundering and cybercrime. The terroristic attacks contributed to change the characteristics of those initiatives, because it modified the perception of the threat itself. Attempts to facilitate greater cooperation in crime control and counterterrorism on an international level started to be strengthened for promoting more communication, establishing guidelines and best practices, and, ultimately for regularising cooperation (Hignett, 2008).

The more substantial aspect of the US contribution to multilateral cooperation in this field is the shifting process from an almost exclusive law enforcement approach to organised crime and terrorism to a more comprehensive strategy, essentially founded on the blurring boundary between internal and external security.

Since the first articulated analysis, made by the Kefauver Committee in 1951, the American perception of organised crime as a domestic issue has significantly changed. Drug trafficking and money laundering were considered as the most important targets as part of the 'narco-terrorism' phenomenon, which has dominated the last decades of the Cold War. The US developed an international strategy which has been essentially based on the protection of American interest, the strengthening of law enforcement and information system, as it reflected the development of internal and international structure of organised crime groups and their intersection with terrorists as a source of founding.

In the aftermath of September 11, the US contribution to the multilateral cooperation increased, since officials started to include counternarcotics in a broader security strategy, focused on lawless zones. Documents issued after the terrorist attacks to the Twin Towers, – the 2002 US National Security Strategy – marked the formalisation of this change and contributed to link new global challenges, including organised crime activities also to *fertile* grounds which can be easily found in weak or failed states. The official launch of the War on Terror was characterised by a very authoritative and militarised language. The list of key security issues consists of terrorist threats, WMD and state failure as key dangers.

Following the military intervention into Afghanistan and the successive invasion of Iraq, the US took the lead but also reminded to the allies of the need to take their own responsibilities. National security is still the main concern but it is no more defined in traditional terms, and associated to globalisation of threats and to greater cooperation. No direct reference to the nexus (as a unique phenomenon) can be found, but the perception of its single components is paradigmatic of the distance which separated the US from other political actors, in the security strategy formulation.

The National Security Strategy, issued by President Obama in 2010, marked an evident shift in the language and establishes new patterns of cooperation. Even though the challenges posed by terrorism is a priority, the use of criminal activities for funding is stressed as well and, more importantly, they are associated to other security threats whose boundaries cannot easily be traced.

The analysis of the reshaped process of US *multilaterability* in tackling crime-terror nexus should be combined with the evaluation of the Strategy to Combat Transnational Organised Crime, released in July 2011 by the US National Security Staff, which represents the most recent policy towards the specific issue on organised crime. It is defined in a very traditional way and in terms of threat to national security of US citizens, but, at the same time, it is presented as Transnational Organised Crime, stressing the fact that the cross-border dimension of alliances and activities is the first feature, in terms of policy.

The US renovated intention to continue multilateral cooperation for strengthening both internal and external security is thus linked to normative potential of cooperation itself, aiming at deepening those principles which have been forged over the decades. More importantly, it is also dependent on the abilities and resources actors are investing.

In this sense, the EU have offered, until now, a wide expertise in the field, based on single Member States experiences, in the framework of the Justice and Home Affairs structures and is currently involved in a process of development of a broader strategy which, within multilateral cooperation, strengthen cross-border security and combines with external dimensions. The process is, probably, still at the beginning, but it is already encouraging.

EU security agenda and the nexus: an added value?

The internationalization of EC/EU crime control started at the beginning of the Cold War, through the development of cross-border policing institutions, and the extension of its own practices to the neighbours. The deepening and widening of the European integration contributed to the increasing of this process.

The nuclear deterrence strategy and arms control negotiations of the Cold War and subsequent détente era contributed to the formulation of national and multilateral defence policies in the 1990s in response to new security threats, like new wars, the rising of civil conflicts, and the proliferation of weapons of mass destruction (WMD). Among the effects of civil conflicts, the opening and widening of illegal markets started to significantly affect national security policies and contributed to the increasing will of the European countries to strengthen their cooperation concerning one of the illegal goods, that is drugs (Shelley, 1995).

As affirmed by the European Monitoring Centre for Drugs and drug Addiction, during 1990s, the number of member countries which started to have national single documents increased and, in the years, a trend in producing joint policies increased, too.

The adoption of the EU Drug Strategy, in December 2004, witnessed the existence of a larger political concern about drugs across the EU countries, beyond the different approaches among Member States. The successive EU Drugs Action Plans, as well as the successive one, scheduled for the period 2009-12 are based on the same set of basic principles: a balanced approach to reducing the supply and demand for drugs, and the founding values of the Union: respect for human dignity, liberty, democracy, equality, solidarity, the rule of law and human rights. In the EU narrative, among the measures prescribed for establishing joint policies, the enhancement of judicial cooperation in the area of combating drug trafficking and law enforcement and the strengthening of Europol, Eurojust and other EU structures are included .[5]

The tradition of close cooperation with underdeveloped countries, in the field of aid and relief offered the already exploited platform and expertise for improving cooperation with third countries and international organisations in the field of drugs through closer coordination of policies within the EU.

In the document *A Secure Europe in a Better World,* issued by the European Council in December 2003, the EU High Representative for Common Foreign and Security Policy, Javier Solana, points out the main elements which are required to build a strong and solid *European Security Strategy* (ESS). The abovementioned set of principles is used also for enlarging EU capabilities and contribution to global security. The ESS stresses European responsibility for global security, the need of effective multilateralism and the extension of the international rule of law, considering that: "*the post Cold War environment is one of increasingly open borders in which the internal and external aspects of security are indissolubly linked*" (ESS, 2003). The ESS lists five key threats to Europe: terrorism, the proliferation of WMD, regional conflicts, failed/failing states, and organised crime. The last one, in particular, is strictly linked to the conditions that cause conflict, fear and hatred, a criminalised economy that profits from violent methods of controlling assets, weak illegitimate states, the existence of warlords and paramilitary groups.

The document was essentially produced in response to the challenges posed by the US about the Union's actions in the sphere of security policies and, in arguing

---

5 Council of the European Union (2008), *EU Drugs Action Plan for 2009-2012*, in OJEU C326/7, 20.12.2008.

that, "*the best protection for our security is a world of well-governed democratic states*" (ESS, 2003: 10), it goes towards the building of a broader and integrated strategy.

Even in the case of the EU, the main character of its contribution is the shifting process from a Home and Justice Affairs approach to a more comprehensive plan, essentially founded on the blurring boundary between internal and external security.

The common objective, which is the protection of citizens and states from risks, explains why the threat of terrorism and organised crime - as the most visible concern for EU citizens – was identified in the ESS which had an explicit external perspective and then appears in the set of documents which constitutes what is commonly described as the Internal Security Strategy (ISS) of the Union.[6] The ISS addresses a wide list of security challenges the European countries face in their domestic borders, including terrorism, organised and cross-border crime, cyber-crime, violence in all its forms, accidents (transport, industrial, etc.) and natural and man-made disasters and implicitly suggests a larger reflection on the *European Security Model*. Therefore, the need to integrate all the existing European strategies relevant to internal security, to strengthen coherence and consistency and to promote truly effective policies is urgently underlined (Attinà, 2013).

The necessity to tackle challenges which go beyond the EU states' national, bilateral or regional capability and which strongly require multilateral efforts have therefore produced two main outcomes.

On one hand, the EU is improving – as already seen – its institutional capacities and actions in a wider framework of international cooperation for preserving its own citizens and its neighbourhood, namely the Mediterranean world and the Western Balkan countries, from increasing domestic political violence by local organised groups. On the other hand, as made clear in the ESS, the rationale on which the fight against crime and terror is based is part of a broader security culture the European countries founded in the early 1990s and deals with the contribution the EU is able to provide for preserving global society.

The constant use of the common actions, in the last decades, has contributed to the rising of a specific international image of EU as a civilian power. The will to build long-term stabilisation, to act through multilateralism, and to be inspired by norms and ideas are the main elements of the global actions the EU has developed in the field of promotion of democracy and security (Duchene, 1972). The more complex set of competences the Treaty of Lisbon has contributed to link this policy to the common security and defence policy and to the civilian and military assets in

6 *Towards a European Security Model*, prepared by the Council and approved at the European Council in 2010 (doc. 7120/10); *The EU Internal Security Strategy in Action: Five steps towards a more secure Europe*, of 22 November 2010 (see Attinà, 2013).

support of peace-keeping missions, conflict prevention and international security outside the Union (TEU art. 42). In particular, "*the Union may use civilian and military means [for] joint disarmament operations, humanitarian and rescue tasks, military advice and assistance tasks, conflict prevention and peace-keeping tasks, tasks of combat forces in crisis management, including peace-making and post-conflict stabilisation. All these tasks may contribute to the fight against terrorism, including by supporting third countries in combating terrorism in their territories*" (TEU art. 43).

The number of military and civilian missions the EU has deployed inside and outside Europe has increased and developed over the years. Since 1991, the EU has deployed a total of 34 missions (19 completed and 15 still ongoing).

Table 1
Missions deployed by the EU (as of February 2014)

Region	Civilian/Military	Ongoing/ Completed	Mission Acronym
Democratic Republic of Congo	M	C	Artemis
Democratic Republic of Congo	M	C	EUFOR RD
Tchad	M	C	EUFOR RCA
Libya	M	C	EUFOR
Guinea Bissau	C	C	EUSSR
South Sudan	C	C	EUAVSEC
Sudan	C/M	C	Amis (AU)
FYROM	M	C	Concordia
FYROM	C	C	EUPAT
Georgia	C	C	EU JUST THEMIS
Bosnia-Herzegovina	C	C	EUPM
FYROM	C	C	EUPOL Proxima
Democratic Republic of Congo	C	C	EUPOL Kinshasa
Aceh	C	C	AMM
Iraq	C	C	EU JUST LEX
Somalia	M	O	EUNAVFOR
Central African Republic	M	O	EUFOR RCA
Mali	M	O	EUTM
Somalia	M	O	EUTM
Horn of Africa	C	O	EUCAP Nestor
Sahel Niger	C	O	EUCAP
Democratic Republic of Congo	C	O	EUSEC
Bosnia-Herzegovina	M	O	EUFOR Althea
Georgia	C	O	EUMM
Kosovo	C	O	EULEX
Ukraine-Moldova	C	O	EUBAM

Afghanistan	C	O	EUPOL
Palestinian Territories	C	O	EUPOL COPPS
Rafah Valley	C	O	EUBAM
Libya	C	O	EUBAM
Democratic Republic of Congo	C	O	EUPOL

European Union External Action, 2014

As Longo pointed out, on one hand, the EU foreign policy put more emphasis on conflict prevention than on management, through political commitment and constructive dialogue. On the other, even though military action is seen as a measure of last resort, the EU developed a structure of crises management and conflict resolution, which is coherent with the global trends about humanitarian intervention and also with its own model of commercial, economic, cooperative, and diplomatic nature (Longo, 2013).

Even though they are envisaged as the last resort, civilian missions have been extensively used for tackling non-traditional threats, including crime and terrorist issue.

Figure 3
EU civilian missions' main tasks

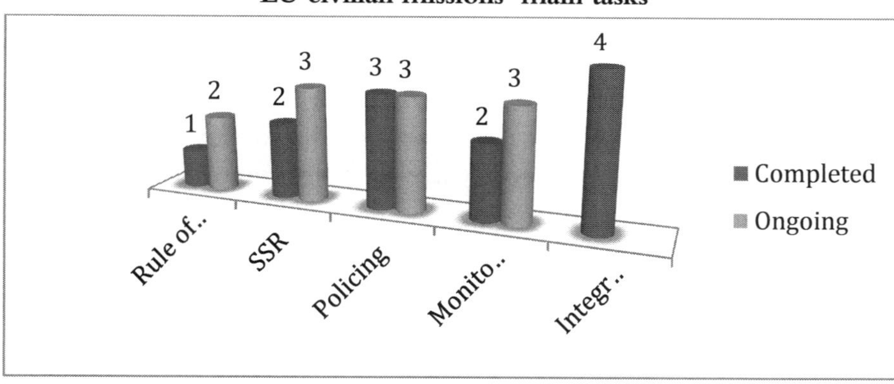

Source: ISIS, 2013; ADISM, CODEBOOK Version 3.2010 CSDP[7]

Within the missions deployed by the EU, Figure 3 includes only those missions which are officially conceived as civilian ones, regardless the place of deployment, either already ended and still active. As clearly demonstrated through data, the number of cases in which threats dealing with organised crime and/or terrorism are

7 ADISM is a dataset on multilateral peace/security operations, made within a research project of the University of Catania. See the website: http://www.fscpo.unict.it/adism/adism.htm

managed through CSDP missions is increasing, especially since 2000 onwards. Also, the tasks are diversifying and becoming more professionalised. Security Sector Reform and Rule of Law may support additional policies or actors (like the EULEX Mission in Kosovo or the EUJUST LEX in Iraq). Therefore, the use of civilian missions constitutes a unique feature of the EU contribution to the multilateral cooperation. Together with shared principles and institutional improvements in this area the EU is – gradually and with difficulty – improving its capacity to dialogue with the US and other actors and to shape the global environment.

Conclusions

This chapter is based on the main assumption that, despite the scepticism which still animates some scholarly debates, the nexus between terrorism and organised crime may represent a renovated kind of security threat and may be relevant for policy purposes. The basic definition, provided by the literature, refers to a strategic alliance between two non-state actors, both able to exploit illegal markets and to influence policy-making on a global level. Such effects may be deteriorating in troubled contexts, affected by war and insurgency, which can constitute safe heaven because ungoverned entities. Failed and weak states do not attract criminals and terrorist *per se* but they can be considered as an additional features, not a constitutive one.

The chapter aims at understanding firstly the kind of threat the nexus still represents for the current global security agenda and, secondly, there is a need to understand how multilateral is the current state of response since challenges are posed to both states and the international system, producing important implications for policy at national and international level, Although criminals and terrorists still remain two separate phenomena, the changing nature of global security and the increasing effects of globalisation have contributed to blur the distinction between political and criminal motivated violence and revealed their operational and organisational similarities. The evanescence of traditional boundaries between internal and external security is currently marking the new manifestations of the nexus and imposing to scholars and policy-makers a re-conceptualisation of the whole phenomenon. It includes on one hand, the flexible set of interactions between separate entities and, on the other, the multi-layered implications they can produce on a regional and global level.

In particular, it is here analysed through three large categories (coexistence, cooperation, convergence) which describe various gradations of intersections between the two illegal actors. While cooperation expresses the traditional way to conceive the nexus, in terms of alliances, forms of co-existence and convergence better represent the more practical use of terrorist techniques by criminals or the illicit activities by terrorist for funding in an occasional and functional perspective.

Empirical data used in this chapter sustain that all categories may be found in both ungoverned or democratic states and can occur in a very fluid way. The challenges the nexus poses to states are definitely marked by the global and regional diffusion and can be placed on a double level. It constitutes a threat to the state capacity to provide security to its citizens and to the regional and international institutions' ability to manage cross-border flows of goods and people. This is the reason why it is listed among those issues of global concern which require a collective response.

If the comprehensive security paradigm can be easily used for analysing the threats posed by the nexus towards the global system, multilateralism can constitute the framework within which the set of responses can be understood. Multilateral cooperation is here considered as a sophisticated form of interaction among states, international and regional organisation, founded on universal principles, equal participation of states in collective mechanisms, and no discrimination in putting principles into action.

In this specific field, the internationalisation of crime and terror control was essentially the export of law enforcement rules – namely the domestic definition of security and of organised crime – from the Western powers to the rest of the global system. Even though they tried to collaborate on various initiatives, since the Cold War, US and EU offered contrasting views of the threat and of the way they should be tackled.

Both the US and EU contributed to shape the international set of definitions and rules in the field of organised crime and terror, by using their different but leading roles. The globalisation process, the rising of non-State actors and the consequent development of the human aspects of security, as well as the events of September 11 pushed the main international political actors to change this composite structure of relations, stressing the blurring boundaries between internal and external dimension of security.

The potential for cooperation between organised crime and terrorist groups should push governments and law enforcement agencies to develop more rational and coordinated counter-strategies. Understanding the factors that contribute to the emergence of organised crime and terrorist groups could make states more resilient, as well as more effective in avoiding that the crime-terrorism nexus becomes more risky and profitable. Multilateralism can represent the only tool for producing this result as well as the only political context within which a coherent and efficient global counterstrategy can be conceived and developed for the overall resilience of states. The potential EU has developed and, in particular, its complex strategy based on an integrated strategy is a promising step for advancing multilateral cooperation.

References

Andreas, P. and E. Nadelmann, *Policing the Globe. Criminalisation and crime control in international relations*, Oxford, Oxford University Press, 2006

Attinà, F., Merging policies as strategy against emergency threats. The EU's institutional response to disasters, risks and emergencies, Jean Monnet Centre, University of Catania, *ReShape Online Papers Series*, Paper no. 01/13, 2013

Attinà, F., *The global political system*. Houndmills, Basingstoke, Hampshire, Palgrave Macmillan, 2011

Attinà, F. and D. Irrera (eds.), *Multilateral security and ESDP operations*. Farnham, Ashgate, 2010

Attinà, F., Introduction: Multilateralism, peace operations, and Europe. In F. Attinà and D. Irrera (eds.), *Multilateral security and ESDP operations*, Farnham, Ashgate, 2010, 1-18

Bonacker, T., T. Diez, T. Gromes, J. Groth and E. Pia, Human rights and the (de)securitization of conflict. In R. Marchetti and N. Tocci (eds.), *Conflict society and peace-building. Comparative perspectives*. London, Routledge, 2011, 13-47

Buzan, B., O. Wæver and J. de Wilde, *Security: A new framework for analysis*. Boulder, Lynne Reinner, 1998

Buzan, B., *People, states & fear*. Pearson, Longman, 1991

Caporaso, J., International Relations theory and multilateralism: the search for foundations. In J.G. Ruggie (eds.), *Multilateralism matters. The theory and practice of an institutional form*. New York, Columbia University Press, 1993, 51-90

Chiottolini, G., The "Private", the "Public", the "State". *The Journal of Modern History*, 1995, 67 (4), S34-S61

Duchene F., Europe's role in world peace. In R. Mayne (eds.), *Europe tomorrow: Sixteen Europeans look ahead*. London, Fontana, 1972, 32-47

EU Commission, *The EU Internal Security Strategy in Action: Five steps towards a more secure Europe*, COM(2010) 673 final

EU Council, *EU Drugs Action Plan for 2009-2012*, in OJEU C326/7, 20.12.2008

EU Parliament, Study on *Europe's Crime-Terror Nexus: Links between terrorist and organised crime groups in the European Union*, PE 462.503, 2012

Finckenauer, J., Problems of definition: what is organised crime? *Trends in Organised Crime*, 2005, 8 (3), 63-83

Hansen, W., *The crime-terrorism nexus*. International Relations and Security Network (ISN), 2012

Hignett, K., Transnational crime and its impact on international security. In M. Shanty (eds.), *Organised crime: From trafficking to terrorism*. Santa Barbara, ABC-CLIO, 2007 pp. 294-298

Holsti, K., *The state, war, and the state of war*. Cambridge: Cambridge University Press, 1996

Irrera, D., Organised crime, non-state actors and weak/failed states. In M. Shanty (eds.), *Organised crime: from trafficking to terrorism*. Santa Monica, ABC-CLIO, 2007, 357-363

Kaldor, M., *New and old wars: Organised violence in a Global Era*. Cambridge, Polity Press, 1999

Keohane, R., Multilateralism: An agenda for research. *International Journal*, 1990, 45, pp. 731-764

Knight, W.A., *Adapting the United Nations to a postmodern era: lessons learned*, New York, Palgrave, 2001

Lake, A. D., American hegemony and the future of East-West relations, *International Studies Perspectives*, 2006, 7 (1), 23-30

Longo, F., The relevance of security sector reform in humanitarian intervention: The case of the European Union in the Mediterranean. *Democracy and Security*, 2013, 9 (1-2), 177-192

Makarenko, T., The crime-terror continuum: Tracing the interplay between Transnational Organised Crime and terrorism. *Global Crime* , 2004, 6, 1, 129-145

Makarenko, T., Terrorist use of organised crime: operational tool or exacerbating the threat?' In F. Allum, F. Longo, D. Irrera, P. Kostakos (eds.), *Defining and defying organised crime: Discourse, perceptions and reality*. London, Routledge, 2009

Migdal, J.S., *Strong societies and weak states*. Princeton, Princeton University Press, 1988

Morris, N., The evolution of humanitarian action. *Refugee Survey Quarterly*, 2008, 27, 1, 24-29

Müller, K., The civil society–state relationship in contemporary discourse: A complementary account from Giddens' perspective. *British Journal of Politics and International Relations,* 2006, 8, 311–330.

Rabasa, A., S. Boraz, P. Chalk P., K. Cragin, T. Karasik, J. Moroney, K. O'Brien and J. Peters, *Ungoverned territories. Understanding and reducing terrorism risks*. Santa Monica, 2007

Rosenau, J.N., *Turbulence in world politics. A theory of change and continuity* New York, Harvester Wheatsheaf, 1990

Ruggie, J. G. (eds.), *Multilateralism matters. The theory and practice of an institutional form,* New York, Columbia University Press, 1993

Shelley, L. and J. Picarelli, Methods and motives: exploring links between transnational organised crime and international terrorism. *Trends in Organised Crime*, 2005, 9, 2, 52-67

Solana, J., *A secure Europe in a better world, European security strategy*. Brussels, 12 December 2003

Strange, S., *The retreat of the state: the diffusion of power in the world economy*, Cambridge, Cambridge University Press, 1996

Telo, M. (ed.), *State, globalization and multilateralism*. Springer, Dordrecht, 2012

Tupman, B., Ten myths about terrorist financing. *Journal of Money Laundering Control*, 2009, 12, 2, 189-205

United Nations (2000), *United Nations Convention Against Transnational Organised Crime*, http://www.unodc.org/documents/treaties/UNTOC/Publications/TOC%20Convention/TOCebook-e.pdf

Wouters, J., S. Basu, S. Schunz, *Meeting the challenges of a multilateralised world? The 'Multilateralibility' of the European Union*. Leuven Centre for Global Governance Studies, Working Paper no. 13, 2008

Reconciling the anti-money laundering compliance duties and the commercial objectives of the bank

Mihaela Sandulescu[1]

Introduction: compliance and banking

The introduction of the anti-money laundering (AML) legislation twenty years ago has significantly changed the way in which banks were used to do business. The shift of responsibility for combating money laundering from the authorities to the financial sector imposed several duties on the financial intermediaries. As such, they have to run several checks before establishing a new business relationship, to attentively supervise their clients' transactions and to make additional investigations if they observe any possible attempt of money laundering. To fulfil these requirements, banks have hired compliance specialists, whose main task is to protect their institution from regulatory sanctions by providing advice and implementing AML risk management systems that correspond to the business focus of the institution. Furthermore, the compliance officer analyses the alerts regarding suspicious transactions and provides guidance for the management and the other employees. Finally, he is an important connection point between the policy maker and the bank -or, as some authors called him, a "gatekeeper" or a "police auxiliary". While the work of the compliance department is vital for an effective management of the bank's risks, the amounts of money that are invested in compliance systems and personnel training are not negligible. KPMG's Global AML survey (2011) points out that compliance costs are continuously rising. More precisely, the respondents indicated an average growth rate of these costs of 45% (for the years 2007-2010). On top of

1 This paper is part of the research project called "*BankAr-Cod*: Argumentative practices adopted by Swiss banks to reconcile AML/CTF supervisory duties with the fiduciary obligations towards the client". BankAr-Cod is funded by the Swiss National Science Foundation under the Division for Interdisciplinary Projects. The project is carried out at the USI-University of Lugano, involving both the Faculty of Communication Sciences and the Faculty of Economics.
Contact at: mihaela.sandulescu@usi.ch

these tangible costs, banks have to consider also the incidence of the intangible costs, for example, by the foregone business opportunities due to increased bureaucracy and privacy violation (Masciandaro *et al.*, 2001 and Johnston *et al.*, 2006).

In some cases, these costs can become a significant burden for the bank, jeopardising its profitability. Finding the right balance between the duty to comply with AML requirements on one hand and the need to boost the bank's profits on the other can create tensions between the defenders of these two different objectives, i.e. the compliance officer (hereafter CO) and the relationship manager[2] (hereafter RM). What follows is that very often these two professionals will hold conflicting views about how certain suspicious cases should be assessed. Sometimes can happen that a transaction/ business relationship does not follow certain predefined parameters in terms of timing, amounts involved, available documents, etc. This deviation, which in most of the cases is not due to criminal activities, can seem suspicious to the CO. As such, the latter will advise the department in charge of opening new accounts not to take the risk of carrying out the transaction. By refusing clients or breaking off transactions that the RM considers to be legally and economically viable, the CO can find himself in conflict with the RM.

This article is part of a larger empirical study focusing on the AML fight in Switzerland. There are several reasons for which the case of Switzerland is particularly interesting. First of all, since the majority of Swiss banks offer private banking/wealth management services, the trust that is created between the client and the RM is pivotal for a successful relationship. Very often, these two can become friends, making it even more difficult for the RM to suspect and report the client. Secondly, even if not much is left of the Swiss banking secrecy, it is still the ground upon which foreign governments criticize Switzerland for having a superficial approach to AML. Thirdly, more than 75% of the assets managed in Switzerland belong to non-residents. This means that the banks must dedicate significant consideration and resources to the due diligence checks. Fourthly, the Swiss AML reporting system is based on the existence of a "well-founded" suspicion. In comparison with the automatic reporting that banks in other countries are required to do, the Swiss banks must first run an "in-house" investigation and gather sufficient objective proofs before reporting to the authorities.

The aim of this article is to provide evidence about the influence that the AML compliance – profit maximisation tension has on the occurrence of a conflict between the CO and the RM. At this point, the conflict is looked at from the CO's

2 This term is frequently used in the private banking sector and it designates the person working at the front desk and managing the clients' business relationship with the bank (i.e. sales person).

perspective. In a further step however, more specific research questions are formulated and data about how the RMs perceive this conflict will be collected as well.

Studying the relation between the CO and the RM is important for at least three reasons. First of all, as previous studies in the AML compliance field have underlined, the CO faces significant challenges when proposing compliance solutions that effectively manage the money laundering risk while supporting the business of the institution (de Koker, 2006; Gully-Hart, 2005; Subbotina, 2009; Verhage, 2011). Secondly, implementing these solutions in practice can prove difficult and can create disputes between the various parties involved in the process. In fact, a recent survey by the Society of Corporate Compliance and Ethics (2012) concluded that compliance professionals are very likely to endure an unhealthy level of stress, as they are in conflict with many of their colleagues. Finally, identifying the drivers of this conflict is important, especially since the continuous update of banking regulation – including AML– keeps compliance matters high on the banks' agenda for the near future (Ernst&Young, 2012).

In order to collect data about the RM-CO conflict, we use a web-based questionnaire. The latter was developed after consulting several compliance specialists, RMs and the law enforcement agency. Using the Swiss Bankers Association's (SBA) member list, a total of 139 banks active in the cantons of Ticino, Geneva and Zurich – the three most important Swiss financial hubs – were contacted for participating in the survey. Subsequently, we specified a logistic regression model in order to understand how the following variables influence the probability of a conflict between the CO and the RM:

1. the perceived contradiction between AML compliance and the commercial interests of the bank;
2. the extent to which the AML duties should prevail when compared to profit opportunities;
3. the percentage of the foreign assets under management in the bank's total assets under management and
4. the decisional authority assigned to the CO.

The model specification does not take into account any behavioural, cultural or organisation-specific factors. Its aim is to investigate whether the conflict is due to the requirements imposed by the AML law.

At the end of the survey period, 46 COs provided information about past conflicts with their colleagues at the front. The regression's results confirm that those COs who perceive a contradiction between the AML compliance requirements and the bank's profit maximisation function are more likely to experience a conflict with their colleagues working at the front office. Variables (2), (3) and (4) instead prove not to be good predictors of the CO-RM conflict, due to the fact that they are not statistically significant.

These findings have important implications for both the banking institutions and the regulating entities. On the one hand, for the banks this conflict represents a cost given by the delay in decisions, distortion of information and the decreased employee performance due to low satisfaction. On the other hand, the amount of compliance that the lawmaker should expect to be observed depends on the costs that the banks must bear.

The rest of the paper is organised as follows: the second section reviews important findings in the field of organisational conflict and presents the reasons why the compliance department's role may lead to conflicts with the front office; the third section presents the data collection method. The fourth section defines the logistic model and the explanatory variables. The results are discussed in the fifth section whereas the potential limitations of the study are outlined in the sixth section. Finally, conclusions and some recommendations are evidenced in the last section.

AML compliance and the potential for internal conflicts

Organisational conflict

According to Brickley *et al.* (2002: 1822) a corporation can be defined as "a collection of individuals. Or more precisely, it is a set of contracts (both explicit and implicit) that bind together individuals with different, often conflicting interests". Hence, beyond any legal form and possible economic purpose, the most important dimension of a company is given by its people. The corporate culture that develops inside each company is supposed to create a common ground for all the employees, such that they share the same behaviours, values and beliefs. More precisely, according to Hofstede *et. al* (1990) organisational culture can manifest at different levels of depth that can be described as an onion diagram: symbols, heroes, rituals and values. In this context, organisational conflict can be defined as a dispute that occurs when interests, goals or values of different individuals or groups are incompatible with each other (Henry, 2009).

After thoroughly reviewing the existent literature on organisational behaviour and management, Rahim (2001) observed that there are two main criteria according to which the organisational conflict can be classified: the *source* of the conflict and the *organisational levels* at which this may originate. With regard to the first criterion, he mentions several sources of conflict: the incompatibility of feelings and emotions regarding a certain issue (Amason, 1996); the disagreements on the tasks to be completed (Eisenhardt *et al.*,1997); the inconsistency between the preferences for the allocation of a scarce resource; the differences in values or ideologies on certain issues (Druckman *et. al*, 1998); the divergent preferences over the decision outcome, etc.

Secondly, inside an organisation conflict may occur at different levels: within the same individual, between two or more individuals, between the individual and the group, and between groups.

Finally, conflict can be either vertical or horizontal; the former occurs within groups of different hierarchical levels, for example managers and subordinates, whereas the latter occurs between individuals of the same level, such as managers of different departments within the same organisation.

In his paper, Corwin (1969) studied the occurrence of a conflict based on several organisational characteristics: structural differentiation, participation in the authority system, regulating procedures, heterogeneity and stability and interpersonal structure.

Contrary to classical organisation theorists like Taylor, Fayol and Weber who prescribed organisational structures in such a way that members would be unlikely to involve in conflict, modern advocates of organisational theory recognize both a negative and positive side of conflict. Conflict can be functional when it stimulates innovation, synergistic solutions to common problems, improvements in organisational decision making and the clarification of points of view. But conflict can be dysfunctional when it causes job stress, burnout and dissatisfaction, fosters distrust and suspicion, increases resistance to change, reduces job performance and loyalty (Rahim, 2001). Moreover, previous studies found that factors like a strong corporate culture, as measured by the consistency of perceptions of company values (Gordon and DiTomaso,1992), the correlation between the attention to an employee's needs and task accomplishment (Hansen and Wernerfelt, 1989) and the strategic decision speed (Baum and Wally, 2003), to name just a few, are all influencing the performance of a company.

Compliance duties under the Swiss AML framework

In Switzerland, the AML framework is given by the following pieces of legislation: (1) the Criminal Code (CC, 1937)–Article 305ter and Article 260quinquies that criminalize the money laundering and terrorism financing offences; (2) the Anti-Money Laundering Act (AMLA, 1997) and (3) the Swiss Financial Market Supervisory Authority Anti-Money Laundering Ordinance (MLO FINMA, 2010).

In addition, the SBA's members can also choose to sign the Agreement on the Swiss banks' Code of Conduct with regard to the exercise of Due Diligence that has been in place since 1977.

Shortly, banks have a general duty of due diligence meaning (a) verifying the identity of the customer and of the beneficial owner when establishing a business relationship and/or whenever there are doubts in the course of the business relationship as to the identity of these two; (b) identifying the nature and purpose of the business relationship wanted by the customer; (c) keeping records of transactions carried out by the customers and (d) adequately training their staff for preventing money laundering. Moreover, Art. 9 of AMLA dictates that if during the due diligence procedures the financial intermediary comes to know/have reasonable grounds to suspect that the assets involved in the business relationship are the proceeds of a crime must immediately file a report with the Money Laundering Reporting Office Switzerland (MROS). The latter will then decide, upon additional investigations, whether to drop the case of forward it to the prosecuting authorities. Alternatively, banks can also use the right to report (Art. 305ter, CC). This is usually the case when there are indications that the funds are the proceeds of crime (i.e. the suspicion is "milder").

A specificity of the Swiss AML system is the freezing period preceding the SAR - *i.e.* for five working days the assets of the reported person will be blocked and the financial intermediary is prohibited from giving any information to the persons affected or third parties of the report (Art. 10 and Art. 10a., AMLA).

The AMLA sets out clear indications regarding the tasks of the AML compliance department. More precisely, this is responsible for: (a) the definition and implementation of the internal AML policy; (b) advising and assisting line managers and the senior executive body in implementing the AML regulations; (c) planning and overseeing internal AML training; (d) defining the parameters for and analysing the alerts generated by the transaction monitoring system; and (e) ensuring that the executive body responsible for making decisions regarding the initiation or continuation of high risk relations is provided with all the necessary information.

In a nutshell, the CO has a central role in minimising the bank's regulatory and reputational risks, by making sure that the institution abides with all the AML provision.

Banks, AML regulation and internal conflicts

Benston and Smith Jr. (1975) defined the financial intermediaries as commercial firms producing specialized financial commodities for the individuals who wish to buy them. Moreover, as any firm operating under productive efficiency, a financial intermediary will try to produce the maximum quantity of financial goods at the lowest cost in order maximise its profit. Among the ordinary operating costs, the costs imposed by regulation may represent a significant constrain, especially since banking is one of the most regulated industries. For a bank, the regulatory costs are given by the total costs incurred for complying with the requirements of a legislation that can refer to: meeting capital requirements, providing the proper disclosure to the clients, restrictions about selling certain investment products, reporting suspicious money laundering transactions, etc.

In almost every bank, the responsibility of keeping these regulatory costs under control by proposing and implementing those compliance policies that correspond to the bank's commercial profile was assigned to the compliance department. Even if AML compliance is the object of interest here, many of the problematic issues discussed below could potentially relate to compliance in general. Moreover, even though the study focuses on Switzerland, several results find support in the international literature.

There are several characteristics that a CO should possess in order to effectively carry out the duties mentioned above. First of all, it is necessary that (s)he has a solid legal background, which makes it easier for him/her to understand the specific legal language. Secondly, a CO must possess strong investigative and analytical skills in order to decide which suspicious cases should be forwarded to the Money Laundering Reporting Office in Switzerland (MROS). Thirdly, when presented with a case, the CO should always objectively analyse the facts, and take a decision based on the results of his investigative research. Finally, on top of these professional requirements, there are also some personal competences that make the CO's work more effective: "to be communicative, discretion, immunity to stress and integrity" (Verhage, 2011:55).

In practice, the implementation of the AML regulations is likely to create an internal conflict for several reasons. The most obvious reason has to do with the profit-maximisation function of the bank. The presence of the compliance department will influence this function in two ways: first, because compliance is a 'cost centre' that needs to be minimised, and secondly, because its inherent role inside the bank is meant to limit certain profit opportunities. The economic costs of AML compliance can be divided in tangible costs – referring to all the physical and human capital needed to perform the due diligence tasks, and intangible costs – given by the inconvenience created to bank's relationship with its clients (Masciandaro et al., 2001 and Johnston et al. ,2006). As Verhage (2011) noted, money is by definition abstract, *i.e.* its value is not dependent on the identity of its owner. As such, money laundering does not harm the commercial interests of the bank: clean or dirty, money can all be part of the bank's investment schemes. Instead, the harm comes from the fact that doing money laundering is illegal. A bank that facilitates money laundering faces important regulatory sanctions, can lose its operating licence and can experience significant reputational damages.

Bearing in mind these premises, the CO is facing both an intra- and inter-personal conflict. The intrapersonal conflict stems from the fact that as an employee of the bank, he cannot be indifferent to the business opportunities that generate profit for his employer but in the same time he cannot allow illegal money to enter the bank.

The interpersonal dimension is the one at which an organisational conflict can mostly manifest itself. As members of the same institution the CO and the RM share a common goal: contribute to the bank's profitability. Nevertheless, as members of different departments, they have different functions, pursue different objectives and as such, they can hold different points of view. In fact, the RM is expected to expand his portfolio of clients and bringing new money to the bank in terms of assets under management (AUM) whereas the CO is concerned with protecting the reputation of the bank by assuring complete rule observance. Several studies have reported that the presence of the CO is translated into an additional layer of control and increased bureaucracy (Pieth *et. al*, 2003; Webb, 2004; Masciandaro *et. al*, 2001). Moreover, Gamson (1966) suggested that specialisations (supported by the authority of distinctive competences) are perceived as targets for hostility and as such, they are positively associated with the incidence of conflict.

In her study of the Belgian AML Complex, Verhage (2011:68) observed that since "*compliance remains a battle between commercial interests on the one hand and rule observance on the other hand (. . .) it has an inherent contradictory characteristic*". Similarly, Favarel-Garrigues et al. (2007:9) noted that "the tension inherent in the AML fight between the commercial ethos and regulatory injunctions can, on the practical level, create dilemmas". To some extent, the presence of the CO is hindering the RM's opportunities of doing business by rejecting those clients whose financial situation is not clear (*e.g.* complex operations, offshore accounts, shell companies). However, this loss is not referring to the illegal money that were forbidden from entering the bank. Instead, it is the long time needed for the verification and certification of the client profile and the origin of his funds that can scare clients off and push them to leave the bank.

Another determinant of the conflict between COs and RMs is the asymmetric degree of interdependence. According to Kumar *et al.* (1995) asymmetric interdependence is verified when parties have different levels of dependence on each other which can affect the level of trust and commitment of the groups. The CO is required to analyse the alerts generated by the transaction monitoring system and to ask the RM for additional documentation. He then combines this information with the details obtained from other sources and decides whether to report the client to MROS. In some cases, the decision to send a Suspicious Activity Report (SAR) will belong to the executive board (*e.g.* if important clients are at stake and the reputational risks must be thoroughly considered). As such, a unilateral dependence develops between the CO and the RM since the former does not need the approval of the latter to carry out his investigation. Moreover, the RM is responsible for dealing with those clients that were reported and whose assets were frozen if they show up at the bank's desk. Being forbidden by AMLA to inform his clients about the SAR, the RM is left with the problem of inventing various excuses why the clients cannot have access to their funds (*e.g.* problems with the payment system).

Another problem with compliance is that it cannot be assessed in terms of turnover (Verhage, 2011; Demetis and Angell, 2007); as such, the added value of this department is debatable. While the performance of the RMs can be easily evaluated by looking at the amount of new AUM, evaluating the compliance department's performance is not straightforward. The best solution is to look at the reputational damages that were avoided due to the CO's ability in identifying and mitigating the risk of money laundering. Even though is impossible to measure the exact cost of reputational damage, Harvey (2004:336) suggested that "it can result in direct costs (loss of income), indirect costs (client withdrawal and possible legal costs) and opportunity costs (foregone business opportunities)".

Research questions

Building upon the observations of Verhage and Favarel-Garrigues *et al.* mentioned above, this article sets out to provide empirical evidence about the internal conflicts generated by the specific requirements of the AML legislation.

First of all, we are interested in testing whether the perceived contradiction between rule observance and the commercial ethos of a bank significantly influences the occurrence of a conflict between the RM and the CO.

Secondly, we will consider whether the CO's propensity to strictly applying the AML provision without considering the commercial component of the transaction makes him more likely to be in conflict with the RM.

Thirdly, we will also control whether the decision authority assigned to the CO has any role in mitigating this conflict.

Finally, since foreign assets must undertake additional controls (and thus the decision making process is more complex) before being accepted, we check whether a higher percentage of foreign AUM is associated with a higher probability of CO-RM conflict.

Data collection

Researchers in the AML field have noticed that the available data – both public and private – is rather limited. International organisations such as FATF, IMF, World Bank, etc. collect only macroeconomic data which can be used for studies tackling the problem of AML compliance at a country level. In addition, it is very rare that a bank will choose to publish information about its internal AML policy, and even in such a case, it will be limited to what they are required to do by law. Finally, corporations can prove very reluctant to provide information to outsiders for research purposes, especially when the subject matter is very sensitive and there is a lack of a "clear organisational payoff" (Verhage, 2011).

Those authors who wished to study a specific AML compliance topic had to resort to a survey in order to obtain the desired information (see for example Masciandaro *et al.* (2001, 2004), Webb (2004), Bührer *et al.* (2005), Verhage (2011), Harvey and Lau (2009)).

We used the SBA's List of members available on-line to select our sample of banks. A total of 139 banking institutions operating in the three main Swiss financial centres – Zurich (ZH), Geneva (GE) and Ticino (TI) – were contacted for completing the on-line questionnaire. This means almost 40% of the total number of banking institutions active in Switzerland. If a bank had offices operating in two/all of these three cantons it was counted only once.

The survey was delivered using the Dillman (2007) procedure: a cover letter describing the study sent one week before the questionnaire became available on-line, a letter containing the password for logging in to the online platform, a first reminder after three weeks and a second and final reminder after another three weeks. Moreover, in each of these four communications, the support of the SBA regarding our study was emphasized in order to improve the response rate.

The final version had a total of 30 questions, collecting information not only about the CO-RM conflict but also about the banks' internal AML policy and the AML law in general[3]. The survey was addressed to specialists working in the compliance department. In those cases in which a CO was not available, a person who had enough knowledge about his institution's internal AML compliance policy was required to complete the survey. For simplification, we will consider all of them COs.

---

3 The results regarding the banks' internal AML policy and the Swiss AML framework are part of another article.

The questionnaire was available on line for a period of eight weeks. The official language of the survey was English but the respondents were given the possibility to choose any of the official Swiss languages: German, French and Italian.

In addition, we also interviewed a total of nine specialists involved in the Swiss AML system: four COs, two MROS officials, two RMs and one executive member of the SBA. Some of them were interviewed both before the survey – in order to understand whether the problems we identified were the case for the actual banking environment but also to provide advice on the template of the questionnaire – and after, to discuss the survey's results. In total, this summed up to twelve individual interviews. All the interviews were conducted in person and were arranged with the agreement that the identity of the banks and individuals will remain anonymous.

Survey sample and population

At the end of the survey period, a total of 52 COs submitted the on-line questionnaire. Nevertheless, not all the submitted questionnaires were complete. Considering the delicate topic of the survey and the well-known discretion that characterises Swiss banks, the respondents were given the option of not answering those questions with which they didn't feel comfortable.

We collected 46 answers with regard to the CO-RM conflict (*i.e.* a 33,1% response rate). Table 1 reports detailed information about the type of banking institutions[4] in which the COs worked at the time of the survey. As we can see, the majority (67,4%) represented foreign-controlled banks[5], while 17,4% of the COs worked in banks that specialise in stock exchange, securities and asset management business. Finally, the rest of 15,2% of the sample represent COs working in cantonal banks (6,5%), major banks (2,2%) private bankers (2,2%) and other banking institutions (4,3%). When considering the canton of residence, we see that almost 57% of the banks were based in Zurich, whereas 28,3% were based in Geneva and only 15,2% in the Italian canton, Ticino.

4 The types of responding banks are defined using the Swiss National Bank's official classification http://www.snb.ch/en/system/glossary#__F

5 A bank is deemed to be foreign-controlled if foreigners with a qualified participation in the bank directly or indirectly hold more than half of its voting shares, or if they exercise a controlling interest in any other matter (www.snb.ch)

Table 1
Number of banks in the population and in the sample by canton and by type of bank

	Sample N	*In % of total*	*Population N*	*In % of total*
Panel A: By canton				
Geneva	13	28,3	50	36,0
Zurich	26	56,5	71	51,1
Ticino	7	15,2	18	13,0
TOTAL	**46**	**100**	**139**	**100**

Panel B: By type of bank				
1. Cantonal Banks	3	6,5	3	2,2
2. Big Banks	1	2,2	2	1,4
3. Banks specialising in stock exchange	8	17,4	28	20,1
4. Other banking institutions	2	4,35	6	4,3
5. Foreign controlled banks	31	67,4	84	60,4
6. Regional and savings banks	0	0,0	1	0,7
7. Branches of foreign banks	0	0,0	5	3,6
8. Institutions with a special field of business	0	0,0	1	0,7
9. Private bankers	1	2,2	9	6,5
Total	**46**	**100**	**139**	**100**

Beside data about the sample, Table 1 contains data about the entire population of banks based in one of the three cantons and that are members of the SBA. By analysing their distributions, we can evaluate the extent in which the sample is a good representation of the population and thus, with what degree of confidence we can generalize the sample's results to the entire population. Regarding the canton of residence, the banks in our sample have a similar distribution to the ones in the population (see Panel A). The same holds true with respect to the type of bank, with some minor exceptions (see Panel B). The latter refers to the branches of foreign banks, private bankers[6] and cantonal banks. Regarding the first category, we do not expect major differences in the conduct exhibited with regard to AML compliance, given that foreign bank branches in Switzerland are obliged to follow not only their home country's regulations but also the Swiss ones. As such, we believe that the

6 Private bankers work in the field of asset management; their partners are jointly and severally liable (www.snb.ch)

possible differences/characteristics attributed to this category are captured by the foreign-controlled banks. Secondly, we collect information from all the cantonal banks. Finally, we have only one observation about private bankers, compared to the nine available in the population. Despite these small differences, the distribution of the three categories that represent more than 80% of the total banks in both the population and the sample is pretty similar (see categories 3 to 5). In conclusion, we can safely generalize our results to the entire population.

Empirical methodology

As emphasized earlier, this study is concerned with understanding whether certain perceptions held by the CO can determine him to have a conflictual relation with his colleagues working at the front. Logistic regression has been increasingly used by researchers for studies in social science related fields which aim was to test the presence or absence of a certain event. Since the data we collect is either binary or categorical, we use a logistic regression to check how the odds[7] of a CO-RM change depending on how strong the CO's beliefs regarding certain matters are. We develop the following logistic model:

$$LogCO\text{-}RM\ conflict_i = \beta 0 + \beta 1 Contradiction_i + \beta 2 AML\_prevalence_i + \beta 3 Decision\_authority_i + \beta 4 Foreign\_AUM_i + \varepsilon_i,$$ where :

CO-RM conflict$_i$ is a binary variable representing a positive "yes" (1) or a negative "no" (0) answer to the question "*Did you ever have any conflictual discussion with your colleagues from the sales department (i.e. front desk)?*"

Contradiction is an ordinal variable corresponding to respondents' answers to the question "*To what extent do you consider that there is a contradictory position between the AML compliance and the commercial interests of the bank?*" The possible values are: 2 for "Large Extent", 1 for "Certain Extent", 0 for "Not sure", -1 for "Limited Extent", -2 for "Not at all".

AML_prevalence is an ordinal variable corresponding to respondents' answers to the questions "*To what extent do you consider that the requirements stemming from the AML law should prevail when compared to the commercial interests of your institution?*". The possible values are: 2 for "Large Extent", 1 for "Certain Extent", 0 for "Not sure", -1 for "Limited Extent", -2 for "Not at all".

---

7 The odds is the ratio of the probability that the event will happen to the probability that the event will not happen (source: Wikipedia)

Decision-authority$_i$ is an ordinal variable corresponding to respondents' answers to the questions "*To what extent you consider that you are given enough authority to make day to day decisions on problems that arouse routinely in the course of applying AML law provisions?*". The possible values are: 2 for "Large Extent", 1 for "Certain Extent", 0 for "Not sure", -1 for "Limited Extent", -2 for "Not at all".

Foreign_AUM$_i$ is an ordinal variable indicating the proportion of foreign AUM inside their institution : 1 for "0%", 2 for "less than 10%", 3 for "10 to 25%", 4 for "26 to 50%", 5 for "51 to 75%" and 6 for "more than 75%".

The first explanatory variable is meant to measure the CO's perceptions regarding one of the most debated conflicts of interest determined by the application of AML regulations. The compliance requirements limit certain business opportunities presented to the RM and, in times of economic turmoil, this limitation makes it even harder for banks to grow. Under this assumption, we expect that the stronger the acknowledgement of a contradiction between rule observance and profit maximization the higher the probability of a conflict between the RM and the CO.

From the interviews conducted prior to the survey we learned that a RM finds it more difficult to interact with a CO if he is too conventional when it comes to applying the law provisions. This conservative behaviour was more obvious in the case of those COs with a legal educational background as they lacked the economic knowledge to understand the bank's commercial needs. We introduced the *AML_prevalence* variable to account for the CO's propensity to strictly apply the AML regulation. We expect the variable's coefficient to be positively related to the occurrence of a conflict.

The variable *Decision_authority* measures the extent to which the CO can independently decide upon daily AML-related matters. To ensure an effective implementation of the law, the lawmaker dictated that the compliance unit should be linked to the executive board; this provision was also supposed to limit potential conflicts of interest (see The Basel Committee on Banking Supervision, 2001). As a consequence, we assume that if one has a high degree of decisional authority, there are fewer opportunities for the others to challenge his decisions (i.e. we will observe a negative coefficient).

The last explanatory variable accounts for the percentage of foreign assets relative to the bank's total AUM. The risk-based approach requires the banks to give special attention to those clients/transactions connected to a high risk jurisdiction/economic activity. As such, we expect more debate between the CO and the RM over the acceptance of foreign funds since it is easier to verify the origin of the local funds.

The limitations of the model together with the potential biases of the study are addressed in a separate section.

Results

Table 2 reports descriptive statistics for all the variables included in this study. Conventionally, for categorical variables the median should be reported but if the categories are ordered the mean can be used as well (Acock, 2008).

On average, the respondents acknowledge the AML compliance vs. profit maximization contradiction (0,375 points) to a certain extent. Furthermore, the mean scores registered for the variables *AML_prevalence* and *Decision_authority* -1,511 and 1,391 points- are very close to the upper bound of the interval. Simply stated, respondents considered that (1) AML compliance should prevail over the commercial interests of the bank and (2) they are given enough authority to take routine decisions. Finally, the majority of the banks in the sample have a high percentage of foreign AUM when compared to the bank's total AUM (i.e. between 50 and 75%).

Table 2
Summary statistics

Variable	Obs.	Mean	Std. Dev.	Var.	Min	Max	Median
CO-RM conflict	46	0,739	0,444	0,197	0	1	1
Contradiction	48	0,375	1,248	1,558	-2	2	1
Foreign_AUM	48	4,958	0,458	2,126	1	6	6
AML_prevalence	47	1,511	0,975	0,951	-2	2	2
Decision_autority	46	1,391	0,856	0,732	-1	2	2

The correlation analysis reported in Table 3 shows that all the explanatory variables are positively and significantly correlated with the dependent variable, except for *Decision_authority*. The latter variable has a negative correlation coefficient, as expected, but it is not significant. Since foreign assets pose a higher money laundering risk, we see that there is a positive and significant correlation between *AML_prevalence* and *Foreign_AUM* (meaning that when a bank accepts foreign assets, it has thoroughly gone through all the AML checks).

Table 3
Correlation analysis

The table reports the Spearman correlation coefficients for the variables used in the logistic regression.
***, **, * denote the corresponding statistical significance at 1%, 5%, and 10% levels.

	Conflict CO-RM	**AML_ prevalence**	**Contradiction**	**Decsion_ autority**	**Foreign_ AUM**
Conflict CO-RM	1				
AML_prevalence	0,2581*	1			
Contradiction	0,3865 ***	-0,0971	1		
Decision_autority	- 0,1631	-0,0616	-0,0171	1	
Foreign_AUM	0,4144 ***	0,4939 ***	0,0664	-0,0855	1

Table 4 reports the logistic regression's results. The univariate models in columns (1) to (4) show that only the odds ratios for *Contradiction* and *Foreign_AUM* are statistically significant[8]: 2,08; p= 0,014 and 2,02; p= 0,016 respectively. As such, they both positively influence the odds of a CO-RM conflict. The odds ratios for *AML_prevalence* and *Decision_authority* are not statistically significant even if they move in the expected direction (1,69; p= 0,116 and 0,59; p= 0,299).

The models in column (5) and (6) show that all the odds ratios are statistically significant and have the expected positive/negative influence on the dependent variable. In model (5) both the perceived *Contradiction* and the belief in *AML_prevalence* positively influence the odds of a conflict between the CO and the RM. They remain significant even after controlling for *Decision_authority* in model (7).

Finally, when including all the variables in model (8), we see that only the odds ratio for Contradiction remains significant (2,26; p= 0,03). This means that if the score for the perceived contradiction AML compliance-profit maximization increases by 1 unit, the odds for a conflictual situation with the RM increase by 126% ((2,26-1)*100). Simply stated, *when the implementation of the AML law create dilemmas about the*

8 An odds ratio smaller (greater) than 1 will negatively (positively) influence the odds of an event.

best courses of action, the parties involved in the implementation process will, most probably, find themselves in conflict with each other.

Table 4

Logistic regression analysis

The table presents the results of the logistic regression having as a dependent variable the CO-RM conflict. All the explanatory variables were described in the Empirical Methodology section. For all the variables we report **Odds Ratios,** (Coefficients) and (Standard Errors). ***, **, * denote the corresponding statistical significance at 1%, 5%, and 10% levels.

	(1)	(2)	(3)	(4)	(5)	(6)	(7)	(8)
Constant	**2.55** *** (0.937) (0.36)	**1.27** (0.236) (0.58)	**6.46** (1.866) (0.89)	**0.17** (-1.785) (1.22)	**0.78** (-0.254) (0.72)	**-2.329** (0.1) (1.45)	**1.40** (0.338) (1.06)	**0.18** (-1.708) (1.71)
Contradiction	**2.08** *** (0.736) (0.3)				**2.48** *** (0.906) (0.34)	**2.24** ** (0.804) (0.37)	**2.24** ** (0.808) (0.34)	**2.26** ** (0.377) (0.38)
AML_ prevalence		**1.69** (0.523) (0.33)			**2.14** * (0.76) (0.41)		**2.09** * (0.738) (0.42)	**1.42** (0.351) (0.48)
Decision_ authority			**0.59** (-0.535) (0.51)				**0.71** (-0.345) (0.48)	**0.75** (-0.292) (0.49)
Foreign_ AUM				**1.83** *** (0.603) (0.25)		**2.02** ** (0.704) (0.30)		**1.7** (0.530) (0.34)
No. obs.	46	44	43	43	44	43	42	40
No. EPV	12	12	11	11	6	5.5	3.7	2.75
Chi2 (logit)	6.9 ***	2.64	0.25	6.78 ***	11.47 ***	12.41 ***	10.74 ***	12.90 ***
Cox-Snell R^2	0.139	0.058	0.030	0.146	0.229	0.251	0.226	0.276
NagelKerke R^2	0.204	0.084	0.044	0.215	0.332	0.369	0.330	0.399
Hosmer –Lemeshow Chi2 (p-value)					5.93 (0.31)	3.28 (0.77)	4.11 (0.85)	2.07 (0.98)

As Verhage (2011) noted, the CO can find himself trapped between "the hammer and anvil" (Verhage, 2011): he has to choose between destroying potential business opportunities and rigidly applying the AML regulations or neglecting his function. According to Rizzo et al. (1970), role conflict (i.e. incompatibility in the role's requirements) may result in intra-person conflict when the individual needs to manage his own values, resources and capabilities to answer all the demands of the role, but it can also lead to conflicts with other people inside the organisation, as they all have different expectations from him (in our case, the RM).

The odds ratio for *AML_prevalence* is positive but not significant (1,42: p= 0,465). Prior to the survey, the RMs we interviewed said they were very often annoyed by the CO's propensity to strictly apply the law, without showing the minimum interest for the commercial priorities of the bank. "*if my client buys a property, the compliance officer will call me and ask for the documents justifying the transaction. He gives me three days of time, even though he knows very well how long is the bureaucratic process until a document is produced in Italy. And still, he insists 'no document, no payment'*" [RM1]. Post-survey however, the COs explained us that even if their job is to safeguard the bank from reputational and legal risks, they are aware of the fact that the bank needs to grow in order for their salaries to be paid. As such, they claim to be helping the RMs, even if they regrettably admit that "*it is very difficult that a true friendship will develop between a CO and a RM*"[CO2].

Moving further, we see that the odds ratio for *Decision_authority* is negatively related to the CO-RM conflict, though not statistically significant (0,75: p= 0,554). The evidence about the causal link between decisional power and organisational conflict is mixed. Corwin (1969) found that the authority to make routine decisions provides more occasions for disputes to arise. On the other hand, the opportunity to participate in the decision-making process gives occasions for expressing minor forms of conflict and might prevent minor irritations from developing into major incidents.

Finally, the odds ratio for *Foreign_AUM* is no longer statistically significant after controlling for *AML_prevalence* and *Decision_authority*; Nevertheless, the fact that the odds ratio is positive suggests that the additional checks that need to be done in the case of foreign funds could increase the probability of a conflict between the back and the front departments. This is particularly relevant for Switzerland, where more than 70% of the assets managed by Swiss banks belong to non-Swiss clients.

Researchers have been often warned that the use of logistic regression can be problematic when the outcome has few events available[9] relative to the number of independent variables included in the model. In such cases, the estimated odds ratios can be biased and the validity of statistical inference may be adversely affected (i.e. the

9 Here, an event refers to the cases belonging to the less frequent category in the dependent variable

final model may be over fitted[10], see Peduzzi *et al.*, 1996). Because of these problems, several authors have drawn guidelines for the minimum events per variable (EPV) required in multivariate analysis. Using a theoretical approach, Harrell *et al.* (1985) suggested that 10 to 20 EPV were necessary. Simulation procedures based on real data employed by Peduzzi *et al.*(1996) and Vittinghoff *et al.* (2006) concluded that 5-10 EPV and 5 EPV respectively, were enough. In our case, the number of EPV is below 5 only in two cases (3,7 and 2,75, see Table 4). Nevertheless, we see that the values taken by our main variable of interest (i.e. *Contradiction*) in these cases does not register significant variations that could be attributed. One could also notice that the number of observations for the different models reported in Table 4 varies. This is because the statistical software uses a list wise deletion by default, meaning that if there is a missing value for any variable in the logistic regression, the whole case will be excluded from the analysis.

In general, the interpretation of the pseudo R-squared is not recommended in the case of logistic regressions. Researchers however, often report the Cox-Snell and the Nagelkerke R-squared as alternatives to the usual (adjusted) R-squared in OLS regressions. When considered individually, only the variables *Contradiction* and *Foreign_AUM* are able to explain a significant portion of the variability in the CO-RM conflict (between 14% and 21%, see Table 4, columns (1) to (4)). In fact, the chi-square statistic is significant only in these two cases (6,9 and 6,78 respectively). When taken together, the variables are able to explain between 27,6% and 39,9% of this variability. Finally, the logistic regression model in column (8) has a chi-square of 12,90 and is significant at 1 percent; this indicates that the combined effect of the explanatory variables is significant and jointly explains the occurrence of a CO-RM conflict.

As an alternative to the chi-square test, I also report the Hosmer and Lemeshow test to check whether the scores predicted by the model significantly differ from the observed scores; since the result is not significant (H-S X^2=2,08, p=0,98), we can conclude that Contradiction, Decision_authority, AML_prevalence and Foreign_AUM reliably distinguished between no CO-RM conflict and CO-RM conflict.

Returning to the research questions, the following conclusions can be drawn regarding the determinants of the CO-RM conflict as a dependent variable. On the one hand, many conflictive situations between these two actors arise due fact that the CO must struggle to find a way to ensure AML abidance while trying not to obstruct

10 For a given set of data, introducing more variables will very likely produce a model that better fits the data.

the bank's business (question 1). On the other hand, the CO's inclination to put first the legal duties does not have any significant influence on the occurrence of the conflict (question 2). The same observation can be made also with regard to the degree of authority that the CO enjoys when solving AML issues (question 3). Finally, regarding our sample of Swiss banks, we cannot conclude that the additional checks that must be ran prior to the acceptance of foreign assets will increase the probability of CO-RM dispute (question 4).

Limitations

This study focuses on the potential conflict between the CO and the RM and it is the first one to empirically assess the origins of this conflict. In particular, I consider the *rule observance* vs. *profit maximisation* contradiction inherent to AML regulations to be the main source of conflict between the CO-RM.

Nevertheless, this conflict could be determined by other factors than the intrinsic organisational role of these two actors - e.g. personality, educational background, culture, age, sex, tenure, professional experience, etc. Moreover, certain organisational characteristics can also influence the occurrence of this conflict; according to Osborn and Hunt (1974) the environmental conditions can influence the effectiveness of the different types of organisational structures. For example, bigger banks put more pressure on the achievement of new clients and this can exacerbate the CO-RM conflict, when the CO impedes the development of certain business opportunities. Furthermore, factors such as the type of clients served, the types of products offered, the degree of differentiation and/or specialization and the organisational culture, will also determine the occurrence of a conflict.

Unfortunately, the use of a questionnaire as a mean for data collection makes it very difficult to obtain information about all the factors listed above. In addition, one must bear in mind that surveys measure beliefs, feelings and perceptions, which can be different from the behaviour in the real life. As such, the COs' answers can be biased, considering the delicate nature of the money laundering subject and the potential reputational damages connected to certain answers.

Finally, it would be interesting to understand whether the CO-RM conflict exists during the normal business relationship with the client or whether it is the reporting duty and the ensuing investigations that triggers its appearance. Furthermore, by observing the frequency or severity of this conflict, one could understand which compliance duties are more likely to influence the emergence of the conflict. Even if the lack of information regarding all the above elements could jeopardize the study of the CO-RM conflict, the aim of this work was to understand whether the specific nature of the AMLA's requirements have any explanatory power. The results presented in the previous section showed that this was actually the case.

Concluding remarks

This paper develops around the assumption that the supervising and reporting duties stemming from the AML legislation can create a conflict between the CO and the RM. By employing a logistic regression methodology, we conclude that the acknowledgement of a contradiction the AML requirements and the usual profit-boosting objectives of the bank increases the odds of a conflictual discussion between the CO and the RM. However, the CO's propensity to strictly implement the law, the decision authority that is attributed to him and the amount of foreign AUM have no explanatory power since their coefficients are not significant.

Overall, this evidence supports the recent findings of the E&Y (2012) "Banking risk management" survey which showed that one of the biggest challenges around banking culture is resolving potential conflicts between the sales driven front office culture and the risk culture.

The existence of this conflict has important implications not only for the financial institutions but also for the regulators. First of all, since the inception of the AML regulations, authors have pointed out that "compliance is a cost centre, not a profit centre" (Gallo and Juckes, 2005). Besides the investment in software and personnel training, one has also to consider the cost of foregone business opportunities. The CO-RM conflict, as any other organisational conflict, can generate additional costs for the financial institution due to: delay in decisions, distortion and suppression of information, and violations of the chain of command (Rizzo, House and Lirtzman, 1970). In fact, Jehn (1997) found that the negative emotionality associated with organisational conflicts leads to poor group performance and low member satisfaction.

Secondly, as Braithwaite *et. al* (2007) point out, if the regulations are to be effective, they should be accepted and considered as needed by the regulated community. This means that if the public and business interests are not sufficiently aligned, compliance is difficult or even impossible to achieve (Gunningham and Rees, 1997). These two recommendations hold true also about the AML laws. The fact that the banks in our sample recognised an ongoing contradiction between AML rule observance and the bank's profit maximisation function should push the regulators to evaluate the grounds upon which they expect to observe a compliant behaviour from the financial institutions. This means understanding the extent to which the requirements are going against the bank's functional purpose and resources. Moreover, a further tightening of the law should consider the efforts and the difficulties incurred by the financial institutions to accommodate them. Finally, the lawmakers should also reconsider the incentives given to financial institutions for compliance. The existent literature on AML compliance has persistently underlined that the main reason for which banks involve in the fight against money laundering is the reputational risk generated by non-compliance (Masciandaro *et al.* (2001), Harvey (2004), Verhage (2011)). As such, the lawmaker should emphasize the adverse impact that the involvement in money laundering has for the banks' reputation.

As a further step, I plan to collect information about the CO-RM conflict as perceived by the RMs. This will allow me to have a complete picture about the determinants of this conflict and also to suggest several directions to solve it.

List of acronyms

CO	Compliance Officer
RM	Relationship Manager
AML	Anti-money laundering
AUM	Assets under management
SBA	Swiss Bankers Association
MROS	Money Laundering Reporting Office Switzerland
FINMA	Swiss Financial Market Supervisory Authority
AMLA	Anti-money Laundering Act
SAR	Suspicious Activity Report
CC	Criminal Code

References

Acock, A.C., *A gentle introduction to Stata*. Second Edition, Stata Press, 2008

Amason, A.C., Distinguishing the effects of functional and dysfunctional conflict on strategic decision making: Resolving a paradox for top management teams. *Academy of Management Journal,* 1996, 39, pp. 123–148

Basel Committee on Banking Supervision, *Consultative Document. Customer due diligence for banks*. Bank of International Settlements, 2001

Baum, J.R. and S. Wally, Strategic decision speed and firm performance, *Strategic Management Journal*, 2003, vol. 24, *no.* 11, pp.1107-1129

Benston, G.W. and C.W. Smith, A transaction cost approach to the theory of financial intermediation. *The Journal of Finance*, 1976, vol. 31 (1), pp. 215-231

Braithwaite, V., K. Murphy and M. Reinhart, Taxation, threat, motivational postures, and responsive regulation. *Law & Policy*, 2007, vol. 29, *no.* 1, pp. 137-158

Brickley, J.A., W.S. Clifford Jr. and J.L. Zimmerman, Business ethics and organisational architecture, *Journal of Banking and Finance*, 2002, 26, pp. 1821-1835

Bührer, C., I. Hubli and E. Marti, The regulatory burden in the Swiss wealth management industry, Swiss Society for Financial Market Research, *Financial Markets and Portfolio Management*, 2005, vol. 19, *no.* 1, pp. 99-108

Corwin, G.R., Patterns of organisational conflict. *Administrative Science Quarterly*, 1969, vol. 14, *no. 4*, pp. 507-520

De Koker, L., Money laundering: control and suppression of financing of terrorism - some thoughts on the impact of Customer Due Diligence measures on financial exclusion. *Journal of Financial Crime*, 2006, vol. 13, *no. 1*, pp. 26-50

Demetis, D.S. and O.I. Angell, The risk-based approach to AML: representation, paradox and the 3rd directive, *Journal of Money Laundering Control*, 2007, vol. 10, *no. 4*, pp. 412-428

Dillman, D.A., *Mail and internet surveys : the tailored design method : 2007 update with new internet, visual, and mixed-mode guide*, 2nd Edition (updated), Hoboken, NJ. Wiley, 2007

Druckman, D. and K. Zechmeister, Conflict of interest and value dissensus: Propositions in the sociology of conflict. *Human Relations,* 1973, vol. 26, pp. 449-466.

Eisenhardt, K.M., J.L. Kahwajy and L.J. Bourgeois, Conflict and strategic choice: How top management teams disagree. *California Management Review*, 1997, 39 (2), 42-62.

Ernst Young, *Global Banking Outlook 2013-2014: Time for bold action.* Ernst & Young Switzerland, 2012

Ernst Young, *Bank Barometer 2012 - Declining optimism at Swiss banks*? Survey results, Ernst&Young Switzerland, 2012

Favarel-Garrigues, G., T. Godefroy and P. Lascoumes, Sentinels in the banking industry - Private Actors and the fight against money laundering in France. *British Journal of Criminology,* 2007, 48 (1), pp. 1-19

Gallo P.A. and C.C. Juckes, Threshold transaction disclosures: access on demand through latent disclosure rather than reporting. *Journal of Money Laundering Control,* 2005, vol. 8, *no. 4*, pp. 328-334

Gamson, W.A., Rancorous conflict in community politics. *American Sociological Review*, 1966, Vol 31, pp. 71-81

Gordon, G.G., N. DiTomaso, Predicting corporate performance from organisational culture. *Journal of Management Studies*, 1992, vol. 29, Issue 6, pp. 783-799

Gunningham, N. and J. Rees, Industry self-regulation: An institutional perspective. *Law and Policy*, 1997, 19(4), pp. 363-414.

Hansen, G.S. and B. Wernerfelt, Determinants of firm performance: The relative importance of economic and organisational factors. *Strategic Management Journal*, 1989, vol. 10, *no. 5*, pp. 399-411

Harvey, J., Compliance and reporting issues arising for financial institutions from money laundering regulations: A preliminary cost benefit study. *Journal of Money Laundering Control*, 2004, vol. 7, *no. 4*, pp. 333-346

Harvey J. and S.F. Lau, Crime-money, reputation and reporting. *Journal of Crime, Law and Social Change*, 2009, vol. 52, pp 57-72

Henry, O., Organisational conflict and its effects on organisational performance. *Journal of Business Management*, 2009, 2 (1), pp. 16-24

Hofstede, G., B. Neuijen, D. Ohayv and G. Sanders, Measuring Organisational cultures: a qualitative and quantitative study across twenty cases. *Administrative science quarterly*, 1990, vol. 35, *no. 2*, pp. 286-316, Cornell University

Health and Safety Executive (HSE). The determinants of compliance with laws and regulations with special reference to health and safety A literature review, prepared by the London School of Economics and Political Science for the HSE, London 2008

Jehn, K.A., A qualitative analysis of conflict types and dimensions in organisational groups. *Administrative science quarterly*, 1997, vol. 42, *no. 3*, pp. 530-557, Cornell University

Johnston, R.B. and I. Carrington, Protecting the financial system from abuse: Challenges to banks in implementing AML/CFT standards. *Journal of Money Laundering Control*, 2006, vol. 9 (1)

KPMG, Global Anti Money Laundering Survey: How banks are facing up to the challenge, KPMG International, 2011

Kumar, N., L. Scheer and J. Steenkamp, The effects of perceived interdependence on dealer attitudes. *Journal of Marketing Research*, 1995, 32 (3), pp. 348-56

Masciandaro, D. and U. Filetto, Money laundering regulation and bank compliance costs: What do your customers know? Economics and the Italian experience. *Journal of Money Laundering Control*, 2001, vol. 5, *no. 2*, pp.133-145

Osborn, R.N. and J.G. Hunt, Environment and organisational effectiveness. *Administrative Science Quarterly*, 1974, vol. 19, *no. 2*, pp. 231-246

Peduzzi P., J. Concato, E. Kemper, T.R. Holford and A.R. Feinstein, A simulation study of the number of events per variable in logistic regression analysis. *Journal of Clinical Epidemiology*, 1996, vol. 49, *no. 12*, pp. 1373-1379

Pieth, M. and G. Aiolfi, Anti-money laundering - levelling the playing field. Working Paper no. 1, Basel Institute on Governance, Switzerland, 2003

Rahim, A., *Managing conflict in organisations.* Third Edition, Quorum Books, Westport, Connecticut, 2001

Rizzo, J. R., R.T. House and S. Lirtzman, Role conflict and ambiguity in complex organisations. *Administrative Science Quarterly*, 1970, vol. 15, *no. 2*, pp. 150-163

Society of Corporate Compliance and Ethics and Health Care Compliance Association, "Compliance and Ethics: A survey", 2012

Subbotina, N. (2009), "Challenges that Russian Banks face implementing the AML regulations", *Journal of Money Laundering Control*, 2009, vol. 12, *no. 1*, pp.19-32

Verhage, A. The anti-money laundering complex and the compliance industry. Routledge Studies in Crime and Economics, Oxon, UK, 2011

Vittinghoff, E. and C.E. McCulloch, Relaxing the rule of ten events per variable in logistic and Cox Regression. *American Journal of Epidemiology*, 2007, vol. 165, *no.* 6, pp. 710-718

Webb, L., A survey of Money Laundering Reporting Officers and their attitudes towards money laundering regulations. *Journal of Money Laundering Control*, 2004, vol. 7, *no. 4*, pp.367-375

AML and the political power weight

Jackie Harvey, Michael Hutchinson and *Adam Peacock*[1]

Introduction: Global AML policing

It is well accepted within the academic literature that the complexity of money laundering makes the task of estimating the extent of the problem challenging (van Duyne, 1994; Johnson and Lim, 2003; and Harvey, 2005a). Sharman (2008) made the telling observation that two decades ago money laundering did not exist within the lexicon of criminology; now the Financial Action Task Force (FATF) Recommendations are applied by more than 180 countries[2] (FATF, 2013). Such devotion to a potential problem suggests it to be of significant threat to the very wellbeing of the global economy, viewed as somehow sinister and dangerous, described by He (2010, p 31) as a '*very secret crime*'.

Many scholars have described the various stages in the process of transforming '*dirty money*' into '*clean money*' (Rhodes and Palastrand, 2004; Simser, 2006; Mei Leong, 2007; Lai, 2010; Hopton, 2009; and Mugarura, 2011). The implication being that money laundering is a crime of such underpinning complexity that its prevention via regulation is manifestly difficult. Such complexity has not, however, stood in the way of the enthusiastic implementation of Anti-Money Laundering (AML) systems.

AML frameworks were first developed in both Europe and the USA primarily due to their more mature legal systems (Tang, 2010) and their common interests in other profit oriented criminality such as the illicit drug trade (Van Duyne and Levi, 2005). This was combined with pressures exerted by the FATF in their recommendations and evaluations. As was intended (by the US) the fight against money laundering took on an international element (Cuéller, 2003) from the start.

---

1 The authors are respectively: Professor of Financial Management and Director of Business Research, Newcastle Business School, Northumbria University; BA Hons Business with Finance Student, 2011 and BA Hons Accounting student, 2013.

2 The FATF has set out its requirements for global AML through the 'Forty Recommendations' first established in 1990 and subsequently updated in 1996 and 2003. The most recent update was in 2012 and launched in February 2013 which has resulted in the incorporation of the additional 9 special recommendations on terrorist financing, formulated in 2001 into the core list.

Sharman (2008) uses diffusion theory in the context of AML to provide an explanation for the speed of global adoption, stating that "*the diffusion of AML policy among developing countries has been driven by discursive, power based mechanisms*" (p. 635). However, acknowledging the paucity of empirical evidence regarding the effectiveness of AML legislation in the prevention of money laundering, he went on to note that AML had been somewhat astutely described as "*politically successful policy failure*", (Peter Andreas, NY Times, June 13, 2004 cited by Sharman, 2008, p. 636). The evident contradiction between political success and policy failure has been tacitly accepted for decades and provides an explanation for the attendant political power weight of the FATF which for some obstinate reason does not translate itself in a commensurate improvement in policy effectiveness.

The focus of this chapter is, therefore, to understand the power wielded by the FATF through an examination of the way in which AML is globally policed and enforced by that organisation. This is achieved through consideration of the inter-relationships between the FATF and member national governments evident through the peer review 'mutual evaluations'. These visits are used to provide an in depth description and analysis of each country's system for preventing criminal abuse of its financial system, in other words, the extent to which it is demonstrating compliance with the FATF Recommendations. Looking through a lens of legitimacy, we aim to investigate the responses of national Financial Intelligence Units (FIUs) to mutual evaluation reports that are deemed to be negative; arguing that these institutions are more interested in demonstration *ex post* compliance in the interest of minimising reputational damage rather than on making substantial changes that will improve the effectiveness of their controls. Hence, contributing to the "*politically successful policy failure*".

Global Regulation of AML Systems

Those who enforce the law are in a difficult situation when deciding how to fight and regulate the criminal activity of laundering. Harvey (2009a) points out that the more the authorities over-estimate the scale of money laundering, the more likely it will be accepted as posing a threat of substantial magnitude. Further, the continued existence of the institutions created to regulate money laundering become predicated upon this image of 'threat' perpetuation and that estimates of global magnitude are used to reinforce their status and claim on resources with which to fight this crime (Harvey, Bosworth-Davies and Elliott, 2013). Indeed, as long ago as 1994, Van Duyne argued "*making bold comments about a problem and demonstrating its actual size are different issues*" (p. 59). Similarly Reuter and Truman (2005, p. 56) note "*large numbers are frequently thrown around without serious support*", consequently "*the alarmist notion of the volume of money laundering being of major significance cannot be objectively challenged*".

Regulation within an industry may be imposed or requested but generally takes place as a correction for market failure (Baldwin and Cave, 1999). The theory suggests that regulation is required primarily for the benefit of the underlying industry but that "[t]*here are regulations whose net effects upon the regulated industry are undeniably onerous*" (Stigler, 1971, p. 3). Biagioli (2008, p. 93) contextualises Stigler's theory in relation to AML noting "*These phenomena are largely overestimated and sometimes used by different subjects (the press, politicians*[..]*etc) for their own interest and purposes*". Within the money laundering arena, the stringency of the laws that are in place to deter money laundering have been questioned with the suggestion that the authorities' continued additions to existing anti-money laundering laws and the commensurate rise in compliance costs lack justification due to a paucity of empirical evidence linking AML to a reduction in crime (Harvey 2005a; Bosworth Davies, 2007). Further it has been argued (Goredema and Montsi, 2002) that the obscure nature of money laundering means that it is extremely hard to eradicate, hence regulation becomes an unwinnable battle.

Regardless of the criticisms of AML legislation and regulation there is little doubt that this crime does exist. Early work on the subject drew attention to the economic benefits available to those embracing AML controls as the existence of money laundering was seen to distort economic data and hence muddy government efforts at macroeconomic policy management (Quirk, 1996, Bowden, 1997). Even with the difficulties of actually determining the level of money laundering, Preller (2008) draws attention to the international coordination required if it is to be tackled. The justification for legislation lies with the belief that separating a criminal from the proceeds of their activities will reduce the number of people who chose to lead that lifestyle (Magnuson, 2009; Harvey, 2009a) with the latter stating, "*the imposition of regulation increases both the costs of laundering and the probability of detection and conviction*" (p. 97). The challenge remains, however, to find the link between the controls, their costs and the prevalence of underlying crime.

The FATF and the FIUs

The FATF is the main body that is responsible for the promotion of anti-money laundering legislation and they note (FATF, 2013) that they are an '*inter-governmental policy-making body*' whose intention is to devise and promote a set of international standards that aim to combat money laundering and terrorist financing. This organisation collaborates with international bodies involved with financial crime and performs mutual evaluations designed to assess different member countries' anti-money laundering policies for compliance with their Recommendations[3]. The FATF also review countries' mutual evaluations to monitor their progress from the initial assessment (Johnson, 2008). While it is the FATF's mission to 'combat money laundering' and promote anti-money laundering legislation on a global basis, it is the actual duty of member countries and their financial intelligence units to implement these Recommendations. Drawing from management literature, little is known of the strategies used to intentionally build and maintain trust (Williams, 2007) but higher than required levels of compliance with regulation can be viewed as an intentional window dressing tactic to instill confidence and reduce insecurities within the market (Adewale, 2013).

Along with way, the FATF have been criticised for contributing to increased levels of regulation. Johnson (2005) noted that Australia had, in 2003, opposed the FATF's revised Recommendations raising concerns regarding the additional compliance burden. However, as an FATF member, the country had little option but to implement as failure to do so would have resulted in identification as being 'non-compliant', something as bad as having leprosy in the Middle Ages.

It is worthwhile reminding ourselves however, that the FATF is and remains, a voluntary organisation and thus implementation of the 40 Recommendations is not mandatory although all members do commit to such action (Boorman and Ingves, 2001). This suggests that the FATF are capable of affecting the reputation a country's financial system, applying reputational pressure to ensure recognition of their standards and thus holding a significant amount of power. "*Mutual evaluation by the FATF countries forces members to become more proactive in their anti-laundering enforcement, implying either ineffective or ineffectual anti-money laundering measures*" (Johnson and Lim, 2003, p. 9). This, therefore, implies that approaches to AML that deviate are deemed ineffective and that the 'Recommendations' provide the best solutions towards tackling money laundering. There is little evidence that actually supports this. Indeed, is there evidence that a western centric approach based on western business models and legal systems would be appropriate in all countries around the globe? Whilst most financial institutions are at best ambivalent about the rules (applying them at least cost to themselves, Harvey *et al*, 2013), it has been suggested that international financial

---

3 There are 34 member countries of the FATF and 2 regional organisations: Argentina, Australia, Austria, Belgium, Brazil, Canada, China, Denmark, Finland, France, Germany, Greece, Hong Kong China, Iceland, India, Ireland, Italy, Japan, Republic of Korea, Luxembourg, Mexico, the Netherlands, New Zealand, Norway, Portugal, Russian Federation, Singapore, South Africa, Spain, Sweden, Switzerland, Turkey, United Kingdom, United States; European Commission, Gulf Co-operation Council.

institutions might gain competitive advantage in their operations within 'newer' jurisdictions having established procedures in place. There is also little doubt that there has been geopolitical influence bought through the ability to sanction non-compliant states (Harvey, 2005a)[4].

Each country the FATF assesses is required to have in place legislation that criminalises money laundering (Recommendations 1 and 2 under the 2003 version of the FATF's Recommendations used for this work[5]). It is ultimately the responsibility of the FIU within each country to ensure compliance with the legislation and promote the required AML measures to all regulated businesses. The purpose of a mutual evaluation is to monitor AML systems within a country for compliance with the Recommendations. The approach has been criticised within the academic community as the FATF sit in judgement on AML systems when little is known on how an effective system should operate and how it should be constituted (Alldridge, 2008; Sansonetti, 2000). Indeed those more powerful members of the FATF 'club' judge others by rules they fail to apply to themselves; such as the US still allowing its Delaware and Nevada companies. It is interesting to observe that up to and including 2002-03, the FATF measured the efficacy and adoption of its Recommendations through a self-assessment survey on compliance with the 28 Recommendations requiring specific action. On the basis of the information provided by FATF members, only 15 jurisdictions were assessed for 2002-03 as having fully implemented the 28 FATF Recommendations requiring specific action. It was a list that excluded both the United States and the United Kingdom (Harvey 2005b, p. 47). Perhaps not surprisingly this approach was superseded by that of peer review. Choo (2012) undertook a similar study for 15 jurisdictions that indicated a significant number of them to be non-compliant or partially compliant with at least five of the Recommendations. Similarly, Alldridge, 2008 (p. 445) noted the failure in compliance of the United States that continues without a murmur of dissent or threat of sanction. Indeed, he goes onto to argue (p 444) that its interference via these controls mask an ulterior agenda of gaining competitive advantage. This fuels the

---

4 One of the early tools employed by the FATF was the use of blacklisting or 'name and shame'. The first blacklist of non-co-operative countries and territories (NCCTs) was produced in June 2000. This group of countries was considered deficient in having effective countermeasures against money laundering. During this process, 23 jurisdictions were listed due to a lack of an effective AML system but all were removed from the list by October 2006. The current focus of the FATF is on identification of high risk jurisdictions, and it continues to name and monitor the efforts of a number of countries.

5 This is now recommendation 3 under the 2012 (revised recommendations published February, 2013).

argument that the FATF can be viewed as being too powerful as they have a significant influence over AML systems within nation states: "*Nonetheless, FATF's power* [. . .] *and its status in the discourse about laundering* [. . .] *has placed it in a dominant position in policy discussion of laundering*" (Alldridge, 2008; 445; Sansonetti, 2000). The consequences of being seen as non-compliant are that trust is lost over the integrity of the financial system, which in turn can lead to large financial costs from loss of business, as other countries are either barred from transaction (in the case of Iran and North Korea) or required to control their financial market exposure against those countries listed as having strategic deficiencies.

The Compliance Culture of the AML Industry

Harvey and Lau (2009; 58) argue that the justification to counter money laundering rests on the theory that it preserves the '*reputation and integrity of the financial system*', arguing that the reputation costs of being seen as non-compliant outweigh the direct compliance costs as money acquired from illegal activities enters into the banking system through legal mechanisms. The theory suggests that money being associated with the term '*laundered*' implies some level of illegality therefore affecting perception. Thus the requirement to maintain trust and reputation helps to enforce AML measures.

Compliance can be viewed as a method used by organisations to satisfy regulators. The general assumption is that the likelihood of sanctions and the severity of them will ensure compliance, however there are both tangible and intangible underpinning motivations driving compliance (Sultinen and Kuperan,1999). Obviously the more regulated an industry is the more likelihood those within are to be compliant so as to avoid sanctions, however, this is seen to be reinforced through internal organisational ethics. "*The sense of moral obligation, it turns out, is very common throughout society and, it appears, may be a significant motivation explaining much of the evidence on compliance behaviour*" (Sultinen and Kuperan, 1999; 174). When assessing the compliance behaviour in the AML industry, Harvey and Lau (2009) suggest that the reputational costs associated with not complying ensure behaviour is in accordance with the FATF 'club rules'. Thus we observe the creation of a culture wherein being *viewed* as compliant takes precedence over ensuring effectiveness of AML measures. This is referred to as '*sanction avoiding*', as opposed to engendering good business practice. As already noted, the literature highlights that compliance with AML regulation does not of itself deliver a reduction in profit oriented crime. Hence, the common assumption that compliance with regulation will produce a successful outcome cannot be relied upon.

Archel, Hussilos, Larrinaga and Spence (2009) noted that legitimacy theory aims to help explain the incentives for organisations engaging in social and economic disclosure activities. Legitimacy theory links organisations with society through an unofficial contract that implies organisations should demonstrate the requirement for their services and how they may be viewed as beneficial (Archel *et al*, 2009). Legitimacy theory has also been used to help explain the link between money laundering compliance and reputation (Harvey and Lau, 2009). They argued that financial institutions would look to disclose their AML systems and controls using compliance as a vehicle to establish legitimacy. Lehman (1992), notes that in the face of criticism, an organisation will generally go out of its way to gather and supply evidence in an effort to reinstate its legitimacy. Just as Harvey (2005a; 339) stated, firms "*demonstrate compliance with their domestic regulators by increasing the number of suspicious activity reports*". Similarly FIUs demonstrate compliance with the FATF by increasing the level of prosecutions or by prompting higher numbers of disclosures from its regulated sector. Thus we set out to answer the following research question: Do FIUs respond to negative international criticism through offering token efforts to improve compliance? Our expectation is that receipt of a negative peer review (through a mutual evaluation) will result in the FIU engaging in window-dressing activity through enhanced disclosure in their annual reports.

Approach to peer assessment

As pointed out by Harvey (2005b; 46) within the prescriptive approach of the FATF, which somewhat grandly describes itself on its webpages as "*the global standard-setter in the fight against money laundering, and the financing of terrorism and proliferation of weapons of mass destruction*" (FATF, 2013), the control measures set out within the Recommendations are used as a mechanism to rate compliance of an individual country's AML framework. There are essentially three critical areas of focus:

- the general AML legal framework that criminalises money laundering;
- mandatory creation of a regime for reporting suspicious transactions (aided by procedures to identify customers; reduce bank secrecy and allow for international cooperation); along with
- the functioning of the FIU.

As with any 'members only club' adherence to the rules is established through a system of peer review or 'mutual evaluations' carried out by teams from other members of that same club. The team is usually composed of four to six experts with legal, financial and law enforcement expertise and two members of the FATF

Secretariat. These reviews provide an in-depth description and analysis of each country's system for preventing criminal abuse of the financial system and are conducted in accordance with a set of Key Principles that were compiled by the FATF in consultation with the FSRBs[6], the IMF and World Bank .The FATF is currently in its third round of evaluations and each assessment takes approximately one year to complete. A statement by FATF President Bjørn S. Aamo at the EU Conference "Fighting money laundering and terrorist financing - New framework, future challenges" that took place in Brussels on 15th March, 2013[7] suggested a shift in emphasis from compliance to 'risk based' focus on effectiveness (although effectiveness has always been a component of these reports). The fourth round of evaluations will begin in 2014 and will be against the new 2012 standards. As in the past, the approach will focus on an assessment of compliance against each Recommendation: scored as compliant; largely compliant; partially compliant; or, non-compliant. The report will further focus on whether the legal and regulatory framework in place is producing the results that would be expected (although quite how such a subjective term will be assessed remains undefined) to be scored as: high-level of effectiveness; substantial level of effectiveness; moderate level of effectiveness; or, low level of effectiveness. The unit of measurement is unspecified which does rather bring into question their usefulness.

Method

Consistent with legitimacy theory and disclosure activity by companies[8], we hypothesise that following receipt of a negative report following a peer review; FIUs will attempt to redress the situation through demonstration of improvements in its regime and that evidence of this would appear in their annual publications.

One of the main areas of focus for the peer review teams when compiling their mutual evaluation reports is reporting of suspicious activity (either reported as SARs or STRs). This indicator is still one of the most widely tracked statistics, despite recognition that there is no causal relationship between the number of disclosures and

6 FATF Style Regional Bodies

7 Statement available at: http://www.fatf-gafi.org/documents/documents/effectivenesshasmovedtothetopofthefatf agenda .html (accessed 26/4/13)

8 Typically, when a listed company receive negative publicity that will impact on share price it will increase efforts to retrieve the situation via publication of positive information and images.

effectiveness of the regime (Harvey, 2008). The fact that even the authorities have moved away from according it the high levels of significance evident early on in the regime has in no way diminished its popularity despite its evident uselessness in reducing money laundering.

The selection of countries for the purposes of analysis followed a non-random purposeful sample method. The process of selection started with a review of all 36 mutual evaluation reports that took place during the third round. This set was then reduced by removing those that took place after 2010 as they were considered too current to allow for a change in response to be evident in ensuing annual reports. The sample was further reduced by removal of those countries for whom either there was no independent information available on the number of suspicious activity reports being filed or where the FIU did not publish annual reports. This left us with usable data for 14 individual countries.

The study firstly considered the mutual evaluation report and then, in a longitudinal study looked for evidence of post-evaluation response gained through review of the FIU's publicly available reports. In particular we were interested in locating evidence of scale and forms of a response to negative feedback within the original mutual evaluation. From this we were able to highlight behaviour patterns within these units after mutual evaluation reports had been issued.

Table 1

List of selected countries and reasons for their inclusion

Country (FIU)	Comments on Selected Countries	Year of Mutual Evaluation	Compliancy Rating for Reporting System
Australia (AUSTRAC)	Very transparent website with clear links to archived annual reports and to the FATF evaluation.	2005	Largely compliant
Canada (FINTRAC)	Interesting criticisms stemming from their mutual evaluation report. The FIU has an annual report containing significant information.	2008	Largely compliant
China (CAMLMAC)	Follow up reports on the FATF website indicating efforts made to rectify problems identified in STR system.	2007	Partially compliant
Denmark (FINANSTILSYNET)	Archived reports back to 1996, extensive information on progress.	2006	Partially compliant

Hong Kong (JFIU)	Website clearly displays STR statistics with response noted in accessible publications. The FIU provides interesting statistics related to their progress from their mutual evaluation.	2008	Largely compliant
Italy (Banca D'Italia)	Clear links in the unit's annual report which can be linked to concerns published by the FATF.	2006	Partially compliant
Norway (OKOKRIM)	Relevant documents were available which also show trends in STRs after the release of their mutual evaluation.	2005	Largely compliant
Portugal (Unidade de Informação Financeira)	Reports found after considerable effort, details of STR and confiscation data.	2006	Largely compliant
Republic of Korea (KoFIU)	Very transparent with clear links to annual reports detailing efforts in relation to FATF's comments post evaluation	2009	Partially compliant
South Africa (FIC)	Very impressive FIU, clear discussion in relation to reporting efforts.	2009	Largely compliant
Sweden (FINANSPOLISEN)	Mutual evaluation report and publications from the FIU are available.	2006	Partially compliant
Switzerland (MROS)	A great deal of criticism in the mutual evaluation report that can be linked to the FIU's annual report.	2005	Largely compliant
United Kingdom (SOCA)	A lot of information available such as FIU's annual report and SAR report.	2007	Compliant
USA (FinCEN)	A large amount of useful information within their annual report, clear discussion about the FATF	2006	Largely compliant

Findings

Country Responses

The summary of findings are presented in Table 2 below. The purpose of this section is to draw attention to some of the underlying details of these responses with a discussion of each country. This Table does illustrate the expected and rather predictable Pavlovian response by the FIUs to direct criticism of their AML regimes, each of which is discussed by individual country.

Table 2
Summary of findings mutual evaluation

Country	Date	Compliancy rating[1]	Total Population (mil)[3]	SARs during evaluation	+1 year	+2 year	+3 year
Australia	2005	LC	20.4	17.212	44%	17%	12%
	Extract from mutual evaluation[2]		*"STRs filed over the past several years and the range of entities reporting is positive and appears to be trending in the right direction with provisions deemed generally adequate. The evaluation team's concern regarding the scope of the terrorist financing offence led the team to be concerned that this could limit the reporting obligation. Expand the definition of the Terrorist financing offence so that transactions are reportable."*				
	Response from FIU contained in annual report		Record level of SARs received post evaluation. FIUs annual reports reference the FATF. Following the report AUSTRAC acquired additional access to extensive data sources enabling it to expand its analysis with the expectation of an increase in reports in future years with the introduction of new suspicious matter reporting obligations under the AML/CTF Act.				
Canada	2008	LC	33.3	210	165%		
	Extract from mutual evaluation[2]		*"The low number of STRs sent by certain financial sectors raise concerns in relation to the effectiveness of the reporting system, the number of staff dedicated to the analysis of potential ML/TF cases in low."*				
	Response from FIU contained in annual report		The jump in STRs is noted by the FIU in their report as being directly resulting from the mutual evaluation.				
China	2007	PC	1317.9	6.450.106	963%	-38%	45%
	Extract from mutual evaluation[2]		*"There is no explicit obligation to report suspicions of terrorist financing, or to report attempted transactions. The rules do not define the basis on which suspicion should be founded and there are significant concerns about the overall effectiveness of*				

			the system and the lack of subjective assessment. Amendments to STR rules should be made at the earliest opportunity. A more subjective STR regime should be implemented once the new sectors become familiar with the overall concepts of suspicious transaction reporting."				
	Response from FIU contained in annual report		Massive response from China's reporting system. Annual reports make reference to the FATF's report in demonstrating its progress with compliance with the recommendations, bringing in changes to legislation to correct the deficiencies identified by the MER				
Denmark	2006	PC	5.4	876	54%	15%	35%
	Extract from mutual evaluation[2]		*"Insufficient monitoring of financial institution participation in the system, the low level of reporting raises effectiveness questions. Danish reporting entities have filed significantly fewer than those in most jurisdictions"*				
	Response from FIU contained in annual report		Statistics showed an increase in STR filing since the MER but concerns that the increased level of reporting is not yet sufficient to fully dispel the concerns about effectiveness of the regime				
Hong Kong	2008	LC	7.0	14.838	8%	23%	3%
	Extract from mutual evaluation[2]		*"while the volume of STRs has increased in recent years, the submission of STRs by DNFBPs could be improved"*				
	Response from FIU contained in annual report		No direct access to annual reports so it is not clear what the response from the FIU was to the MER. There is evidence of pressure exerted on FIs to comply with STR reporting				
Italy	2006	PC	58.9	9.838	24%	17%	45%
	Extract from mutual evaluation[2]		*"need to increase the levels of suspicious transaction reporting from nonbank FIs the number of reports from bureaux de change, the postal banks, stockbrokers, investment funds and trust companies and the insurance sector is abnormally low"*				
	Response from FIU contained in annual report		The report of the FIU notes the increase in STRs with emphasis on the discussion around financial intermediaries				
Norway	2005	LC	4.6	4.893	44%	7%	20%
	Extract from mutual evaluation[2]		*"there are some concerns about the effectiveness of the reporting system, the number of STRs being reported by nonbank financial institutions is very small and the number of STRs being reported by banks themselves is also decreasing"*				
	Response from FIU contained in annual report		Record number of STRs received in the year following the MER, implementation of electronic monitoring systems in commercial banks and savings banks contributed to the increase				
Portugal	2006	LC	10.9	584	34%	16%	38%

	Extract from mutual evaluation[2]		*"The low number of STRs filed by the financial entities raises the issue of effectiveness. The evaluation team had concerns regarding the scope of the TF offence, this could limit the reporting obligation"*				
	Response from FIU contained in annual report		Efforts by the FIU to raise awareness of AML and CFT is seen as contributing to the increase in both the number of STRs and the range of business sectors reporting suspicious cases.				
Republic of Korea	2009	PC	49.2	136.282	73%		
	Extract from mutual evaluation[2]		*"limitations in scope of predicate offences, it is recommended that POCA be amended to incorporate all offences as it limits the scope of STR reporting."*				
	Response from FIU contained in annual report		Increase in STRs following the report is attributed to the enhanced awareness of the AML system by major FIs, the FIU submitted an action plan to the FATF to correct deficiencies identified by the MER				
South Africa	2009	LC	49.3	29.411	26%	45%	
	Extract from mutual evaluation[2]		*"leasing and financing companies have not yet implemented reporting obligations. Authorities should work with dealers in precious metals and stones and the real estate sector to determine whether they are adequately identifying and reporting suspicions."*				
	Response from FIU contained in annual report		The introduction of an enhanced compliance regime produced an increase in the number of STRs, with the vast majority coming from financial institutions.				
Sweden	2006	PC	9.1	6.359	-5%	116%	-30%
	Extract from mutual evaluation[2]		*"the large majority of STRs have been filed by a small number of FIs. The assessors had concerns over the effectiveness of this recommendation."*				
	Response from FIU contained in annual report		The report acknowledges the decrease in STRs but notes this was from a historically high level, although there is a significant increase the following year. The report discusses the increase in reports being filed by financial institutions in comparison to prior years				

Switzerland	2005	LC	7.4	729	-15%	28%	7%
	Extract from mutual evaluation[2]		*"The system of reporting of suspicious transactions raises very serious problems of effectiveness especially the low numbers of reports."*				
	Response from FIU contained in annual report		Record level of SARs reached in 2009, despite the dip in the year following the evaluation				
UK	2007	C	61.0	220.484	4%	5%	3%
	Extract from mutual evaluation[2]		*"the amount of SARs analysed by the FIU is small compared to the amount of SARs received. The FIU does not conduct sufficient proactive analysis on SARs, the UK FIU should continue to increase its staff."*				
	Response from FIU contained in annual report		The UKFIU increased efforts to reduce unnecessary reporting.				
USA	2006	LC	298.4	1.051.162	10%	14%	0%
	Extract from mutual evaluation[2]		*"low number of filings from the securities sector. There is $5.000 threshold to reporting suspicious transactions for casinos as the only DNFBP sector that is required to report suspicious transactions. recommend FinCEN remove the threshold from the reporting obligation."*				
	Response from FIU contained in annual report		Increase in filings from the commercial real estate sector.				

Sources: Data compiled from various reports contained within (i) FATF website extracted from (http://www.fatf-gafi.org/documents/documents.jsp?lang=en) and (ii) from each of the FIU's websites

1. The compliancy rating (column 3) given to the country's reporting system is based on an analysis of each of the countries' STR systems compared against the ideal reporting system noted in the FATF's Recommendations. The possible gradings are 'compliant' (C) where the Recommendations are fully observed with respect to all essential criteria, largely compliant (LC) where there are only minor shortcomings, with a large majority of the essential criteria being fully met, partially compliant (PC) where the country has taken some substantive action and complies with some of the essential criteria and non-compliant (NC) where there are major shortcomings, with a large majority of the essential criteria not being met.
2. The column headed Extracts from Mutual Evaluation Reports provides example quotations that highlight the main criticisms contained in the review, drawing attention to any concerns and recommendations in relation to the FIU's STR system.
3. This column provides an estimate of population recorded in the year of the mutual evaluation (The World Bank data, available at: http://data.worldbank.org/indicator/SP.POP.TOTL).

4. The SAR system was then analysed to identify the change in reporting levels since the assessment (columns 7-9). Chaikin (2009, p. 241) reports that the FATF believe SARs will produce, '*quantitative and qualitative law enforcement outcomes*'. This column notes the number of reports received by the unit on the year of evaluation. The following columns display the percentage change in number of reports over the subsequent years. The importance of reporting suspicious activity is clearly emphasised by the FATF in their recommendations, if criticised it is expected that there will be increases in subsequent reporting periods.
5. The final column encapsulates the response of the FIU. This column summarises the results post-evaluation and notes any specific reference to the comments of the FATF.

Australia

AUSTRAC was recorded as largely compliant although as noted in the extract from their report reproduced in Table 2, the evaluation team was concerned that the scope of the terrorist financing offence would limit the reporting obligation. Their recommendation was that the definition of the offence be expanded, which would presumably result in an increase in reporting. Indeed STR data shows an increase from 17.212 reports filed in 2005 (the year of the Mutual Evaluation Report - MER) to 24.785 for 2006 with subsequent annual increases even though the new reporting obligations under the AML/CTF framework did not come into effect until December 2008. The MER also criticised the low level of prosecutions related to money laundering offences, although it did not indicate what it would regard an appropriate rate to be or indeed if some a measure could be set.

Canada

Canada was noted as being largely compliant, however the MER (2008) criticised the low level of STRs submitted by certain financial sectors, in consequence STR disclosure rose by 346 or 165% the following year (FINTRAC 2009). Canada has a significantly lower level of reporting relative to their population[9] which in part would have prompted these comments, illustrative of the view that higher levels of reporting correlate with effectiveness of the regime. The response from the FIU noted that they had altered their system so as to improve the quality of reports as well as their ability to analyse them more efficiently.

China

CAMLMAC was rated as only partially compliant with serious concerns over the effectiveness of the STR system; although the FIU had only been established in 2006, so had only been in operation for a limited amount of time. The MER recommended that changes be made as soon as possible so that reporting entities

---

9 Population is used to provide a simple and crude measure of scale.

could be in no doubt about their responsibility to report suspicious activities. In 2007 the FIU released new reporting rules that addressed this. Subsequently there was a significant jump in the level of reports being made, however, the annual report notes that although these resulted in a significant number of investigations and prosecutions "*no data exists to confirm whether these were money laundering cases*".[10]

Denmark

Denmark was reprimanded in 2006 in respect of their low level of reports relative to other jurisdictions and associated concerns over 'effectiveness'. The report criticised the FIU's handling of the STR reporting system, indicating failings in the standard of analysis of the suspicious activity reports and inadequate guidance on how such reports should be submitted. The 2009 annual report of the Danish FIU is highly enthusiastic about the improvements they consider to have been made in their system of reporting (with development of standardised forms and electronic reporting) supported by additional legislation. It also specifically comments on the rise in STRs from 876 in 2006 to 2.095 in 2009 specifically drawing attention to this increase as evidence of the development of their reporting system.

Hong Kong

The MER criticised the scope of the SAR requirement as well as the low level of reports originating from the non-financial sector. Review of data from the JFIU indicated a subsequent increase in the level of SARs and draws attention to both the level of arrests in connection with money laundering offences as well as to the amount of assets confiscated by the Unit.

Italy

Italy was criticised in 2006 for the low level of reports being submitted by non-bank financial intermediaries, as well as over the way in which reports were processed slowing down feedback to reporting entities. The report of the FIU in 2009 draws attention to changes made to the format of reports such that they contain far more details. It further draws attention to the progress of the criticised sectors, highlighting the growth in their reports. There was a reported increase overall in each of the subsequent three years of 24%, 17% and 45% respectively.

---

10 China Anti-Money Laundering Monitoring and Analysis Center (CAMLMAC) Annual Report, p 70, 2007 available at: http://www.pbc.gov.cn/english/chubanwu/nianbao/2007/en19.pdf

Norway

The MER praised the authorities for the high rate of prosecution of money laundering offences. However, attention is drawn to apparent ineffectiveness due to the low level of SARs received from non-bank financial institutions and the falling level received from banks. Not surprisingly their subsequent annual report draws attention to the growing number of reports filed by companies operating within the identified sectors.

Portugal

The MER reflected concern about the level of reporting and the 'effectiveness of the reporting requirement', in particular focusing on the low number of STRs filed by financial institutions. The response of the FIU was to raise public awareness of both AML and CFT issues. The FIU subsequently draw attention to the number of different business sectors that were reporting suspicious cases and to the increase in the number of reports that were received which doubled over a four year period.

Republic of Korea

The MER noted that the list of predicate offences in POCA did not cover all the categories of offences required by the FATF and further that the STR obligation is only mandatory above a threshold equivalent to $10.000. In response to this, the number of reports has risen year on year and the growth from 275 filed in 2002 to 136.282 in 2009 is viewed as evidence of compliance by the FIU as Korea strives to obtain full membership of the FATF.

South Africa

The MER highlighted deficiencies in certain sectors in compliance with AML. The FIU indicates that it views compliance with the FATF to be of great importance and the number of reports in the year after the assessment increased by 6.649 (a jump of 29%). This increase is directly attributed to increased awareness and promotion by the unit, although there is no specific mention of the delinquent sectors identified by the MER.

Sweden

The MER drew attention to the fact that the majority of the STRs emanated from a small number of financial institutions with half of Swedish banks making no reports at all. Thus the level of reporting was viewed as inconsistent with other jurisdictions having similar sized financial sectors. There was concern over the low number of convictions and what were regarded as being 'weak' penalties for money laundering, though the FATF has nothing to say about the independent judiciary. The FIU was criticised for limited guidance on the correct form of reporting which was seen as slowing down the time taken to analyse their content. Subsequent annual reports by the FIU provided guidance on their requirements for the standard format of future reports, and drew attention to the increase in STRs (following an initial small decline) in particular and not surprisingly, those emanating from the banking sector.

Switzerland

Similarly, Switzerland was criticised for the low level of suspicious transaction reports in 2005, though there appears to be an increase in the level of reports received in subsequent years (albeit with an initial dip in 2006) with a rise of 28% recorded in 2007. The report by the Money Laundering Reporting Office of Switzerland (MROS) 2009 also notes its interest in sponsoring amendments to their national legislation to achieve a higher level of compliance with international standards.

United States

The MER notes the significant progress that the country had made to establish 'an effective AML system' but drew attention to the need to remove the *de minimis* reporting threshold and to extend the scope of the legislation to embrace sectors that were currently excluded. The securities sector was specifically mentioned as having low reporting numbers. The FinCEN reports drew attention to the consequent increase in reports it received in particular, from the securities sector which increased by 58%. There is no mention of the Delaware and Nevada companies which still appear to dodge the FATF recommendation concerning know your customer.

United Kingdom

The UK was the only country in our sample that was rated as compliant. The criticism within the MER was not for lack of reporting but for failure on the part of the FIU to effectively analyse the number of reports received although this was attributed to the inadequate level of staffing. This information was used by the FIU to lobby for an increase in resource with the 2008 annual report specifically commenting upon the increase in staffing levels.

Discussion

Drawing this together we can make a number of observations. Namely that the main area of criticism relates to the small number of suspicious transaction reports being made and that this directly translates to the label of 'ineffectiveness' being applied to the regime without searching for further evidence. The one country that was not criticized for this failing (the United Kingdom) was reprimanded for inability to analyse the volume of reports being received! There is occasional criticism of the number of prosecutions for money laundering offences and of the leniency of sentencing (although this falls outside of the mandate of the FATF). What appears missing from the scope of the mutual evaluation reports is discussion of the overall quality of the reports and the role that they have played in prevention of criminal activity. A more significant criticism can be laid at the door to the FATF club, however, in that they appear to readily accept the tokens of compliance as meaningful.

Largely, these data would suggest that the FATF and their mutual evaluation process had a clear impact on countries and their AML systems. There are obvious examples within the majority of FIU's annual reports where they have altered their AML policy due to the criticism they have received from the FATF mutual evaluation missions. STRs are viewed by the FATF as providing evidence of effective compliance and thus supporting the legitimacy theory of publically displaying compliance as measured by this standard (Lehman, 1992; Harvey and Lau, 2009). Indeed the majority of countries report a jump in reporting levels which, consistent with this theory, allows for the provision of evidence that seeks to address the shortcomings identified within the mutual evaluation reports. Interestingly the increase is proportionally greater for countries with lower ratings which must be related to their lower baseline.

The FATF appear to have 'captured' regulation and are able to use their influence effectively. The possibility of damaging the reputation of a country's financial system ensures compliance, indeed the majority of FIUs referenced the MER criticism as a motivation for their efforts if not as argument to plead for an increase in staff. Therefore, the FATF are able to promote and enforce their Recommendations on AML systems, although this says nothing on improvements in standards, nor indeed that compliance will produce a successful reduction of criminal activity. The FATF is also prepared to go one step further and to arrogate itself to comment negatively on the sentencing policy in money laundering cases.

Table 2 highlights some interesting points, especially regarding trends of reports received by the units after evaluation. Lehman (1992) discusses the efforts made by an organisation to restore their legitimacy in the eyes of their stakeholders following a negative incident. The unit's disclosure of their activities is an integral tool used to emphasise their compliance with the regulator. For example, the Italian mutual evaluation noted that there was an abnormally low quantity of reports stemming from certain industries. The Italian FIU's annual report then specifically dedicated a section to displaying the progress of reports originating from these industries. Throughout the analysis there is continual evidence to support that FIU's are attempting to display their compliance with the FATF and their Recommendations. All want to present themselves at the very top of the class and do so by simply increasing the SAR numbers.

The data gathered suggests that a compliance culture is very much present within the AML industry. It also appears that compliance is a highly regarded technique to sustain reputation. Concerns or criticisms stemming from the regulator are acknowledged seriously and action is promptly taken. It is interesting that the peer review teams continue to view an increase in reports as synonymous with 'effectiveness' when clearly the only real method to judge efficacy of the system would be through a drop in underlying crime and the subsequent prosecution and asset recovery data. There is also a tendency to benchmark countries against each other in the belief that there is some 'magic ratio' of reporting that should be achieved. It is not entirely clear how we can arrive at such a ratio. If focus is placed upon the population divided by the number of SARs, as has been suggested by World Bank, no account is taken of the financial transaction density in a country. Apart from that, what does a high ratio mean given the conception that the AML measures should prevent money laundering? The coveted high compliance could then rather be interpreted as evidence of the ineffectiveness of the AML system. It all rather looks like chasing numbers without appropriate thought and reflection.

Data would suggest the FATF have significant influence over countries and their legislations regarding money laundering. The main aim of the FATF is to promote a global set of measures to combat money laundering, while it should not directly interfere with individual countries' legislations. However, the results imply that any direct criticism generally forces the country in question to alter their AML policy. The criticism is considered to be seriously detrimental to a country's reputation and their financial system (Johnson, 2005; Harvey and Lau, 2009). Therefore, countries would rather comply than incur reputational damage. This effectively paints an image of the industry working in harmony and successfully achieving their overall mission as measured by a high score of SARs. In reality, the evidence suggests, this merely ensures countries take precautions to help prevent money laundering occurring without fully knowing whether they are actually productively impacting on criminal activity.

References

Adewale, A., Corporate Governance: a comparative study of the corporate governance codes of a developing economy with developed economies. *Research Journal of Finance and Accounting*, 2013, *4* (1) pp 65-77

Alldridge, P., Money laundering and globalization. *Journal of Law and Society*, 2008, *35* (4), pp. 437-463.

Archel, P., J. Hussilos, C. Larrinaga and C. Spence, C. (2009). 'Social disclosure, legitimacy theory and the role of the state', *Accounting, Audit and Accountability Journal*, 2009, *22* (8), pp. 1284-1307

Baldwin, R and M. Cave, *Understanding regulation: theory, strategy and practice.* 1st edn. New York, Oxford University Press, 1999

Biagoli, A. Financial crime as a threat to the wealth of nations: a cost-effectiveness approach. *Journal of Money Laundering Control.* 2008, *11* (1), pp. 88-95.

Boorman, J. and S. Ingves, *Financial system abuse, financial crime and money laundering.* International Monetary Fund, Washington, DC, 2001

Bosworth-Davies, R., Money laundering- chapter five: The implications of global money laundering laws. *Journal of Money Laundering Control*, 2007, *10* (2), pp. 189-208

Bowden, S., *Money laundering: key issues and possible action.* 1st edn. London, Commonwealth Secretariat, 1997

Chaikin, D., How effective are suspicious reporting transaction systems? *Journal of Money Laundering Control*, 2009, *12* (3), pp. 238-253.

Choo, K., Designated non-financial business and professionals: A review and analysis of recent financial action task force on money laundering mutual evaluation reports. *Security Journal,* (23 April 2012) doi:10.1057/sj.2012.9

Cuéllar, M., The tenuous relationship between the fight against money laundering and the disruption of criminal finance. *The journal of criminal law and criminology*, 2003, *93*, 2/3 pp 311-466

Duyne, P.C. van,. Money-laundering: estimates in fog. *Journal of Financial Crime*, 1994, *2* (1), pp. 58-74

FATF(2013) *About the FATF* Available at*:* http://www.fatf-gafi.org/pages/aboutus/. *(Accessed 3/3/13).*

FATF (2013) "*FATF issues new Mechanism to Strengthen Money Laundering and Terrorist Financing Compliance*" available at: http://www.fatf-gafi.org/topics/fatfrecommendations/documents/fatfissuesnewmechanismtostrengthenmoneylaunderingandterroristfinancingcompliance.html (accessed 26/4/13).

Goredema, C. and F. Monsti, Towards effective control of money laundering in Southern Africa: Some practical dilemmas. *African Security Studies*, 2002, *11* (1); 5-15

Harvey, J., An evaluation of money laundering policies. *Journal of Money Laundering Control*, 2005a, 8 (4), pp. 339-345

Harvey, J. (2005b) "Controlling the Flow of Money-Laundering or Satisfying the Regulators", Chapter 3, pp.43-64. In P.C. van Duyne, K. von Lampe, M. van Dijck, and J.L. Newell (eds.), *The organised crime economy: Managing crime markets in Europe*. Wolf Legal Publishersm, Tilburg, The Netherlands. 2005

Harvey, J., Just how effective is money laundering legislation? *The Security Journal*, 2008, Vol. *21*, pp. 189 – 211

Harvey, J., The search for crime money – debunking the myth: facts versus imagery. *Journal of Money Laundering Control*, 2009, *12* (2), pp. 97-100

Harvey, J and S.F. Lau, Crime money, reputation and reporting. *Crime Law and Social Change*, 2009, *52* (1), pp. 57-72

Harvey, J., R. Bosworth-Davies and M. Elliott, M., AML compliance: Rituals of engagement or improvements in integrity? pp 227-247. In P.C. van Duyne, J. Harvey, G.A. Antonopoulos, K. von Lampe, A.Maljević and J. Spencer (eds.), *Human dimensions in organised crime, money laundering and corruption*. Wolf Legal Publishers, Nijmegen, 2013

He, P., A typological study on money laundering. *Journal of Money Laundering Control,* 2010, 13 (1), pp. 15-32

Hopton, D., *Money laundering: A concise guide for all business*. 2nd edn. Surrey, Gower Publishing Ltd, 2009

Johnson, J. and Y. Lim, Money laundering: has the Financial Action Task Force made a difference? *Journal of Financial Crime*, 2003, *10* (1), pp. 7-22

Johnson, J., Australia's response to the FATF's 2003 40 recommendations. *Journal of Money Laundering Control*, 2005, *8* (4), pp. 297-304

Johnson, J., Third round FATF mutual evaluations indicate declining compliance. *Journal of Money Laundering Control*. 2008, *11* (1), pp. 47-66

Lai, L. (2010). 'Misuse of securities and futures markets by money launderers- a general overview', *Journal of Money Laundering Control*, 2010, *13* (1), pp. 66-69

Lehman, C., *Accounting's changing roles in social Conflict*. New York and Princeton: Markus Wiener Publishing Inc, 1992

Magnusson, D., The costs of implementing the anti-money laundering regulations in Sweden. *The Journal of Money Laundering Control*. 2009, *12* (2), pp. 101-112.

Mei Leong, A., Chasing dirty money: domestic and international measures against money laundering. *The Journal of Money Laundering Control*. 2007, *10* (2), pp. 140-156

Mugarura, N., The global anti-money laundering court as a judicial and institutional imperative. *The Journal of Money Laundering Control*, 2011, *14* (1), pp. 60-78.

Preller, S., Comparing AML legislation of the UK, Switzerland and Germany. *The Journal of Money Laundering Control*, 2008, *11* (3) pp. 234 – 250

Quirk, P., Macroeconomic implications of money laundering *IMF Staff Working Papers* WP/96/66, 1996 June, IMF Washington

Reuter, P. and E. Truman, Anti-money laundering overkill? *International Economy*, 2005, *19* (1) pp. 56-60

Rhodes, R. and S. Palastrand, A guide to money laundering legislation. *Journal of Money Laundering Control*, 2004, *8* (1), pp. 9-18

Sansonetti, R., The mutual evaluation process: a methodology of increasing importance at International Level. *Journal of Financial Crime*, 2000, 7 (3), pp. 218-226

Sharman J.C., Power and discourse in policy diffusion: anti-money laundering in developing states. *International studies quarterly*, 2008, *52* (3), pp. 635-656

Simser, J., The significance of money laundering: the examples of the Philippines. *The Journal of Money Laundering Control*, 2006, *9* (3), pp. 293-302.

Stigler, G., The theory of economic regulation. *Bell Journal of Economics and Management Science*, 1971, *2* (1), pp. 3-21

Sultinen, J. and K. Kuperan, A socio-economic theory of regulatory compliance. *International Journal of Social Economics*, 1999, *26* (1/2/3), pp. 174-193

Tang, J., Combating money laundering in transition countries: the inherent limitations and practical issues. *Journal of Money Laundering Control*, 2010, *13* (3), pp. 215-225

Williams, M., Building genuine trust through interpersonal emotion management: A threat regulation model of trust and collaboration across boundaries. *Academy of Management Review*, 2007, *32* (2), pp. 595-621

Greedy of crime-money
The reality and ethics of asset recovery

Petrus C. van Duyne, Wouter S. de Zanger and *François H.G. Kristen*[1]

Threat and greed of crime money

"Money makes greedy" is a platitudinous observation and of almost universal validity. It applies to individuals, corporations as well as states. Greed is a powerful motive and its satisfaction is frequently at odds with what is ethically and legally admissible, in particular if satisfied by crime. This leads to the second platitude: "Crime should not pay". This is the basic principle to deny law breakers the ill-gotten gains they obtained from their deeds. In addition, there are many subsidiary reasons for reclaiming those illegal profits. In the past decades these subsidiary reasons have attracted more attention than the simple crime-should-not-pay principle for which reason we bring this to the fore in this introduction.

These subsidiary reasons for attacking crime-money concern unwanted law enforcement and economic effects of leaving the crime-monies with the offenders. In terms of law enforcement it may lead to an erosion of the rule of law while saved crime-money remains available for re-investments in new criminal undertakings. That concern applies mainly to the underground economy of prohibited substances; most economic crimes, such as VAT or environmental fraud do not require must investment (Pashev, 2008). There are also unwanted macro-economic side-effects: the erosion of the integrity of the financial industry, destabilisation of the financial system and inflation because of the circulation of black money (Tanzi, 1996; Quirk, 1996; Barlett, 2002, ch. III).

These economic effects have been central in the presentation of the crime-money problem by the IMF: it sketched a kind of financial doom hovering above us, as a matter of fact, for decades. These have been widely accepted. But have they come true? Reuter (2013) looked for historical evidence, but found no unambiguous

---

1 The authors are: Professor of Empirical Criminal Law, Tilburg University; PhD Candidate at Utrecht University and Professor of Criminal Law, Utrecht University. The project has been funded by the Dutch Central Recovery Agency.

confirmation: yes there are many laundering scandals but no evidence of macro-financial systemic instability due to laundering.[2] Actually, these crime-money threat messages rather remind us of the prophesied doom of the biblical Nineveh by Jonah. But Nineveh was saved because its inhabitants converted to the 'right path', which is not a likely scenario in the world of criminal finances and crime-entrepreneurs. Instead, criminal finances continue to play a role in our society though their effects remain a matter of speculation: there are no indications the economists' doom prophesies have come true. In contrast, it was not the *existing* crime-monies in circulation, but the phantom credits deceptively created by greedy bankers *that* wreaked havoc on the global financial system. The deceptive creation of this phantom money proved to be more dangerous than stealing and laundering 'existing' money. Surprisingly, there is not a single line of reference in the money laundering literature to a potential laundering of the proceeds of this bankers' intentional deception.[3]

Despite this difference, virtually all jurisdictions have enacted a legal system to reclaim ill-gotten funds (not bankers' bonuses) as their undisturbed availability is considered a threat to society, whether in terms of jeopardising upperworld finances or undermining the morality of the financial system.

Following the IMF and later the FATF (gu)estimates, there are strong internationally held beliefs about the staggering volume of crime-money earned each year of which an unspecified part is 'available for laundering' (FATF, 1990; Keh. 1996; UNODC, 2011). Such strong beliefs cannot but strengthen the threat image as well as the expectations about the potential volume of recoverable crime-monies. How far are such expectations free of greed? Naturally, from the perspective of restorative justice ill-gotten profits should be returned to the victims and the public in general. However, there are indications that law enforcement recovery enthusiasm is also fuelled by greed or bounty hunting (Rasmussen and Benson, 1994; p. 137;). Extravagant manifestations of asset recovery in the US should be taken as a serious warning that the greed of the authorities may grow on a par with that of criminals. Criminal assets recovery policy turned into a budget targeting independent of the principles of restoring justice (Blumenson and Nilsen, 1997).

2 Reuter refers the mention by the IMF of Latvia in the 1990's and the Dominican Republic in 2002, to which he adds that it remains unclear whether financial problems should not be attributed to the predicate offences.

3 Though the selling of pretended triple A mortgages to clients was a 'white money' business, the trade and thereby the profit was based on criminal deception of the clients, contemptuously called 'muppets'. This profit is proceed. Likewise, the profits made from the Libor-fraud produced proceeds and receiving these in the form of a 'white' bonus fall under the definition of laundering.

Is the Dutch criminal asset recovery policy exempt *from* such tendencies? Not *a priori*, though examples of US-style excessive confiscations are lacking. Nevertheless, this does not rule out a greedy policy driven by unrealistically high expectations leading to unfounded criminal assets recovery targets. Is that only window dressing or has it also practical consequences? This chapter will investigate the practice of the Dutch criminal asset recovery system, its turnover, yield and its extra coercive powers against the background of (high) expectations and related targets.

High expectations

As elsewhere, Dutch policy makers and politicians share the general belief of the existence of a (threatening) huge volume of criminal funds. Since reports issued by the United Nations estimated the amount of crime-money worldwide at one trillion US dollar *per year*, this has become a kind of the official tenet (Keh, 1996; Van Duyne *et al.*, 2005), though some zealots go beyond this number (Walker, 1999; Walker and Unger, 2009). Governments elaborating or implementing legislation against crime-money and laundering have no reason to question this official international stand which justifies their efforts. This also applies to the Dutch government: the Ministers of Justice and Finance equally expressed their strong belief of the vast amounts of crime-money in The Netherlands. This belief was strengthened by a research project conducted by Unger *et al.* (2007), commissioned by the Ministry of Finance, the FATF-portfolio holder and not likely to deviate from the official FATF stand.[4]

Given this official stance it is interesting to observe the creation of a political reality. Unger's research project worked with a debatable hypothetical economic model[5] and filled here and there some blanks with hypothetical numbers of money flows and also some empirical observations of diverse reliability. Based on this mixture of hypothetical assumptions and observations the report concluded there was a hypothetical volume of crime-money of € 18,5 billion *either transiting* through or being laundered within the Netherlands. Irrespective of this ambiguous formulation, in the end the figure of € 18,5 billion obtained a political 'reality by citation' in the subsequent parliamentary debate on crime-money in the Netherlands (see Harvey, 2011)._Though such a creation goes against the idea of 'evidence based' policy

4 Unger e.a., *The amounts and the effects on money laundering. Report for the Ministry of Finance*, Den Haag 2006.

5 Walker, 1996. Reuter (2013) points at the incredibly high profit margins. Van Duyne and Soudijn (2010) point at grave methodological flaw, such as ratings by unqualified officers who have no broader view than the little desk they are sitting at.

making, it is not exceptional. This shift from 'maybe' to fact could already be observed with the wording of the FATF 1990 report and the following debate: the report's wording is in the subjunctive mode – '*may*' and '*could-be*' – which in the general debate soon turned into the indicative *is*-mode (Van Duyne *et al.*, 2005) and after a few rounds of citations turned into an iron cast truth.

Unsurprisingly there proved to be a gap between belief and reality: the (gu)estimate of € 18,5 billion versus about € 30 million recovered at the time (2011).[6] As belief usually prevails, this did not lead to a reassessment of expectations but to a strengthening of the existing belief, because "there *must* be more!" and: "criminals are always one step ahead of us". This bolstered conviction found its expression in the political debate and policy-making concerning this topic. In the parliamentary introduction to enhanced (legislative and policing) efforts, references were made to these assumed flows of illegal proceeds to justify this more severe policy.[7] High expectations of the rise of income for the state from confiscations can also be found in the parliamentary debate preceding the amendment of the bill on the Extension of Recovery Possibilities (2011). Under the heading 'financial consequences', the Minister wrote that due to the proposed amendments of the law[8], the expected revenues from assets recovery will rise to € 30 million in 2011 and then structurally to € 35 million as of 2013.[9] However, it was pure feel-good speculation and window dressing. When members of the liberal party (VVD) asked for an explanation as to the source of these numbers[10], the minister evaded a clear answer: the numbers were simply extrapolated from the sums recovered in the previous years, and it was expected that the increased intensification of the combat against financial crime would lead to a further (linear) increase of the recovered proceeds.[11] This did not satisfy all MPs. An MP (Recourt, PvdA-labour party) confronted the minister of Justice with the 'fact' that the amount of criminal assets is estimated at around € 15 billion, while only around € 35 million was budgeted as prospective recovery (discussion March 2012). In the ensuing discussion the minister promised to increase

---

6 *Kamerstukken II* 2009/10, 32 194, no. 3, p. 19 (Memorie van Toelichting).

7 *Kamerstukken II* 2009/10, 32 194, no. 5, p. 2-3 (Verslag), *Handelingen II* 2009/10, 77, 15 April 2010, p. 6565, 6567, 6570, 6575,

8 De *Wet Verruiming mogelijkheden Voordeelsontneming*. Staatsblad 2011, 171. It concerned, among others, the introduction of a legal presumption concerning the illegality of proceeds (*bewijsvermoeden*) and the extension of the seizure possibilities of property under a third person (*anderbeslag*).

9 *Kamerstukken II* 2009/10, 32 194, no. 3, p. 19 (MvT). This expected rise in income for the state was at that point already accounted for in the budget of the Ministry of Justice.

10 *Kamerstukken II* 2009/10, 32 194, no. 5, p. 15 (Verslag).

11 *Kamerstukken II* 2009/10, 32 194, no. 6, p. 20 (Nota naar aanleiding van het verslag).

the amount of recovered assets and in addition promised to achieve concrete targets: while € 48 million was recovered that previous year (2011), the target was to increase with around 100%, to € 100 million the following year (2013).[12]

This was little else than a juggling with figures, let alone an educated guess, rather a kind of thoughtless political reflex: reassuring Parliament by raising unfounded expectations gullibly accepted by them without any further questions. Certainly not a display of evidence based policy making. A driving factor was not only an understandable concern about the extent of crime-money in the economy, but also the consideration of filling the state coffer by intensified asset recovery. Concrete and detailed expectations of potential income for the state were expressed. With such high expectations (or greed) and lofty promises few asked whether this was realistic.

An important underlying driving force is the 'organised crime' theme which has an enormous policy making leverage. Measures that serve the fight against 'organised crime' (and terrorism) are easier justified or less criticised than if put forward under another more general criminal policy umbrella.[13] From the beginning of the anti-organised crime policy in the late 1980s, this theme has been ever present in policy documents and parliamentary history (Van Duyne, 2004).[14] However, this time the organised crime issue was juxtaposed by another theme: *financial crimes* as an additional source of recoverable criminal assets. It is interesting to observe that less attention was paid to the right of *victims* (enterprises and persons) to compensation from the recovered assets. While the principle of restorative justice was referred to (bringing criminals back to their financial *status quo ante*), the emphasis also was on the revenues for the state: as mentioned, wishful thinking without facts or figures. No questions were raised about the effectiveness of the present criminal assets recovery regime or the functioning of the most important agency in this field, the *Central Recovery Agency* (CRA).

This CRA is the essential executive body in the chain of freezing, confiscation and the execution of the recovery orders. Functioning literally as a final stop in the criminal revenue recovery procedure, its 'yield' can be considered as a proxy for criminal wealth still available after conviction. Apart from the normal – civil law – debt recovery powers, the CRA has a special power to 'induce' debtors to pay: it can request the Public Prosecution to address the Court to apply a *coercive custody of*

---

12 *Handelingen II* 2011/12, 68, 27 March 2012, p. 11. There is some confusion: according to a press release that figure would be reached in 2018 (ANP 26-1-2011).

13 For example the Law on Integer Decision Making in the Administration (BIBOB, 2003).

14 Among many others: proposal for a Directive of the European Parliament and of the Council on the freezing and confiscation of proceeds of crime in the European Union, COM(2012) 85 final, p. 3 and *Kamerstukken II* 2009/10, 32 194, no. 3, p. 1.

maximum three years for defaulting convicts who are suspected of 'unwillingness to pay'. That is not a punishment but a (tough) recovery measure that is intended to yield full payment. What are its effects in terms of recovered assets? And how does that reflect on the high expectations and targets set by policy makers?

The Dutch recovery procedure in a nutshell

According to the Dutch criminal system the Public Prosecutor can file a request for a recovery of the illegally obtained profits. With the exception of fiscal offences, the recovery order can concern all kinds of criminal offences and all profits (even if spent or lost) which are plausibly derived from crime ("sufficient indications"). The recovery Court has much latitude in determining the amount of the criminal profits, which also includes saved expenses. The judge can deduct some (not all) of the criminal business costs in which he is rather free to use assumptions and 'rules of thumb' which is characteristic for the whole criminal profit assessment procedure. Some of these rules of thumb are debated as they may lead to a higher recovery sum than what the convict has actually earned: for example extrapolating the turnover by multiplying one the weekly average by the number of weeks the dealer was assumed to be in operation irrespective of periods of slack trade. The judge is also free to moderate the amount of the recovery sum if there are reasons for such a moderation, *e.g.* a disabled drug dealer without capacity for paid work.

Once the recovery order is final, the CRA gets the task to execute it.[15] To that end it can first of all sell off the confiscated assets. If that is less than the recovery sum or if there are no confiscated assets, the convict is summoned to pay. If the latter claims to have no money and no income he can file for a payment reduction or even remission of debt to the Court. The CRA can also settle for an instalment scheme. If the CRA has serious doubts about the sincerity of the defaulting debtor, for example it has reasons to suspect that assets are hidden somewhere, it can propose the Public Prosecution to file a request at the Court to apply the measure of *coercive custody*. If the Court shares the opinion of the Public Prosecutor that the non-payment is due to lack of willingness it can impose a number of "coercive custody days", proportionate to the amount of unpaid money with a maximum of 3 years. This is not a "replacement custody", serving time instead of paying: this has been abolished in

15 The CRA has the legal obligation to execute all financial sanctions. It functions 'on behalf of' the Public Prosecutor's Office and under the responsibility of the Minister of Security and Justice.

2003 (for recovery orders only) but is still applied to cases finalised before September 2003. If the convict is still at large without known residence an arrest warrant can be issued. Otherwise he can be put on the 'wanted list' (a system not changed by the 2003 law).

Once the coercive custody is imposed the convict still can negotiate a settlement with the CRA: suspension or release in exchange for a down payment and/or an instalment scheme. If the convict fails to comply with the instalment scheme he can be arrested to serve the remainder of his custody days. This system allows for much flexibility to coerce convicted criminals to pay off the recovery order. This indicates that the full execution of a recovery order can take much time and effort: getting crime money cost money and time. We will provide more details in a later section.

Method of research

This chapter presents the selected outcomes of a larger research project that consisted of a legal study and analysis as well as an empirical investigation. This chapter will only present the findings of the empirical part of the project for which reason, we will only elaborate the methodological aspects concerning the analysis of the data from the CRA database and criminal files. These consist of the administrative database of the CRA and a selection of criminal recovery files.

The CRA database

The CRA provided the research team with two separate sub-databases: *finalised* and *on-going* recovery cases. The databases have identical variables, but despite that they cannot be fused: the '*on-going* database' contains only cases from an initial recovery sum of € 10.000 and more. This means that the low-end tail of the frequency distribution is cut off. This has consequences for the comparison of the finalised with the on-going cases of which the 'lower legs' have been cut off.

Another impediment is the large number of missing values, particularly concerning the *predicate offences* which were very often missing. This means that cross-break analyses with the predicate offences as one of the lead variables resulted in a significant reduction of the number of cases. The total number of *finalised cases* is 10.012 with 2.377 (23,7%) missing values on the *offence* variable. In terms of money involved: the total initial recovery sum for *all* cases is € 133.027.389, while the deduction of records because of missing values (offences and other) resulted in a shrunken database of 7.635 cases with a recovery sum of € 63.454.861. That implies that with the criminal offence variable failing, more than half of the total value of all the finalised recovery orders remains in the 'missing value box'.

This is not the only *caveat.* The fact that a case has been marked as 'finalised' does not imply that all the money mentioned in the column 'initial recovery sum' has actually been paid. In fact, in 1.204 cases (12%) the last category of 'finalising activity' contains mode of *non*-payment. For example, 640 convicted debtors were imprisoned under the old regime of '*replacement* custody' ('sitting' instead of paying); 131 died before (full) payment; in 203 cases the Court reduced the debt without the amount recorded in the database; or the case terminated as "uncollectable" (94), etc. In these 1.204 cases, € 29.783.748 remained unpaid. That is 75,2 % of the total payment obligations in these cases.

Furthermore, in 121 other cases the Court in the execution phase had already mitigated the payment obligation before the finalising activity. So, when taken together with the 1.204 mentioned cases above, a total of 1.325 (13,2%) finalised cases ended without ever being fully paid: in total € 33.291.401 remained unpaid in these cases. This represents 25% of the total initial payment obligation in all the (10.012) finalised cases. So the column under the heading 'finalised' does certainly not mean 'paid'. Indeed, 25% remained unpaid. A little more than twelve million Euros have been 'earned' by criminals by doing time in replacement custody. Almost 11 million Euros was reduced from the main debt by the Court in the execution phase on the request of the debtor in view of his insolvency.

Of the *on-going* cases 7% went into the box of 'inactive' and 'bankrupt' cases, representing 20% (€ 44.103.131) of the *unpaid* debt. Though this represents a considerable part of the total recovery sum, the databases still do not make clear how much has to be written-off (see section a, Table 1).

The sub-database of the *on-going* cases does not show the defect of missing values on the offence variable: of the 2.756 cases there are only 98 with missing values on the offence variable. However, as mentioned above, the subset of < € 10.000 cases have not been included, allegedly being the 'easy' recoveries (which is questionable in view of the processing time of small debts: see section b table 3). If we were allowed to extrapolate from the *finalised* database the estimate would be that this recovery class could be about 79% of the on-going cases. This is hypothetical as there are too many uncertainties for such an extrapolation from one database to another. All together a clear warning never to take an official database for granted.

Apart from a unique case number, codes for the court region, birth date, confiscation and the initial recovery sum, date of inflow and the predicate offence(s) (if not missing and otherwise in many cases more than one), both databases mention the last recorded recovery activity such as: "preparing for settlement", "monitoring settlement", "putting on the warrant list", preparing for "coercive custody". The *on-*

going database mentions also the sum still unpaid at the time of the last recovery activity. Naturally in these on-going cases this is only a temporary mention. The *finalised* database contains the date of finalisation and the way of finalising the case, such as "payment to the bailiff", "payment to the police", "death of debtor", "custody", "uncollectable", etc.

The offence variable consists of four columns which provides room for multiple offences per case. In the official criminal statistics offences are usually listed in order of decreasing seriousness according to their maximum penalty. In these two databases it was uncertain whether this order was also maintained. In addition, various offences were 'instrumentally connected' in the sense that one offence is enabling the commission of the main profit making offence. For example, cannabis growing requires much energy which is very often obtained by illegally tapping into the electricity grid. This is recorded as 'theft' or 'breaking' (if the meter is broken) as a secondary offence. Subsequently handling the revenues from the cannabis growing counts as laundering, being the third offence. All this can be done in cooperation with other perpetrators, which results in the additional offence of 'participating in a criminal organisation'. We simplified this complexity by taking the most likely *money making* offence and inspected whether it was mentioned in conjunction with *participation in a criminal organisation* (+OC). For example we created the two categories: 'soft drugs' and 'soft drugs + OC'. Further differentiation with additional offences was possible, but would lead to ever smaller absolute numbers and to half empty cross-breakdown tables.

The criminal file analysis

In addition to this statistical survey of the two total databases it was considered of interest to explore how the threat of custody worked in real life cases. To this end a sample of 35 cases has been drawn from 738 'coercive custody cases' (a coercive measure was prepared or executed) for more detailed examination. This was not a *random* but a layered selection to get a cross-section through the levels of criminal revenue in the recovery set. Our main interest concerned the cases with the high recovery sums: the supposedly 'rich' criminals to find out how the coercive recovery worked at this criminal echelon. Therefore, the largest group (20 criminal files) facing a coercive custody threat or actual custody had a high recovery order: above € 300.000. Five cases had a lower recovery sum around the general midpoint of € 15.000 and five cases were at the absolute low end of the recovery distribution, ranging from € 400 – 570. Besides these thirty cases, five additional cases with a *successfully applied coercion* were studied to explore the contribution of coercion to a successful finalisation.

Findings

a. General overview and uncertainties in the databases

The general overview has to be divided into the two sets of on-going cases and finalised cases. As explained above, the truncated on-going database lacks the < € 10.000 cases for which reason it cannot be fused with the set of finalised cases. This implies that presenting the cases by year of inflow has to be done separately.

Table 1 provides an overview of the total on-going recovery cases from 1995 onwards.

Table 1
***On-going* cases: number, recovery sum and unpaid proportion**

Year inflow	N	Recovery order €	Unpaid €	% of recovery sum unpaid
1995	3	53.474	36.159	68
1996	17	693.417	450.854	65
1997	12	450.957	333.800	74
1998	13	509.985	270.012	53
1999	18	983.441	730.682	74
2000	26	2.343.612	1.484.138	63
2001	13	1.193.587	1.050.758	88
2002	41	4.332.347	2.103.522	49
2003	79	10.648.244	8.112.032	76
2004	197	47.956.571	41.846.582	87
2005	213	19.595.277	12.667.599	65
2006	269	22.099.917	18.135.362	82
2007	349	45.548.337	22.438.427	49
2008	368	24.864.186	20.525.061	83
2009	345	43.375.372	38.307.596	88
2010	349	24.939.109	22.406.882	90
2011	434	42.601.592	37.958.858	89
2012*	10	298.139	298.139	100
Total	2.756	292.487.565	229.156.464	**78**

* The database was produced in March 2012: Therefore 10 cases in that year are still open.

As Table 1 shows 78% of the imposed recovery sums in the set of on-going cases is still not paid (2012). Is there a 'coercive custody effect'? If we take September 2003, the year of the introduction of the coercive custody measure as the dividing line, the average unpaid custody sum before 2004 is 69%. From 2004 onwards 79% of the recovery sum is still unpaid, which does not look like an improvement. However, the time factor may compound the outcome: older cases (before 2003) tend to be more often settled. There is a moderately significant correlation between year of registration and the percentage of unpaid recovery sum: Spearman's rho = 0,56; sign. 0,024. However, there are extreme values that can affect the outcomes per year. For example, the exceptional high rate of payment in 2007 is determined by one case with a recovery sum of € 22,5 million of which € 18 million was paid (the remainder went into the 'inactive stock').

If we look again at differences of the recovery sums between the years, we observe a steep rise in the recovery sum of the case inflow but also a relative rise in unpaid debts. Can we differentiate the years before and after the 'coercive custody law'? With all reservations, looking at the averages per year we find substantial differences before and after 2004: for 1995-2003, a mean of unpaid debts of € 65.639 and for the 2004-2011 time span, a mean of € 107.361. Is this a coincidence or a causality?

Table 2
***Finalised* cases: number and statistics of initial recovery sum**

Year inflow	N	Mean €	Median €	Sum €	Maximum €
1995	86	25.497	5.604	2.192.732	850.838
1996	141	15.550	5.445	2.192.488	453.780
1997	244	28.184	4.538	6.877.000	3.785.339
1998	192	10.425	3.310	2.001.561	181.512
1999	331	14.110	3.442	4.670.259	695.320
2000	305	24.781	3.959	7.558.110	1.878.650
2001	411	10.760	3.403	4.422.450	453.780
2002	613	10.656	3.015	6.532.047	920.000
2003	1.052	11.785	2.723	12.397.822	593.998
2004	1.076	12.764	2.990	13.733.728	1.183.137
2005	1.110	10.869	3.000	12.064.680	1.250.000
2006	1.162	13.811	3.500	16.130.226	1.486.514
2007	1.053	10.422	3.414	10.974.477	945.000
2008	842	10.669	3.469	8.983.190	600.000
2009	634	14.686	3.287	9.311.036	1.217.000
2010	450	20.557	3.820	9.250.531	2.273.844
2011	309	12.007	4.000	3.710.054	565.760
Total	10.011	13.286	3.310	133.002.389	3.785.339

When we look at the database of finalised cases, as presented in Table 2, we find interesting differences between the central indexes of mean and median.

As can be observed, the difference between the mean and median is large indicating a *skewed* distribution. This means that lower sums have a high frequency and high recovery sums are rare. Of the maximum recovery sums for each year, in only seven years it is above one million Euros, while the median as midpoint remained roughly around € 3.500. The mean shows a larger deviation over the years: from € 10.422 in 2007 to € 28.184 in 1997. The skewness of the frequency division is visualised in figure 1.

Figure 1
Recovery sum intervals and their frequencies of finalised cases

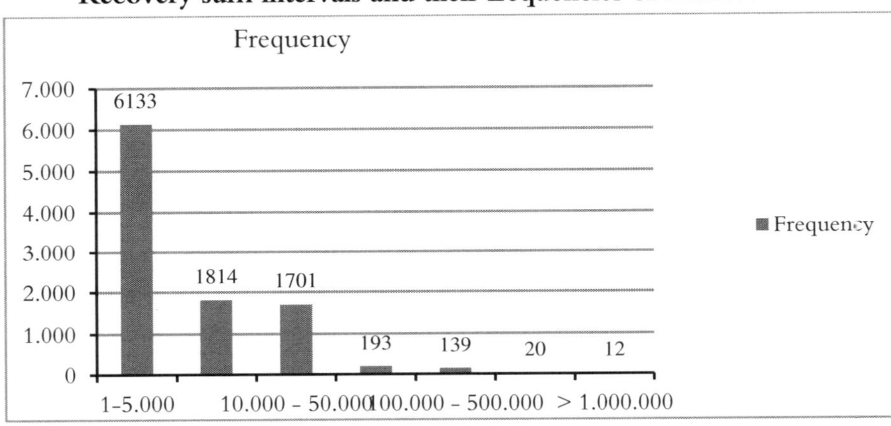

Against 6.133 cases of less than € 5.000 on the low end we have 364 cases with recovery sums of € 50.000 or more of which only 12 are more than one million Euros. This is not unique: the recoveries received by the UK Asset Recovery Agency had an equally skewed distribution: 50% was under £ 50.000 and 6% in the interval of > £ 1 million (National Audit Office, 2007).

When we repeat our question concerning the potential effects of the 2003 coercion custody law and compare the averages between the two time spans of 1995-2003 and 2004-2011 in this finalised database, we do not observe any noticeable difference: the respective means are € 14.472 and € 12.684. This contrasts with the on-going cases where the effect was negative: a larger proportion of unpaid debts after 2003.

b. Getting the money: how long does it take?

From an efficiency perspective it is important to know how much time it takes to get the recovery orders fully paid. We have already seen in Table 1 that *on-going* cases can have a long history: the oldest stemming from 1995 while 45% of the cases was older than 5 years measured from end 2011. This gives already an indication that it takes time to achieve a full payment of the recovery orders. Therefore we have to look at the *finalised* cases for the full execution time. This is represented in Table 3 in which the execution time is broken down by intervals of the recovery sum.

Table 3
Execution time (in years) of finalised cases by recovery sum interval

Intervals of the recovery sum in €	N	Mean year	Median year	Maximum years
1-5.000	6.133	2,3	1,2	16,1
5.000-10.000	1.814	2,8	1,8	15,9
10.000-50.000	1.701	3,1	2,1	16,1
50.000-100.000	193	3,5	2,5	14,9
100.000-500.000	139	3,5	2,8	12,0
500.000-1.000.000	20	3,7	2,1	16,1
>1.000.000	12	3,5	1,8	14,6
Total	10.012	2,6	1,5	16,1

As is clear from Table 3, making criminals pay takes time: on average 2,6 years (median 1,5). As the comparison of the mean and median shows, not only the money variable, but also the time distribution is skewed with a few number of extremes pulling the mean to the high end: 18,6% lasted more than 5 years; four cases of them lasted 16 years; other cases ended after 14 and 15 years with custody; or finally with the admission that further execution efforts will be fruitless.

If we look at the median we see that biggest deviation from the mean, and therefore high extremes, can be found in the ≥ € 1.000.000 cases though their absolute frequencies are low. However, taking the median values, the main delays are not found within this highest recovery category, but lower, in the € 100.000 – 500.000 group followed by the next lower group. The low recovery category of € 1 - 5.000 had the shortest execution time, but still on average 2,3 years (median 1,2 years also indicating large extremes). The correlation between execution time and recovery sum was low: $r = 0{,}053$, but still significant at .05 (due to a large N). If execution time could be interpreted as a proxy-indicator to the inability (or unwillingness) to pay, this seems to be spread across all debt levels of the criminal debtor population.

What is the picture of the *on-going* cases? Naturally we cannot speak here of an execution time span, though we can measure the time between the entry date of the cases and the latest known recovery task, which we call the '*arrear time*'. We remind again of the *caveat* of not having the lower interval cases (< € 10.000) in this data base. This is reflected in the higher arrear time average: 2,8 year; median 2,1 year (compare: finalised cases 2,5 year; median 1,4).

The recovery tasks that have the longest arrear time are: issuing an arrest warrant plus monitoring it (5,3 years: 20 cases) and monitoring the execution of the coercive custody (4,6 years). A special category is the 'inactive work stock': 4,6 years. One may also call them 'sleeping cases' to be reactivated when the debtor is able to pay or emerges again. There was no correlation between the volume of the recovery sum and the arrear time (R = 0,017). Again: making criminals pay is apparently at all levels a time consuming task. A further differentiation according to crime type is presented in section d.

c. 'Squeezing' the criminal debtor: coercive measures (or not)

1. *The general picture*

As few profit oriented criminals will hand in their ill-gotten gains because of pangs of conscience, the awareness of some ultimate 'strong hand' measure in the form of the coercive custody can act as an anticipating 'encouragement' to comply with the recovery order. This would imply that with such an awareness coercion may remain in the background. This is not always the case: the criminal debtor can pretend not to be able to pay when he has hidden the 'loot'. Or he has squandered the criminal revenues on the usual trinity of slow horses, fast cars and expensive women. But extravagance and dissipation does not liberate him from the duty to pay his ill-gotten revenues back: as long as he has some income he is supposed to have a 'payment capacity', either to pay in full or in agreed instalments and if he defaults on this arrangement the threat of the coercive custody is activated (again) and suspended as a kind of 'sword of Damocles' – but without any prospect of debt reduction: doing time does not wipe out debt. But that does not come down unexpectedly: it is suspended with a lot of warnings and rattling while the criminal debtor has the opportunity to explain to the Court that he is willing but 'really' insolvent. How often is that threat invoked and how does that work?

The threat of coercion is not often used. It appears that most cases could be finalised without rattling 'Damocles' sword': only in 6,8 % of the cases was custody threatened or actually applied with a total recovery sum at stake of € 12.887.948 which is 9,7 % of the recovery sum of the finalised cases.

In the on-going cases the use of coercive measures occurred (thus far) in 337 cases which is 12% of the cases (above € 10.000) and in which € 40.596.178 is involved. That is 14% of the recovery sum in on-going cases. Because of the 'amputation' of the < € 10.000 category in the on-going database, a very large subset, we restrict the rest of the analysis to the finalized cases.

What is the precise picture of the coercion cases, taking account of the amount of money, execution time, type of offences and coercion? Table 4 provides a first more detailed overview of the finalised coercion cases with the imposed recovery sums divided in intervals.

Table 4
Coercive measures broken down by intervals of recovery sum & mean and median of the recovery sums

Coercive measure	€ 1- 5.000	€ 5.000- 10.000	€ 10.000 - 50.000	€ 50.000- 100.000	€ 100.000 - 500.000	€ 500.000- 1.000.000	€ >1. million	Total N	Mean €	Median €
Preparation custody (incl. replacement)	76	20	17	3	2	1	1	120	25.863	3.244
	63,4%	16,7%	14,2%	2,5%	1,7%	0,8%	0,8%	100%		
Submission custody request	10	5	4	1	1	0	0	21	22.589	5.000
	47,6%	23,8%	19%	4,8%	4,8%	0	0	100%		
Issuing arrest war-rant	15	6	6	0	2	0	0	29	15.438	4.538
	51,7%	20,7%	20,7%	0%	6,9%	0	0%	100%		
Forwarding and monitoring arrest warrant	154	49	103	14	13	0	0	333	19.318	5.604
	46,2%	14,7%	30,9%	4,2%	3,9%	0	0%	100%		
Monitoring custody execution	85	40	43	6	4	0	0	178	13.649	5.433
	47,8%	22,5%	24,2%	3,4%	2,2%	0	0%	100%		
Total coercion	340	120	173	24	22	1	1	681	18.925	5.000
	49,9%	17,6%	25,4%	3,5%	3,2%	0,1%	0,1%	100%		
Coercion in % of finalised cases	5,5	6,6	10,2	12,4	15,8	5	8,3	6,8		
Total finalised	6.133	1.814	1.701	193	139	20	12	10.012	13.287	3.311
	61,3%	18,1%	17,0%	1,9%	1,4%	0,2%	0,10%	100%		

The coercive measures appear to be the smaller part of the activities to collect the recovery sums: as mentioned they occurred in 6,8% of the cases (681). These coercive actions concerned: 'preparing' the coercive custody procedure (120 cases[16]), actually executing the custody order (178) or putting someone on the warrant list (333 cases after a court order of a custodial term *in absentia* and no known residence). The total initial recovery sum of the coercion cases is € 13 million.

Exerting coercion (encompassing all actions from light to severe: from preparing to locking up) occurred relatively most often in the € 100.000 - 500.000 interval: 15,8%, but rarely in the next higher level; € 500.000-1.000.000. In the lowest interval (< € 5.000) the least coercion cases occurred: only 5,5% though this interval accounts for 61% of the total finalised database. Nevertheless, it should be noted that the measure of coercive custody is not reserved for the 'high earners': 48% of the 178 *executed custody* orders concerned debts of less than € 5.000.

Compared to the frequency distribution of all the coercion cases, in the cases of filing a request for custody or executing a custodial order, there appears to be a small overrepresentation in the € 5.000 - 50.000 intervals. The same applies to arrest warrants. Otherwise the coercive custody measures (and follow-up steps such as arrest warrant) is applied proportionally across the whole range of debtors and are not only reserved for 'high earners', of which there are not many anyhow.

2. *Execution time and coercion*

An important aspect of the recovery procedure is the relationship between the various execution steps and the execution time as has already been indicated above. Table 5 provides a picture of the execution times broken down by the coercion steps.

Table 5

Coercion and execution time of *finalised* cases. In years.

Coercive measures	N	Mean	Median	Maximum
Preparation replacement custody*	22	7,9	7,2	14,3
Preparation coercive custody	98	2,8	2,4	7,7
Issuing arrest warrant	29	5,1	3,9	13,7
Submission custody request	21	3,8	3,4	7,1
Forwarding and monitoring arrest warrant	333	6,3	5,8	14,8
Monitoring custody execution	178	6,9	6,6	15,0
Total	681	5,9	5,5	15,0
All cases	10.012	2,6	1,5	16,1

* Cases under the old recovery regime of replacement custody before Sept. 2003

16 These included 22 cases of replacement custody under the pre-2003 law.

Unsurprisingly, cases which finally lead to coercion measures last on average longer: they take twice the execution time than is the case with non-coercive cases: 5,9 years compared to 2,6 years (median 1,5 year). This is partly due to the old cases under the previous recovery law of replacement custody (till Sept. 2003). But apart from that, it is clear that putting debtors in jail (letting the sword of Damocles come down = 'monitoring custody execution'), occurs only after a very long processing time: on average almost seven years.

Coercive measures, or the threat thereof, also occurred in on-going cases. A direct comparison with the finalised cases is not possible as with on-going cases the last recorded recovery task of threatening custody can be followed up by one or more others execution actions. Nevertheless, it is of interest to compare the execution time as a temporary delay concerning coercive measures. In 161 cases, no execution time till the coercive measures was known. Because of these missing values the total N is therefore 2.595 instead of 2.756.

Table 6

Execution time till coercive measures: *on-going* cases. In years

	N	Mean	Median	Maximum
Preparation replacement custody*	1	4,0	4,0	4,0
Preparation coercive custody	127	3,1	3,0	7,9
Submission custody request	93	2,6	2,1	7,1
Forwarding and monitoring arrest warrant	20	5,3	4,3	14,5
Monitoring custody execution	96	4,6	4,2	13,8
Total	337	3,5	3,2	14,5
Total all ongoing case	2.595	2,8	2,1	15,8

* Cases under the old recovery regime of replacement custody before Sept. 2003

Also in this database, the coercive cases last on average longer than is the case with the total set, although the difference is less substantial than with the finalised cases. Also, the distribution is less skewed. It is a matter of speculation whether these distribution characteristics will disappear as soon as these on-going cases reach the 'finalised' status.

3. *Outcome of coercive actions*

What is the outcome of the coercive actions? What happens as a response to the decision to prepare coercion measures, such as submitting a request to the Court or subsequently, issuing an arrest warrant or finally executing a custody order? The outcomes are displayed in Table 7. It presents what happened after the last recovery action: whether paid or not and the outcome of the last recovery action.

Table 7
Last recovery action and results of coercion cases: defaulting and paying debtors

	Outcome of defaulting debtors					Paid		
Last recovery action with coercion	Custody	Reduc tion	Other	N	Initial recovery sum €	Settled sum €[17]	N	Total initial recovery sum €
Preparation replacement custody	1	1	5	7	33.770	214.231	15	248.001
Preparation coercive custody	0	7	5	12	248.005	2.607.613	86	2.855.618
Submission custody request	0	4	0	4	381.881	92.493	17	474.374
Issuing arrest warrant	2	0	1	3	26.029	421.671	26	447.700
Forwarding & monitoring arrest warrant	150	0	3	153	3.568.751	2.864.011	180	6.432.762
Monitoring custody execution	73	3	2	78	1.314.479	1.115.014	100	2.429.493
Total	226	15	16	257	5.572.915	7.315.033	424	12.887.948

As can be observed in Table 7, most debtors found the means to pay: 424 (62,3%): being aware of an arrest warrant (180) or actually facing imprisonment. Of the 257 debtors who still could not or did not want to pay most served time: 226 (33% of all coercion cases = 681). Against most of them an arrest warrant was issued (153). 15 cases resulted in a request for debt reduction, in 4 cases the prosecution waved further execution and 9 debtors died pending the custody procedure. In terms of money value the 'success' was less pronounced: the initial sum for which the debtors settled (62,3% of these cases) represents 56,8% of the total recovery sum of this coercion subset.

17 The debt settlement does not necessarily imply that the whole debt has been paid: there could be a reduction which was not recorded. It only says: "remaining debt = 0".

It is clear that the coercive custody remains a pressure tool while to most of the debtors it is also clear that it is a real sword of Damocles which has to be averted because of its reality value. Nevertheless, from these figures one cannot deduce any yardstick for estimating efficiency or effectiveness.

d. Recovery per crime category: money, time and coercion

Table 8
Recovery sums and execution time of finalised cases. In € and years per crime category

			Recovery sum €			Execution time in years	
Offences	**N**	**Total €**	**Mean €**	**Median €**		**Mean years**	**Median years**
Soft drugs	3.497	20.568.406	5.882	3.000		1,6	0,8
Soft drugs + OC	81	1.507.043	18.605	5.370		2,0	0,8
Hard drugs	1.468	13.831.956	9.422	3.000		3,2	2,1
Hard drugs + OC	116	2.579.115	22.234	5.913		3,5	2,7
Fraud and other	641	7.281.597	11.360	2.500		3,4	2,6
Fraud and other + OC	33	2.051.202	62.158	15.429		4,8	5,8
Property crime	1.120	3.550.909	3.170	1.361		3,8	3,3
Property + OC	56	1.114.288	19.898	8.612		3,6	1,9
Hum. traff. & smuggling	73	830.969	11.383	3.403		2,6	1,2
Hum. traff. & smuggl + OC	17	386.407	22.730	3.959		3,2	2,7
M. laundering	210	1.693.900	8.066	1.825		2,4	1.1
M. laun.+ OC	9	160.466	17.830	10.494		3,5	1,8
OC + other	28	2.352.666	84.024	8.177		3,2	2,0
Other crimes	286	5.545.937	19.391	2.711		1,6	0,2
Total	7.635	63.454.861	8.311	2.723		2,5	1,3
Missing values	2.377						

In the previous sections we grouped all the predicate offences together, thereby hiding potential differences related to the nature of the crimes. In this section we will differentiate according to offence categories we have designed on the basis of the reported criminal codes. As described in the section on methodology, in cases of multiple offending we took the main money making crimes with the highest maximum penalty and subsequently looked whether "participation in a criminal organisation" was also mentioned which is coded in the table as "+ OC", as presented in Table 8. We remind that the number of missing values on this offence variable is large: 2.377 which restricts the potential for extrapolation.

The breakdown of the outcome variables (money and time) by type of crime allows more detailed observations, assuming that the missing values (no crime recorded) is equally divided over all crime categories. The categories with the highest (total) recovery sums are the soft and hard drug cases (not in organised setting). But they do not have the highest average: that is to be found with 'organised crime + other offences' (mean € 84.024 but median € 8.177) and 'organised fraud' (mean € 62.158 and median € 15.429). Further, the money and time variables are per crime type (again) very skewed, though the degree of skewness is more pronounced with the *money* variable: there are in all categories many low and moderate and a only few very high recovery sums. This is particularly the case with convictions for the commission of crimes mentioned in conjunction with *participation in a criminal organisation* (+ OC).

As far as the *execution time* variable is concerned, we observe a less pronounced skewness: the mean is 2,5 year and median 1,3. There are some marked differences between the average execution times per crime category. The execution times of convicted *soft drug* dealers or growers, whether or not in organised setting, is the lowest: median 0,8 year or a mean of 1,6 year (non-organised) or two years (in organised setting). The '*other crimes*' category shows a record low execution time of less than three months (median). But *fraudsters*, in particular in organised crime setting, prove to be very tenacious in handing in the illegal profits (or had nothing left). It should be observed that – contrary to common findings – in this fraud category the median is higher than the mean implying that the frequency distribution for this category is not determined by a few occasional stragglers (unwilling or incapable debtors), but by many, shifting the median upwards above the mean.

As remarked before, coercive custody is and remains a credible and not a fictional sword of Damocles. Nevertheless, it must be used parsimoniously. Letting that sword down and executing the custody order should not be considered a success: putting a defaulting debtor in prison must be considered an expense in the execution: about € 180 per day. Therefore, we should look at the cases in which the threat of custody worked by inducing the debtor to settle his debt as well as where it failed and the custody order had to be executed.

Table 9
Coercive measures (from preparing to execution) and Settling/payment of recovery order

Crime category	N cases 'coercive acts'	N settled settled debt	% settled	Total initial recovery sum €	Initial recovery sum settled* €	% of initial order
Soft drugs	119	95	*80*	781.094	476.018	*60,9*
Soft drugs + OC	2	2	*100*	13.239	13.239	*100*
Hard drugs	114	59	*52*	1.644.668	853.655	*51,9*
Hard drugs + OC	18	12	*67*	327.461	232.992	*71,2*
Fraud and other	86	54	*63*	1.033.906	336.815	*32,6*
Fraud and other + OC	3	3	*100*	28.112	28.112	*100*
Property crime	115	66	*56*	412.902	193.637	*46,9*
Property + OC	6	4	*67*	171.211	122.657	*71,6*
Hum. traff. & smuggling	2	1	*50*	6.353	454	*7,1*
Hum. traff. & smuggl + OC	1	1	*100*	20.420	20.420	*100*
Money laundering	10	7	*70*	72.179	46.087	*63,9*
Money laundering + OC	0	0	*0*	0	0	*0*
OC + other	1	0	*0*	4.538	0	*0*
Other crimes	8	4	*50*	20.514	12.430	*60,6*
Total	485	308	*64*	4.536.597	2.336.515	*51,5*
Missing values	196					

* In this table 'settled' means a finalisation other than reduction, remission, bankruptcy, death and other "non-payment" finalisations. The settled sum is that of the initial recovery order, though part of it may have been paid as instalment before defaulting and the 'announcement' or initiation of coercion measures.

As can be observed from the figures of Table 9 the missing values reduced the number of coercive cases to 485 which is now our 100%. As Table 9 shows, the coercive activities of the CRA 'worked' in 64% of the cases in which the threat of a execution became real. But in terms of the paid debts the success rate was less shining: the money received represented only 51,5% of the outstanding recovery sum (of this subset).

The soft drug offenders, hard drug offenders (in organised setting), property offenders (in organised setting) and money launderers paid on average more often: > 60%. From *fraudsters* and property offenders (without an organised setting) a comparatively lower portion of the total debt was received: about 30% and 47% (but these represented 63% and 56% of the offenders). Success of coercion appears to be crime category dependent.

Does this crime category differentiation also apply to the execution time? For the total database we have already observed that there are differences in average execution times per crime category. Does this also hold for the 'coercion cases'? Table 10 presents the breakdown of time and crime category.

Table 10
Execution times of all 'coercion cases' per crime category in years

Crime category	N cases with 'coercive acts'	Mean execution time	Median execution time
Soft drugs	119	4,2	3,9
Soft drugs + OC	2	5,3	5,3
Hard drugs	114	6,6	6,3
Hard drugs + OC	18	5,7	5,0
Fraud and other	86	5,9	5,6
Fraud and other + OC	3	7,6	7,7
Property crime	115	6,9	6,6
Property + OC	6	6,9	6,1
Hum. traff. & smuggling	2	9,2	9,2
Hum. traff. & smuggl + OC	1	8,1	8,1
Money laundering	10	5,1	4,5
Money laundering + OC	0	0	0
OC + other	1	12,9	12,9
Other crimes	8	7,1	6,1
Total	**485**	**5,9**	**5,6**

As can be observed there is little difference between the mean and the median execution times in this subset of coercion cases, for which reason we use the mean, which is 5,9 years. The range around the mean is large: from 7,6 years for fraud in organised setting (but only three observations), 6,9 years for property crimes, to 'only' 4,2 years for the soft drugs group. A comparison of these outcomes with the average execution times for the whole database, differentiated by crime category as presented in Table 8 accentuates the long execution times of the coercion cases which for most crime categories more than doubled.

Summarising the coercion findings: the picture is that it is relevant for 6,8% of the total debtor population; it yields about 57% of the recovery sum of these coercion cases; but which on average takes about five years and eleven months to realise. Indeed, there are not many 'easy pickings'. The range of the execution time was large: from more than four years for the 'easy' soft drug cases to over eight years and more for human trafficking cases.

Before continuing with the more detailed study of criminal case files one may wonder whether this statistical analysis can provide a justification of an extra investment in 'squeezing capacity'. That is not the case: these statistical outcomes do not shed light on cost-benefit issues and cannot give a formula to estimate the extra gain from an extension of staff. They highlight that collecting money from reluctant or insolvent criminals is a time consuming costly process, and as the next section will make clear, often an arduous job.

e. A closer view on recovery in action

Apart from full access to the raw database for statistical analysis, we also had access to the criminal recovery files. This provided us the opportunity to explore directly the recorded steps and processes of collecting the ill-gotten gains. The collection of the files took place in the office of the CRA where we used their computer. This gave us the opportunity to experience directly the daily work of the "Serious Crime Team" (tasked with cashing debts of more than € 100.000.) Studying criminal files is a time consuming undertaking, which implied that we had to make a selection. As we expected that cases with high recovery sums would contain convicted criminals with a high degree of stalling and struggling to avoid payment or real insolvency, we selected 20 cases of the € 100.000 + class in which the CRA *considered or initiated a coercive custody request*: these represent real 'squeezing cases'. For reasons of comparison we also studied 10 files of lower recovery classes: five cases around the median and five cases "at the bottom" of the recovery scale: about € 500. In addition to these 30 cases five custody cases with the *highest fully paid* recovery orders (the 'success cases') were investigated, adding up to a total of 35 cases.

1. *The 'high earners'*

The assessed criminal income to be recovered from the 'high earners' ranged from € 310.830 to € 1.942.000. The division is as follows:

1. 5 cases > € 1 million, highest € 1.942.000
2. 4 cases € 500.000 – € 1 million
3. 11 cases € 310.830 – € 500.000

The first question is: How successful was the CRA in coercing these 'rich' criminals, allegedly 'sitting on their assets', to pay the recovery sum? This is a misleading picture, if only because of the time span elapsed between the money-making offences and the final 'pay day': that was on average *nine* years and *six* months (in four cases more than twelve years), part of it spent in prison. This means that much can happen with the assets during nine to twelve years since they were acquired: some got divorced and complained that the 'ex' took everything (or the divorce was a construction to frustrate recovery); others still supported their school going children; but conversely two were supported by their family ('living with mom')[18] because 'there was nothing left'.

The wide variety of financial adventures is reflected in the ways coercive recovery measures are applied and its eventual success. That proved to be meagre: in only one case was the debt fully paid; the others recoveries are still pending. However, this was not because these are all wily evading criminal debtors. Some were: those whose home country was out of the reach of the Dutch authority, withdrew to that safe haven: Turkey (2x), Togo or Singapore. A few others 'withdrawers' who tried to hide assets abroad had a less secure escape country in the EU: Belgium, Spain and Portugal, which rather led to a considerable delay then to a lasting successful frustration of the recovery.

There is one surprise: an *absent* phenomenon. In all this struggling and evading to keep the loot out of the hands of the CRA we miss the 'exotic' offshore centres or other kinds of sophisticated constructions which abound in the money laundering literature. There were no loan back constructions or complicated structures of multiple corporate layers. Instead, we find simple constructions such as an 'ex' in whose name the assets were placed. This was not only shallow, but sometimes also dangerous as the 'ex' could eventually become a *real* ex instead of the 'divorced' faithful partner playing her or his role: "My properties have been snatched by my ex!" (which can be a lie too). Nevertheless there were constructions to put companies and assets in the name of ex-s or other relatives permitting the debtor to

[18] Paraphrased from S.D. Levitt and S.J. Dubner (2005): ch. 3; *Why do drug dealers still live with their moms?*

use corporate assets such as cars in the name of the firm of his ex-partner. All to no avail: the custody threat remained as it is 'laundering neutral'.

Opposite the hiding-withdrawing debtors we have the sad dopes with high recovery obligations and no money left to pay, living "at mom's" (disabled) or in a miserable student room on social security (2x) or without permanent address. Two debtors declared bankruptcy (to the disadvantage of the CRA), divorced (all assets in ex's name). In two cases the debtor declared never to have received the criminal revenue for which they were convicted (€ 538.182 and € 380.000). Though the Court rejected this defence on formal grounds, the financial situation and non-payment lend some credibility to this claim. Three of them have been taken into custody, which failed to make them pay. One debtor even stayed in prison for 642 days, which made the CRA and the Prosecution more nervous than himself. So they arranged a meeting to talk about a debt settlement of € 150 per month. However, appearances can be deceptive as three years later a house is confiscated in Spain which appeared to be in his name. The other two cases of executed custody (180 and 189 days) had to be interrupted too, "because the debtor did not pay". It appears that though the sword of Damocles has a 'three years length' threat, when it is put to the test by an insolvent (or recalcitrant) criminal debtor.

Between these extremes we have a varied category of 'wheelers and dealers': much irregular income and few assets, if at all, and an endless arguing, stalling, evading and last minute proposals to avert immediate execution. Execution of the recovery was also sometimes halted because of a new detention elsewhere for new crimes.

Summarising the financial outcome of the recovery from these 'high earners': one case was fully paid (of which later), in thirteen cases the recovery remained below 10% and in six cases on average 26% of the recovery sum was paid; three debtors were detained for a long term. The sword of Damocles can also be blunt.

2. *The 'median and low earners'*

The vicissitudes of these ten criminal debtors is determined by social-psychology and the 'warrant list'. As far as the social-psychological variable is concerned, half of this groups consists of '*les misérables*': two of them live at the Salvation Army and are under financial supervision of social workers (recovery sum: € 15.000 and € 400); one is in an AA-group (€ 500), another (€ 440) is mentally defective with more fines than he is able to count and finally there is one 'normal' small drug dealer who still had to pay € 410. The latter would have been detained if he was not 'rescued' by his new girlfriend who intervened, telephoned the CRA and arranged a payment by instalment with the CRA.

The other cases (one small embezzler for € 570 and four 'median' earners of slightly more than € 15.000) had also varied outcomes. In two cases the payment failed: one debtor moved to Germany and stopped after his first instalment of € 150. The CRA rattled loudly with Damocles' sword, but nothing happened. In a second case the CRA made three times a formal mistake in serving the writ. The two other cases ended with a successful recovery due to the 'warrant list' factor which made the debtors pay as soon as they were apprehended for the execution of the coercive custody days.

3. *The threat effect*

Knowing to be on a warrant list for direct arrest appears not to be taken lightly: the debtors know that any police contact, traffic control or otherwise can lead to immediate apprehension and detention. And if detained they know they may have to serve a considerable time in prison unless they pay the whole recovery sum or make an acceptable and credible proposal for payment by instalment. It is a threat which prompted many reluctant debtors to pay.

> A major drug entrepreneur was convicted for wholesale cannabis growing and had to pay € 392.066. All the moveable assets had been reported as 'stolen in a burglary' (but no traces of forcible entry), planes (used for dropping drugs in England) suspected being his property were registered in the name other people while his house was in the name of a firm of which his partner was managing director. He had no permanent home or address. He filed several requests for reduction of his payments, which were rejected. In the end the Court ruled 540 'custody days'. Then he paid an instalment of € 145.700 which suspended the execution of the custody. But he failed to pay the remainder and was placed on the 'warrant list'. Arrested during a traffic control he was detained for the execution of his 540 'custody days'. After two days he paid the full outstanding debt of € 244.021.

Four other debtors also paid: either under the threat of immediate execution of the coercive custody or after having spent a short spell behind bars. They were able to pay directly the recovery sum ranging from € 18.000 to € 80.000 despite the fact that shortly before they filed a petition for reduction or a full remission of their debt.

Do these observations justify the conclusions that these criminal debtors are just dragging their feet while 'sitting on their money' and are only moved to pay when Damocles' sword was dangling dangerously on a very thin thread? That would be a rash conclusion. In two cases that may have been the case, but then there are indications that they wasted much of their ill-gotten fortunes on incompetent barristers to stay out of prison. This was held against them as evidence that they were not incapable to pay the recovery sum: € 25.000 in one case and € 185.000 in another case were paid for legal aid. In the last case it was paid to a notoriously dishonest lawyer who was later disbarred because of grave misconduct and neglect of client's interest. Indeed, with a wrong lawyer their ability to pay (if present) evaporated quickly.

Is the threat of being locked up for not paying effective? Though our set of selective cases is small and used for illustrative purposes to shed light on the functioning of this regime, it cannot be denied effectiveness. To many reluctant debtors who are stalling and evading a clear sign is given: "with us your hiding, disguising and delays don't work anymore. If we don't believe you are incapable to pay, we have you incarcerated!" On the other hand, there can be a negative side: the debtor has to spend his custody days while he is really insolvent. In some cases the CRA had to admit this, but then the debtor had served his custody already: coercion proved to be unjustified.

Conclusion

Juxtaposing the empirical findings from the CRA data and the political expectations reveals a gap which is difficult to bridge. On the one hand, we have the political expression of high expectations concerning what can be exacted from the 'criminal wealth'. On the other hand, we have the empirical findings of this research project, casting a different light on that 'criminal wealth'. They show that coercing, up until custody, is not ineffective, but that there are reasons to admonish moderation of expecting flows of money from 'rich' criminals. As far as the criminal wealth is concerned, the empirical findings are in line with the results of earlier studies: yes there is a large amount of crime-money but its distribution is very unequal (Levi and Osofsky, 1995; Van Duyne and Miranda, 1999; Van Duyne *et al.*, 2009; Van Duyne and Soudijn, 2010). Whether we look at the ownership of real estate, valuables, cash or bank accounts, the frequency divisions have a similar inverted J-like shape: a high frequency at the low-value end and a low frequency at the high-value end. It would not be exaggerated to state that the 'criminal wealth distribution' is as skewed as wealth and income is in the licit upperworld. Perhaps it is not too farfetched to project a criminal proletariat, a 'middle class' and a few top level earners.

Of course, this 'class division' may be unrealistic as it tacitly assumes a financial stability or criminal wealth consolidation as far as the higher earners are concerned. But how much criminal wealth consolidation can be observed? Apart from studies on

Italian organised crime (Paoli, 2003), relevant empirical data are scarce and mainly anecdotal.[19] Naturally, our view is biased as we see only 'known' cases in which the authorities have intervened. Also, we must recognise that after the intervention of law enforcement, many criminals entered into a phase of 'downward wealth mobility'. This can be a protracted phase. A time span of ten years between the last money generating criminal act, prosecution and final recovery (with evasions or insolvency) is not uncommon. With time passing by much earnings may have 'evaporated'. Perhaps with the exception of property, that does not evaporate of course, but can be put in the name of a third person, for example the 'ex' with the risk that she turned into a *real* ex. Many convicts, 'rich' as well as poor, had to resort to a payment by instalment settlement while facing a coercive custody procedure. This became a reality for only a small minority, but sufficiently often to be taken seriously.

Were these non-payers just braving the authorities with wily tricks? With a few exception we observed that the ways they try to dodge new incarceration were anything but manifestations of a self-confident attitude or a stoic resignation. Looking at our 'end of the journey' data when convicted criminals finally have to pay back their ill-gotten gains, we only find intermittent examples of a suspected consolidated criminal ownership, often in the form of real estate, bank accounts, cash and valuables (in that order of recovery importance). These cases coincided with the opportunities to hide assets as well as the own person abroad.

Opposed to these empirical findings since 1999 we find a public image of a huge accumulated criminal wealth as derived from speculative extrapolations from economic models (Unger *et al.*, 2007). These are often characterised by broad ranges and fuzzy definitions, particularly concerning such an important concept like 'organised crime' (Schneider, 2012). At a more concrete level we have the figures of the Financial Intelligence Units concerning unusual and suspicious transaction – still to be proven really criminal of which we know little due to lack of feedback from the police or prosecution. We also have the accumulated confiscation figures, though without proper conversion of into what remains of them in the eventual recovery procedure. There is also the claim that criminals are getting smarter (an eternal complaint) and that they use increasingly off-shore corporate vehicles in which they figure as vanishing 'ultimate beneficiary owners'. That may be true, but in this database of more than 15 years we found less than a handful of cases in which legal persons have been used, all easily traceable. This is in line with previous research

19 This is largely due to the non-cooperative attitude of the authorities requested to release (anonymised) data for research. Levi (2013) observes that The Netherlands are in this regard the most open country for doing criminological basic research.

(Meloen *et al.*, 2003; Van Duyne; 2003) which revealed some financial itineration along off-shore centres, but mainly determined by own social preferences.

All these statements and 'observations' convey a similar message: there is so much crime-money while the authorities constantly fail to exact their 'pound of flesh'. Is that true? Does law enforcement really fail? Or does it rather face a financially disorderly and floating criminal reality of which one should not have too high expectations of tapping it orderly to the full? Much can end differently than intended or simply go wrong: in our database 25% was partially or fully not cashed. This is part of the job and part of the costs of recovering. But what is known about recovery costs? How do we integrate the cost element into the whole recovery balance sheet? Levi (2013) indicates that instead of making a net profit, we may be happy if law enforcement becomes a bit less costly. Setting profit targets may lead to disappointments: it was expected that the UK Asset Recovery Agency (ARA) would become self-financing by 2005-06, but it failed to reach this target. One of the reasons was the high costs of the receiver, whose case handling exceeded 15% of the value of the assets: they constituted the second largest expenditure of the ARA: £ 6,9 million in 2005-06 (National Audit Office, 2007; p.8). The expectation of a self-financing criminal justice agency proved to be a fallacy.

The expectation of a net income from recovery may be based on the tacit assumption that criminals still possess the revenues they once acquired: they 'sit on it' and just have to hand it over at no or low costs. As a matter of fact, few criminals proverbially 'sit' on their money. But whether criminals 'sit' on their money or on empty bags, the execution of the recovery orders takes much time and effort with rich and poor criminals alike. Irrespective of the amount to be paid, the execution time last in half of the cases more than 1,5 to 2,5 year (median or mean), but sometimes up to 16 years. That is the general picture. In cases in which coercion has to be threatened or applied the execution time more than doubles. Whether in these cases the recovery costs also double is in the absence of data difficult to determine, but given the involvement of the CRA staff, a Public Prosecutor and the Court (two to four staff) all high-qualified and paid, the coercive custody procedure is expensive, even if one abstracts from the custody costs per day the debtor spends in jail. Perhaps we should be satisfied to learn that a proper recovery policy makes law enforcement less costly and reflect on one of the basics of asset recovery: restoring justice which should not be determined by the amount of money that can be raked in.

There is no single formula to address this dilemma as the population of the criminal debtors is too heterogeneous, that is, measured by the nature of their offences, persons as well as outcome variables. For example, the soft drug entrepreneurs' cases represent an 'easy' subpopulation: their cases are reasonably quickly dealt with (50% within nine months) but the average yield is low. In contrast to this 'easy' group, cases with fraudsters in organised setting took on average more than five years to finalise: 50% more than five years and nine months.

Law enforcement has to face the fact that the execution of asset recovery orders covers a chaotic spectrum ranging from the once rich criminal who ends broke and the low earner who proves to be a tenacious feet-dragger and in between per crime type much procedural variety. One could greet this observation with some sober resignation. However, this contrasts with the prevalent political landscape. Instead of resigning to the world of facts we find the well-tried threat images of criminal finances and a self-reinforcing political activism. In some jurisdictions this has contributed to setting recovery targets or to provide incentives to law enforcement agencies (Levi, forthcoming). This is not objectionable as such, however, in the absence of proper evaluation figures to assess the added value of incentives and target setting, this approach is at risk of leading to deceptive success inflation or reporting mainly the 'easy pickings', such as cash seizures from low level drug dealers while the costs of the procedural aftermath is left out of the books: "The great majority of these [confiscations] are low value cases, which currently have to be expensively adjudicated in Crown Courts" (Levi, 2013). This means that policy makers please the audience with high confiscation figures from only the first stage of the lengthy recovery procedure while omitting the sequel. What remains of the seized wealth and claimed criminal revenues after the full criminal procedure: that is from first instance to cassation followed by the recovery procedure (see Meloen *et al.*, 2003; ch. 4)? The initial high targets are set and publicised, figures of the realised (shrunken) targets and recovery expenses remain hidden.

In the UK this target setting has been abandoned by now. How surprising is it that the Dutch authorities (Minister of Safety and Justice) actually embark on this target setting policy. Neither demonstrating any knowledge of this experience abroad, nor being informed (or letting themselves to be so) of the outcomes of previous research, they jump to questionably high targets. € 100 million has to be confiscated from 2018 onwards[20] while extra staff (officers of the Fiscal Police and National Police) have to earn back three times their salary. One may question the ethics of this political endeavour and wonder whether this is a display of irresponsible, greed driven day-dreaming or knowingly embarking on an unrealistic policy.

20 RTL Nieuws | 08 januari 2013

References

Barlett, B.L., *The negative effects of money laundering on economic development.* Asian Development Bank, May, 2002

Blumenson, E. and E. Nilsen, *Policing for profit: the drugs war hidden agenda.* 1997. Http://www.fear.org/chicago.html

Duyne, P.C. van, Money laundering policy. Fears and facts. In: P.C. van Duyne, K. Von Lampe and J.L. Newell (eds.), *Criminal finances and organising crime in Europe.* Nijmegen, Wolf Legal Publishers, 2003

Duyne, P.C. van, The creation of a threat image: Media, policy making and organised crime. In: P. C. van Duyne, M. Jager, K. von Lampe and J.L. Newell (eds.), *Threats and phantoms of organised crime, corruption and terrorism.* Nijmegen, Wolf Legal Publishers, 2004

Duyne, P.C. van and H. de Miranda, The emperor's cloths of disclosure: hot money and suspect disclosures. *Crime, Law and Social Change*, 1999, *no. 3*, 245-271

Duyne, P.C. van, M. Soudijn and T. Kint, Bricks don't talk. Searching for crime money in real estate. In: P.C. van Duyne, S. Donati, J. Harvey, A. Maljevic and K. von Lampe (eds.), *Crime, money and criminal mobility in Europe.* Nijmegen, Wolf Legal Publishers, 2009

Duyne, P.C. van and M. Soudijn, Crime-money in the financial system: what we fear and what we know. In: M. Herzog-Evans (ed.), *Transnational Criminology Manual, Volume 2*, Nijmegen, Wolf Legal Publishers, 2010

Duyne, P.C. van, M.S. Groenhuijsen and A.A.P. Schudelaro, Balancing financial threats and legal interests in money-laundering policy. *Crime, Law and Social Change*, 2005, vol. 43, *no 2-3*, 117-147

Financial Action Task Force on Money Laundering, *Report on money laundering*, Paris, 1990

Harvey J., Money laundering, phantoms, imagery and facts. In G.A. Antonopoulos, G., M. Groenhuijsen, J. Harvey, T. Kooijmans, A. Maljevic, and K. von Lampe (eds), *Usual and Unusual Organising Criminals in Europe and Beyond.* Maklu, Antwerp, 2011

Keh, D.I. *Drug money in a changing world: economic reform and criminal finance.* Vienna, UNDCP, 1996

Levi, M. and L. Osofsky, *Investigating, seizing and confiscating the proceeds o crime.* London, Home Office Police Research Group, 1995

Levi, M., *Drug Law Enforcement and Financial Investigation Strategies.* International Drug Policy Consortium, September 2013

Levitt, S.D. and S.J. Dubner, *Freakonomics.* London, Penguin books, 2005

Meloen, M., R. Landman, H. de Miranda and J. van Eekelen, *Buit en besteding.* Zoetermeer, Elsevier Overheid, 2003

National Audit Office, *The Assets Recovery Agency. Report by the Comptroller and Auditor General.* London, the Stationery Office, 2007

Pashev, K., Organised VAT fraud in an enlarged Europe. In: P.C. van Duyne, A. Maljević, M. van Dijck, K. von Lampe and J. Harvey (eds.), *Crime business and crime money in Europe. The dirty linen of illicit enterprise.* Nijmegen, Wolf Legal Publishers, 2007

Quirk, P.J., *Macro economic implications of money laundering.* IMF Working paper, IMF, 1996

Paoli, L., *Mafia brotherhoods. Organised crime Italian style.* Oxford, Oxford University Press, 2003

Rasmussen, D.W. and B. Benson, *The economic anatomy of a drug war. Criminal justice in the commons.* Lanham, Rowman and Littlefield, 1994

Reuter, P., Are estimates of the volume of money laundering either feasible or useful? In: B. Unger and D. van der Linden (eds.), *Research handbook on money laundering.* Cheltenham, Edward Elgar Publishing, 2013

Schneider, F., The hidden financial flows of organised crime. In: C.C. Storti an P. de Grauwe (eds.), *Illicit trade and the global economy.* Cambridge (Mass.), The MIT Press, 2012

Tanzi, V., *Money laundering and the international financial system.* IMF Working paper, IMF, 1996

Unger, B., *The scale and impacts of money laundering.* Cheltenham, Edward Elgar, 2007

UNODC, *Estimating illegal financial flows resulting from drug trafficking and other transnational organized crimes.* Vienna, 2011

Walker, J., 1999. How big is global money laundering?, *Journal of Money Laundering Control*, 1999, vol. 3, *no. 1*, 25-37

Walker, J. and B. Unger, Measuring global money laundering: "The Walker gravity model". *Review of Law and Economics*, 2009 Vol. 5, no. 2, 822-853

Land of opportunities
The illicit trade in cigarettes in the United States

Klaus von Lampe, Marin Kurti and *John Bae*[1]

Introduction

The illegal cigarette trade is a global phenomenon. The smuggling and sale of contraband cigarettes is pervasive in many parts of the world and trafficking routes span the globe. Much of the recent criminological research, however, has focused on the situation in just a few regions, namely Australia, China, Europe and Canada.[2] Comparatively little attention has been paid to the cigarette black market in the United States even though the US has been associated with a major problem of cigarette smuggling. According to recent estimates the US has the third largest illegal cigarette market in the world in terms of the absolute number of illegal cigarettes traded, only surpassed by China and Russia. In relative terms, the same estimates suggest that between 13% and 25% of US smokers purchased illegal cigarettes in 2007 (Joossens, Merriman, Ross & Raw, 2009: 10, 12).

The purpose of this study and review is to examine and to interpret the illegal cigarette trade as it pertains to the United States against the backdrop of developments in Europe. A close-up look will be taken at New York City, arguably the largest local cigarette black market in the country. It seems that the state of affairs over the past few years is somewhat reminiscent of the situation of the illegal cigarette

---

1 Klaus von Lampe is Associate Professor at John Jay College of Criminal Justice, New York, Department of Law, Police Science and Criminal Justice Administration; Marin Kurti is a doctoral student at the Rutgers School of Criminal Justice, Newark, New Jersey; John Bae is a student in the joint BA/MA program in Criminal Justice and a McNair Scholar at John Jay College of Criminal Justice.

2 On the situation in Australia, see Geis, Cartwright & Houston (2004). On the situation in Canada, see Beare (2002; 2003). On the situation in China, see Shen, Antonopoulos & von Lampe (2010) and von Lampe, Kurti, Shen & Antonopoulos (2012). For a collection of criminological writings on the illegal cigarette trade in Europe, see Van Duyne & Antonopoulos (2009). See also Antonopoulos (2006; 2008), Coker (2003), Griffiths (2004), Hozic (2004), von Lampe (2006; 2010).

trade in Europe in the 1990s, marked by the exploitation of cross-jurisdictional tax differentials by bootleggers and some degree of connivance on the part of the tobacco industry. At the same time there are features that are specific to the United States. This includes the role of Native American reservations and the concentration of cigarette black markets in deprived inner city areas.

Basic parameters of the illegal cigarette trade

The illegal cigarette trade, at its core, is a form of tax evasion. The taxes imposed on cigarettes create incentives for criminal suppliers and consumers to seek ways to circumvent taxation. Four main schemes can be distinguished by which cheap cigarettes are currently made available for illegal distribution: bootlegging, large-scale smuggling, counterfeiting, and so-called *cheap whites*.

Bootlegging involves the purchase of cigarettes in low-tax jurisdictions. The cigarettes are obtained with taxes paid and are then transported to a high-tax jurisdiction for illegal distribution.

Large-scale smuggling takes advantage of the fact that cigarettes destined for export are not subject to taxation until they are introduced to the final consumer market. These untaxed 'in-transit' cigarettes are diverted from international trade channels to the black market. The term 'large scale' is used because typically 'in-transit' cigarettes are obtained and smuggled in large consignments of millions of sticks at a time.

Counterfeiting involves the illegal production of brand cigarettes without permission by the trademark owner and without paying taxes. The counterfeiting of cigarettes needs to be distinguished from the counterfeiting of cigarette tax stamps. Counterfeit tax stamps have been affixed to different kinds of illegal cigarettes (i.e., bootlegged, smuggled and counterfeit), apparently in an effort to increase their marketability by appearing as a legitimate product on which taxes have been paid. For example, cigarettes bootlegged from Virginia, may bear a counterfeit combined New York City and New York State tax stamp to hide the source of origin and to fool law enforcement into believing that local city and state taxes have been paid.

Cheap whites are cigarettes that are legally produced in other states under unique brand names or no brand name at all. They appear to be destined primarily for illicit distribution and are largely absent in legal distribution channels. The constellation is similar to large-scale smuggling in several respects. In both cases, *legally* produced untaxed cigarettes are made available for illegal distribution in large consignments at low costs. Likewise, in both cases there is some degree of connivance on the part of manufacturers. However, in the case of cheap whites the manufacturers are for all intents and purposes an integral part of the illegal cigarette trade.

Developments in Western Europe since the 1990s

In Western Europe since the 1990s, namely in Germany and the UK, the cigarette black market seems so have evolved through four partially overlapping phases, marked, respectively, by one specific procurement scheme (Joossens and Raw, 1998; 2008; von Lampe, 2006).

The emergence of extensive cigarette black markets in Germany and the UK appears to have been fuelled initially by bootlegging between Poland and Germany, respectively across the British Channel. Along the way, bootlegged cigarettes were partly replaced by diverted 'in-transit' cigarettes that the major tobacco companies had sold into dubious channels. In the early 2000s, as a result of political and legal pressure exerted on the tobacco industry, the supply of 'in-transit' cigarettes to smugglers was largely cut off. The resulting vacuum was filled in part by counterfeit cigarettes originating from China and other South-East Asian countries (von Lampe, 2006: 247).

Counterfeits were commonly inferior in quality and threatened to undermine the reputation of the affected premium brands like "Marlboro" and "Benson & Hedges". This brought the tobacco manufacturers into a natural alliance with authorities in Europe and Asia. Considerable state and industry resources have gone into curbing the influx of counterfeit cigarettes. At the same time it seems that because of the low quality of the counterfeit cigarettes their marketability in Europe has been limited, perhaps with the exception of the UK and Ireland (von Lampe, 2006: 237; von Lampe, Kurti, Shen and Antonopoulos, 2012: 57-58).

The mounting efforts to suppress the marketing of counterfeit cigarettes paved the way for the emergence of cheap whites. These cigarettes do not challenge the integrity of the major cigarette brands. Likewise, because of their status as legal manufacturers the producers of cheap whites, located in various Eastern European non-EU countries, were largely immune from law enforcement intervention. In essence, authorities could act only once cheap whites illegally crossed the border into the EU. Ironically, the success of cheap whites has made them a lucrative target of counterfeiters (World Customs Organization, 2013: 20), providing yet another example for the dynamic nature of the illegal cigarette trade.

Without arguing that the development in the Western European cigarette black market is the only possible course of events, it can serve as a point of reference for assessing the evolution of the illegal cigarette trade elsewhere, namely in the United States.

The data reviewed in this chapter suggest that the development in the United States has so far largely remained in the bootlegging phase with the primary modus operandi being the transport of genuine brand cigarettes between states within the US. The question is to what extent large-scale smuggling, counterfeiting and cheap whites are likely to become more prevalent.

The tobacco-tax regime in the US

Similar to the situation in Europe and elsewhere, cigarettes in the US are a highly taxed good with taxes making up the major component of the retail price (GAO, 2011: 10). Also similar to the situation in Europe (see Hornsby & Hobbs, 2007: 554), the United States is characterized by a patchwork of different tobacco-tax levels. Just as tobacco taxes vary from country to country in Europe, tobacco taxes in the US vary from state to state and sometimes even on the local level. However, the state-to-state tax differentials are greater than cross-country differences in the EU, and overall the average tax burden on cigarettes in the US is significantly lower than in the EU. In 2010, on average, taxes made up around 78% of the retail price of a cigarette in EU Member States (European Commission, 2010: 7). In comparison, in the US this share was only around 53% (GAO, 2011: 10). While the federal government collects a uniform excise tax on cigarettes ($1,01 in 2010), state excise taxes on cigarettes vary greatly. In 2010, Missouri was the state with the lowest rate of $0,17 per pack compared to $4,35 per pack in the state of New York (GAO, 2011: 10-11).

In addition to federal and state excise taxes, some local governments impose taxes on cigarettes. In New York City, a further $1,50 is added to the price of a pack of cigarettes, accounting for the highest tax burden and accordingly the highest retail prices for cigarettes nationwide at around $12-13 per pack (Kurti, von Lampe and Thompkins, 2013).

The illegal cigarette trade and the US: an overview

From all that is known, the illegal cigarette trade in the United States has been fuelled primarily by domestic bootlegging which exploits retail-price differentials between low-tax and high-tax jurisdictions. To what extent other schemes besides bootlegging have played any substantial role, is difficult to discern. Given the fragmentation of law enforcement in the United States, no comprehensive data on the nature and extent of the cigarette black market and on the prevalence of large-scale smuggling, counterfeit cigarettes and cheap whites are available. Research, mainly driven by a public health agenda has likewise remained fragmented; and the tobacco industry, which may have more complete data, is not willing to share these publicly.

Inter-state bootlegging

The United States has a long history of inter-state bootlegging. As early as 1949, federal legislation in the form of the Jenkins Act aimed at curbing illicit cigarette sales across state lines (Alderman, 2012: 8).

It was not until the mid-1960s, however, that cigarette bootlegging emerged as a significant problem, especially in the Northeast. By that time price differences had increased substantially between the tobacco-producing states Kentucky, North Carolina and Virginia, on one hand, which kept their cigarette taxes low, and states like New York, on the other, which raised their taxes rapidly in part to increase revenue and in part to discourage smoking. The policy to reduce smoking by increasing the costs of cigarettes had been inspired by a now legendary 1964 report issued by the Surgeon General on the health hazards of smoking (Advisory Committee, 1977).

Large-scale smuggling

Since the 1960s, bootlegging within the United States has remained the main modus operandi for procuring cigarettes for illicit distribution. Large-scale smuggling of genuine brand cigarettes never seems to have played a dominant role for the domestic cigarette black market.

The diversion of untaxed 'in-transit' cigarettes has often been identified as a potential problem and some cases have been detected over the years. But there does not appear to be any evidence that large-scale smuggling has ever been the main source of contraband cigarettes as it has been for the EU in the 1990s and early 2000s (Joossens & Raw, 2008; GAO, 2011: 18; Lafaive, Fleenor, & Nesbit, 2008: 8). This is remarkable especially because large numbers of US-manufactured 'in-transit' cigarettes have found their way into illegal distribution channels in other parts of the world, namely China, Europe and South America (Holzman, 1997; Joossens & Raw, 1998).

The smuggling of genuine brand cigarettes from other countries into the US appears to be confined largely to the US-Mexican border, significantly impacting only the four southern border states of California, Arizona, New Mexico and Texas (Lafaive & Nesbit, 2010: 12). At the US-Canadian border, the problem is reversed. Here, the US has long been a source and trans-shipment country for contraband cigarettes going into Canada (Beare, 2002; Lafaive & Nesbit, 2010: 12).

Counterfeit Cigarettes

Similar to large-scale smuggling, there is no clear evidence that counterfeit cigarettes play a major role in the cigarette black market in the United States. Some attention has been paid to counterfeit cigarettes being seized at US ports and surfacing on local cigarette black markets. However, there does not appear to be a trend towards an increasing market share of counterfeit cigarettes. A 2004 report by the Government Accountability Office (GAO), for example, noted that the problem of cross-border cigarette smuggling is particularly one of counterfeit cigarettes, following a sharp increase in the number of counterfeit cigarettes seized by US authorities in the years 1999 and 2000 (GAO, 2004: 21). In contrast, another GAO report on illegal cigarettes presented in 2011 mentioned counterfeit cigarettes more or less only in passing as one of many schemes to evade tobacco taxes (GAO, 2011: 17).

This corresponds to published tobacco industry estimates that suggest that counterfeit cigarettes might play a much lesser role in the US and the Western Hemisphere than in other parts of the world. A report issued by British-American Tobacco (BAT) on the prevalence of illegal cigarettes in various world regions claimed that in the Americas in 2008, 2% of illegal cigarettes were counterfeit, compared to 4% in the Asia-Pacific region, 7% in Africa and the Middle East, 12% in Western Europe, 49% in Eastern Europe, and 80% in China (British American Tobacco, 2010: 18). Unfortunately, these estimates have not been broken down to the level of individual countries, not to mention individual parts of countries.

Native American Reservations

The landscape of the illegal cigarette trade within the United States has been complicated by the role of Native American reservations that are scattered across the country. These tribal lands have some level of legal autonomy that can only be limited by the US Congress. The state where a reservation is located has no authority to regulate business activities or to collect taxes from tribal members (Alderman, 2012: 5). As a result, cigarettes can be sold to tribal members on a reservation exempt from state taxation. However, tribal businesses have not only sold cheap cigarettes to Native American customers but also to non-tribal members through retail stores on reservations and online.

Purchases of cheap cigarettes from Native American Reservations have originally been primarily a problem for states in the Western parts of the country, in particular for Washington state (Advisory Commission, 1977: 12; Svogun, 1980: 252). Over the course of the 1980s and 1990s, the centre of gravity of the tribal cigarette business shifted to reservations located in New York State. The mail order and internet sale of cigarettes in particular is said to be dominated by businesses based in upstate New York reservations (DeCicca, Kenkel & Liu, 2010: 8).

Some reservations have become main importers of brand cigarettes disproportionate to their population size (DeCicca et al., 2010; GAO, 2011; Walker Guevara & Willson, 2008). This situation is similar to the role countries like Andorra or Cyprus have played for the illegal cigarette trade in Europe during the 1990s. Andorra with a population of 63.000, for example, became a trans-shipment centre for billions of brand cigarettes that were legally imported and then illegally exported through various smuggling routes to Spain and the UK (Joossens & Raw, 2000: 948-949).

The cigarette black market in New York City

The nature of the illegal cigarette trade in the United States can perhaps best be observed in a close-up look at New York City. It is here where the most salient features of the cigarette black market converge and fall, it seems, on particularly fertile grounds.

Factors conducive to illegal cigarettes in New York City

New York City, as indicated, has the highest tobacco taxes and the highest retail prices for cigarettes in the US. This creates a demand for cheap illegal cigarettes, particularly in socioeconomically deprived neighbourhoods (Chernick & Merriman, 2013).

At the same time, New York City is in close proximity to a number of potential sources for contraband cigarettes. Several Native American reservations that sell cigarettes are nearby. Low-tax states such as Virginia are also within driving distance. A round-trip by car, including purchasing cigarettes at one of many cigarette retailers takes about 10 hours. In addition, the New York City area is home to one of the largest container ports in the world, the Port of New York and New Jersey, through which counterfeit and 'in-transit' cigarettes could be smuggled, for example from China or from Paraguay. Paraguay, importantly, is a major producer of illicit cigarettes for black markets in Latin America (Ramos, 2009: 23; World Customs Organization, 2013: 28-29).

A potentially countervailing factor is the decreasing smoking prevalence in New York City. Under mayor Bloomberg (2002-2014) the city has seen a relentless campaign against smoking which is credited with bringing down adult smoking rates from 35% in 2002 to 14% in 2010 (New York City Department of Health and Mental Hygiene, 2011). During the same time period legal sales of cigarettes in New York City fell by about two-thirds (Chernick & Merriman, 2013: 657). It is not clear, however, what impact this trend has had on the volume of the cigarette black market in either relative or absolute terms.

The history of the cigarette black market in New York City

The city of New York has a long history of cigarette trafficking dating back to the year 1938 when a temporary tax of 1 cent was added to the price of about 15 cents for a pack of cigarettes. The response of many smokers was, reportedly, to either buy their cigarettes outside of the city or to draw on bootleggers for a supply of cheap cigarettes. The state of New York followed with a cigarette tax of its own in 1939. This led to smokers and bootleggers going to the neighbouring state of New Jersey, which did not tax cigarettes until 1948 (Fleenor, 2003: 2).

Cigarette taxes remained at a relatively low level throughout much of the 1940s and 1950s. Then, combined city and state taxes on cigarettes rose quickly from 4 cents per pack to 14 cents between 1959 and 1965 (Fleenor, 2003: 3). This is when cigarette smuggling is said to have shifted from small-time operations of independent smugglers to 'organised' bootlegging with the involvement of members and associates of the New York Mafia, also known as Cosa Nostra. A contemporary report by the Advisory Commission on Intergovernmental Relations provides the following illustrative example of one mafioso turned bootlegger (Advisory Commission, 1977: 23-24):

> As early as 1966, Anthony Granata was known to be involved on a large scale in transporting and selling untaxed cigarettes in the City and State of New York. Originally his operation was located in the Bath Beach section of Brooklyn, N.Y. Granata is listed by law enforcement officials as a member of the organised crime family headed by Joseph Colombo. His criminal record reflects 12 arrests, four of

> which were connected with cigarette bootlegging. He has been convicted of criminally receiving stolen property as well as use of a forged driver's license.
> Initially, Granata's operation consisted of small-scale bootlegging. As the years went on, it developed into a full-sized operation. In the period from September 1966 to April 1967, Granata, based upon his own records seized by law enforcement authorities, was responsible for smuggling 1.109.920 cartons of cigarettes into New York State. Tax assessments against him totalling $2.422.510 were levied by New York State and City authorities for this period, as provided by law. These assessments remain uncollected.
> Granata operated his business on a professional level with over 30 employees. He was known to have dispatched drivers on a 6-days-a-week schedule to North Carolina. Orders were placed and all necessary arrangements were handled by clerical employees in New York City. He also employed an expediter or traffic manager, stationed in North Carolina, to manage that end of his operation. Typically, drivers were paid $100 per trip and an additional $95 expense money if they were long-haul drivers (all the way to North Carolina). Short-haul drivers (to Pennsylvania) received $60 per trip, plus expenses. A short-haul driver would be used when arrangements had been made with the North Carolina supplier to transport the cigarette loads to selected points in Pennsylvania. The short-haul driver would meet the shipment, transfer it to his vehicle, and bring it into New York.
> All legal costs arising from the arrests of drivers, such as lawyers fees, bail, and fines, were also handled, wherever the jurisdiction, from Granata's headquarters. Fraudulent driver's licenses and other false identification were supplied. Among other devices used to avoid detection, Granata constructed a truck disguised as a lumber transporter. Dummy corporations also were formed to further conceal his cigarette bootlegging business.

Reportedly, Cosa Nostra members and associates like Anthony Granata pushed small-time bootleggers out of the market through violence and intimidation (Fleenor, 2003: 6; Svogun, 1980: 245). The mafia dominance over the cigarette black market in New York, however, did not last long. Later analyses of the situation make little or no mention of mafia involvement and point to a wide range of individuals and groups engaged in the smuggling and selling of illegal cigarettes (Fleenor, 2003: 14; Walker Guevara & Willson, 2008).

One reason for the fragmentation of the cigarette black market might have been the passage of the Contraband Cigarette Trafficking Act (CCTA) in 1978 that increased the risk for large inter-state bootlegging operations. The act made the transport and distribution of contraband cigarettes a crime punishable by up to five years in prison. It also authorized the seizing of vehicles used in smuggling activities (Fleenor, 2003: 11; Svogun, 1980: 259-260).

A significant uptick in cigarette black market activity occurred in the aftermath of tax hikes in the year 2002 (Walker, Guevara and Willson, 2008). In March 2000, New York State taxes were increased from $0,56 to $1,11 and in April 2002 to $1,50 per pack of cigarettes. Shortly thereafter, New York City raised its tax in a single step from $0,08 to $1,50 per pack. This led to a drop in legal sales of cigarettes by more than 50% in the first few months following the tax hike (Fleenor, 2003: 3, 13). A further growth of the cigarette black market is alleged to have been triggered by tax hikes in 2008 when New York State raised taxes from $1,50 to $2,75 per pack (Chernick & Merriman, 2013), and also by a tax hike in 2010 that led to an increase of New York State taxes by $1,60 to the current level of $4,35 per pack (Montero, Fasick, & Bennett, 2010).

The role of Native American Reservations in New York State

The most significant development that accompanied the New York City and New York State tax increases of the 2000s was the emergence of Native American Reservations as the main source of contraband cigarettes reaching the New York City black market.

This development is reflected in sales data of untaxed cigarettes in the state of New York that were provided by the New York State Department of Taxation and Finance. These data show a steady increase in the number of untaxed cigarettes going to Native American reservations through the 1980s and 1990s and peaking in the year 2005. In 1984, about 200 million untaxed cigarettes were delivered to Native American reservations in New York State. In 2005 that number had risen to 9,5 billion untaxed cigarettes (Figure 1 next page).

Figure 1
Native American untaxed cigarette purchases
(cartons per 200 sticks) 1-01-1984 till 31-08-2012

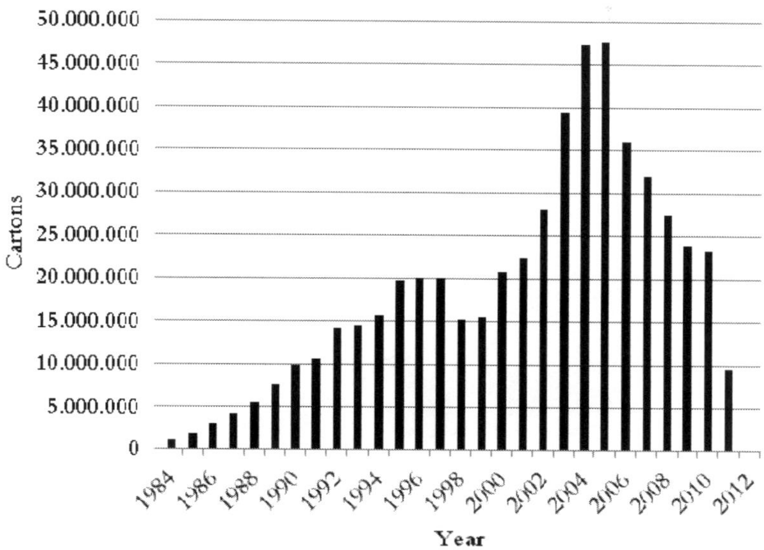

Source: New York State Department of Taxation and Finance

It is obvious that by far most of these cigarettes were sold on to non-tribal members. Otherwise each of the some 30.000 tribal members on the New York reservations would have had to smoke more than 40 packs of cigarettes a day. Particularly telling is the example of a reservation on Long Island close to New York City. This reservation with a territory of one square mile (2,5 km^2) and a population of 283, according to the New York State Department of Taxation and Finance, imported a total of more than 59 million cartons of untaxed cigarettes (11,8 billion sticks) between January 2001 and June 2011. This means that on average some 3,6 million cigarettes per tribal member were delivered to this tiny reservation annually, equalling a per-capita consumption of close to 500 packs per day. A large portion of these shipments passed through one business, that of a native of Costa Rica who had married into the reservation. Other shipments went to addresses on the reservation that were literally no more than a sign post by the street, and some delivery addresses were entirely fictitious. In other words, the reservation essentially served as a trans-shipment centre (Saul, 2008). Non-tribal consumers either came to the reservation directly or bootleggers, typically using minivans and cars for transportation, would pick up cigarettes and bring them to retail sellers in New York City (Walker, Guevara and Willson, 2008).

Figure 2
Native American untaxed cigarette purchases:
Share of New York State sales volume: 1-01-1984 till 31-8-2012

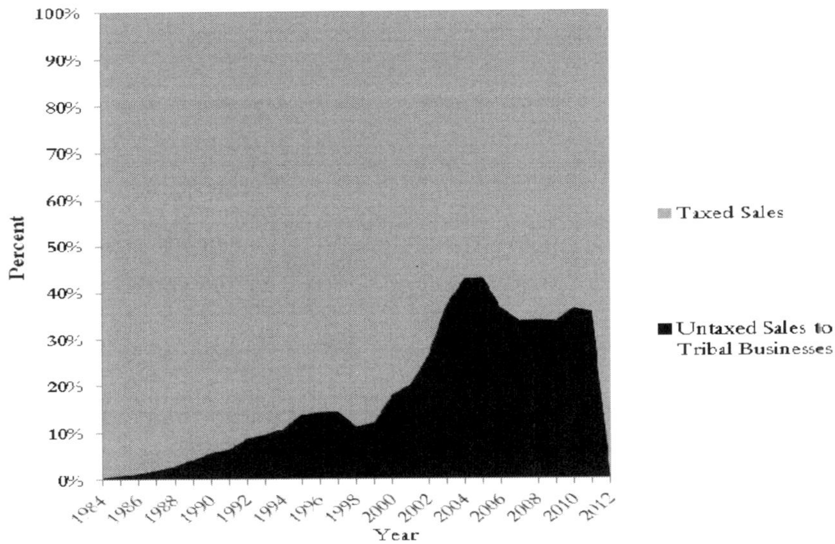

Source: New York State Department of Taxation and Finance

The Role of the Tobacco Industry

The cigarettes passing through the Native American reservations eventually made up a substantial part of the business of the tobacco industry in New York State. Figure 2 shows the trends in the delivery of cigarettes from non-tribal tobacco manufacturers to Native American Reservations from January 1984 until August 2012, the last month for which data where made available at the time of writing this chapter. Significant is the overall steady increase from 0,5% of tribal purchases in New York State in 1984 to close to 15% in the 1990s and 20% in 2001. This was followed by a sudden increase between 2002 and 2005 when the share of wholesale cigarettes in New York State going to tribal stores reached 43,2%. After 2005 the share first decreased slightly to a level of about 35% between 2006 and 2011, then abruptly dropping to 0,01% in 2012 when untaxed cigarettes purchases by Native American reservations were regulated by the New York State Department of Taxation and Finance under amended New York Tax Law § 471 and § 471-e.

The tobacco manufacturers, prominently among them R.J. Reynolds, Lorillard and Philip Morris, would sell their products, such as Camel, Newport and Marlboro cigarettes, to a small number of wholesalers who in turn would deliver the cigarettes to the reservations. At the same time, the tobacco manufacturers are said to have also been in regular direct contact with tribal businesses 'to check supply and product placement, update signs, and discuss discounts' (Walker, Guevara & Willson, 2008).

As indicated in Figure 2, in the mid-2000s up to more than 40% of cigarettes sold in New York State were untaxed purchases by businesses on tribal lands. Native American reservations seem to have been particularly important for Lorillard and its Newport brand which is popular among smokers in socio-economically deprived areas of New York City such as the South Bronx (Walker Guevara & Willson 2008). In a survey of a purposive sample of 254 South Bronx smokers conducted in May 2011[3] by Marin Kurti, a co-author of this chapter, almost all respondents (91,6%) reported that Newport was their preferred brand (Kurti, 2011). Likewise, a survey of discarded cigarette packs conducted in March 2011 in 30 randomly selected census tracks in the South Bronx found that Newports held a market share of 86%. The study also showed that 76,2% of cigarettes smoked in the South Bronx were not legally purchased with payment of New York City and New York State taxes. In light of 42% of discarded packs not having any tax stamp and 15,9% bearing counterfeit tax stamps the study concluded that most illegal cigarettes had most likely come from Native American reservations (Kurti et al., 2013).

How much Lorillard depended on reservation sales in absolute terms and relative to other tobacco manufacturers is shown by data for 2007. In that year Lorillard sold 2,88 billion *taxed* cigarettes in New York State compared to 2,02 billion *untaxed* cigarettes going to Native American reservations. This means that 41,2% of Lorillard's business in New York State went to tribal stores in a year when industry wide the share of untaxed sales to tribal stores had already dropped to 33,9%. In comparison, the shares of untaxed sales to tribal businesses of the two other major tobacco manufacturers, R.J. Reynolds and Philip Morris, in the year 2007 were only 29,7% and 17,6%, respectively (Walker Guevara & Willson, 2008). In the end, 5% of the entire national volume of Lorillard's Newports reportedly flowed through just one tiny reservation closest to New York City, long after Philip Morris had ceased supplying cigarettes to the tribal stores there in an effort to distance itself from the bootlegging business (Buiso, 2011).

---

3 In May 2011, 254 surveys were distributed in three commercial zones in the South Bronx. Respondents were purposively selected according to their residency status (12 or more months), smoking status (one or more cigarette per week) and age (18 years and older).

Efforts to curb bootlegging from Native American Reservations to New York City

The developments between 2005 and 2011, when the overall share of sales to tribal stores began to decline and eventually dropped to 0 can be ascribed to various measures undertaken by the State of New York. The first two measures were taken in 2005 and aimed against the sale of cheap cigarettes from Native American reservations over the internet. The New York attorney general joined forces with other states' attorneys general and the U.S. Bureau of Alcohol, Tobacco, Firearms and Explosives (ATF) to reach an agreement with the major credit card companies and PayPal to stop processing internet purchases of cigarettes. Shortly thereafter, the New York attorney general successfully pressured private carriers, including FedEx and UPS, into stopping the delivery of cigarettes (Ribisl, Williams, Gizlice & Herring, 2011: 2). Congress followed up on this agreement with a law going into effect in 2010, the Prevent All Cigarette Trafficking Act (PACT), which prohibited the US Postal Service from delivering cigarettes (Lafaive & Nesbit, 2010: 9).

The decisive measure that effectively cut off supply from Native American reservations to New York City, however, was legislation passed by the state of New York in the same year, 2010 (Chapter 134 of the Law of 2010). This law mandated that all cigarette packs delivered to tribal stores had to bear a New York State tax stamp. Tax-exempt purchases by tribal members in New York State continued to be possible, but only through a coupon or prior approval system that effectively limited the volume of tax-exempt sales to tribal members.

After a legal battle the new law was upheld by the New York State Supreme Court in June 2011, which put an immediate stop to untaxed cigarettes being supplied to tribal stores. In fact, it practically ended the supply of non-tribal brand cigarettes to tribal stores altogether. Between June 21, 2011 and August 31, 2012, according to data provided by the New York State Department of Taxation and Finance, a total of only 1.140 cartons of cigarettes (228.000 sticks) were delivered to Native American reservations under the new prior approval system.

This left only Native American brand cigarettes as a potential supply from reservations to the black market in New York City. However, the new law did not affect cigarettes produced on tribal lands. Only cigarettes delivered to reservations have to bear a New York State tax stamp, not cigarettes that originate from reservations. However, as of this writing there is no indication that Native American brands have gained any significant share of the cigarette black market in New York City.

Supply channels for illegal cigarettes since 2011

Theoretically, the void left by brand cigarettes funneled through Native American reservations could have been filled by a number of sources of illegal cigarettes. With a view to developments in Europe one could have expected large-scale smuggling, cheap whites or counterfeit cigarettes conquering the cigarette black market in New York City. None of this has happened, however, as of this writing.

a. Bootlegging to New York City since 2011

All available information points to genuine brand cigarettes bootlegged from low-tax states such as Virginia dominating the black market in New York City once again, similar to the situation in the 1960s and 1970s (Caruso, 2013; Davis, Grimshaw, Merriman, Farrelly, Chernick, Coady, Campbell, & Kansagra, 2013).

One recent high profile case illustrates the current scale of inter-state bootlegging. In May of 2013, authorities broke up a smuggling ring made up of 16 Palestinian immigrants with alleged terrorist ties. The suspects are charged with selling more than 274 million cigarettes in New York City and in New York State over a period of about two years. The cigarettes were purchased in bulk from a legitimate wholesaler in Virginia under the ruse of supplying stores in Virginia. The cigarettes were then transported to a public storage facility in Delaware. A group member shuttled back and forth between the storage facility and New York, bringing about 20.000 cartons (4.000.000 sticks) per week to nine distributors who in turn took the cigarettes to various storage facilities in New York City from where the cigarettes were sold to markets and grocery stores (Hays, 2013; Mekeel, 2013; Powell, 2013).

Beyond anecdotal evidence, systematic research based on the analysis of littered cigarette packs points to a resurgence of inter-state bootlegging as the main procurement scheme for the New York City cigarette black market since June 2011. A survey of discarded cigarette packs undertaken in New York City in 2008 found only 14% of packs with tax stamps from other states (Chernick & Merriman, 2013: 644). In comparison, a study using a similar methodology in New York City in 2011 found a share of 49,1% of discarded packs with known non-local tax stamps or no tax stamps. Among cigarette packs with non-local tax stamps or no tax stamps approximately 62,6% of discarded cigarette packs were from other states (Davis et al., 2013: 3).

The shift to bootlegging from low-tax states is even more evident in research carried out in the South Bronx. Pack surveys were conducted in March 2011, shortly before the New York State Supreme Court upheld the new legislation preventing untaxed cigarettes from being funnelled through reservations, and again in March

2012. The 2011 survey found a low share of 15,8% of discarded packs in the South Bronx with tax stamps from other states (Kurti et al. 2013). One year later, about nine months after the supply of cheap cigarettes coming through Native American reservations had been cut off, the share of packs with tax stamps from low-tax states had increased to 57,6%. The share of cigarettes from Virginia alone increased between March 2011 and March 2012 from 9,1% to 48,6%. At the same time, the share of cigarettes with no tax stamps or counterfeit New York City tax stamps decreased from 56,1% in 2011 to 16,8% in 2012 (Johnson, von Lampe & Kurti, 2012).

b. Counterfeit Cigarettes on the New York City Market

The 16,8% of packs with either no tax stamp at all or a counterfeit New York City tax stamp that were found in the 2012 survey are significant because they arguably mark the greatest possible extent to which counterfeit cigarettes have penetrated the cigarette market in the South Bronx as of March 2012. This assumption is based on the notion that most cigarette packs that were found in 2011 with no tax stamps or counterfeit tax stamps came from Native American reservations and that it would make no sense to market counterfeit cigarettes in New York City with any counterfeit tax stamps other than those imitating New York City tax stamps. It is doubtful, however, that the share of counterfeit cigarettes in the South Bronx was indeed as high as 16,8% in 2012. These cigarettes could also have been bootlegged from states that do not use tax stamps, namely North Carolina, South Carolina and North Dakota (Chernick & Merriman 2013: 640). Other possibilities for the absence of tax stamps, respectively the presence of counterfeit tax stamps include the cigarettes coming from duty free stores or stamps from other states having been removed and replaced by counterfeit New York City tax stamps.

As far as can be seen, no estimates have been published about the prevalence of counterfeit cigarettes in New York City except for a press report from 2010 which mentioned in passing that tobacco manufacturers believe up to 2% of the New York cigarette market might be counterfeit (Crudele, 2010). Interestingly, this corresponds to the BAT estimates for the entire Western Hemisphere cited above. No litter pack survey has examined if the cigarette packs themselves are counterfeit. Knowledge of counterfeit cigarettes are reserved for tobacco companies who have their own ways of verifying 'unauthorized products' (UP), as they call them, including forensic examination of tear tape and foil (Unauthorized Product Strategy, 2000).

A systematic review of media reports in the three daily New York City papers *The New York Times*, *Daily News* and *New York Post* covering the time period January 1995 to September 2012[4] suggests that various attempts have been made by suppliers of counterfeit cigarettes to penetrate the New York City black market without sustained success. The first reported incidents of counterfeit cigarettes in New York City date back to 2002, which is relatively late considering the sharp increase in the seizure of counterfeit cigarettes in the US nationwide as early as 1999 and 2000.

The first reported New York cases were linked to Chinese businesses and the Chinese community in New York City. One case, for example, involved an alleged $5 million operation supplying fake Marlboros and other brand names originating in China to stores in Canal Street in Chinatown (Graham, 2002; Shifrel, 2002).

Counterfeit cigarettes being sold by Chinese businesses have been a recurrent theme in media coverage (see, e.g., Medaglia, 2007). Another recurrent theme has been the introduction of counterfeit cigarettes into the same illicit distribution channels through which also bootlegged cigarettes from Native American reservations and from low-tax states have been funnelled to the black market in New York City. In one case, for example, 28 mostly Middle-Eastern men were arrested for selling cigarettes bootlegged from Native American reservations as well as counterfeit cigarettes obtained from Chinese suppliers. The cigarettes went to store owners in New York City and the neighbouring town of Yonkers (Wilson, 2005; see also Crowley, 2006).

Some of the counterfeit cigarettes appearing in New York City have reportedly been delivered to legitimate stores, complete with counterfeit tax stamps, and have then been sold to unwitting consumers at regular prices (Weir, 2007). However, it seems that more typically counterfeit cigarettes have been sold under circumstances, including price and venue, that made the illegal nature of the cigarettes more or less obvious to customers, if not by the often low quality of the fake brand products (Graham, 2002; Medaglia, 2007; Weir, 2007; Seifman, 2012). This means that the retail sale of counterfeit and other contraband cigarettes tends to be an illegal transaction in which sellers and buyers collude. Accordingly, seller-buyer relationships at the retail level are an integral part of the illegal cigarette trade.

---

4 Using the Lexis-Nexis database of news publications, media reports from 1 January 1995 to 20 September 2012 printed by The New York Times, Daily News (New York) and The New York Post were retrieved using various combinations of keywords (cigarettes; cigarette; tobacco; counterfeit, fake, illegal, illicit, bootleg, pirated, smuggled). The initial search netted 4.204 articles that included any of the keywords in the content; upon further review, 190 articles were identified as having relevant content.

c. Retail selling of illegal cigarettes

In New York City the organisation of retail selling of illegal cigarettes seems to have gone through different phases. Early reports speak of retail sellers opportunistically searching for customers at public places where smokers likely converge in large numbers, for example at factory gates or at train stations (see, e.g., Pileggi, 1987: 57). This seems to have been the prevalent pattern throughout the 1960s, 1970s, 1980s and 1990s. In the 2000s, following the tax increases of 2002, stationary vendors operating at particular public and semi-public places appear to have been the most common manifestation of the retail sale of illegal cigarettes. Dubbed '$5 Man', these vendors became a common sight 'on street corners, in busy shopping areas, outside subway entrances, and in apartment buildings' particularly in low-income neighbourhoods (Shelley, Cantrell, Moon-Howard, Ramjohn and VanDevanter, 2005: 1484).

For reasons that are not entirely clear, since the late 2000s, the retail sale has shifted from street vending to sales out of grocery stores, commonly called 'bodegas'. The New York City Sheriff's Office Tobacco Task Force, which has conducted over 1.700 cigarette retail inspections between August 2011 and 2012, found that approximately 42% of bodegas sold illegal cigarettes (Virginia Crime Commission, 2012). Law enforcement data also suggest that bodegas that sell contraband cigarettes tend to be geographically located in socio-economically deprived neighbourhoods with largely African-American and Hispanic minority populations[5] (New York City Sheriff's Office, 2013; see also Walker, Guevara and Willson, 2008). Bodegas in these areas are typically owned and operated by recent immigrants from the Middle East which may explain in part why many of the bootlegging and wholesale operations that have been detected in recent years are also made up primarily or exclusively of individuals with Middle Eastern roots (Crudele, 2011).

One can speculate that a reason for the apparent shift from street vendors to bodegas might have been that street vendors became associated with low quality (counterfeit) cigarettes. In contrast, smokers might have been more confident to obtain high quality genuine cigarettes from bodegas. At the same time, in light of rising legal prices for cigarettes it appears plausible that bodega owners have increasingly felt a need to sell cheap (illegal) cigarettes in order to maintain customers (Guart, 2002). Especially for smokers in socio-economically deprived areas it has become more and more difficult to afford a pack of cigarettes at prices of well over $10. Once one bodega in an area starts selling illegal cigarettes, as anecdotal evidence

---

5 Hot spot analysis of seizures from cigarette retailers from August 2011 to March 2013 indicates that they are saturated in low-income census tracts of New York City.

suggests, this creates substantial pressure on nearby bodegas to also sell illegal cigarettes (Montero, Fasick & Bennett, 2010).

It appears evident that the sale of illegal cigarettes enjoys some level of social acceptance in poor neighbourhoods (Shelley et al., 2005). At the same time law enforcement pressure has been described as relatively low and the penalties for black market participants are seen to be lenient, especially in comparison to drug dealing (Alderman, 2012: 4; Caruso, 2013).

Conclusion

The illegal cigarette trade in the United States has for the past decades been marked primarily by the exploitation of cigarette price differentials between high-tax and low-tax jurisdictions. In the case of New York City, arguably the most important local cigarette black market in the country, inter-state bootlegging, and for a historical period of some twenty years ending in 2011, the bootlegging from Native American reservations have been the main modes of procurement of cheap cigarettes. Against the background of developments in Europe since the early 1990s, two aspects are remarkable.

First, it is important to note that according to the available evidence neither large-scale smuggling, nor counterfeit cigarettes, nor so-called cheap whites have taken over the black market and that the illegal cigarette trade continues to be defined by the least sophisticated procurement scheme.

Second, it is peculiar to find major tobacco manufacturers implicated in the illegal cigarette trade at a time when in Europe the tobacco industry seems to have completely desisted from supplying cigarettes into dubious distribution channels. Apologetic statements by Lorillard at the height of their involvement in untaxed sales, claiming that "cigarette manufacturers should not be expected to police the trade in untaxed cigarettes" (Saul, 2008), remind one of the stance taken by manufacturers in Europe before they succumbed to political and legal pressure exerted by the European Commission and others in the late 1990s and early 2000s. Perhaps this is something that should be kept in mind should the tobacco industry be implicated in shady schemes in the future.

From a scholarly perspective, the United States is not just another case of criminals taking advantage of the taxation of cigarettes. The variations in the patters of illicit activity across space and time involving a commodity which remains constant in shape, size and weight invite future research into the organization of crime for profit from a comparative angle.

References

Advisory Committee on Intergovernmental Relations, *Cigarette Bootlegging: A State AND Federal Responsibility*. Washington DC: ACIR, 1977

Alderman, J., *Strategies to Combat Illicit Tobacco Trade.* St. Paul, MN: Tobacco Control Legal Consortium, 2012

Antonopoulos, G.A., Cigarette smuggling: A case study of a smuggling network in Greece, *European Journal of Crime, Criminal Law and Criminal Justice,* 2006, *no. 3*, 239-255

Antonopoulos, G.A., The Greek Connection(s): The Social Organization of the Cigarette-Smuggling Business in Greece, *European Journal of Criminology*, 2008, *no. 3*, 263-288

Beare, M., Organized corporate criminality: Tobacco smuggling between Canada and the US, *Crime, Law and Social Change*, 2002, *no. 3*, 225-243

Beare, M.E., Organized Corporate Criminality: Corporate Complicity in Tobacco Smuggling, in: M.E. Beare (ed.) *Critical Reflections on Transnational Organized Crime Money Laundering and Corruption*, Toronto, ONT: University of Toronto Press, 2003, 183-206

British American Tobacco. Illicit Trade: examining the problem and advocating solutions. Anti Illicit Trade Unit. British American Tobacco (Holdings) Limited. 2010

Buiso, G., Butt-Leggers, *New York Post*, 12 June 2011

Caruso, D, NYC cigarette tax fight hampered by low fines. *Associated Press*, 5 May 2013. Retrieved from http://bigstory.ap.org/article/nyc-cigarette-tax-fight-hampered-low-fines

Chernick, H. and D. Merriman, Using littered pack data to estimate cigarette tax avoidance in NYC. *National Tax Journal*, 2013, *no. 3*, 635-668

Coker, D., Smoking may not only be hazardous to your health but also to world political stability: The European Union's fight against cigarette smuggling rings that benefit terrorism. *European Journal of Crime Criminal Law and Criminal Justice*, 2003, *no. 4*, 350-376

Crudele, J., Counterfeit smokes, unchecked, growing in NY. *New York Post*, 27 July 2010

Davis, K.C., V. Grimshaw, D. Merriman, M.C. Farrelly, H. Chernick, M. Coady, K. Campbell, and S.M. Kasagra, Cigarette trafficking in five northeastern US cities. *Tobacco Control,* 2013, doi 0.1136/tobaccocontrol-2013-051244

DeCicca, P., D. Kenkel, and F. Liu, Reservation prices: An economic analysis of cigarette purchases on Indian reservations, 2010. Retrieved from:

http://www.economics.mcmaster.ca/documents/reservation-20prices_may14_2010_tables_appendix.pdf

Duyne, P.C. van and G.A. Antonopoulos (eds.), *The criminal smoke of tobacco policy making: Cigarette smuggling in Europe*. Nijmegen: Wolf Legal Publishers, 2009

European Commission, Excise Duty Table, Part III - Manufactured Tobacco, January 2010. Retrieved from: http://ec.europa.eu/taxation_customs/resources/documents/taxation/excise_duties/tobacco_products/rates/excise_duties-part_III_tobacco-en.pdf

Fleenor, P., Cigarette taxes, black markets, and crime: Lessons from New York's 50 year losing battle. *Policy Analysis, no. 468*, 6 February 2003

GAO (General Accounting Office), Cigarette Smuggling: Federal Law Enforcement Efforts and Seizures Increasing. Washington DC: GAO, 2004

GAO (Government Accountability Office), Illicit Tobacco: Various Schemes Are Used to Evade Taxes and Fees. Washington DC: GAO, 2011

Geis, G., S. Cartwright and J. Houston, Public wealth, public health, and private stealth: Australia's black market in cigarettes. Centre for Tax System Integrity, Australian National University, Working Paper No. 55, February 2004

Graham, J., Cops flick butt-leggers. *New York Post*. 28 September 2002

Griffiths, H., Smoking guns: European cigarette smuggling in the 1990's. *Global Crime*, 2004, *no. 2*, 185-200

Guart, A., Burning issues steam the apple - Butt-leggers' sell illicit cigs under cops' noses. *New York Post*, 18 August 2002

Hays, T., New York cigarette smuggling ring may have funneled money to Hamas, say officials. *Huffington Post*, 16 May 2013. Retrieved from: http://www.huffingtonpost.com/2013/05/16/new-york-cigarette-smuggling-hamas_n_3288536.html

Hornsby, R. and D. Hobbs, A zone of ambiguity: The political economy of cigarette bootlegging. *British Journal of Criminology*, 2007, *no. 4*, 551-571

Hozic, A.A., Between the cracks: Balkan cigarette smuggling. *Problems of Post-Communism*, 2004, *no. 3*, 35-44

Johnson, J., K. von Lampe and M. Kurti, The illegal cigarette market in the South Bronx: After a tax amendment. *American Society of Criminology Annual Meeting*, Chicago, IL, 26 November 2012

Joossens, L. and M. Raw, Cigarette smuggling in Europe: who really benefits?. *Tobacco Control*, 1998, *no. 1*, 66-71

Joossens, L. and M. Raw, How can cigarette smuggling be reduced? *British Medical Journal* 321, 2000, 947-950

Joossens, L. and M. Raw, Progress in combating cigarette smuggling: controlling the supply chain. *Tobacco Control*, 2008, no. 6, 399-404

Kurti, M., K. von Lampe and D.E. Thompkins, The illegal cigarette market in a socioeconomically deprived inner-city area: The case of the South Bronx. *Tobacco Control*, 2013, *no. 2*, 138-40

Kurti, M., Where there's smoke, there's fire: The illegal cigarette market in the South Bronx.(Master's thesis), 2011. Retrieved from WorldCat

LaFaive, M. and T. Nesbit, *Cigarette taxes and smuggling: A Statistical analysis and historical review*. Midland, MI: Mackinac Center for Public Policy, 2008

LaFaive, M. and T.Nesbit, *Cigarette taxes and smuggling*. Midland, MI: Mackinac Center for Public Policy, 2010

Medaglia, A., Cigarettes are costly, but often less so in Chinatown. *New York Times*, 18 September 2007

Mekeel, T., Cigarette-smuggling case forces Lancaster County wholesaler into bankruptcy. Lancaster Online, 31 May 2013. Retrieved from: http://lancasteronline.com/article/local/856146_Cigarette-smuggling-case-forces-Lancaster-County-wholesaler-into-bankruptcy.html

Montero, D., K. Fasick and C. Bennett, Burned by bootleg smokes. *New York Post*, 26 November 2010

Montero, D., K. Fasick and C. Bennett, It pays to cheat. *New York Post*, 26 November 2010

New York City Department of Health and Mental Hygiene, Trends in Cigarette Use among Adults in New York City, 2002-2010. Epi Data Brief, No. 12, November 2011. Retrieved from: http://www.nyc.gov/html/doh/downloads/pdf/epi/databrief12.pdf

Pileggi, N., *Wiseguy: Life in a Mafia Family*. London: Corgi, 1987

Powell, N., Ramadan bros. taken to NY for cig smuggling. *Ocean City Today*, 24 May 2013. Retrieved from: http://www.oceancity.com/ocean-city-today/ramadan-bros-taken-to-ny-for-cig-smuggling

Ramos, A., Illegal trade in tobacco in MERCOSUR countries. Centro de Investigacion de la epidemia de tabaquismo Uruguay. Working Paper, June 2009

Ribisl, K.M., R.S. Williams, Z. Gizlice and A.H. Herring, Effectiveness of state and federal government agreements with major credit card and shipping companies to block illegal internet cigarette sales. *PLoS One*, 2011, *no. 2*, e16754

Saul, S., Suits claim wide reach of cigarettes from tribes. *New York Times*, 2 October 2008

Seifman, D., Cig-tax cheating stores burn city. *New York Post*, 8 June 2012

Shelley, D., M.J. Cantrell, J. Moon-Howard, D. Ramjohn and N. Vandevanter, The $5.00 man: the underground economic response to a large cigarette tax increase in New York City. *American Journal of Public Health*, 2007, *no. 8*, 1483-8

Shen, A., G.A. Antonopoulos and K. von Lampe, 'The dragon breathes smoke': Cigarette counterfeiting in the People's Republic of China, *British Journal of Criminology*, 2010, *no. 2*, 239-258

Shifrel, S., Bogus butts pinched in Queens. *New York Daily News*, 28 September 2002. Retrieved from http://www.nydailynews.com/archives/news/bogus-butts-pinched-queens-article-1.501478

Svogun, T., Cigarette bootlegging: The problem, civil and criminal remedies. In: G. Blakey and J. Robert (ed.), *Techniques in the Investigation and Prosecution of Organized Crime*. Volume One. Cornell Law School, 1980, 241-271

Unauthorized Product Strategy for USA, 23 March 2000. http://legacy.library.ucsf.edu/tid/sew99h00/pdf?search=%22unauthorized%20product%22

Virginia State Crime Commission, SJRR 21: Illegal Cigarette Trafficking, 2012. Retrieved from: http://vscc.virginia.gov/FINAL_Cigarette%20trafficking%20November%20presentation.pdf

von Lampe, K., The cigarette black market in Germany and in the United Kingdom, *Journal of Financial Crime* , 2006, *no. 2*, 235-254

von Lampe, K., Preventing organised crime: the case of contraband cigarettes, in: K. Bullock, R.V. Clarke and N. Tilley, (eds.) *Situational Prevention of Organised Crimes*. Cullompton, UK: Willan, 2010, 35-57

von Lampe, K., M. Kurti, A. Shen and G.A. Antonopoulos, The Changing Role of China in the Global Illegal Cigarette Trade. *International Criminal Justice Review,* 2012, no. 1, 43-67

Walker, G.M. and K. Willson, Big tobacco's New York black market. Tobacco underground, 2008. Retrieved from: http://www.publicintegrity.org/investigations/tobacco/articles/entry/1084/

Weir, R., Illegal cig operation is busted. *Daily News*, 14 August 2007

World Customs Organization, *Illicit trade report 2012*. Retrieved from: http://www.wcoomd.org/en/topics/enforcement-and-compliance/activities-and-prgrammes/~/media/WCO/Public/Global/PDF/Topics/Enforcement%20and%20Compliance/Actities%20and%20Programmes/Illicit%20Trade%20Report%202012/WCO%20REPORT%202013%20-%20BR.ashx

Human trafficking policy making and the politics of international criminal justice A case study of sexual exploitation

Jon Spencer[1]

Introduction

Contemplating attending a conference on Human Trafficking this year or next? All you need to do is a cursory web search and there are numerous choices. Conferences in the USA on the global problem of trafficking, conferences in Europe that seek to address the issues with a law enforcement perspective and national conferences that address the issues of human trafficking victims. The past twenty years or so has seen high levels of policy activity to combat human trafficking. The underpinning view is that it is a problem of global proportions and a lucrative source of income for organised crime. The aim of this paper is to place under scrutiny the hegemony of ideas that prevail in the trafficking debate and policy making.

The policy area of human trafficking for sexual exploitation has been a global criminal justice policy activity with the United Nations, European Union and many national governments all of which engage in 'strategic responses' to the problem. These three domains of policy-making interact and reproduce policy definitions, responses and interventions that legitimate the problem within the parameters of the existing debate. Therefore, decisions in one policy domain are influential on policy decisions and actions in the other domains. However, much of this policy structuring and decision-making is fundamentally flawed as the databases used to construct policy frameworks, and the operational interventions, are polluted.

Quantitative data, whether or not from polluted bases may be of moderate interest to policy makers. The policy responses to the 'problem' of human trafficking for sexual exploitation are mainly built on the foundations of international protocols and agreements. The 2011 EU Directive on "*Combatting human trafficking and*

1 The author is Director of the Anglo-Baltic Criminological Research Unit, University of Manchester.

protecting victims" (European Union 2011) says that human trafficking is a serious crime and ". . . often committed within the framework of organised crime". However, an Institute of Public Policy Research (IPPR) Report stated:

> "Rather than perceiving it (Human Trafficking) as an issue dominated by organised criminal networks, it must be understood as a crime often perpetrated by people known to or, in many cases, related to the victims who may otherwise live their lives in an outwardly respectable way." (IPPR 2013:4)

This not only confounds law enforcement claims of the role of 'organised crime' but also demonstrates that the complexities of how people are moved and exploited are ignored by the EU Directive. However, the Directive squarely identifies that the signatories are of the view that the Directive and their commitment to it is ". . . part of global action against trafficking in human beings" (EU 2011). What we see is an attempt to co-ordinate responses that weave national, European and International policies into a joined up response. However, these approaches are over-focused on 'organised crime' and over-estimate the size of the problem. This results in serious flaws in international policy initiatives to address human trafficking.

Policy directives and protocols in this area are based on incomplete data and this has contributed to the flawed approach of a narrow and relatively ineffective response. One of the key reasons for this lack of effectiveness is because policy activity on human trafficking for sexual exploitation has been firmly placed within the domain of law enforcement. The whole complex dynamic of migration is hidden, or only partially recognisable, because within this policy domain migration is a focus of enforcement and regulatory action which migrants naturally seek to evade. This paper first addresses the issue of prevalence and then goes on to consider the underpinning policy making trends. Finally in a consideration of 'trafficking cases' an argument is developed that urges a more critical approach to the 'problem' of human trafficking with an overall conclusion that what is required is a broader and more flexible approach that takes account of the complexities of migratory movements.

The 'Wicked' Problem of Human Trafficking

One approach to social problems is to understand them either as wicked or benign problems. Wicked problems:

> ". . . are unstructured. This means that causes and effects are extremely difficult to identify and model, thus adding complexity and uncertainty and engendering a

> high degree of conflict because there is little consensus on the problem or the solution." (Weber and Khademian 2008: 336)

'Wicked' problems are messy and do ". . . not stay still'" (Ritchey 2011:1), they cut across different "policy domains and levels of government" (Weber and Khademian 2008:336), and "are inescapably connected to other problems" (Weber and Khademian 2008:336). There are many such problems within criminal justice, for example, at an international level the problems experienced by law enforcement in addressing 'organised crime' is a 'wicked' problem due to shifting definitions, changing crime patterns and a lack of consensus concerning the 'nature' of the problem (Paoli 2002).

The lack of an accurate assessment of the prevalence of human trafficking also adds to the 'wicked' nature of the problem. As Tyldum and Brunovskis (2005) argue research on human trafficking is complex, demanding and difficult. However, if public policy is to be informed and shaped by research then getting the research right is critically important:

> "Uncritically using or publishing findings not based on sound methodologies may result in misinformation and hinder the creation of relevant policies and appropriate programmes." (Tyldum and Brunovskis 2005:18)

The United Nations Office of Drugs and Crime (UNODC 2009) in its *Global Report on the Trafficking of Persons* provides no numerical estimate of the scale of the problem but claims that the problem is significant and requires immediate action (UNODC 2009). The UNODC 'Global Report into Trafficking in Persons' provides a country by country analysis and argues that:

> ". . . sharing human trafficking data on a global basis is possible and can yield valuable insights, *despite the inherent limitations of the criminal justice figures*." (UNODC 2009: 8 *my emphasis*).

The report (UNODC 2009) further recognises the difficulty in estimating the size of the problem:

> "Without a sense of the magnitude of the problem, it is impossible to prioritize human trafficking as an issue relative to other local or transnational threats, and it is difficult to assess whether any particular intervention is having effect…Far more knowledge is needed before the true size of the market for human beings can be estimated . . ." (UNODC 2009: 12)

The report goes onto estimate that in 2008 that there were 21.400 victims of trafficking identified[2] in 111 reporting countries. In the same year in the UK The Home Affairs Select Committee (Home Office 2009) reported that there was approximately between 100.000 and 800.000 thousand people, the majority of them women, trafficked into the EU each year and of these 5.000 are in the UK (Home Office 2009:3). If this figure is to be believed it means that, on average, each of the twenty-seven EU member states receives each year in excess of 20.000 trafficked people, the majority of them women. Furthermore, Central Eastern European Countries are generally defined as source and not receiving countries for trafficking. This being the case we should expect Central Eastern European countries to have lower levels of inflow of trafficked victims than the identified receiving countries, for example the UK and Germany. If the Home Affairs Select Committee figures are accurate there must be a majority of receiving countries where the number of trafficked women must be substantially higher than the average. What is also apparent is that across Europe there are low levels of victim identification. If we use the Home Affairs Select Committee (Home Office 2009) and UNODC (2009) figures for the number of identified victims it represents approximately 2% of the total trafficked population. There are two possible explanations for this low percentage: either law enforcement is ineffective and incompetent or the figures of people trafficked are substantially lower than claimed as the UNODC (2009) estimates for 2008 indicate.

These estimates of the 'trafficked population' require arithmetic gymnastics that render any attempt to size the trafficked population unreliable. For such figures to be accurate it would mean that in some of the receiving countries human trafficking must be at epidemic proportions. All of this suggests that the sizing of the trafficked population is problematic, however, many of the assumptions that policy decisions are based upon utilises versions of these unverified data, as Tyldum and Brunovskis note ". . . the only thing worse than no data is wrong and misleading data" (Tyldum and Brunovoskis 2005:30).

One simple and relatively crude way to estimate the prevalence of trafficking, for example, is the number of convictions of traffickers as there may be some relationship between recorded offences and actual offences. The UK figures for human trafficking for sexual exploitation are surprisingly low, as are the figure for exploitation of prostitution[3] (see Table 1 below), especially when taking account of the substantial

2 The manner in which victims are identified and defined is highly problematic.

3 This offence is included as it may be an alternative charge where an offence of trafficking for sexual exploitation cannot be proved but where there is evidence of exploitation of prostitution, there are no details in the England and Wales figures of the country of origin of the victims of these crime types.

resources invested in combating this type of crime (see Spencer and Broad 2010). The UNODC (2009) *Global Trafficking Report* provides conviction figures for the UK and these are low. The low conviction and recorded offences figures could suggest that either the problem is relatively small or, we must conclude that UK law enforcement agencies are incompetent in only managing to secure a 1% recorded offence rate.[4] This latter interpretation is especially so if the Home Affairs Select Committee estimated figures are anywhere near accurate.

Table 1
Recorded offences – trafficking & prostitution:
Number of recorded offences

Year	**2002**	**2003**	**2004**	**2005**	**2006**	**2007**	**2008**	**2009**	**2010**
Trafficking for sexual exploitation	No recorded figures	No record ed figures	21	33	43	57	52	58	67
Convictions[5] for Trafficking for sexual exploitation			3	21	32	23			
Exploitation of Prostitution	127	186	117	153	190	184	173	148	153

(Source: *Crime in England and Wales 2010-2011*. Home Office 2011).

However, the lack of verifiable data does not dissuade those that consider trafficking to be a significant problem arguing that the conviction and prosecution figures are not the result of low incidence or law enforcement incompetence but of the problems of obtaining evidence. Therefore, they argue, that the small numbers of prosecutions and convictions do not accurately reflect the scale of the problem (UNODC 2009).

Those who promote such an account of human trafficking claim ‘good intelligence’ concerning the strategies used by ‘traffickers’ in their criminal operations. However, apprehending and prosecuting the ‘traffickers’ seems to be exceptionally problematic. For example, the United Kingdom Human Trafficking Centre’s

4 The sentencing data does not disaggregate those sentenced for exploitation of prostitution and trafficking for sexual exploitation from within the ‘Other Sexual Offences’ category, so it is difficult to calculate the number of offenders responsible for these offences and the sentences they received.

5 This data is partial because it is included from the reported data in the UNODC Global Trafficking Report 2009

(UKHTC) Pentameter II operation is often credited with the successful identification of 163 victims, and 406 suspects arrested with 67 of these being charged with human trafficking offences. Of this final figure it is claimed 15 (9%) were convicted (UKHTC 2008). However, the investigative journalist Nick Davies (Guardian 2009) argues that the Pentameter II operation did not result in one conviction for trafficking:

> "Internal police documents reveal that 10 of Pentameter's 15 convictions were of men and women who were jailed on the basis that there was no evidence of their coercing the prostitutes they had worked with. There were just five men who were convicted of importing women and forcing them to work as prostitutes. These genuinely were traffickers, but none of them was detected by Pentameter . . ." (Guardian 2009)

This lack of success in terms of the number of convictions by law enforcement indicates that human trafficking into the UK may be much less than the official account suggests, despite of the resources, for example, the lavish funding of the UKHTC and SOCA's activities on immigration crime (see Spencer and Broad 2010).

Goodey (2008) argues that four things have happened in the development of law enforcement policy in response to trafficking. First it has become victim centred so that there are many accounts of victims. Second, trafficking of human beings is located, in the 'migration, crime, and security nexus'. Thirdly there is little information on the trajectories or antecedents of the men and women involved in the act of trafficking. Finally, there is a lack of reliable data on the demand side of the trafficking equation (Goodey 2008). However, despite all of these concerns the claims by official agencies that human trafficking is prevalent appear to be influential in the policy-making process. Such claims, media reports and institutional interests contribute to the construction of societal problem imagery. (Spencer 2008) This construction of the 'problem' of human trafficking does not rely on creditable statistics to estimate the size of the problem or reliable data concerning the 'traffickers'. Furthermore there is little knowledge concerning the structure of the markets, both in terms of supply and demand. This lack of knowledge and data does not curb the repeated calls for international action (Van Duyne and Spencer 2011). In the official account human trafficking remains a sizeable problem but there seems little evidence that it is as large and 'wicked' as claimed. So, with such poor evidence the research question arises, and which still remains to be answered is: how has the hegemony of human trafficking policy developed?

International policy approaches to human trafficking

The Palermo Convention

The United Nations Convention Against Transnational Organised Crime (Palermo Convention) was agreed in 2000. The Convention has three protocols, one that is focused on the movement of firearms, and another which is concerned with people smuggling and the final protocol that is concerned with the trafficking of persons, especially women and children. Wharton (2010) comments on the development of 'anti-trafficking' policy in the USA during the late 1990s and early 2000s and demonstrates that much of it was the outcome of what Boswell *et al.* (2010) would identify as a *policy narrative* (see also Dozema 1998). That narrative articulates the anxiety that young women are at a high risk of sexual exploitation and looks like a reminiscent of the fear of white female trafficking in a century ago. The response was the swift introduction of national and international legislation and protocols. The relevant Palermo Protocol is one such piece of internationally agreed policy.

This protocol is evidence of a globalised criminal justice policy-making process. Dozema (2005) discusses the process of how the protocol was agreed and comments on the absence of the sex worker's voice. The protocol is an outcome of competition between different women's groups, some of which advocate that sex workers are unable to give consent because all prostitution is rape (Agustin 2006 and see Spencer 2008). Alternatively, many sex workers agree to sex work argue that *consent* is the critical factor in determining their own agency in undertaking the work they choose (Doezema 2005). The absence of the sex worker's voice in the preceding discussions and consultations of the Palermo Protocol is critical in determining the discourse of policy, Doezema argues:

> "As the space for consent dwindles to nothing, the myth of trafficking grows to encompass all prostitution, and every woman selling sex becomes mythically positioned as a slave." (Doezema 2005:74)

This notion of all non-national women selling sex as trafficked victims, as enslaved women, is an important feature of the policy making process and the reproduction of the human trafficking discourse.

The Palermo protocol defined the trafficking in human beings in the following way:

> "Trafficking in persons" shall mean the recruitment, transportation, transfer, harbouring or receipt of persons, by means of the threat or use of force or other forms of coercion, of abduction, of fraud, of deception, of the abuse of power or of a position of vulnerability or of the giving or receiving of payments or benefits

> to achieve the consent of a person having control over another person, for the purpose of exploitation. Exploitation shall include, at a minimum, the exploitation of the prostitution of others or other forms of sexual exploitation, forced labour or services, slavery or practices similar to slavery, servitude or the removal of organs." (United Nations 2000)

Taking as an example the UK the approach to the Palermo Protocol has been to develop law enforcement co-operation strategies. In the UK in 2005 there was a concern about European Union enlargement and whilst workers from the accession countries would be admitted, to meet labour shortages, this clashed with the 'little England' sensitivities concerning immigration of some members of the political establishment and some of the print media. In the UK, the call to adopt anti-trafficking legislation does not solely originate within the anxieties concerning immigration but also from those anxieties that are deeply entrenched in attitudes to prostitution and the sex industry. There are two different discourses, one concerning migration, the other prostitution, that utilise human trafficking as a means of influencing policy decisions. These points of influence are in part a result of different coalitions of interest. In the UK law enforcement plays an active part in the building of this coalition that structures the discourse in a particular strategy of power, namely by the omission of certain key actors, in this case sex workers, as indicated by the UKHTC website:

> "The UKHTC's partners include police forces, the UK Border Agency, HM Revenue & Customs, the Crown Prosecution Service, the Gangmasters Licensing Authority, non-Governmental organisations (NGOs) and *many charitable and voluntary expert groups*." (SOCA 2013 emphasis added)

But where are the sex workers? The majority of these 'partners' are official government agencies. The remainder are not named and so are drawn from the charitable and voluntary sector that provide support to those defined as having been 'trafficked'. The questions of who is it that decides upon which charities are included and who the experts are in the field? What appears to occur is the selection of these charities and experts by the official agencies of the state thus, no doubt, reinforcing the dominant political discourse. So, the policy narratives by this process are exclusionary but adherence to the trafficking narrative highlights powerful coalitions that pressure the government to take action.

b. The European level

The anxieties about trafficking are also found at the European Union level. Europol has a clear mission to combat human trafficking, but the problems of definition are acknowledged:

> "The scale and nature of THB (Trafficking in Human Beings) in the EU is not easy to define because of very fundamental reasons. Criminal activity related to trafficking in human beings can be hidden within other criminality, such as prostitution, illegal immigration and labour disputes, for example. This often results in instances of trafficking not being investigated or recorded as trafficking cases." (Europol 2011:3-4)

This is the classic narrative that is provided to create and sustain the problem: human trafficking is much more widespread than the numbers suggest because of its hidden nature. It is also important to note where it is hidden: within prostitution, border transgression and labour disputes. However, in many member states these actions are not necessarily criminal. What is criminal about a labour dispute? In many member states prostitution is not criminal; it is the soliciting that is against the law. However, EUROPOL's mission statement makes a connection to those broader anxieties, as outlined in the UK example, of migration and with it labour issues and prostitution. There is, also, an acknowledgement of a lack of reliable data. However, again this does not dissuade policy makers from tackling the problem at the European Union level because there is a supporting international protocol that claims that trafficking is a problem of organised crime.

The human trafficking narrative

The issue of human trafficking acquires a certain narrative of its own that surrounds the victim. In many cases the victim is described as young innocent woman duped into migrating through either a supposed 'boyfriend' or with the promise of legitimate work. The impetus to migrate is explained simply in terms of either push and pulls factors or a 'romantic' interest. But there is little or no accurate knowledge about the 'traffickers'.

Much of the official narrative fails to engage with the complexities and flexibilities of people movement networks across Europe. For example there is little discussion of the demand side and how this works or of the experiences of the 'traffickers', nor is there much discussion of the migratory trajectories of the women (see for example EUROPOL 2011). If the woman fails to conform to the trafficked stereotype then she is viewed as a migrant working as a prostitute, and if an irregular migrant, she is viewed as an offender and returned to her country of origin. The policy deliberations, strategic decision making and the use of law enforcement techniques to 'combat' trafficking have resulted in the relocation of the lived experience of migration into the arena of criminal justice. This is because the narratives and policy questions are predominantly framed within a criminal justice context. It is for these reasons that the narratives of the women and the men involved in the migratory project are rendered silent other than when they conform to the dominant narrative structure. As Agustin articulates:

> "In recent years, the field of migration studies has opened up to diverse theories; . . . So it is strange that a whole category of migration should be discursively shunted or perhaps tidied away into another domain. I refer to women who leave their countries and later are found selling sex in someone else's, at which point they disappear from migration studies (where they would be migrants) and reappear in criminological or feminist theorising (where they are called victims)." (Agustin, 2006: 29)

Agustin (2006) is addressing the global facet of migration and how in these instances it becomes a globalised approach to the criminalising of migration flows, with migrant women as victims and perpetrators[6] and migrant men as mainly perpetrators of trafficking. This process of criminalisation is through the use of international instruments and agreements. There is a connection between the Palermo Protocol that establishes the narrative structure for the criminalising process, to the EU responses to migratory flows from North Africa and the subsequent Dublin Accord, which was an attempt to strengthen and reinforce the Schengen Agreement[7]. At the localised level the inclusion of trafficking and exploitation offences in the UK's Sexual Offences Act 2003 (HMSO 2003) is, in part, a legacy of these international and European protocols and directives.

However, all of these protocols, international agreements and national laws locate trafficking within a criminal justice narrative rather than one of migration. One consequence of this is, as Paoli and Fijnaut (2006) argue:

> ". . . migrants today [having] a harder time accessing the legal economy and, due to the restrictive policies adopted by most Western European states, are more

6 There are cases of where trafficked women (victims) become traffickers (perpetrators).

7 One rationale of the Schengen Agreement was to ensure the free movement of people within Europe to ensure the meeting of labour demand.

likely to find a means of survival only in the informal and illegal economies." (Paoli and Fijnaut, 2006: 318)

So, the policy making approaches, influenced and shaped by protocols and so on, are a critical factor in shaping the day-to-day lived experience of the migrant in the labour market. The lack of access to formal economic activity and the easier access to informal and illegal economic activity potentially places migrants in the realm of criminal justice. Consequently, generally, internationally, the criminal justice response is to understand issues of migration within the framework of trafficking. This shaping of criminal justice responses has been assisted by the very broad and inclusive terms of the Palermo Protocol.

The policy narratives that emerge through international pressure groups and criminal justice policy entrepreneurs have supported this strategic approach. These actors in the policy-making discourse have parallel agendas in relation to the sex industry and migration; for criminal justice entrepreneurs there is a need to establish a narrative that makes international criminal justice strategies indispensable to the management of migration policy initiatives and for international pressure groups their sphere of influence and in some cases access to funding is determined by the ability to sustain narrative structures and policy questions.

Four case histories

The following section discusses four cases where the influence of the policy-making hegemony is apparent. The first case is that of the *Demarku Brothers*; the second the case of *Aurel Zlate*, 46, and his wife *Alexandra Oaie*; the third case is of *Telus Dumitru* and finally the case of the *Cuddles Massage Parlour*. These brief case studies raise questions of the nature of the understanding of the concept of trafficking. Is trafficking an organised criminal action reliant on networks and criminal groups, or is it individual and opportunistic?

A particular case 1: the Demarku brothers

In December 2005 the Demarku brothers and a family friend were sentenced to prison for offences of human trafficking for sexual exploitation. They originated from Albania. Neither official records nor press accounts specify whether they were in the UK legally or as irregular migrants. All five of the defendants were convicted at Southwark Crown Court in December 2005 for offences of trafficking, as defined within the Sexual Offences Act 2003. They all received substantial prison sentences, ranging from 5 to 18 years. The facts of the case, as established by the court, were that a 16-year-old woman was deceived with a promise of work into coming to

London from Lithuania. She travelled with two Lithuanian men and on arrival at London Stansted Airport she was met by two Albanian men (neither of whom was a Demarku). The woman's papers were taken from her and she was forced to work in a brothel in Sheffield. After five days she returned to London Stansted Airport and there she met three of the Demarku brothers, along with other women who were arriving to work in the sex industry voluntarily. From there she was driven to a brothel controlled by the Demarku brothers where she was forced to work as a prostitute in order to repay her 'debts'.

The young woman's mother became concerned at the lack of contact with her daughter and she contacted the Lithuanian police and a Lithuanian television channel which made contact with the BBC in London. The BBC decided to investigate the story and it was during this time that the police were informed of the victim's whereabouts in Hounslow. The police kept the brothel under surveillance and discovered that the Demarku brothers were 'managing', or had links to a further six establishments and moving women between them. In one of these establishments there were two women who were working against their will as prostitutes, one of which was the young Lithuanian woman. All the other women working at the brothels were free to leave and were remunerated for their work, though none of them were UK nationals.

The media reporting of this case was extensive and the news reports used familiar constructions in reporting the case; the Demarku brothers were a 'gang,' (BBC 2005), *The Sun* used the term ". . . gang of Albanian traffickers" (The Sun 2009). *The Guardian* picked up on the judges comment of the Demarku brothers being a "family firm" (The Guardian 2005) and *Sky News* dubbed the Demarku brothers as the "Sexual Exploitation Gang" (Sky News 2005). Some of the news reports make particular reference to the extensive profits, in excess of two million pounds it is claimed, that the brothers were alleged to have made and remitted to Albania.

One of the key ingredients of this case is that of ethnicity. The Albanian identity of the brothers is a key factor that is reported in the press in relation to this case. In many instances Albanians are viewed as being the originators of trafficking and it is their 'signature' organised crime. The Demarku brothers' victim provides a model for future victim constructions. In the Demarku case the victim is presented as young and innocent. She is duped into making the trip to London and the 'trafficker' gains the trust of the girl's parents. It is only when she has surrendered her passport and arrived in the UK that the full horror of what is expected of her is clear. The victim stereotype rests upon an innocent yet naive victim, with trusting but unworldly parents

The Demarku brothers were not the traffickers, they did not arrange the travel or entice the young woman to come to the UK. However, they were clearly part of a network of male brothel keepers who were 'employing' women from Central Eastern Europe. The Demarku brothers took the opportunity to increase their profit by paying for the passport of the young woman and using this control and power to sexually exploit her.

Aurel Zlate and his wife Alexandra Oaie

The second case is different in that it concerns a Romanian couple, Aurel Zlate and his wife Alexandra Oaie. They were convicted of trafficking a young Romanian girl of 7 to the UK to act as an unpaid domestic servant. The young girl had ". . . been sent to Britain by her penniless mother in the hope of a better life" (*Daily Mail* 2013). There were also allegations against the couple of abusive treatment to a 53-year-old Romanian man who had been central in securing the young girl's freedom. This was a very serious case of abuse and exploitation. This case falls within the 'trafficking' definition and technically it is such a case. However, Zlate and his wife were not organising trafficking crimes on any scale: their criminal actions rather seemed to have been opportunistic in that they were able to convince the girl's mother that she would have a better life in the UK.

This couple, guilty of offences of trafficking, appears to have gained the opportunity to enslave the seven year old by duping the girl's mother. None of the reports of the case suggest that Zlate and his family were involved in the trafficking of young people into the UK for domestic servitude. This is the case of an unscrupulous couple and their family wilfully exploiting a minor.

Telus Dumitru and child begging

The third case is that of Telus Dumitru who was convicted of offences of benefit fraud. Essentially Dumitru designed a means of applying for and receiving a range of benefits that he was not entitled. The Guardian (2011) reported that Dumitru was the central figure in an organised crime gang that was trafficking children from Romania to the UK to beg in the streets. Dumitru, it was argued had a pivotal role in the scam:

> "Southwark crown court heard that Dumitru "controlled and directed" the benefit fraud activities of at least seven other adult Romanians in the UK who were linked by blood or marriage." (The Guardian 2011)

The suspicions of child trafficking are not the subject of the charges against Dumitru but form a significant part of the Guardian report and place him within an organised crime framework.

> "Dumitru is believed by police to be the most senior UK-based figure so far brought to justice from a Roma gang from south-east Romania whose members are accused of trafficking children who then beg and steal across the south of England." (Guardian 2011).

Dumitru was arrested during 'Operation Golf', an anti-trafficking Joint Operation between the Metropolitan police and the Romanian Police and the criminal group that Dumitru was connected to was essentially geographically located in Tandarei, which is a small town in South East Romania. It seems that Dumitru was connected to the other members of the criminal group through familial ties and that this was a targeted and organised approach to benefit fraud with the majority of the money being remitted back to Tandarei. The press report is vague in its reporting of the trafficking issue as it maybe that there was some complicit actions between the parents of the children and the criminal group. There are also suggestions that there was some use of intimidation (Guardian 2011).

This case is one of systematic fraud, however, there are no charges of trafficking against Dumitru. The organisation of the trafficking of children to beg on the streets does not appear to be the central element of the criminality and the discussion of trafficking in the press report is very circumspect and appears to rely heavily on police briefings.

The Birmingham parlour

The final case concerns a massage parlour in Birmingham. It was raided by the police in September 2005 and it was claimed that the 19 women working there, who were foreign nationals, had been trafficked:

> "Nineteen women from 10 countries, believed to have been tricked into working in the sex trade, were under police protection yesterday after a raid on a massage parlour. Detectives think the women may have been held against their will behind locked doors and an electric fence at premises in Birmingham." (Guardian 2005)

However, it transpired that none of the women had been trafficked. The women were working at the massage parlour 'voluntarily'. It is apparent that the women were encouraged to come to the UK and that they were procured by 'brokers' who recruited the women in their home countries and then passed them onto brothel owners who paid them for procuring the women[8]. This case has similarities to the

---

8 For a detailed description of the case see R. v Makai (Atilla) [2007] EWCA Crim 1652

Demarku case in that the Demarku brothers appear to have used a broker to recruit the women for their brothels and it is through the broker that they were offered a woman that could make them a greater profit.

In the Cuddles case the conviction of Carl Pritchett for Managing a Brothel was referred to the Criminal Cases Review Commission because:

> "The judge said: "There is information in there undermining the conviction, that the police were in possession of a statement revealing people were working in these premises voluntarily 16 days before the raid took place." (Stourbridge News 2011)

The issue of trafficking had been central to the conviction and was on appeal considered undermined because of a failure of the police to disclose witness statements.

These case studies demonstrate that human trafficking is a complex crime and that in many cases the definition of trafficking is so expanded that crimes which are abusive and for which there exists adequate legislation become corralled into trafficking. The offences of trafficking now seem to be so broad in their definition that every type of offence related to prostitution can be described in some way as trafficking.

Policy to practice relevance

The implementation of policy is a political process and the practitioners responsible for implementation range from enthusiastic to compliant through to subversive. The action of implementation is where practitioners are influential in the making of policy by the way in which they respond to the official demands for implementation. Policy is subject to competing discourses gaining prominence on the interpretative frame (Turnbull 2006) and also how the contradictions between these different narratives is given space in the formation of policy that can allow for the dominance of one narrative over another (Spanger 2011). The dominant policy narrative becomes exclusionary of other associated narratives and one consequence is that policy implementation is exclusionary as its foundations are embedded within the dominant narrative. When the data and research underdetermines the dominant narrative there is little move away from the dominant narrative form and no accommodation of an alternative, and at times, competing narrative.

In the UK the established policy narrative is through criminal justice, and so it is the criminal justice professionals and NGO activists with their varying agendas that become dominant voices within the trafficking policy narrative. This shapes and structures the interventions and the implementation of policy. However, there are, off-stage, other policy narratives that have been trying to be heard that offer a different analysis to that of the main narrative, for example the International Union of Sex Workers in giving written evidence to the Home Affairs select committee on trafficking commented on policy:

> "The majority of the evidence related specifically to the sex industry already taken by the Committee is from the perspective that all prostitution is violence against women. This is the view of the Poppy Project and of Harriet Harman. This ideological position, *their entirely subjective opinion*, necessarily impacts their estimation of the scale of abuses within the sex industry and distorts their proposals for appropriate responses to those abuses as they consider everyone who offers us a place in which to work to promote violence against us . . ."
> (Home Affairs Select Committee 2008:Para13 *italics in original*)

Criminal justice practitioners who are operational in the field express a different narrative form to that of the dominant discourse. Research completed under the AGIS Programme of the EU (Spencer *et al* 2010) highlights a significant discrepancy in the accounts of trafficking given by senior law enforcement official and operational 'frontline' staff. The former are 'on message' with the official narrative whereas the operational staff are much more sceptical:

> "For example, the UK qualitative data with border guards suggests that the main focus of work is on facilitation and on individuals attempting to breach the border by individual enterprise. This is far removed from the official policy that is focused on organised crime and systematic forms of illegal movement of people."
> (Spencer *et al* 2010:53)

These oppositional narratives generally go unheard and feature little in policymaking discussions, however, there now seems a body of evidence that suggests that policy is structured around a set of questions that are probably more to do with anxieties concerning migration and prostitution than they are with an anxiety over trafficking, for as Spanger (2011) has noted the dominant discourses are most often concerned with constructions of morality.

Conclusion

The argument developed in this paper is that 'policy solutions' to the issue of human trafficking that are expressed in the Palermo Protocol on human trafficking are a significant contributory element in the criminalisation of migration and have shaped law enforcement responses at the level of the nation state. However, the human trafficking for sexual exploitation policy-making process has a foundation based on incomplete data and this has contributed to a flawed international approach to the problem.

Human trafficking for sexual exploitation has been the dominant narrative in law enforcement policy making. In the UK governments have established funding streams and agencies (for example REFLEX followed by the UKHTC) to work across disciplines to address and combat the human trafficking for sexual exploitation problem. In the 2012 SOCA threat assessment human trafficking is one of the identified threats (SOCA 2012). Consequently much of the academic literature has been concerned with sexual exploitation (see for example Agustin 2008 and Weitzer 2007 for a critical appraisal). It is only recently that there has been an emerging focus on labour exploitation (see for example Jokinen *et al.* 2011).

This focus on sexual exploitation has significantly influenced the shape of the 'problem' of human trafficking, which in turn is influenced by the relevant Palermo Protocol to the United Nations Declaration on Transnational Organised Crime. The responses to the Palermo Protocol over the past decade have been the establishment of law enforcement networks to combat human trafficking. The development of the anti-trafficking infrastructure has occurred at two levels:

- At the *international level* the United Nations has developed the policy initiatives by the UNODC and the website UN.GIFT (United Nations Global Initiative to fight Human Trafficking) both of which have a 'worldwide' brief.
- At the *EU level* the European Commission has established a National Rapporteur system and an Anti-Trafficking Co-ordinator, the role of the latter as being that of policy co-ordination.

The National Rapporteur system has received a mixed response from member states with only eleven of the twenty-seven having in place an identifiable system with a 'named' person to collect and report upon the relevant data.

What both of these strategic approaches demonstrate is that human trafficking falls within the policy remit of law enforcement but that it draws from a number of policy domains. The role of Anti-Trafficking Co-ordinator acknowledges this difficulty as their role is viewed as being critical to the development of a coherent EU approach across different policy domains:

> "An effective EU policy on the fight against trafficking will need to draw from many different policy fields, such as police and judicial cooperation, protection of human rights, external relations, migration policies and social and labour law. It will be the task of the anti-trafficking coordinator to ensure coherence between all these policy fields." (European Union 2010)

Within this EU approach it can be argued that there is recognition of other competing policy domains and that this introduces a level of complexity into the policy making that requires co-ordination and mediation between the different conflicting policy domains.

In the UK the approach to human trafficking does not claim any sophistication as the policy approach is unquestionably, and perhaps exclusively, placed in the law enforcement domain. The responsibilities for addressing the problems of trafficking are those of SOCA and more specifically within SOCA at the UKHTC. The latter is multidisciplinary in its approach and provides ". . . a central point of expertise and coordination in relation to the UK's response to the trafficking of human beings" (SOCA 2012). The positioning of the UKHTC within SOCA reinforces the argument that human trafficking is located firmly within 'crime security nexus' (Goodey 2008) and all the problems that this brings with it. In the UK the publication of the Coalition Government's strategy on human trafficking defines the activity in this way:

> "Traffickers use threats, force, coercion, abduction, fraud, deception, abuse of power and payment to control their victim. *And most traffickers are organised criminals*. It is estimated that 17% of organised criminal networks operating in the UK are involved in organised immigration crime, of which a *small proportion is human trafficking*". (Home Office 2011:6 *emphasis added*)

It is interesting to note how, in the above quote, human trafficking is elided into organised immigration crime. They are not one and the same, as the latter can be the smuggling of people across borders where the criteria of the Palermo Protocol are not fulfilled. This only serves to indicate how confused and contradictory the policy definitions of human trafficking are and how governments use the terms interchangeably when they are anything but interchangeable.

The UK strategy has stripped out of the equation the explicit policy areas recognised by the EU and explicitly links immigration crime with human traficking and 'organised crime'. The consequence of this approach is to make law enforcement the dominant narrative within policy development. Further evidence for this, at the local level, is that the UK's National Referral Mechanism (NRM) is a strategy to identify and assist victims of trafficking. The mechanism works by authorised agencies, for example all police forces, social services departments and some NGOs, referring cases that they consider potential trafficking cases (the identified victim is required to sign the referral form). The referral is forwarded to one of two Competent Authorities, the UKHTC or the United Kingdom Border Agency (UKBA) for a decision on the probability of the individual having been trafficked.

So, an agency that is active in the policy debate and has interests in promoting the problem has a significant level of responsibility in deciding which of those people referred are possible victims. Both of these agencies subscribe to the law enforcement narrative and this is reflected in Coalition government policy (Home Office 2011). It is here that we witness Verschuere's (2009) idea of 'complementarity' in action. So rather than moving outside of the confines of this policy narrative into a narrative space that is more dynamic and complex (Spencer and Broad 2011) the well known rhetoric of the law enforcement narrative is sustained as the dominant narrative form in the UK.

The conclusion that we can draw from this policy making process is that the shadow of Palermo, which represents the international policy making process through the United Nations, is cast over the policy constructs and strategies at the nation state level. There is a calling point at Brussels (the European Union) to ensure a form of policy solidarity between member states, which are subscribed to with varying degrees of enthusiasm. However, the structure and implementation of this globalised policy is hidden only by the merest hint of a national flavour.

This globalised policy response to human trafficking has reproduced an over-concentration on sexual exploitation. Consequently the interpretative framework and the policy narrative often exclude the complex problems of migration as being driven by the demands of a global economy. As Bosworth and Guild (2008) argue it is critical to understand the policy narrative of 'non-citizens' through border control strategies. The reproduction of the law enforcement policy narratives is essentially suspicious and criminalising of migration. Such narratives locate law enforcement at the centre of the strategic response, which in turn reproduces the narrative by emphasising the criminality of human trafficking, as though it is not a strategy of migration, but of organised crime. Once this law enforcement legitimating loop of the policy narrative is closed there is no need for data to evidence the problem; only a requirement of numbers to justify the internal logic of the policy narrative. Such an approach has within it many 'blind-spots' (Dorn 2010), or perhaps supporting silences (Yannow 1995), that results in a policy failure to take other forms of labour exploitation and unfree labour than sex services (Strauss 2012) as being in need of policy responses.

As long as a criminal justice narrative dominates the focus of international policy making the policy response to human trafficking will fail to address the problems that are a consequence of the global economy and the exploitative and degrading practices inherent in labour exploitation.

References

Agustin, L., The disappearing of a migration category: Migrants who sell sex. *Journal of Ethnic and Migration Studies*, 2006, 32 (1) 29-47

Boswell, C., A. Geddes and P. Scholten, The role of narratives in migration policy-making: A research framework. *The British Journal of Politics & International Relations*. 2011, Vol. 13: 1–11

Bosworth, M. and M. Guild, Governing through migration control: Security and citizenship in Britain. *British Journal of Criminology*. 2008, Vol. 48, *No 6*:703-719

Doezema, J.. Forced to choose: Beyond the voluntary v. forced prostitution dichotomy. In K. Kamala and J. Doezema (eds.), *Global sex workers: rights, resistance, and redefinition*. Routledge, New York, 1998

Dorn, N., The governance of securities: Ponzi finance, regulatory convergence, credit crunch. *British Journal of Criminology* Vol.50: 23-45 2010

Duyne, P.C. van and J. Spencer, The traded body: the ultimate commercial option. In P.C. van Duyne and J. Spencer (eds.), *Flesh and Money*. Wolf Legal Publishers. Nijmegen Netherlands 2011

Europol, *Knowledge Product: Trafficking in human beings in the european union*. Europol The Hague 2011

Guardian, *Inquiry fails to find single trafficker who forced anybody into prostitution* Guardian Newspapers October 20th 2009

Hoffman, J., Implicit theories in policy discourse: An inquiry into the interpretations of reality in German technology policy. *Policy Sciences* Vol28 No2;127-148 2005

Home Affairs Select Committee, *Written evidence to the Home Affairs Select Committee enquiry into Human Trafficking* from the International Union of Sex Workers 19 December 2008. House of Commons London 2008

Home Office, *The House for Commons Home Affairs Select Committee Report. The trade in Human Beings: Trafficking in the UK*. HC 23-1 The Stationery Office. London 2009

Home Office, Human *Trafficking: The Government's Strategy*. Home Office London 2011

HMSO, *Sexual Offences Act*. Her Majesty's Stationery Office London 2003

Jokinen, A., N. Ollus and K. Aromaa, *Trafficking for forced labour and labour exploitation in Finland, Poland and Estonia*. HEUNI Report No 68. HEUNI Helsinki, Finland 2011

Mai, N., *The psycho-social trajectories of Albanian and Romanian 'traffickers'*. ISET Working Paper 17. Institute for the Study of European Transformations, London 2010

McKie, A., F. Baguley, C. Guthrie, C. Jackson, P. Kirkpatrick, A. Laing, S. O'Brien, R. Taylor and P. Wimpenny, Exploring clinical wisdom in nursing education. *Nursing Ethics,* 2012, Vol19: 252

Melossi, D., 'In a peaceful life' Migration and the crime of modernity in Europe/Italy. *Punishment & Society*, 2003, vol 5; 371

Page, E., *How public policy is really made.* Public Management and Policy Association, London 2006

Paoli, L., The paradoxes of organized crime. *Crime, Law & Social Change,* 2002, 37, 51–97

Paoli, L. and C. Fijnaut, Organised crime and its control policies. *European Journal of Crime, Criminal Law and Criminal Justice*, 2006, 14 (3) 307-327

Ritchey, T., *Wicked problems structuring social messes with morphological analysis*. Swedish Morphological Society, 2011, (Downloaded from: www.swemorph.com accessed 15.04.2012)

SOCA (Serious Organised Crime Agency) 2012 http://www.soca.gov.uk/about-soca/about-the-ukhtc accessed 10.07.2012

SOCA (Serious Organised Crime Agency) 2013 http://www.soca.gov.uk/about-soca/about-the-ukhtc accessed 02-05-2013

Spencer J. and R. Broad, Lifting the veil on SOCA and the UKHTC: Policymaking responses to organised crime. in *Cross-border crime inroads on integrity*, (eds.) P.C. van Duyne, G. A. Antonopoulos, A. Maljevic, T. vander Beken, K. von Lampe and J. Harvey. Nijmegen, Wolf Legal Publishers 2010

Spencer J., R. Broad, K. Aromaa, M. Junninen, A. Markina, J. Saar and T. Viljanen, *Organised crime, corruption and the movement of people across borders in the new enlarged EU: A case study of Estonia, Finland and the UK*. HEUNI Report No 69 HEUNI Helsinki 2010

Spencer J. and R. Broad, The 'Groundhog Day' of the human trafficking for sexual exploitation debate: New directions in criminological understanding. *European Journal on Criminal Policy and Research*, 2012, Vol.18(3) , 269-281

Spencer J., Media constructing organised crime concepts in an extended criminal Europe: Trafficking women for sexual exploitation. In P.C. van Duyne, J. Harvey, A. Maljevic, K. von Lampe and M. Scheinost (eds.), *European crime markets at cross-roads: extended and extending criminal Europe.* Nijmegen, Wolf Legal Publishers 2008,

Strauss K., Coerced, forced and unfree labour: Geographies of exploitation in contemporary labour markets. *Geography Compass*, 2012, vol. 6, *no3*: 137–148

Turnbull N, How should we theorise public policy? Problem solving and problemasticity. *Policy and Society*, 2006, 1, 3-22 2006

Turner J. and L. Kelly, Trade secrets intersections between Diasporas and crime groups on the constitution of the human trafficking chain. *British Journal of Criminology*, 2009, vol 49, 184 – 201

Tyldum, G. and A. Brunovskis, Describing the unobserved: Methodological challenges in empirical studies on human trafficking. *International Migration*, 2005, vol. 43, *no 1/2*: 17-34

United Kingdom Human Trafficking Centre, *United Kingdom Pentameter 2 Statistics of Victims recovered and Suspects arrested during the operational phase*. UKHTC. Sheffield 2008

United Nations, *Protocol to prevent, suppress and punish trafficking in persons, especially women and children, supplementing the United Nations convention against transnational organized crime* United Nations. New York 2000

UNODC, *Global Report into the Trafficking of Persons*. United Nations Office of Drugs and Crime. Vienna, 2009

Vaiou, D., Gendered mobilities and border-crossings: from Elbasan to Athens, *Gender, Place & Culture: A Journal of Feminist Geography*, 2011

Verschuere, B., The role of public agencies in the policy making process: rhetoric versus reality. *Public Policy and Administration*, 2009, vol 21:1

Weber, E.P. and A. Khademian, Wicked problems, knowledge challenges and collaborative capacity builders in network settings. *Public Administration Review* March - April 2008

Wharton R.L., A New Paradigm for Human Trafficking: Shifting the Focus from Prostitution to Exploitation in the Trafficking Victims Protection Act, 2010, *William & Mary Journal of Women and Law*, 16, 753-780

Weitzer R, The social construction of sex trafficking: Ideology and institutionalization of a moral crusade *Politics and Society* 35 (3) 447-475 2005

Yanow, D., Practices of policy interpretation, *Policy Sciences*, 1995, 28: I 11-26

Young, J., To these wet and windy shores: recent immigration policy in the UK. *Punishment & Society*, 2003, *5*: 449- 462

The death of the legitimate merchant? Small to medium-size enterprises and shady decisions in Greece during the financial crisis

Georgios A. Antonopoulos and Steve Hall[1]

Introduction

In mainstream criminology, representations of illegal markets tend to rest on two specific assumptions: firstly, that illegal markets are monopolised by – very often foreign – 'organised crime' groups with the objective of expanding illegal markets to an international level; and, secondly, that 'organised crime' groups engage in campaigns to corrupt fiscal structures (see Potter, 1994). As Van Duyne (2010) notes, in most of the 'organised crime' literature the threat of enormous criminal finances being invested in the legal sector, affecting the integrity of the fiscal system and undermining fair competition in the business sector, has a prominent position. The bulk of these 'criminal finances' are allegedly invested in terrorist and 'serious' organised criminal activities (see Lowe, 2006). Although these tenets have been criticised by a number of theorists and researchers (see for example Smith, 1975; Hobbs, 1988; Naylor, 2004), they continue to exert a powerful influence in official and media discourses. This influence has been further intensified in the context of the current 'financial crisis'. In Greece, for example, a report on organised crime trends and policy countermeasures in 2011, which echoes official and media perspectives from the beginning of this financial crises (see, Kolonas, 2008), suggested that "*[i]llegal trades undercut the turnover of legal merchants and shop-owners . . . thus contributing to the continuation of adverse economic conditions for the legitimate economy*" (Michaletos, 2011). Recently it has been suggested – with increasing frequency and fervour among primarily political, media, and business circles – that if Greece (and by extension the rest of the world) is to get out of the vortex of the financial crisis, the role of

1 Georgios A. Antonopoulos and Steve Hall are Professors of Criminology in the Teesside Centre for Realist Criminology, Teesside University, UK. The authors would like to thank the reviewers and Simon Winlow for their constructive comments on earlier drafts of this chapter.

'entrepreneurial ethics' should be paramount because it 'provides solutions' to the financial crisis (Gortzis, 2013; NET, 2013).

However, this orthodox 'analysis' is too simplistic. What we try to do in this chapter is highlight the complexity of the situation by introducing another type of criminal entrepreneur to the discussion: the 'reluctant criminal undertaker'. By this we mean legal entrepreneurs who are normally involved in the provision of legal commodities/services but dabble in illegal markets within the confines of their legal businesses simply to sustain financial viability. This is part of an on-going project on illegal markets and the informal economy in Greece and beyond. Our research is based on interviews with entrepreneurs who became reluctantly involved in illegal markets in an effort to sustain their legal businesses amid the financial pressures that have exerted themselves throughout Greece since the current crisis took hold. In this way, we hope to contribute to the discussion about the wide range of illegal behaviours associated with the financial crisis as it is manifested in Greece.

After discussing the methodology, we summarise the current financial and entrepreneurial situation in Greece. It is not our intention to provide a finely detailed account of the Greek financial crisis and the bailouts. This would require a whole book. Instead, we offer a basic account of the situation in Greece from late 2009 until the signing of the memorandum with the IMF/ECB/European Commission, the measures taken by the Greek Government, and their impact on Greek society and economy. Although the signing of the memorandum is by no means the end of the story (additional fiscal adjustment and austerity measures were introduced in subsequent waves in 2011 and 2012), policies enacted in the period 2009-2010 laid the foundations for the current fiscal and entrepreneurial environment in Greece.

In a later section we present a short summary of the characteristics of the set of cases which this chapter is based upon as well as two representative empirical case studies highlighting the 'reluctant undertaking' of criminal activities. The case studies will provide the reader with an existential insight into the motivations and actions of these criminal entrepreneurs. We end the article with a theoretical contextualisation that criticises the common notion that ethics can be reinstated at the core of markets without disturbing fundamental political and socioeconomic arrangements.

Methods and data

The data in this article derive from interviews with thirteen legal entrepreneurs in Greece who became involved in illegal markets in order to sustain their businesses. The interviews are drawn from an overall data-set that consists of initial material from an on-going ethnographic analysis of the criminogenic consequences of the collapse of the Greek economy. Table 1 offers an overview of the participants in this study. Two case studies have been selected: a confectioner who runs his own shop and small-scale production facility, and the owner of an internet café. The data from these selected cases are presented more fully in Table 1. In line with colleagues who have used a limited number of case studies in their work (e.g. Carlsson, 2012), we have selected these two because they clearly express characteristics that can be found throughout the whole sample and because the details associated with the case study data is integral to the overall analysis.

Table 1
Overview of the interviewees

Name of participant (pseudonym)	Age (at time of the interview)	Legal (primary) business	Illegal business	Time of involvement in illegal business	Criminal record?
Nick*	24	Confectioner's shop	Dark chocolate	2010	N
Chris*	25	Internet café	Online gambling	2010	N
Michael	57	Jeweller's shop	Gold and silver	2010	Y
George	43	Café	Coffee	2010	N
John	45	Kiosk	Cigarettes	2010	N
Costas	49	Haberdashery	Cigarettes	2010	N
Alex	33	Haberdashery	Cigarettes	2010	N
Aristos	50	Kiosk	Cigarettes	2010	N
Maria	39	Fast-food shop	Meat	2010	N
Tom	51	Garment factory	Jackets	2010	N
Peter	55	Butcher	Meat	2010	N
Paul	63	Alcohol wholesaler	Alcohol	2010	N
Dimitris	52	Petrol station	Oil	2010	N

*Indicates the case studies extensively presented in the chapter.

The motivations for involvement in illegal markets represented in these two case studies also appeared throughout the whole sample. Although space limits the number of case studies, we should not underestimate the value of data that they can offer or the initial signs of clear emergent tendencies that are worth following up on a larger scale (see Hall *et al.*, 2008).

Participants in all 13 interviews were identified through the researcher's social network, and opportunities for interviewing were taken at social occasions (see

Hobbs, 2013). It is indicative for this approach that one of the authors was introduced to the confectioner at a wedding. As there are no obvious benefits for those concerned in revealing their practices and motives, the role of the intermediaries – the people who brought the researcher and the interviewees together – was crucial. The intermediaries performed the roles of introducing both parties to each another, which led to an initial disclosure of criminologically relevant information, and 'vouching' for the trustworthiness of both parties, which accelerated the process of access and made the generation of revealing data possible. The arranged interviews were informally conducted and the interviewees were given autonomy in introducing their own concepts and terms regarding the legal and illegal aspects of their business. All interviewees were briefly informed about the objectives of the research and their rights as participants, after which they agreed to participate.

The reliability and validity of the interviewee's accounts is an issue that warrants some attention. There can be no guarantee whatsoever about the reliability of the accounts provided. There may be instances in which participants simply do not remember, instances in which issues are concealed from the researcher or instances where the accounts become confused and unclear. In order to validate some information we used the process of 'member checking', "where collected data was 'played back' to the informant to check for perceived accuracy . . . " (Cho and Trent, 2006: 322). In addition, crucial aspects of the accounts provided by some of the interviewees were verified by individuals who were known to both the researcher and the interviewees, and also to those who acted as the initial points of contact.

'The plagues of the economy & the Golgotha of entrepreneurship'

The current financial & entrepreneurial landscape in Greece

In the period 2001-2007 the Greek economy's average annual growth rate of 4,2% was one of the most rapid in Europe. However, this was not due to correspondingly increased competitiveness, a factor that is reflected in the growth of current account and trade deficits for this period (Katseli, 2008). It was primarily a result of unrestricted access to cheap capital from the financial markets and increased investor confidence after the country joined the Eurozone in 2001. This capital was used to pay for budget and trade deficits and government spending, and to counterbalance low tax revenue rather than establishing a job-creating productive basis to increase exports and the competitiveness and real wealth of the Greek economy as a whole (see Nelson *et al.*, 2011). According to McKinsey & Co. (2012), consumption accounted for approximately 97% of cumulative GDP during this period (almost 20 percentile points of GDP higher than other European countries) and this was fuelled by a high domestic demand that was artificially sustained by credit and a large public sector.

However, Greece was not unusual amongst other Western nations in its shift to a consumption-based economy. Although some economies, such as Germany, retained productive manufacturing industries, the West in general was feeling the effects of an epoch-making structural shift. This can be interpreted as a US-led global economic policy that orchestrated a reversal of the global flows of trade and capital after 1971. This was a complex process, but, as the majority of primary job-rich manufacturing centres were relocated to the East, the upshot is that all Western nations became to varying degrees dependent on consumption of commodities produced elsewhere, deficits and fiscal stimulus; the so called 'neoliberal' project revolved around a distinctively Keynesian core (see Varoufakis, 2011).

This development, founded on the creation of fragile bubble economies in the West, quickly collapsed. The financial crisis in 2007/2008 triggered a major recession, which would have been worse than the Great Depression had it not been for the global financial institutions such as the IMF, World Bank and European Central Bank and the quantitative easing mechanisms now built into the system as safeguards (Varoufakis, 2011).

This economic convulsion had an enormous negative effect on Greece. Two of the main industries, shipping and tourism, entered into a vortex, which fuelled a persistently high trade deficit resulting in a 15% reduction of revenues in 2009 (Business Week, 2012). This was the start of the most severe financial crisis since the restoration of democracy in the country in 1974. The crisis was exacerbated by irresponsible bank lending and a combination of political and institutional weaknesses.

Together, these problems have plagued the economy, contributing to Greece's poor productivity, lowering foreign investment and weakening competitiveness. They revealed an unsustainable economic model with a very high debt burden (214% of GDP in 2008) and the highest public debt and consumer lending in Europe (McKinsey & Co, 2012). Adding a further pathogenic problem to the economy was what appeared to be an endemic tax evasion: only 43% of traders declared an income of up to €5.000 in 2007 (To Vima, 2008). Funds from tax evasion by big companies were diverted to political parties in return for the award of state contracts at overpriced rates (see Telloglou, 2009). Yet more pathogenic factors included a big informal labour market, the formation of cartels, speculation in important commodity markets (e.g. milk, flour), the inadequacy of the state's attempts to protect small/medium-size entrepreneurship, a complex and unfair tax system that consistently disadvantaged those with smaller incomes (Tsiros, 2008), and what appeared to be a remarkable disconnection between academic/governmental research and the national economy (OECD, 2012). Excessive and often outdated market government interventions, poor investment and low resource allocation in crucial industries, excessively lax quality standards, low early stage entrepreneurial activity, and the failure of the Greek state to promote products and services effectively in the international arena have all contributed to the current parlous condition of the Greek economy (see OECD, 2007).

Corruption and a nexus of many contradictory and ambiguous laws and 'red tape' which deter investors should not be ignored. According to a European Commission (2012a) report, the cost of bureaucracy in Greece is estimated at approximately 22,3% of the country's GDP in 2010 as opposed to 10,9% in 2009. The wages of public sector workers can be a significant factor in boosting consumer demand, but this is offset by the fiscal cost of the bureaucratic apparatus and the pressure it places on wage-driven inflation. The latter limits the profit-making and job-creating abilities of legitimate businesses in the private sector. The bureaucracy also significantly neutralises the already weak competitiveness of the Greek economy by providing practical obstacles to businesses in terms of administrative expenses and delays in the initiation of a business.[2]

Looming over these obvious micro-economic factors was the overarching and currently inescapable neoliberal macro-economic structure: in a global context of trade and capital-reversal most manufacturing start-ups are in developing countries that compete with low wages and taxes, and retain the ability to devalue currencies to boost exports. The West's manufacturing strength now lies in specialist hi-tech production, which tends to be less labour-intensive than primary production. Thus, inward investment into weaker Western economies to fuel genuine wealth-creating industry is very difficult to secure. This race to the bottom has left most Western economies unable to compete as production centres and, therefore, over-reliant on credit, consumption and financial services. The upshot is that Greece is one of the weakest of a group of Western economies that are finding it almost impossible to compete in an unforgiving global market in which national capital exchange controls have been abandoned and capital is entirely free to be invested wherever higher returns are more likely.

2 According to Politis (2007), trying to start up a business in Greece is an expensive and time-consuming process: the average start-up capital is double the European average. It is also very risky for the individual: on average 53% of the investment costs comes from the aspiring entrepreneur's savings/own capital, and 50% of the remainder tends to come from close family members.

In October 2009, the newly elected (pseudo)-socialist government of Greece announced that the deficit of the country exceeded the national income by 12 per cent. By early 2010 it was more than obvious in international financial circles that Greece would have to seek external assistance to avoid a default (Varoufakis, 2011). Initially, the Greek government informally asked for assistance from the EU but this request was met with opposition by the German Chancellor Angela Merkel. For five months Greece had to borrow at usurious rates from the financial markets, something that worsened the country's financial situation (Varoufakis, 2011).

In the meantime, two austerity packages were implemented in Greece. The first followed the signing of memoranda with the International Monetary Fund (IMF) and the European Central Bank (ECB) regarding a loan of €80 billion. The package, implemented in February 2010, included a 'freeze' in the salaries of all government employees and a 10% cut in bonuses, as well as reductions in the numbers of public employees (Eleftherotypia, 2010). The second package, implemented in March 2010, was a response to mounting fears that the country would become bankrupt after pressure by EU economic affairs commissioner Olli Rehn, who visited Greece in March 1, 2010 (Reuters, 2010). Parliament passed a Bill on 'National Economy Protection' (L.3833/2010). The Bill's purpose was to save €4,8 billion by implementing measures such as 30% cuts in Christmas and Easter bonuses and the cancellation of leave of absence payments, an additional 12% cut in public bonuses, a 7% cut in the salaries of public and private employees, a significant rise in VAT and petrol tax rise and other painful measures (Taxhaven, 2010). After the implementation of the second package, which also proved unsuccessful in helping Greece to meet fiscal targets, the European Commission (EC), the IMF and the ECB set up a tripartite committee (known disaffectionately as the 'Troika') to prepare an appropriate programme of economic policies that would impose upon the nation the conditions of austerity required to secure a larger loan. Since the root of the problem was structural weaknesses that the Greek government was simply unable (or unwilling) to deal with, inevitably the weight of this programme was to fall on the public (Kazakis, 2011).

On 1 May 2010, the Greek government announced a series of austerity measures to persuade primarily Germany to sign on to a larger EU and IMF loan package. On 2 May 2010 the EC, the ECB and the IMF agreed to a three-year €110 billion loan with a 5,5% interest rate that, according to Varoufakis (2011: 207), was 'high enough to make it very unlikely that the Greek public purse would be able to repay this new loan as well as the existing ones'. An important condition was attached to this loan: that the Greek government would implement an additional series of austerity measures alongside the previous two. Simultaneously, the credit rating agencies in the financial market (Moody's, S&P and Fitch) immediately downgraded Greek governmental bonds to an even lower 'junk' status (see Ewing & Healy, 2010). Further tough austerity measures finally introduced – primarily general budgetary savings or tax increases – included:

- *Cuts in pay, pensions and jobs* (e.g. cuts on public sector allowances in addition to the two previous austerity packages and pay cuts for public sector utilities employees, etc.)
- *Revenues increases through direct and indirect taxation* (e.g. a 'special' tax on high pensions, extraordinary taxes imposed on company profits, rise in the value of property (and thus higher taxes), rise of an additional 10% tax for all imported cars; increases in VAT (ranging for diverse products) to 23% (from 19%), 11% (from 9%) and 5,5% (from 4 %); a 10% tax increase in luxury commodities and additional taxes on alcohol, cigarettes, and fuel)
- *Increase in the average retirement age for public sector workers from 61 to 65* (OECD, 2011).

This memorandum was reviewed and 'revised' at least twice in August and November 2010 to include: cuts in public investment, the sale of some units of the *Public Power Corporation*; the implementation of business contracts instead of sector contracts between employers and employees (which deregulated the labour market and was an initial blow to employment rights); the reduction of expenditure on health and public utilities as well as the support of the Greek banking system towards the promotion of liquidity in the Greek economy. Despite the last intervention, the banks were reluctant to lend money due to fear of 'bad loans', a situation commonly referred to as a 'liquidity crisis'. This was further exacerbated by two additional factors: (a) Greek banks are heavily reliant on ECB loans and the majority of Greek banks' assets are tied up with devalued Greek government bonds; and (b) the tendency among the Greeks to withdraw savings in order to cover basic household needs but also not to deposit money into banks due to mistrust of the banking system and fear of its possible collapse (Bank of Greece, cited in Tsipouras, 2012).

Despite the measures introduced, in 2010 Greece's public debt *increased* by €41,8 billion (see Marias, 2011). Moreover, this deadly cocktail of a global recession, negative psychology in Greece and beyond, and severe austerity measures, the cornerstones of what Kotzias (2010: 18) calls 'aggressive neoliberal capitalist reconstruction', have had rapid and abrupt traumatising effects on the economy and the everyday lives of Greek citizens.

Firstly, the destructive effects of imposed neoliberal restructuring impacted on the country's economic activity and GDP growth. Whereas growth was 4,2% from 2000 to 2007, from 2008 onwards the economy has been continuously shrinking (- 0,1% in 2008, - 3,3% in 2009, - 3,5% in 2010 and – 6,9% in 2011) (IMF, 2012). Membership of the Eurozone prevented the Greek government from devaluing the currency, which could have assisted in the country getting back on the track of development by boosting exports, but the 'race to the bottom' described earlier means that there was no guarantee of success in this endeavour. With a high risk of failure in or out of the EU, Greece was trapped in a negative double-bind.

Secondly, the effect has been reflected on unemployment and plummeting living standards. From a peak of 4,5 million employed Greeks in 2008, half a million had lost their jobs either through redundancies or the closure of the small-medium enterprises that constitute the backbone of the Greek economy. The result has been a steep decline in employment in the country and the creation of a large number of unemployed or underemployed people (particularly those under 25) (graph 1) (EL.STAT, 2011). Apart from an increase of young Greeks considering emigration (Malkoutzis, 2011) and the slow erosion of the Greek middle-class, unemployment was the primary cause of an increase in the number of people who are considered 'poor', and an increase in the number of those driven to 'extreme poverty' when the 12-month period of unemployment benefit elapses. Many of the latter group have become over-reliant on informal/family networks, churches and NGOs. Specifically, 20,1% of the population in Greece are now estimated to live below the poverty line as opposed to 9% in the Czech Republic, 12,3% in Hungary, 12 % in Slovakia and 17,6% in Poland (see Sotiropoulos, 2012).

Graph 1
Unemployment in Greece, 2006-2011

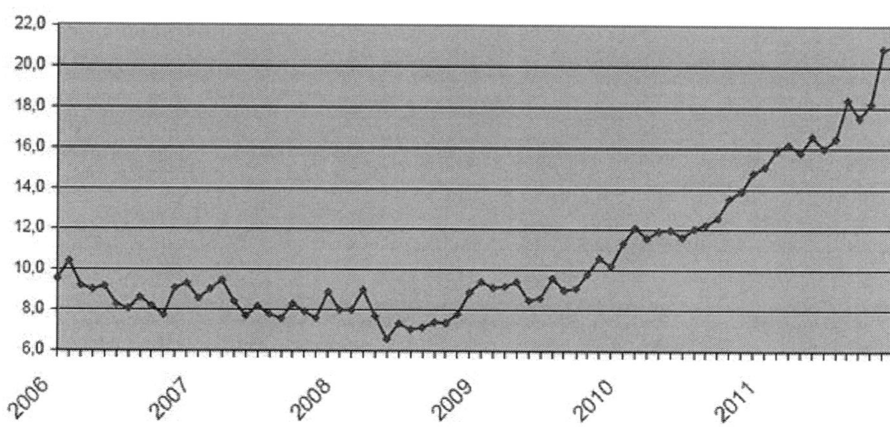

Source: EL.STAT (2011)

Thirdly, the additional tax measures and high inflation, which in August 2010 reached 5,5% from 1,3 % in 2009 (which at the time was below the EU average of 1,4%), led to a drop in consumption even in traditionally strong sectors of the economy such as car sales and fuel distribution (POPEK, 2010; Nautemporiki, 2010).

The estimated negative (or, at best, zero) growth rate of the income in many employee categories led to a significant reduction in the buying power of the Greek public in late 2009 and early 2010, which in turn led to negative psychology (IOBE, 2010) and a steep reduction in the consumer confidence of the Greek public (graph 2).

Graph 2
Greek consumer confidence, October 2009-December 2010

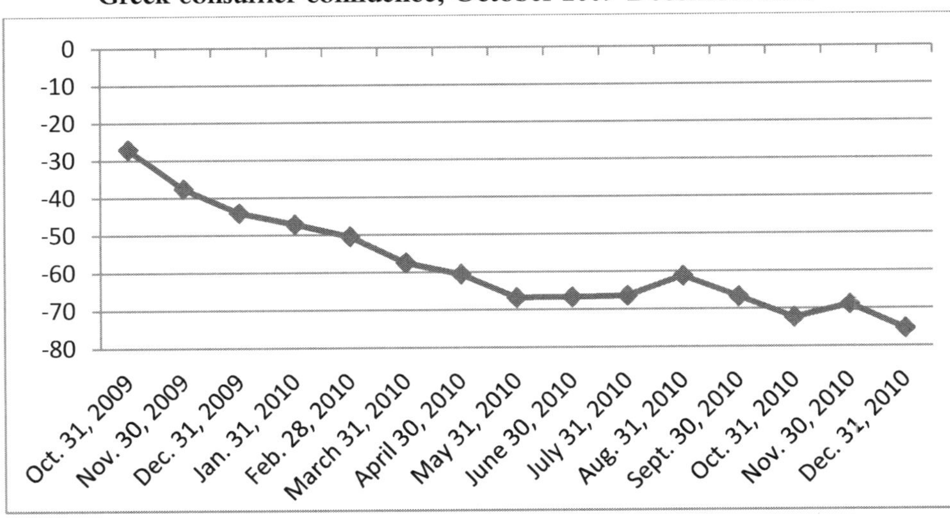

Source: Data compiled from European Commission (2012a)

According to a report by the Greek *Foundation for Economic and Industrial Research* (IOBE) in November 2010, Greek consumers have been in a state of constant depression since 'they see no light at the end of the tunnel'. Buying power was significantly reduced and consumer confidence reached its lowest point in October 2010, with 95% of households believing that unemployment would increase in the following year, whereas 75% of households suggested that they would further reduce their consumption in the same period. Moreover, 83% of households estimated that they would not be able to save any money in the following 12 months (Georgas, 2010).

The reduction in consumption primarily in the first half of 2010 was unprecedented for Greek standards. It affected not only the vast majority of small-medium enterprises, which inevitably downsized by sacking employees or reducing their wages in order to survive (Malkoutzis, 2011), but also the traditionally 'healthy' big transnational enterprises such as Coca-Cola Hellenic (see Kitsios, 2010). In this context the Greek government has been unable (or unwilling) to understand that high taxation had the double effect of the reduction in consumption and an increase in smuggling which prevented an even stronger consumption decline. This double effect impacted negatively on the state income. In addition the tax increase also increased the cost of production and transportation of commodities whilst simultaneously fuelling inflation, which further depressed consumer confidence. The result was the complete failure of the state to increase revenues, which was one of the main objectives of the restructuring programmes (see Marias, 2011).

As a result, according to the World Bank's (2010) study 'Doing Business', in 2010, Greece was in 109th place among 183 countries when it came to 'entrepreneurial environment', and scored worse than all other EU countries as well as countries such as Kazakhstan, Zambia and Rwanda. This hostile environment has not only created obstacles to aspiring entrepreneurs but also resulted in the breakdown of trust among existing entrepreneurs and obliged some to go up their 'Golgotha' to sustain their businesses. Chief financial officers from mid-sized companies with growth ambitions put Greece at the top of the list of contexts perceived as "most risky for investment", and consider Greece less attractive than war-torn Syria, Libya, Nigeria and Yemen (BDO, 2012). It is unsurprising that when it comes to "low business confidence" and "fear of the business failing" Greece is considered the 'world champion' (Politis, 2007; European Commission, 2012b).

Less fortunate entrepreneurs were 'obliged' to become financially less diligent. Data from 'Teiresias', the inter-banking company which processes information reflecting the economic behaviour of individuals and companies aiming at promoting bank-provided credit and reliable transactions in Greece, revealed that there were huge increases in bounced cheques and unpaid bills of exchange in 2009 and 2010 (Teiresias, 2012). This significantly affected intra-market trust and led to business introversion in a sociocultural climate of increasing suspicion and cynicism. Many other entrepreneurs were forced to cease their activity. According to the National Confederation of Greek Commerce (2012), 68.000 small and medium-sized enterprises in Greece have gone out of business since 2010, which is considered by the Confederation as a significant downturn for Greek small and medium entrepreneurship. This is almost double the 38.000 businesses that shut down over the preceding seven-year period of 2003 to 2009 (IOBE, 2012).

From 'free' market to 'dead' market to 'illegal' market: Evidence from the sample and the two case studies

All 13 interviewees were Greek nationals. 12 were male and only one was female (7,7%). Their ages at the time of the interviews varied from 24 to 63 (mean = 45 years). With the exception of Michael, the jeweller who had a criminal record for an offence he was not willing to disclose, the rest of the interviewees did not have criminal records. None were persistent offenders with problematic behaviour and involvement in property and violent offences from an early age. As legal entrepreneurs before 2010, they were involved only in the archetypal 'offence' for (Greek) business people, tax evasion.

Very importantly, these criminal entrepreneurs had extremely short criminal careers, and before 2010 they were neither involved in the illegal businesses described in this chapter nor in illegal markets distinct from their legal business. The involvement of all participants in illegal business at more or less the same time in 2010, was a response to the financial crisis as it is currently manifested in Greece. The illegal activities took place only in the final stage of a process which involved prior measures, such as asking a reduction in property rent, using savings, sacking employees, reducing their hours and paying them less, as well as cutting down on raw material or diluting the primary commodity (e.g. Paul, the alcohol wholesaler). The sole objective of *all* the participants in this study was survival in an adverse entrepreneurial environment. However, while all participants evaded apprehension, few were able to make their businesses survive. We have been unable to follow the latest developments in all the participants' business activities (legal and illegal), but we know that Chris and Dimitris have definitely gone out of business.

All the participants' stories highlight how primary occupations constitute a platform on which opportunities for illegal business can present themselves. The criminal entrepreneurs interviewed do not engage in alternative business activities but attempt to maximise potential within their own businesses. In a way, although reluctant and perhaps 'atypical' compared to the motivations of illegal marketers in general, these interviewees are in a sense 'typical' criminal entrepreneurs 'extending' their business with illegal 'branches' (see van Duyne (1991; 1993) within their legal businesses. Practically and psychologically speaking, this is what is to be 'expected' of them: an obvious and available solution that suits their skills, contacts and knowledge of the businesses, and their peculiarities and regulation (see van Duyne and Block, 1995).

What follows in this section are detailed accounts of two owners of small-medium size enterprises; a confectionary shop with an adjoining workshop (Nick), and an internet café (Chris). These businesses had been doing quite well but suffered significant loss of custom as the Greek economic crisis deepened.

'The survival of the sweetest' - Nick, the confectioner

Nick is 24 years old and lives with his parents in a town on a large island in southern Greece. His father is a retired confectioner who, in the late 1980s, established a confectioner's shop in the biggest, busiest, and most central street of the town; a shop that is, according to local people, 'the best shop of its kind in the town if not the whole island'. The reason for the shop's success was that Nick's father ran the place with a particular business philosophy that was valued by customers.

> "*My father was the best confectioner . . . The most important reason for his success was that he always used good quality raw materials. Only the best chocolate, only the best sugar, only the best biscuits, only the best milk . . . Anything that was not of excellent quality did not enter his workshop. And this is what he always used to say to me: 'If you want to succeed in this business, always use the best materials'. Do you know what others in this business do? They get low quality materials and the customers see that. For example, what others do when they make ice-cream is that they use milk powder or they buy ice-cream from factories that is made of milk powder. My father used only normal milk like the one we drink. You need a bigger quantity but it is worth it . . . Dark chocolate. That's very important. What others, for example [name of chain confectionery shop], do is that they mix small quantities of dark chocolate with vegetable oil and make it look thicker. In this way they can make many more small chocolate bars* ('glyka kerasmatos'), *you know those with nuts or fruits . . . But the customers know when they taste them . . . Plus after a few days, the chocolate bars don't look well because of the vegetable oil... This is why the others have always been second to my father . . .*"

After immense pressure from his father, Nick rather reluctantly enrolled in a private confectionery school. He is the only child of the family and was expected continue the family business. When Nick was student in that school, and specifically towards the end of his studies, his father fell seriously ill and he could not continue running the shop. Nick's cousin George, also a confectioner who was working in the same workshop, assumed responsibility for producing the bulk of the merchandise until Nick's graduation. When Nick completed the theoretical part of his studies (May 2010), he immediately applied himself to the business. In the beginning, with George's help, all day-to-day practical problems were solved. However, the most difficult challenge was not Nick's parents' production-related expectations for their son but the already rapidly declining sales.

> *"Generally, with George's help, I did not have any significant problems in making the stuff. He is really good and hardworking. But people nowadays do not buy as much as they used to. Two years ago [meaning 2008] those who came into the shop used to say 'I want a kilo of this, a kilo of that, a kilo of the other. Nowadays [late summer 2010], the whole environment has changed . . . Small chocolate bars . . . they [customers] say 'a piece of this small chocolate bar, a piece of the other small chocolate bar, one small piece of this cake' . . . stuff we previously used to give as tasters! And others may come in to buy one cup of ice-cream while before they'd buy a kilo, maybe more . . . People do not consume as much anymore, even the richer of our customers who used to buy stuff for their houses . . . Some come and ask 'can you 'write them' [meaning to get the merchandise on credit] and I will pay you at the end of the month?"*'.

The significant reduction of sales and profits occasioned Nick to cut down on the functional expenses of the business. Evading some more tax was almost impossible and he already owned the property on which his shop was located. Cutting down on functional expenses was done in various stages. The initial move was to reduce the days his employee attended work before eventually sacking her, and immediately after that to keep merchandise longer in the shop.

> *"In the beginning I told to the Albanian girl working in the shop to come at the weekends, maybe big name days when there are more customers. Then I told her 'we are not doing anything, we can't collaborate anymore . . .'. My mother has been helping a bit with the sales. Then we started keeping stuff for longer. For example, we started keeping 2-3 days old cakes, which are not as fresh anymore, in the refrigerator so that they last longer. Some years ago, we'd give those cakes to customers for free, and that was good marketing too! Or my mother would take them to my grandmother at the village to give to her friends . . . We are even more conscious of losses now that the sales are low. If something bad happens you have a serious problem. A few years ago another girl we had working in the shop forgot the door of the refrigerator open, the ice-cream melted and we had a loss of 1.500 euros. Five years ago we'd say 'these things happen, it's part of the business'. If something like this happened now, we'd probably have to close the shop".*

Those steps were also insufficient to guarantee some profit to Nick given the gradual reduction in consumption. Having no employees – other than the experienced George who significantly contributed to production and acted as pillar of support – and no intention to further compromise the quality of his merchandise and consequently jeopardise the 'name' of the business, Nick took an important decision. He approached the island representative of a legal wholesaler who had a personal relationship with his cousin, and asked him to provide significantly cheaper dark chocolate, Chocolate is a luxury product, is subjected to numerous layers of taxation in Greece providing some margin for cost reduction.

> "*I thought we needed to make some more reductions in the expenses of the shop. George is too important until I can fully stand on my feet. You cannot cut down on electricity, of course . . . 50% of the shop, if not more, is its refrigerators and fridges . . . So the next thing you can cut down on is raw materials. But I did not want to ruin the 'name' of the family by making low quality products. The last thing I wanted was people to say '[name of shop] is not as good as it used to be'. Once your customers get used to a level of quality, you can't offer them anything less. So, I went to this friend of my cousin's who is representative of [name of company] in [name of island], they are confectionery material wholesalers in Athens, and asked where I could find 'cheaper' but good dark chocolate. Do you know what I mean? He said 'give me a few days and I will get it for you. How much do you want?'*".

Nick initially ordered one ton of raw dark chocolate, which was transported by boat from Piraeus to the island, and delivered to him a few days later in big barrels (as opposed to the 'normal' wrapped 10-kilo plaques of dark chocolate) at the location he suggested: his grandmother's small warehouse at the back of her house in her home village a few kilometres away from the town. Nick is not aware of the origin of this dark chocolate, although he suspects it is stolen from a well-known specialist company's warehouse in mainland Greece. He, however, verifies not only that the quality of the merchandise is excellent but also that this illegal transaction was very convenient because, in Greece's current financial and entrepreneurial conditions, legal intra-trade exchanges between wholesalers, procurers and shop owners have become rather inflexible due to the decline in the commercial trust that had traditionally been an integral part of the trade.

> "*The quality is excellent and it is cheap . . . why should I care where it comes from?. . . I can buy it in that price. Listen, George, we give a battle every day here. When you do business normally with invoices etc., the wholesalers, even those who know you for years, now ask for cash upfront only; there are no cheques, no credit, as it happened previously, nothing . . . just cash. There are so many bounced cheques in the market that no one trusts anyone else anymore . . . And who has this much cash to give upfront now?*"

Nick keeps only the necessary (for a few days' or a week's work) quantity of raw dark chocolate in the shop in order to avoid the possibly unpleasant scenario of the financial police paying him a visit for an inspection. His mother transports small quantities of chocolate during her numerous visits to Nick's grandmother. He was not willing to disclose the exact amount of money that was saved from buying dark chocolate in the black market this one time although, as he suggested, it was substantial enough to lift some of the financial burdens that were jeopardising his business.

"... We are not talking about big profit here. Enough to 'cover some holes' in the business and survive in these times ... The times when the shop made a lot of money enough for my parents to live very well, pay for my school, go on holiday, buy stuff, and even have savings, are long gone ... Before, there was not a single night that I did not go our even for just one drink in a bar. Now, I may go out for a coffee once a week ... A few years ago my father, my mother and I even considered expanding the business to [name of nearby town]. A confectioner's shop with the same name that George would be in charge of. Back then we could get a loan from the bank and that was it. But this is not going to happen now ... Now we are marginal. We pay bills, standard expenses, the accountant, and there is hardly any profit ... We just survive now."

'In greed he trusts' - Chris, the internet café owner

Chris is 25 years old and lives in a city in Western Greece with his father, mother and brother. When he was 18 he took pre-university exams and was accepted in Forest Science School in a small, semi-rural town with a technological institute. As a student he was not particularly diligent, and he failed many academic years as he spent most of his time with friends in cafés and bars, and in houses where they consumed drugs and played video games. Chris was perceived as a 'dealer' by his social circle and was the link between his friends/classmates from the institute and a cannabis dealer in the town, who he had met in a bar. He used to get a small commission from his friends and classmates whenever he delivered the 'goods'. He was once asked to collect a substantial package of drugs for this particular dealer from the town's coach station in order to obtain a larger quantity of cannabis – about half a kilo – on credit. This instance, which resulted in Chris almost being arrested by the police, was the turning point in his entrepreneurial activities. Chris's drug troubles, which had been known to his family from the time when a particularly serious incident had led to Chris's hospitalisation, made his father decide to establish a small business for him in his hometown so that Chris could stay away from 'bad company' and 'trouble'. In early 2009 Chris's father obtained a business loan from a bank and opened an internet café on a busy road in a suburb of his hometown.

"My father was disgusted by me and the drugs case and told me 'that's it. You are coming back to [name of hometown] and we'll see what you will do. Do you want to have a shop and be the boss in it? How about an internet café? You will do almost nothing'. I replied 'sure ... why not'. It is not much else I could do anyway. And what was I supposed to do after I graduated? There is not much you can do as a forest scientist anyway."

Chris's internet café was opened in the summer of 2009. For a relatively short period of time business it was reasonably successful. The primary customers were initially teenagers from the wider neighbourhood playing PC games, supplemented by the occasional older internet and Facebook users who did not possess a computer.

> "*In the beginning, and for about 5-6 months, it was not bad at all. It took about a month for the business to take off but after that we were full. Mostly teenagers playing 'Counter-Strike' 'Call of Duty' or football the whole day and then someone who did not have a computer at home and wanted to book a flight, print the ticket or mess about in Facebook. Business was so good that me and my father were not enough to run the place and we hired a girl to help with coffees, and the refreshments and sandwiches but also to have a beautiful woman in the place.*"

The normal pattern of the business changed significantly in the beginning of 2010, however, to the point that there were many days in which either no customers entered the premises, or, when they did, it was primarily for socialising more than using the services offered. This was especially true for local teenagers over the weekend. This steep downturn in customers exerted such pressure on Chris and his father that they were forced to consider whether they should keep the business.

> "*At a point, in the beginning of 2010, things changed dramatically. There were days in which not a single customer entered the shop. OK, we are not in the centre of the city, in a place which everyone sees but it is a relatively busy road. I don't know what happened with the kids, maybe they all got their own PC and did not have to come here to play. But did they all get their own PCs at the same time? After a point, a few of those who used to come and play for the whole day, would now come to play for an hour but they would not get even a drink, not a single coffee, nothing . . . I know what has been going on in Greece, etc. etc. etc. But still . . . not a single customer for whole days?! . . .*"

If the business investment was to yield returns, the adverse conditions in which Chris and his father were experiencing required immediate action. Initially, while they covered expenses and basic family needs by using savings, they asked the owner of the property to reduce the rent by €200 per month. The property owner agreed to a €50 discount only as he counted on the rent to pay off the monthly instalments of a bank loan. The discount did not make much of a difference, and thus additional measures had to be taken.

> "*We thought we were completely destroyed . . . we had already 'burned too much fat'* (meaning they already used much of their savings) . . . *We fired the girl that was working here. We told her 'you do a good job here but there are no customers . . . We are about to close down, sorry Helen . . .' And the girl understood.*"

Firing the employee was quite 'relieving' for the enterprise as Chris and his father did not have to find her wages, but the financial problems continued as business remained remarkably low and pressure from the bank to pay off the loan, in addition to the external pressures felt throughout the nation, intensified. Chris' father came up with the idea of transforming part of the business. A number of computers previously used almost exclusively for PC games were converted into gambling machines (the so called *'froutakia' – jackpot slots* - in Greece).

> "*We saw that were not going anywhere with the internet café. And the bank 'had put the knife on our throat' with the loan. You can't win with the bank . . . And we had to pay more and more taxes . . . We would have to close down and my father said to me one night: 'what do you say? Shall we ask my friend John, who works in electronics, to tell me how we can change the computers to 'froutakia'? I heard that he knows people who do it'. I replied 'yes, it is a good idea'. What else could you do with these computers anyway? The Greeks love gambling. Give them gambling, and take their soul. Have a look at them next door at the 'Propotzidiko'* ('Betting Forecast Shop') *. . . betting and betting like mad the whole day. So, I thought 'yes, let's try this too, and see . . ,*'"

The electronics expert managed to introduce Chris's father to a colleague who could transform the computers into jackpot slot machines controlled by a central server by using a software package that was quite expensive (approximately €30.000). Thus, Chris and his father had to sell a small piece of land in the countryside as well as use the family's final batch of savings.

The 'new' business worked with a relatively small number of trusted customers who were acquainted to Chris and/or his father, or individuals who occasionally entered the premises with those acquaintances. Two very frequent and good customers were introduced to Chris by his uncle, himself a regular patron to an illegal card games 'club'. Visitors to the café were quickly 'scanned' upon entry to the premises. This 'scanning' required Chris or his father to act as a lookout at specific times, operating with a special remote control. This remote control, which the lookout kept to hand, turned over the jackpot slots on the screen to a random website page or turned off the system altogether when a unknown visitor was present. The lookout sat in a small office next to the entrance of the shop. This office was fitted with a one-way mirror so that those in the office could see out but those outside could not see in. Gambling sessions were not initiated in Chris's café when 'new faces' were present unless they came with a trusted patron who wanted to gamble. Cash was accepted as a deposit. It was converted into the equivalent number of credits, which were inserted into the customer's computer-cum-slot machine. In addition to the genuine internet user, the business initially worked with an average of five gambling customers a day. These customers gambled enough money for the business to be sustainable, and the owner to make a small profit. Given the clearly illegal nature of the business, advertising the service was not an option.

> "*It was not as good as I expected. To be honest I expected many customers but OK, I don't complain . . . It is not like it is a totally legal business, and maybe it is better this way. A few but good customers that I now. Customers who are willing to play 50 euros, 100 euros or even a couple of hundred euros every time they come in. It does not mean that this is the profit! They play many times every time they come, 5 euros, then another 5, then 10 euros and that's how it goes, and they have to win sometimes. And sometimes we have to give them 'air'* (meaning to give them a free 'starting bonus'). *Do you get me? They have to be 'sweetened' so that they come again. But it is much better now with the 'froutakia' than before . . . We are not rich now, you see how the people get by in Greece now, and we still have problems. But it is better than before . . . we are not closing down . . . for now, at least . . .*"

Chris's initial suspicion of this rather quixotic business effort materialised. Despite his attempt to adapt to the harsh entrepreneurial environment, Greece's enormous economic problems were eventually to triumph. The already limited numbers of gambling customers were not in the position to spend more money on the type of services offered in the café; their 'bankroll', to use the gambling vernacular, was drying up. Thus, in the first part of 2011, Chris had to close down the business.

Discussion

What we have encountered in our project is a type of criminal entrepreneur that we call the 'reluctant criminal undertaker' influenced by Sombart's (1967) cult of the 'undertaker', the pragmatist who simply seeks to 'get things done' on behalf of the interests of the self, and according to the logic of the market's 'dark heart', in the midst of 'inherited' or artificially created circumstances, no matter how brutally competitive and unforgiving they might be. There is a hard core of 'undertakers' who operate relatively successfully in capitalism's socio-economic nodes and arteries, often straddling the boundary between the legal and the illegal, as the influential and committed reproductive agents of the undertaking itself. The successful 'undertakers' lead initially reluctant others into new forms of economic shadow-activity, a reality that permeates the new (urban) economies and their socio-economic relations. Where Pitts's (2008: 39) 'reluctant gangster' is a 'product of, and an actor in, a world demarcated by poverty, socio-cultural and racial exclusion, illegitimate opportunity, and big city corruption' as well as a response to insecurity, the 'reluctant criminal undertaker' is the product of the pre-emptive fear of losing one's finger-hold on the economy and ending up in that situation. Ultimately, both are the products of an aggressive neoliberal restructuring, deep austerity, and what Fisher (2009) calls 'capitalist realism': the new dominant ideology based on the principle that no feasible alternative to the current form of political economy is possible.

There is an overall ideological climate of resignation and cynicism in which our distressed small businessmen, Nick, Chris, and the rest of the entrepreneurs we interviewed can see only one real choice: to participate in illegal activities or close their businesses and face the likelihood of material poverty and loss of social status. This is not the intrusion of 'anomie' (normlessness) at the core of society displacing traditional values and norms but the opposite, the emergence of a *new norm* based on ideological resignation to the corrupt anti-values at the logical core of the market system (see Žižek, 2010; Hall, 2012).

Commercial competition is one of capitalism's fundamental principles. Other confectioners must have been put out of business by the success of Nick's father; we cannot argue that he is undeserving of success or that market competition has not functioned effectively to deliver the best ice-cream to the customers on the island. At a fundamental level, however, Nick is dying by the same sword that killed his father's former competitors, but in a situation where alternative commercial ventures or replacement employment are far more difficult to come by. As our discussion of Nick's situation suggests, for example, there is no 'love' and 'trust' amongst actors in the marketplace in the current economic reality. Neither customers nor fellow shopkeepers will buy more ice-cream or somehow club together to save his business, there will be no surprise gift from a wealthy benefactor and, in the grip of the Troika, no help from the government. There are no values or manufactured consent at the heart of markets, merely subjects resigned to an unsentimental logic. In times of slump, the values of social cohesion evaporates, exposing the myth of its moral core.

In simple terms, as our analysis of Nick and Chris's situation (as well as the situation of the rest eleven interviewees) appears to confirm, businesses must continue to make profits or die, and in difficult circumstances this imperative can override the ethical restraints that can exert greater influence on socioeconomic action in more prosperous times. Karstedt and Farrall's (2006) answer to the growth of 'market anomie' is the reinstatement of ethics and rules, rather like Weber's preference for 'good business' over 'bad business'. This is a perception shared by many in Greece, but it is a misconception of the operation of the market (and its legal and illegal manifestations) at many levels. There is an accompanying perception that a clear boundary exists between the *legal* and the *illegal* markets, the *upperworld* and the *underworld* (Van Duyne, 2005), a view at the heart of the conceptualisation of 'illegal markets' as a *negative*, *imported* feature that is at least partly responsible for the current financial crisis. However, illegal marketers are there not to subvert the legal system but only to exploit opportunities for profit, but to benefit from the legal sector (van Duyne and Block, 1995). Legal businesses also benefit from illegal marketers in various ways. The illegal markets presented in the current chapter are not always antagonistic (Passas, 2002) to their legitimate counterparts or the legal sector as a whole. Moreover, what is also interesting to note here is that the legal businesses are the setting in which 'loyalty is borrowed' (von Lampe, 2007) and/or legal business relationships are transposed into criminal business relationships.

What Karstedt and Farrall (2006) suggest is also a misconception in relation to the principal human drivers of the market. Neither are moral but, respectively, *logical* and *thymotic* (Hall, 2012): enterprises survive by beating competition and making profits. Entrepreneurs do not enter markets primarily for moral reasons or to provide services to communities, but to grow wealthy and achieve or maintain status. In the absence of strong social ties and political solidarity, and thus expecting no voluntary support, the beleaguered yet driven entrepreneur facing the unforgiving logic of a global capitalist economy administered by unsympathetic neoliberal governance will repress moral injunctions and reluctantly resort to unethical acts in order to ensure the survival of the business.

As circumstances become more trying in specific economically distressed regions, which are not temporary aberrations but likely to be fragments of a shared future (Žižek, 2010), ethico-cultural restraints are buckling under the strain placed upon them by corrosive forces that are not imposed on the system by unethical politics, 'foreign' intruders or aberrant social actors but welling up from inside the system's enduringly pathogenic core (see Hall, 2012). Neoliberal political economy and the ideology of capitalist realism have combined to present us with the only game in town. We should not be too surprised when some individuals in the most difficult circumstances resort to deception simply to shore up their financial viability and cultural status for one more day. The way things are going in the neoliberal world this could catch on in a big way.

References

BDO, *Ambition Survey 2012*. Brussels: BDO, 2012

Business Week, 'Greece – Bankruptcy', *Business Week,* October 18, 2012 http://www.businesstoday-eg.com/case-studies/case-studies/greece-bankruptcy.html

Carlsson, C., Using turning points to understand processes of change in offending. *British Journal of Criminology,* 2012, *52*, 1-16

Cho, J. and A. Trent, Validity in qualitative research revisited. *Qualitative Research*, 2006, *6* (3), 319-340

EL.STAT. Labour Force Survey, December 2011. 2011. Available online at: http://www.statistics.gr/portal/page/portal/ESYE/BUCKET/A0101/PressReleases/A0101_SJO02_DT_MM_12_2011_01_F_EN.pdf

Duyne, P.C. van, Crime-enterprises and the legitimate industry in the Netherlands. In C. Fijnaut and J. Jacobs (eds.), *Organised crime and its containment: A transatlantic initiative*. Deventer, Kluwer, 1991

Duyne, P.C. van, Organised crime and business-crime enterprises in the Netherlands. *Crime, Law and Social Change*, 1993, *19*, 103-142

Duyne, P.C. van, Crime and commercial activity: An introduction to two half-brothers. In P.C. van Duyne, K. von Lampe, M. van Dijck and J.L. Newell (eds.) *The organised crime economy: Managing crime markets in Europe*. (pp.1-17) Nijmegen, WLP, 2005

Duyne, P.C. van, Organised crime (threat) as a policy challenge: A tautology. *Varstvolsovie*, 2010, 12(4), 355-366

Duyne, P.C. van and A. Block, Organised cross-Atlantic crime: Racketeering in fuel. *Crime, Law and Social Change*, 1995, *22*, 127-147

Eleftherotypia, Pagoma Misthon kai Perikopes Epodimaton Anakoinose I Kyvernisi. *Eleftherotypia*, February 9, 2010

European Commission, Greece Consumer Confidence Indicator. 2012a. Available online at http://ycharts.com/indicators/reports/european_economic_sentiment_indicator

European Commission, 'Greece Business Confidence'. 2012b. Available online at: http://www.tradingeconomics.com/greece/business-confidence

Ewing, J. and J. Healy, Cuts to debt rating stir anxiety in Europe. *New York Times*, 27 April 2010

Fisher, M., *Capitalist realism*. Winchester, Zero, 2009

Georgas, V., 'IOBE: 3 sta 4 Noikokyria Sfiggoun ki Allo to Zonari', *Eleftherotypia*, November 4, 2010, p.53

Gortzis, A. 'I Epixeirimatiki Ethiki Fernei Lyseis', *Eleftherotypia*, April 17, 2013

Hall, S., *Theorizing crime and deviance: A new perspective*. London: Sage, 2012

Hobbs, D., *Doing the business*. Oxford, OUP, 1988

Hobbs, D., *Lush Life*. Oxford, OUP, 2013

IMF, *World Economic Outlook*. Washington, D.C.: IMF, 2012

IOBE, The Greek Economy. *Quarterly Bulletin*, 2010, No.61, pp.1-128

IOBE, *I Epiheirimatikotita stin Ellada 2010-2011*. Athens: IOBE, 2012

Karstedt, S. & Farrall, S., 'The Moral Economy of Everyday Crime', *British Journal of Criminology*, 2006, 46, 1011-1036

Kathimerini, Nearly a third of businesses in central Athens closed due to recession. *Kathimerini*, 25 September 2012

Katseli, L., Greece 2020: Researching a Greek developmental model. In T. Giannitsis (ed.), *Researching a developmental model for Greece.* (pp. 11-23) Athens, Papazisis, 2008

Kazakis, C., *H Elliniki Pompeia.* Athens, Pontiki, 2011

Kitsios, C., Syrriknonontai gia na Epiviosoun. *Oikonomia,* 22 August 2010, p.10

Kotzias, N., Epithetiki Kapitalistiki Anasygrotisi. *Kyriakatiki Eleftherotypia,* 22 August 2010, p.18

Malkoutzis, N., *Greece – a year in crisis.* Berlin, Friedrich-Ebert-Stiftung, 2011

Marias, N., *To Mnimonio tis Hreokopias kai o Allos Dromos.* Athens, Livanis, 2011

Maruna, S. and A. Matravers, 'N=1: Criminology and the person. *Theoretical Criminology*, 2007, *11*(4), 427–442

McKinsey & Co., *Greece 10 years ahead.* Athens, McKinsey & Co., 2012

Michaletos, I., Organised crime in Greece: Statistics, trends and police countermeasures in 2011. 2011. Available online at: http://www.balkanalysis.com

National Confederation of Greek Commerce, 'Deltio Typou tis ESEE gia to Neo Anaptyksiako Nomo'. 2010. Available online at: http://www.esee.gr/page.asp?id=3338

National Confederation of Greek Commerce, 'I Troika Vlaptei Sovara tin Ygeia'. 2012. Available online at: http://www.esee.gr/page.asp?id=3903

Nautemporiki, 'Evale Opisthen in Agora Autokinitou, Nautemporiki, 26 August 2010, p.19

Naylor, R.T., *Wages of crime.* New York, Cornell University Press, 2004

Nelson, R., Belkin, P. &Mix, D., *Greece's Debt Crisis.* Washington, D.C: CRS, 2011

NET, 'Netweek', *NET,* April 22, 2013

OECD, *Economic Survey: Greece.* Paris: OECD, 2007

OECD, *OECD Economic Surveys: Greece.* Paris: OECD, 2011

OECD, 'OECD Science Technology and Industry Outlook: Greece 2012', 2012 http://www.oecd.org/greece/sti-outlook-2012-greece.pdf

Pitts, J., *Reluctant gangsters.* Cullompton, Willan, 2008

Politis, T., Entrepreneurship in Greece. Presentation at the LSE, London, March 13, 2007

POPEK, 'I Katanalosi Kaysimon Ypohorise Kata 30%', *Desmos ton Venzinopolon,* June, 2010, p.14

Potter, G., *Criminal Organisations.* Prospect Heights, Ill.: Waveland Press, 1994

Reuters, 'Timeline: Greece's Economic Crisis', *Reuters,* March 3, 2010 available online at: http://www.reuters.com/article/2010/03/03/us-eurozone-greece-economy-timeline-idUSTRE62230T20100303

Smith, D., *The Mafia mystique.* New York: Basic Books, 1975

Sombart, W., *The quintessence of capitalism: A study of the history and psychology of the modern businessman.* New York, Fertig Howard, 1967

Sotiropoulos, D., A democracy under stress: Greece since 2010. *Taiwan Journal of Democracy,* 2012, *8*(1), 27-49

Taxhaven , To Psifisthen Nomoschedio gia tin 'Prostasia tis Ethnikis Oikonomias', *Taxhaven,* 8 March 2010. Available online at: http://www.taxheaven.gr/news/news/view/id/5693

Teiresias, Statistics 2003-2011. 2012. Available online at: http://www.tiresias.gr

Telloglou, T., *To Diktyo-Fakelos Siemens.* Athens, SKAI, 2009

To Vima, Epicheirein gia 5,000 Euro Etisios. *To Vima (Oikonomia),* 5 August 2008, p.1

Tsipouras, D., Molis sto 75,5% tou AEP oi Synolikes Apotamieuseis. *Avgi,* 6 July 2012

Tsiros, T., Pos tha tin Plirosoun oi Marides. *Oikonomia,* 31 August 2008 p.5

von Lampe, K., Criminals are not alone: Some observations on the social microcosm of illegal entrepreneurs. In P.C. van Duyne, A. Maljevic, M. van Dijck, K. von Lampe and J. Harvey (eds.) *Crime business and crime money in Europe: The dirty linen of illicit enterprise.* (pp.131-155) Nijmegen, WLP, 2007

Varoufakis, Y., *The global minotaur.* London, Zed, 2011

World Bank, *Doing business.* Washington, D.C , Palgrave/World Bank, 2010

Žižek, S., *Living in the end times.* London: Verso, 2010

Inner contradictions of economic crime control

Matjaž Jager and *Katja Šugman Stubbs*[1]

Introduction

In this chapter we borrow the Marxist philosophical concept of "inner contradiction" and apply it to the area of economic crime control. In light of this concept we ask whether it is possible to identify any systemic internal contradictory and opposing developments in the way economic crime control operates today. If the answer is yes, the next question that can be raised is whether these contradictory forces that we can identify indicate some future evolution in the way economic crime control is carried out?

One can point out several features of the modern economic crime control that could count as inner contradictions. Some of them lie just beneath the surface. At the more basic level we point to the contradictory role of the modern liberal capitalist state as an agent of control. In its Janus like face the state needs to regulate economic activities and release the regulatory burden on economic actors at the same time. This situation triggers the attempts from all sides to secure the privileged treatment which in practice amounts to a competitive advantage. In its contradictory role, the state, despite the declarations of democratic participation and equality among its citizens, responds to the special interests. At the end of the day it mostly endorses the preferences of most powerful, affluent and influential actors.

On the other hand, one can point out contradictions in the role of the modern criminal law as a policy tool against most harmful economic crime, including massive labour law violations and Ponzi finance.

---

1 Matjaž Jager is Director and senior fellow at the Institute of Criminology at the Faculty of Law Ljubljana and Associate Professor at the Faculty of law University of Ljubljana. Katja Sugman-Stubbs is Professor of Law at the Faculty of law University of Ljubljana and senior fellow at the Institute of criminology at the Faculty of Law, Ljubljana.

We conclude our tentative exploration of this analogy, which no doubt raises as many questions as answer, by speculating on the transforming potential of these inner contradictions for the future of economic crime control.

In search for contradictions

If we persistently contradict ourselves in communicating with others our lives will soon become burdensome and complicated, to say the least. Clearly, sometimes we just cannot make up our mind, sometimes we may be indifferent as we do not care, but affirming one option and at the same time its exact opposite will make communication problematic. If I sit down in a café and order coffee and at the same time negate my order it will make me look strange. In a public debate, someone who contradicts himself, needs, technically speaking, to choose between his two opposite statements or perhaps take some time off to think it over and/or remain silent. Contradictory positions make standard logical compulsion impossible: stating A and non A at the same time can mean at best that only one of them may be true. In everyday life, in public reasoning and, last but not least, in logic and science contradicting oneself means bad news.

On the other hand the related but different concept of "inner contradiction" as borrowed from Hegel's dialectics and developed in Marxist philosophy denotes a feature of potential future transformation and does not necessarily mean 'bad news'.[2] Simply put an inner contradiction is an active force of self-transformation of something from within; the transformation springs from the clash of opposites tied together (*e.g.* Bhaskar, 1993: 56).

In other words, what a certain thing or a phenomenon will become depends most of all on the dynamics of its inner contradictions. Let's take the main example that Marx used: the explanation of the whole historical development. He believed that – put in a very abstract way - inner contradictions of political-economic formations, *i.e.* "epochs" like feudalism and capitalism, drive the historical development forward. In his view capitalist societies, for example, suffer from irresolvable inner contradictions that will eventually bring about the transformation of

2 While addressing the cyclical crises in the capitalist economy Marx, for example, pointed out the futile attempts of some economists to cover the contradictions up: »In order to deny crises, they assert unity where there is conflict and contradiction. They are therefore important in so far as one can say they prove that there would be no crises if the contradictions which they have erased in their imagination, did not exist in fact. But in reality crises exist because these contradictions exist.« (Marx, 1968: 519)

this socio-economic formation in the direction of socialism and, in the final distance communism. But we need not dwell upon his historical predictions here. What interests us is the idea of opposing inner contradictions that might have the potential to develop the economic crime control.

Is it then possible, looking at this segment of crime control, to identify something similar, *i.e.* systemic inner tensions, oppositions or "contradictions" with a transformative potential?

Two contradictions at first sight

It appears that economic crime control abounds with inner contradictions; some can be spotted even just beneath the surface. It is the only area of crime where the criminals or the potential criminals try to influence the definitions and the reach of the law. They try to influence them and many times do succeed in this. Notorious 'regulatory capture', 'revolving door problem' and similar phenomena recently attract increasing attention from criminologists and the critical media. One of the most notorious specific examples is the case of Berlusconi, but more systemic ways of exercising undue influence are manifold. These kinds of captures and conflict of interest can go a long way. Describing the recent financial crises Dorn, for example, writes about the regulatory capture process in the US and the UK involving rating agencies and the entities rated. Not only did the rating agencies that needed to objectively rate the risk of various "financial products" got paid by the clients they rated. They also became entrenched in the mutual thinking models and understandings. Things went so far that, as Dorn observed, in such a "mood of unity private interests regulate the regulatory bodies, their thinking, models, data and rule making" (Dorn, 2010: 243-245, 252).[3]

On the other hand, the globalized world of international trade, globalized economy and the globalised financial markets in particular highlight another, let us call it the local-global contradiction. This is the contradiction between the paradigmatic primarily local regulatory and repressive response to the economic crime 'events' on the one hand, and the *de facto* global playground in which the perpetrators of high level economic-financial crime operate. The system of local responses based on the initiative of nation states is in opposition to the need for a global regulatory, preventive and repressive mechanism that can, at least in theory,

3 For a fascinating recent documentary that illustrates the revolving door problem with the Goldman Sachs »alumni«, see Fritel and Roche (2012).

match the globalized playground of these people (See, *e.g.*, Aas, 2007: 123-126). But this last opposition may not be typical for high level economic and financial crime only, we find it in areas of 'classical' organised (economic) crime and internet crime as well. Here, on the level of the law in the books international policy makers have responded with a number of international (UN) conventions, the broadest being the Convention on Transnational Organized Crime (2000). In the area of international financial crime one recent initiative that goes into the right direction is the European Parliament resolution on Fight against Tax Fraud, Tax Evasion and Tax Haven (2013).[4] But this initiative is limited to the EU member states and is legally speaking only a resolution.

A more basic contradiction perhaps: one state with two opposing missions

To us the fundamental contradiction in the area of economic crime control concerns the dual role of the modern state. The state's mission follows two mostly opposing goals: backing the maximisation of profits of economic actors and enforcing regulations upon them.[5] Faced with these clashing goals the policy makers many times opt for 'pragmatic' solutions enabling *ad hoc* exceptions in the application of regulatory and criminal law which by definition ought to be general and universal. The power of making an exception reflects the need for establishing convenient loopholes in the principled area of (criminal) law. The examples are manifold. Let us present in some detail two Slovenian ones.

The 'highway cross' cartel

A couple of years ago the Slovenian state turned a blind eye on what turned out to be the greatest building cartel in Slovenian history established for the purpose of building the Slovene 'highway cross' (Cf., Jager, 2011). The cartel that lasted for more than a decade siphoned off huge amounts of public money.[6] The higher cartel price that was charged to the state was reflected in one of the most expensive

4 See, European Parliament resolution of 21 May 2013 on Fight against Tax Fraud, Tax Evasion and Tax havens (2013/2060(INI)).

5 Calavita and Pontell (1990, 337) single out authors who stressed this structural problem in the area of occupational safety and health standards.

6 For the similar Dutch building cartel, see, van Duyne and van Dijck (2007).

kilometre of highways in Europe. There are many indications that the state not just turned a blind eye: it facilitated and encouraged the formation of a cartel that united the domestic building firms, big and small. The idea was that by allowing the domestic building firms a special treatment the Slovenian national economic interest will be best served. The crucial element of the whole design was of course that this arrangement would never get public; the representatives of the state publicly and stringently endorsed a globalised competition and the façade of the competitive bids. At the same time they secretly endorsed the criminal building cartel, actively or passively. At the end all came out and ended with huge detrimental effects for the Slovene building sector as a whole. But, the enforcement of this illegal cartel is not an isolated case. The second example comes from the field of labour law.

The social insurance swindle

The Slovenian Criminal code covers the most severe violations of the Slovenian labour law, among them the non-payment of pension contributions. Article 202 entitled "*Violation of social insurance rights*" incriminates intentional non-compliance with social security legislation and prescribes imprisonment of up to one year or monetary penalty or both.[7] At the beginning of the recent financial crises media started reporting on the fast growing number of cases where the firms unilaterally stopped paying the social security contribution for their workers and in many cases even deceived them. For example, the monthly instalments were recorded on their pay checks as paid. Thus many victimised employees became aware of this only after their firm went bankrupt. Due to media pressure the Slovenian prime minister openly acknowledged that he knew that round 3.000 firms stopped paying pension and social security obligations for their workers. According to some estimates round 100.000 employees were victimized.

Some independent state institutions did raise their voice: the Ombudsman has been notifying various bodies about this problem for years, but with no success (Hanžek, 2010). The State Prosecution Service refused to press criminal charges *ex officio* claiming that according to its interpretation of the law, in most cases they cannot qualify this activity as a criminal offence. The Ministry of Justice joined this legal opinion that clearly disregarded the very straightforward wording of this incrimination defined in no ambiguous way. Only after the indignation of the public and the critique of this legal opinion in the professional press (Cf., Kovačič Mlinar, 2010: 6) the Ministry of Justice and more importantly the State Prosecution Service

---

7 The Criminal Code (KZ-1), Ur.l. RS No. 55/2008, 66/2008 – correction.

finally changed their position 180 degrees and started enforcing the criminal law that was not maintained up till then. Two years later The Supreme court confirmed this last interpretation of the criminal code.[8]

The more or less deliberate passivity of the state to protect workers' rights reflects in our opinion the unstated understanding among the policy makers that employees in Slovenia are overprotected, in any case that the labour market is 'too rigid'. But since, at the time, reducing labour law standards by law would be highly unpopular for the centre left government, they decided to push into the direction of greater flexibility by elegantly not enforcing the law. In this way they preserved the façade of the law in books and at the same time effectively undermined its promises by not enforcing it in practice to the detriment of the disadvantaged segment of its citizens.

The policy maker's leaning to one side

These examples illustrate how the state is caught between two, in many aspects contradictory goals. On the one hand, it imposes all kinds of regulations on the market economy and business actors. The regulation of these norms ought to facilitate the economy but in an important part the rules simply limit the freedom of choice of these actors.

On the other hand, policy makers struggle to establish the so called 'business friendly environment' in order to create conditions in which the present business activities will flourish and new business activities will be attracted to its (fiscal) jurisdiction. Being friendly to business and its maximisation of profits is a must.

So on the one hand, it has to impose the barriers and limitations to 'free market economy' and on the other hand, reduce them as much as possible. Policy makers need to regulate and release the 'regulatory burden' at the same time. In some cases, as explained above, the state imposes regulation and at the same time either facilitates its violation or chooses to passively ignore the violations of its own norms and in this way 'resolves' this contradiction.

The way the contradiction is resolved is very important because it is not done randomly or based on equal and fair treatment. On the contrary, it is systematically done in favour of more powerful economic players and systematically to the detriment of the less powerful players on the economic market place. In our cases the state did not keep its promises to those with less power and influence: be it a foreign

8 Judgement of the Supreme court of the Republic of Slovenia No. I Ips 22840/2011-52 from the year 2012.

building firm bidding in Slovenia or be it workers cheated for their social security payments.[9]

To be able to manoeuvre, the policy makers do not want to be completely bound by their own criminal law, nor by its regulations at large. The reason for this uneasiness in relation to its own 'legislative child' lies in the very uncompromising, principled nature of criminal law. The criminal code solves a selected number of value judgements and value conflicts in advance and once and for all so to say. As a consequence, it prohibits certain acts and omissions *per se*: it is by definition binding for the future – no matter what. The more detailed and specific it is, the more predictable it becomes. Its role reflects a *meta* policy wisdom: that it makes sense to have principled constraints on policy making set up in advance. A principle example of such a policy constraint mechanism is of course a written constitution.

However, the average policy maker in power does not particularly like any such absolute and principled constraints on their every day decision making. Any pre-commitment narrows down their choices. Because of this they try to interpret in their favour, narrow down, bend or simply ignore the legal order so as to maximize some imminent interest, more or less adequately labelled for example as 'the national interest' or the economic or other interest of an influential social group.

At first sight, one could draw here a rather common analogy with the notion of the highest level of moral development. The position of pragmatic policy makers resembles in a certain way the position of a most highly morally developed human person. Such a person creates his or her own principles of decision making. In Kohlsberg's stages of moral development a person of the highest, so called post-conventional stage does not stick to the rules no matter what (Kohlberg, 1981). He realises that law itself can be immoral, relative and partial; instead of that he is strongly committed to the universal morality of the worth and dignity of every human being (Kohlberg, 1984: 180). "While the person at postconventional stage does also recognize fixed legal-social obligations, recognition of moral obligations may take priority when the moral and legal viewpoints conflict." (Ibid.). At first glance it may seem that both – pragmatic politicians and most highly moraly developed decision makers - tend to bend the legal norms or moral norms according to their views and beliefs. The crucial distinctive criteria however is the basis for their position.

Taking into account Kohlberg's theory, it is easy to asses what is in the interest of a society: policy makers with post-conventional moral reasoning. Only such

---

9 Keeping its promises is the essence of the rule of law. As, for example, Pitamic put it: The legal order must be effective in the real world or at least we can reasonably count that the law will most of the time keep its promises, if necessary with the use of legal force. (Pitamic, 2009: 7-9.)

personalities would not be influenced by his or her own egoistic personal, family, group or partial special interest but would only be devoted to universal justice based on a universal respect.[10]

But the great majority of citizens never reach that level of moral enlightenment; they are interested in making a little exception for themselves while the others should stick to the rule. The fundamental question rooted in the very basic dilemma of living together in a society can thus be framed also in the 'free rider discourse' asking, for example "Why should self-interested utility maximisers refrain from acting as free riders on the cooperation that has arisen based on social norms?" (Cf., Rothstein, 2005: 141). Because of this pressure to make an exception for himself, so called 'universal institutions' such as the impartially working, legitimate legal order are weak and precarious, because, in light of the self interested actor theory, it is in no-one's interest to defend them (2005: 143- 145). The cooperative, universalistic systems such as the modern state are a prey of the special interest groups. The perception that everybody is out there to make a little exception for himself is undermining social trust needed for the cooperative rules to function at a satisfying degree. The proclamations and actions of the policy makers and economic actors are not aligned. As Rothstein observed in the corporate world: "In theory, all firms and industries are in favour of full and open competition, while in practice, they generally act to promote state establishment of various forms of subsidies and rules that limit competition in their particular field." (Id., 143). Free riders and policy makers, both affluent, do not walk their talk.

On the practical and empirical level the recent research focused on the amount of political participation of various strata of the American population illustrates this. The disturbing picture of the American democratic participation is this: the American government does responds to the special interests and its response is heavily in favour of high income groups (Cf., Gilens, 2012, 2005, Page *et.al*, 2013). For example, Gilens' empirically grounded conclusion is that "when Americans with different income levels differ in their policy preferences, actual policy outcomes strongly reflect the preferences of the most affluent but bear virtually no relationship to the preferences of poor or middle-income Americans." (Gilens, 2005: 778).

---

10 A person on the level of post-conventional thinking has already outgrown his tendency to gratify only his (or his immediates') egocentric, individual needs. By taking a political decision he genuinely wants to take interest of everyone into account, tending to make his decision universally just and fair regardeless of the position in which he finds herself at the moment. Sometimes, of course, policy makers' motives are hard to analyse in the midst of the retoric of the 'economic interest', 'common good', 'national interest' and similar.

Left on its own the government will succumb to the will of the powerful at the expense of the less powerful. Adam Smith observed this tendency in his landmark *An Inquiry into the nature and Causes of the Wealth of Nations* and warned us in this respect well before Marx (Smith, 1976 (1776), 292).[11] In other words the government will, without an adequate counter pressure, be most tempted to govern the public affairs rather in line with the interest of the powerful and influential citizens than in the interest of the poor and disadvantaged. For that reason we need to count on a "natural" inclination on behalf of the government to slip into serving special interests.

Dissuasive criminal law penalties of most harmful corporate crime as contradictio in adiecto

In dealing with high level economic and financial crime the repressive response is the tool of the day. It is most of the time, apart from civil law remedies, framed in administrative or criminal law framework or both. The idea is to reduce and if possible prevent this kind of crime by threatening with criminal law sanctions. It is embedded in the broader fact that the prevailing assumptions of the present day criminal justice systems are those of the classical criminological school. These assumptions on the purpose of punishment are presently expressed by the default formula of the international criminal law conventions urging state parties to impose "effective, proportionate and dissuasive" criminal law penalties in order to secure the implementation of this or that policy. The assumption behind is that we can control or at least channel human's choices with the threat of punishment attached to deviant choices. Thus we reduce future social harm by dissuading others not to do so: "effective and dissuasive" criminal law penalties serve as a policy tool.

Most people would agree that if there is one area of crime where rational choice perspective would fit in, it is the area of economic and financial crime. Even more,

---

11 On the clash of special interest with the public interest he writes: "The interest of the dealers, however, in any particular branch of trade or manufactures, is always in some respects different from, and even opposite to, that of the public. To widen the market and to narrow the competition is always the interest of the dealers." (Smith, 1976: 292). And similarly: "The proposal of any new law or regulation of commerce which comes from this order, ought always to be listened to with great precaution, and ought never to be adopted till after having been long and carefully examined, not only with the most scrupulous, but with the most suspicious attention. It comes from an order of men, whose interest is never exactly the same with that of the public, who have generally an interest to deceive and even to oppress the public, and who accordingly have, upon many occasions, both deceived and oppressed it." (Ibid.)

high level economic and financial crime appears to be a perfect fit for the more or less hard version of the rational choice perspective. Economic and financial crime is perceived as a prototypical instrumental crime where the costs and benefits are assumed to be carefully weighed. If the perpetrator of this kind of crime is not a perfectly rational economic calculator, he or she is still responding to incentives and remains basically reasonable, as we say. (Cf., Korobkin and Ulen, 2000, McAdams and Ulen, 2009).

Now, as Bentham and others have analysed in great detail, in order for the punishment to have a dissuasive effect on a potential perpetrator it needs to prevail over the impelling motives that are driving him into offending. This is the central idea of the theory of rational choice and the backbone assumption of the classical school in criminology. And indeed this assumption is at least an unspoken assumption of the mainstream criminal law reaction to (economic) crime. The belief in "effective, proportionate and dissuasive" penalties formula embodies it.

We would, therefore, expect some version of rational choice theory to be the most influential explanation in the area of economic and financial crime control. This commonsensical victory would then be reflected in the practice of criminal justice systems of the world, at least in those countries that purport to practice rational policy making. However, the reality appears to contradict this: what we find in practice are relatively low punishments prescribed by law and relatively low sentences actually imposed in most cases that end up in courts or are settled. On top of this the possibility of detection and prosecution of these cases is generally low or very low. For example, in Slovenia, up until recent more energetic responses of the police triggered by the change in the political will, we had, as our president of the Commission for the prevention of corruption described it "a zero risk environment" (Klemenčič, 2013).

In the area of economic and financial crime which could cause round 50% of all monetary damage due to all crime[12], where in theory the normative idea of "effective, proportionate and dissuasive" penalties is universally accepted and proclaimed, the practice testifies to the contrary. In our efficiency and market rationality driven societies the reaction to this kind of crime does not follow theory. Even more: this is the only area of crime control that has not witnessed the rising punitive pattern evident in most western market economies in the last couple of decades. In his book on neoliberal government of social insecurity Wacquant offers the following condensed explanation of why this might be so: "'Class advantage' a la

12 This Slovenian approximation is based on the average estimates made by the Slovenian police for the years 1999-2011, see, Keršmanc (2013: 300-302).

Sutherland, rooted in the socio-cultural affinity of justice officials with bourgeois offenders, an edge in juridical resources available to corporate scofflaws, and laws promulgating restrictive definitions of economic crime and favouring civil remedies for them, have combined with the inherent complexity and furtiveness of white-collar crime as violations of trust in complex chains of agency to shield corporate criminals from the renewed zeal of the penal state." (2009: 126). [13]

In the light of what has been said so far about the dual and partial role of the state this contradiction between words, law-on-paper and deeds should not surprise us. The modern policy makers show uneasiness with the idea of applying all available deterrence tools against the perpetrators coming mostly from the powerful and influential socio economic groups. On the other side it does not show this uneasiness when dealing with the crimes of the poor.

But even if . . .

But even if we could remedy this undemocratic bias against the interests of poor and disadvantaged, the idea that deterrence works in general and, in the case of most harmful economic crime in particular, remains deeply problematic. Let us point out just two "inner contradictions" that we can observe. The first has to do with the assumption of the threat of punishment as a communication. The system assumes that the potential offenders know the law and get its message. The problem with this point has been eloquently addresses by Mathiesen a couple of decades ago. He pointed out factors of a successful communication that remained forgotten: the sign structure that the message lands in and its interpretation. Looking at general prevention as communication he argued that many times

> "the sign structure which the preventive message lands in and is interpreted within, the context of interpretation within which the signal is picked up and understood, is such that the signal is not effective, and the message not understood as the sender has meant it . . . , the signal is not interpreted as a (threat of) deterrent sanction or an educational message. Rather, it is for example

13 Speaking of "restrictive definitions of economic crime« in light of the present Ponzi finance crises Dorn believes pessimism is in place regarding criminalisation of the harms of capital . . . meaning that 'it ain't gonna happen': one would have to attack not isolated individuals but the whole social swathes . . . Yes, there is public anger, but trying to stoke it higher is likely to result in bringing just a few vulnerable individuals, whilst further distracting attention from the historical dynamics that have brought us to this juncture." (Dorn, 2010: 255).

interpreted as more oppression, more moralising, and more rejection." (Mathiesen, 1995: 231.)

In the world, or perhaps a subculture of transnational corporations and finance this could mean that "That part of the business community which largely keeps away from grey or black (*i.e.* semi-legal or illegal) economic activity on normative grounds, lives in a normative sign structure or a moral context of interpretation which at the same time makes the threat of punishment appear as a deterrent sanction or a sensible educational message. Those who are not kept back on normative grounds, however, live within a normative sign structure which neutralises the deterrent effect of punishment." (Ibid.). In other words, and from the opposite perspective, why do people obey the law in the first place? Is fear of punishment the prevailing motivator or is it something else? Tyler showed us that maintaining social order through what he calls "command and control model" faces serious problems (Tyler, 2006). Instead of fear from punishment, his empirical research suggests, the assessment of fairness or legitimacy of a legal rule prevails as a main factor of adherence to a social order (Cf., Tyler, 2006: 272).[14] So, to summarise this contradiction with Mathiesen, may it be the case that "general prevention functions in relation to those who do not 'need' it. In relation to those who do 'need' it, it does not function." (Mathiesen, 1995: 231.)

The second inbuilt barrier to the general prevention effect of criminal punishment in cases of most damaging economic crime is the inflexibility of punishment itself. One could call it the contradiction between the requirement of dissuasiveness and proportionality. Hence, even if we assume for the moment that the general prevention idea of influencing future behaviour works perfectly and even if we assume for a moment that the state would be zealous to employ it against economic crime (which, as we saw is now systematically not the case), *i.e.*, that it would technically speaking, with great certitude, severity and swiftness target high level economic and financial crime, this 'remedy' would hit into its own inner barrier.[15] Having at disposal the three variables of the deterrence tool "certainty, celerity and severity", the politicians most of the times choose to bet on the increase

14 In a setting of corporate employees his research led him to the conclusion that:«Employees followed policies and obeyed rules when they viewed the corporation as legitimate and entitled to be obeyed... Employees were also influenced by their judgements about the degree to which the policies of their companies were consistent with their own moral values. Self-regulating strategies to influence employee behaviour have a stronger effect than fear of punishment based approach. (Tyler, 2006: 272, 2005).

15 For the general overview of the classical Becker's model of optimum punishment from the rational choice theory perspective, see, e.g. Albertson and Fox (2012: 36-57).

in severity of proclaimed punishment. Why? Because it is most convenient for them. It is the fastest – just changing the law will do – and it also looks the cheapest in the short run as it does not necessarily trigger additional increases of the police and other personnel. And one appears to be 'tough on crime'.

Proportionality is not, as some have noticed, a limiting principle of the administrative penalties only; at some point in the increase of severity the administrative penalty may reach the threshold reserved for the criminal law (Cf. Ogus, 2004: 49-50.) Equally valid within the domain of criminal law, the proportionality principle is traditionally entrenched into the modern criminal justice systems. It is true that the actual application of this principle in criminal sentencing depends on the concrete criminal justice system. Proportionality is a relational concept whose sensible application depends on the underlying philosophy of punishment, be it for example mostly retributive or mostly utilitarian, which can lead to several jurisprudental issues that cannot be addressed here. At the bottom line however this sentencing limiting principle prevents the almost never-ending increase of criminal law sanctions as could be dictated by the idea of effective dissuasiveness of the threat of punishment.

In other words, if the government decides to increase severity of punishment it will sooner or later (depending on the point of departure and depending on its punitive aspirations) hit the barrier imposed by the principle of *proportionality*. In the context of high level economic crime the rewards expected will many times be so high that lots of it will remain perfectly rational even if the proportionality requirement is stretched to the limit.[16]

In practice a generally low certainty of punishment, *i.e.* low detection and conviction rate would have to be offset by yet additional increase in severity which would mean for example that severity would have to be doubled if the probability of punishment is at very high 50% (assuming that the perpetrators are risk neutral, while the opposite may in fact be the case in many cases of overconfidence). The threat of punishment that ought in theory to secure the deterrent effect would have to become so high that it may be declared excessive in relation to the punishments prescribed for other crimes.

Thus in this case the state, being forced to implement the effective and dissuasive punishment on the one side, and proportionality principle of punishment on the other side, is confronted with a contradictory task: the threat of punishment cannot be increased indefinitely as it hits the systemic inner barrier at some point. Beyond

16 On the many theoretical issues concerning the requirement of proportionality – the primarily retributive requirement that the punishment should fit the crime - see, e.g. Frase (2004), Plesničar (2012, pp. 12-13).

that barrier dissuasiveness simply is absent by theory. So, even if certainty, severity and swiftness of punishment in these cases would be considerably higher than today – which is highly unlikely for the reasons explained above – the most damaging crimes of this sort would still remain to be undeterred.

In other words, based on its own assumptions the repression of high level economic and financial crime through criminal punishment based deterrence suffers an inbuilt barrier created by the proportionality principle. Because of this even in the most optimistic scenario lots of most harmful (and rewarding) economic crime would still look rational from the rational (economic) man point of view.[17]

Conclusion: is the mix of contradictions near the tipping point?

Borrowing from Marx and his notion of inner contradictions we sketched some potential examples of such contradictions in the area of economic crime control. They appear on various levels and in various interrelations. Perhaps the fundamental contradiction concerning the policy goals reflects the dual role of the state. The modern state has to regulate economic activities and create a business friendly (read 'deregulated') business environment at the same time. In addition, the policy makers in this dual role are most of the time not neutral and not in the pursuit of the common good of all citizens. They mostly favour policy options that favour those with power and influence. Thus in its dual, opposing role the state formally proclaims equal and fair treatment of all but in reality undermines it.

On the other hand considering the policy tools, criminal law remains the prevailing and most exposed instrument against serious economic crime. In this area criminal law sanctions are again discriminately applied. But even if the state would function in a non-partial and bias free manner, the general prevention idea might not function for those that "need it". On top of that even if we assume that deterrence works, *i.e.*, that the threat of punishment deters those who "need it", the inbuilt barrier of proportionality of criminal sanctions would mean that the most damaging economic crime would remain under deterred.

17 This does not mean that other potential socio-economic damages tied to criminal prosecution do not frighten the potential perpetrators. The impact of these factors is however mostly out of the picture in discussions that focus primarily on (increasing) the severity of punishment that will »finally« bring about the holy grail of the dissuassive effect.

Paraphrasing Oscar Wilde we could simply acknowledge that "Only shallow areas of crime do not contradict themselves". On the other hand the transforming potential of observed contradictions in the area of high level economic and financial crime control remains a matter for debate. May these contradictions under suitable circumstances trigger a dialectic transformation in the paradigm of economic crime control from within? If the answer is yes, when will the mass of inner contradictions become critical and what will such 'resolution' of opposites bring about?

Are, on the other hand, the observed contradictions just a peripheral reflections of core inner tensions of the present day globalized financial capitalism? In this respect Dorn discussing the recent Ponzi finance crises predicts the following: "On the wider canvass, changes in markets and their regulation will occur as part of wider geo-political processes, involving the de-centring of western power and the rise of new historical forces (including 'class' forces, for those wishing to try to integrate that aspect into the social and cultural analysis)" (Dorn, 2010: 255). Very probably so, but it remains to be seen.

For the time being some worries remain. Writing in 1990 in the aftermath of the Savings and Loan scandal in the US, Calavita and Pontel noted that piecemeal regulatory reforms that followed the scandal did not touch the root causes that brought about the crises and pictured a grim perspective: "The future is likely to bring more of the same" (1990, 338). A quarter of a century later their prediction came true. In the aftermath of being hit by "much much more of the same" Dorn again put it on the record: "If changes are not made, we might as well sit back and wait for a replay." (Dorn, 2009: 3). Therefore, to borrow the philosophical vocabulary for the last time, the future will show whether we are already destined for the dialectical transformation of some sort or we remain stuck with the Nietzschean "eternal recurrence".

References

Aas, K.F., *Globalization & Crime*. Los Angeles, Sage, 2007

Albertson, K., C.Fox, *Crime and economics: An introduction*. London and New York, Routledge, 2012

Bhaskar, R., *Dialectic: The pulse of freedom*, London, New York, Verso, 1993.

Bonger, W.A., *Criminality and economic conditions*, Horton, H.P. (transl.), Boston, Little, Brown and Company, 1916

Calavita, K. and H.N. Pontell, "Head I win, tails you lose": deregulation, crime and crisis in the savings and loan industry. *Crime & Delinquency* 1990, vol. 36, *no. 3*, 309-341.

Duyne, P.C. van and M. Dijck, All in the Dutch construction family: cartel building and organized crime. In L. Holms (ed.), *Terrorism, organized crime and corruption: Networks and linkages*. Elgar, Chelterham, 2007, 109-129

Dorn, N., Ponzi finance and state capture: The crisis of financial market regulation. In P.C. van Duyne, G.A. Antonopoulos, J. Harvey, A. Maljevic, T. Vander Beken and K. von Lampe (eds.), *Cross-border crime and inroads on integrity in Europe*, 2010, pp. 235-260

Dorn, N., Financial market systemic regulation: Stability through democratic diversity, VoxEU.org – policy portal of the Centre for Economic Research, funded by the EU, 8. December 2009. http://www.voxeu.org/index.php?q=node/4411

Frase, S.R., Excessive prison sentences, punishment goals and the Eight Amendment: "proportionality" relative to what?, *Minnesota Law Review*, 2004, vol. 89, pp. 571-651

Gilens, M., *Affluence and influence: Economic inequality and political power in America*. Princeton, Princeton University Press, 2012

Gilens, M., Inequality and democratic responsiveness. *Public Opinion Quartery*, vol. 69, *no. 5*, Special Issue 2005, 778-796

Fritel, J., M. Roche, Goldman Sachs: La Banque qui dirige le monde, (documentary), Arte France/Capa, 2012

Hanžek, M., Pravna in socialna država. *Pravna praksa.no.33*, 2010, 3

Jager, M., The politics of the Zemono building cartel on the sunny side of the Alps., In G. Antonopoulos, M. Groenhuijsen, J. Harvey, T. Kooijmans, A. Maljevic and K. von Lampe (eds.), *Usual and unusual organising criminals in Europe and beyond: profitable crimes, from underworld to upper world: Liber Amicorum Petrus van Duyne,* Apeldoorn, Antwerpen, Portland, Maklu, 2011, pp. 105-117

Keršmanc, C., Preslepitve na meji in onkraj pregona: konceptualni selekcijski mehanizmi pri pregonu goljufivih preslepitev v gospodarstvu, Doctoral thesis at the Faculty of Law University of Ljubljana, Ljubljana, 2013.

Klemenčič, G., Dejansko smo v vojnem stanju, intervju z Goranom Klemenčičem (Meta Roglič), *Objektiv*, 16. 3. 2013

Kovačič Mlinar, B., Kaznivo dejanje kršitve pravic iz socialnega zavarovanja v praksi: primer delavcev Steklarne nove v stečaju, Pravna praksa, no. 22, 2010, 6-8.

Kohlberg, L., *The philosophy of moral development: Moral stages and the idea of justice*. San Francisco, Harper & Row Publishers, 1981

Kohlberg, L., *The psychology of moral development: The nature and validity of moral stages.* San Francisco, Harper & Row Publishers, 1984

Korobkin, R.B. and T.S. Ulen, Law and behavioral science: Removing the rationality assumption from law and economics. *California Law Review*, vol. 88, 2000, 1051-1144

Marx, K., *Theories of surplus value.* vol. 2, Moscow, Progress Publishers, 1968

McAdams, R.H. and T.S. Ulen, Behavioral criminal law and economics. In N. Garoupa (ed.), *Criminal law and economics.* Cheltenham, UK, Northampton, MA, Edward Elgar, 2009

Mathiesen, T., General prevention as communication. In R.A. Duff and D. Garland (eds.), *A reader on punishment*, New York, Oxford University Press, 1995.

Ogus, A., Enforcing regulation: do we need the criminal law? In H. Sjogren and G. Skogh (eds.), New perspectives on economic crime. Cheltenham, UK, Northampton, MA, Edward Elgar, 2004, 42-56

Plesničar, M. M., Uklonilni zapor končno na ustavnosodnem rešetu, *Pravna praksa*, 2012, 12-13.

Page, B. I., L.M. Bartels and J. Seawright, Democracy and the policy preferences of wealthy Americans. *Perspectives on Politics*, vol. 11, *no.1*, March 2013, 51-73

Pitamic, *Država*, Ljubljana, GV Založba, 2009 (1927)

Rothstein, B., *Social traps and the problem of trust.* Cambridge, Cambridge University Press, 2005.

Smith, A., *An inquiry into the nature and causes of the wealth of nations*, R.H. Campbell and A.S. Skinner (eds.), 2 vols., Glasgow edition of the works and correspondence of Adam Smith 2, Oxford, Oxford University Press, 1976.

Tyler, T.R., *Why people obey the law* (With a new afterword by the author), Princeton, Princeton University Press, 2006

Tyler, T.R., Promoting employee policy adherence and rule following in work settings: The value of self-regulatory approaches. *Brooklyn Law Review*, vol. 70, 2005, 1287-1312.

Wacquant, L., *Punishing the poor: the neoliberal government of social insecurity.* Durham and London, Duke University Press, 2009

Bestiarum vocabulum of economic crime: excerpts from the Slovene volume 1996-2010

Ciril Keršmanc[1]

Introduction to a (post)modern bestiary on economic crime

A bestiary, or a Bestiarum Vocabulum, could loosely be defined as an illustrated encyclopaedia of beasts that was quite a popular genre in the Middle Ages. Very often a moral lesson was attached to the description of the beast in question:

> *"A bestiary is a book of real and imaginary beasts, though its subject often extends to birds, plants and even rocks. Long perceived merely as rudimentary natural histories, medieval bestiaries actually reflect the belief that the natural world was designed by God to instruct mankind. They describe the physical nature and habits of animals in order to elaborate on the moral or spiritual significance of these characteristics . . . [B]estiaries typically contain abundant depictions of animals that reinforce or add to their description in the text. Word and image work together and individually to communicate morally edifying material, such as might be included in medieval sermons, in an appealing and accessible manner." (Runde, n.d.)*

By using the form of a modernised (and agnostic) version of the medieval bestiaries, this paper aims to present some of the results of a yearlong in-depth qualitative analysis of economic crime in Slovenia.

Generally the definitions of serious[2] economic crimes in criminal codes tend to differ from the definitions of classic serious crimes because they are much more likely

---

1 Ciril Keršmanc, LL.M., Ph.D.; Researcher at the Institute of Criminology at the Faculty of Law, Ljubljana [ciril.kersmanc@pf.uni-lj.si]. This paper is based on my doctoral research and my Ph.D., Keršmanc, 2013a.

2 The adjective 'serious' is used to differentiate between more serious crimes and lesser crimes. In some jurisdictions terms felony and misdemeanor are used in others the terms indictable offence and summary offence. The main differentiating factor between the two categories is usually the type/duration of the sentence that is prescribed by the legislator for a specific criminal act. The other important distinction between the two categories is the type of criminal procedure that follows and how

to use malleable terms. This effectively means that their exact content is more open to interpretation (relative to classical crimes) and that it is more likely to change through time even though there is no change in the wording of the legislator's definition of the specific economic criminal norm itself. This has been described as a "deficiency that one needs to be conscious of and has to endeavour to minimise it, but a deficiency that is nonetheless *unavoidable* when dealing with economic criminal law" (Kobe, 1973: 281).

This observation also applies to abuse of position, because what counts as such and what is considered to be a deceptive business practice is relatively open for interpretation, widening the margins of discretion for the interpreter. The latter is not only the judge who ultimately fixes the (economic) criminal norm, but also the injured party, the police and the state prosecutor as they are the ones who start the wheels of criminal justice and keep them spinning.

The question that this paper will address is: what kind of dangers for the criminal justice system this (unavoidable) increased margin of discretion entails? We will try to find the answer by a closer examination of two economic criminal norms through the case law or rather exemplars that they produced in a selected national jurisdiction.

More specifically, our research focused on two crimes pursuant to the Slovene Criminal Code [SCC], namely "Business fraud [BF]"[3] and "Abuse of position or trust in business [APTB]"[4]. Both of them are covered in the section of SCC dealing

---

much discretion the prosecutors have when deciding to prosecute or not – with serious crimes, at least in Slovenia, their discretion is limited to those instances that are expressly prescribed by law.

3 Pursuant to Art. 228 of SCC (Kazenski zakonik, KZ-1B), BF is defined as: "Whoever in the performance of an economic activity, when concluding or implementing a contract or service, defrauds another by representing the obligations as that they will be fulfilled, or by concealment of the fact that the obligations will not be or will not be able to be fulfilled, gains property benefit or causes loss of property to a client or a third person on account of such partial or complete non-fulfilment of obligations shall be sentenced to imprisonment for not more than five years." Second and third paragraph deal with qualified and privileged forms in case the property loss/benefit is of considerable (more than € 50.000) or negligible (less than € 500) amount.

4 APTB is defined in Art. 240 of SCC (Kazenski zakonik, KZ-1B) as: "Whoever in the conduct of business activities abuses his position or the trust placed in him by another, acts beyond the limits of the rights inherent in his position or fails to perform his duties originating from a state law or other state prescription, prescriptions of the legal entity or his contractual obligations vis-a-vis the management of other's property or benefits with a view to procuring an unlawful property benefit for himself or for a third person or to causing damage to the property of another, shall be sentenced to imprisonment for not more than five years." The second paragraph prescribes a harsher penalty of up to eight years imprisonment in case of substantial property loss/illegal benefit (more than € 50.000), while the third paragraph criminalises also

with economic crime while there are important quantitative and qualitative differences between the two which makes them even more suitable for our analysis. These differences and the rich diversity of 'beasts' one can find in the deep dark forest of economic crime are the topical focus of this paper.

A quantitative snapshot of divergence within the concept of economic crime

There is a rather obscure provision in the Slovene State Prosecutor Act [SPA] which states that Slovenian State Prosecutor General may allow access to archived "raw" prosecutorial files and registers to an individual who demonstrates that he needs access to conduct scientific research.[5] Such a request was filed and access was granted.[6] What follows is an overview of research that was conducted *in situ* of The District Prosecutor's Office in Ljubljana [DPOL] between 30-6-2011 and 27-6-2012 with some of the more picturesque exemplars that were gathered. To my knowledge this is one of the longest, if not the longest, qualitative studies dealing with economic crime inside the prosecutorial "black box"[7] in Slovenia. However, before we begin the hunt for the 'economic bestias', let us first briefly present (a) the outlay of the land and (b) more specifically the part of the forest where we did our hunting (b).

a. The general quantitative context – The "Matryoshka analysis"

This part of our analysis was named "Matryoshka analysis", because the chosen method bears an underlying resemblance to the traditional Russian doll Matryoshka.

---

the instances where the conduct defined above results in non-property benefit for the perpetrator with an imprisonment for up to two years.

5 Now second paragraph of Article 181 of the SPA (ZDT-1), previously first paragraph of article 69.a of the SPA (ZDT-UPB5).

6 The request was filed 16-6-2011 and granted 21-6-2011 with an official reply from the Office of the State Prosecutor General, Nb. Tu 35/2011-05.

7 In contrast, when analysing Serbian anti-corruption policy, for example, Van Duyne used a more quantitative approach, followed by a qualitative analysis, noting that Serbian "institutions of prosecution and the judiciary are still a kind of *black box*. That may not look positive, though in experimental psychology it is a neutral concept used to denote the 'mind' which is closed to direct observations and therefore a 'black box'. All we can do is to observe [input and output]. In between we must speculate about inner mechanisms. The same approach can be used to address the prosecution and courts embedded in a surrounding anti-corruption strategy" (Van Duyne, 2013: 330).

For those unfamiliar with it, Matryoshka is a layered doll: after opening the bigger doll you find a smaller one inside it and an even smaller one inside the next one and so forth . . . We will try to present economic crime with the two chosen serious crimes (BF and APTB) within the general statistics on crime in a similar fashion through a visual representation. The source of data for this part of the analysis are yearly publications by the Slovene Ministry of Interior [MNZ]. We shall not dwell on the critique of MNZ's methodology of gathering and recording data[8] too much as we rather uncritically used their numbers and their statistical classifications ourselves. In the grand scheme of things numbers as mere numbers are not what interests us in this subsection. Also, for example, when talking about damage caused, the police data are inherently subjective because it is either based on their own estimates or the estimates of the person filing the criminal complaint.

Table 1
Official statistical crime data gathered by MNZ

	All Crime			Economic Crime		
Year	**No.recorded crimes**	**Damage caused in €**	**Damage recorded crime**	**No. Economic crimes**	**Damage caused in €**	**Damage per recorded crime**
1999	61.693	82.916.666	1.344	4.922	45.416.666	9.227
2000	67.617	122.083.333	1.806	6.337	54.166.666	8.548
2001	74.794	142.762.875	1.909	7.215	55.818.708	7.736
2002	77.218	139.684.416	1.809	8.527	71.121.833	8.341
2003	76.643	115.000.000	1.500	7.168	49.210.750	6.865

8 Even though the shortcomings of police data are pretty well known and have been covered elsewhere in more detail (see for example Markowska and Serdyuk, 2013:430-433 for the Ukrainian perspective), let us nonetheless add the Slovenian experience to the pile, especially because it is directly relevant for the data we used in our research. Svetek who used to compile the data for the MNZ had remarked the following in one of his last reports: "[MNZ data] show above all the activity of the police and not the picture of criminality from a security point of view . . . Slovenia does not have a developed model for measuring and determining the level of criminality with which one could with a high degree of accuracy and scientifically sound results identify the scope of various kinds of crime in different layers of our society . . ." (Svetek, 2006a: 95-98). As far as economic crime is concerned he pointed out that: "in the long term evaluation of economic crime trends one should only consider those socially unacceptable acts whose definition does not change considerably through time due to their well established and typical incriminations." (2006a: 98). For an in depth look at the methodology of gathering and recording data by the MNZ see also Svetek (2006b).

2004	86.568	162.916.667	1.882	5.825	100.656.666	17.280
2005	84.379	172.500.000	2.044	5.322	44.880.750	8.433
2006	90.354	168.333.333	1.863	6.696	42.276.500	6.314
2007	88.197	265.600.000	3.011	6.748	77.544.920	11.492
2008	81.917	175.000.000	2.136	6.701	96.639.640	14.422
2009	87.463	278.000.000	3.178	6.787	179.152.570	26.396
2010	89.489	577.300.000	6.451	9.448	466.324.270	49.357
2011	88.722	271.800.000	3.064	8.539	151.470.950	17.739
Average	**81.158**	**205.684.407**	**2.461**	**6.941**	**110.360.068**	**14.781**

	Business Fraud			**Abuse of Position or Trust in Business**		
Year	**No. of all BFs**	**Damage caused in €**	**Damage per recorde d BF**	**No. of all APTBs**	**Damage caused in €**	**Damage per APTB**
1999	171	3.700.000	21.637	55	6.275.000	114.091
2000	231	3.933.333	17.027	81	220.833	2.726
2001	771	12.102.791	15.698	333	12.221.500	36.701
2002	2079	19.515.458	9.387	185	17.014.166	91.968
2003	1672	11.036.125	6.601	201	20.691.583	102.943
2004	1054	21.302.500	20.211	207	39.405.833	190.366
2005	982	12.904.166	13.141	145	13.827.125	95.359
2006	1412	27.854.583	19.727	175	17.567.083	100.383
2007	993	10.131.740	10.203	231	47.817.140	207.001
2008	1595	8.966.940	5.622	169	54.719.370	323.783
2009	1940	23.763.760	12.249	351	58.012.180	165.277
2010	3880	33.736.050	8.695	246	255.538.270	1.038.773
2011	4232	33.878.880	8.005	161	65.150.230	404.660
Average	**1.616**	**17.140.487**	**12.939**	**195**	**46.804.639**	**221.079**

(Source of data: Ferme and Kebe, 2012; Lukan, 2007-2009; Lukan and Kolenc 2010, Lukan et al. 2011; Svetek 2000-2006a, also officialy published data from MNZ)[9]

We are more interested in the question of whether we can make any relevant deductions regarding the relationships between various categories where

9 The data was aggregated from yearly police reports and their regular analysis in the Journal of Criminalistics and Criminology, an SSCI journal that is published by the Slovenian Ministry of Interior MNZ.

methodological errors in principle cancel themselves out. We believe the answer is positive as can be seen from Figure 1. In it we visualised the basic relationships between different categories in terms of their individual shares or sizes compared to each other.

Figure 1

Crime in general vs. Economic crime vs. APTB vs. BF

(Frequency and damage estimates: Source of data, see Table 1)

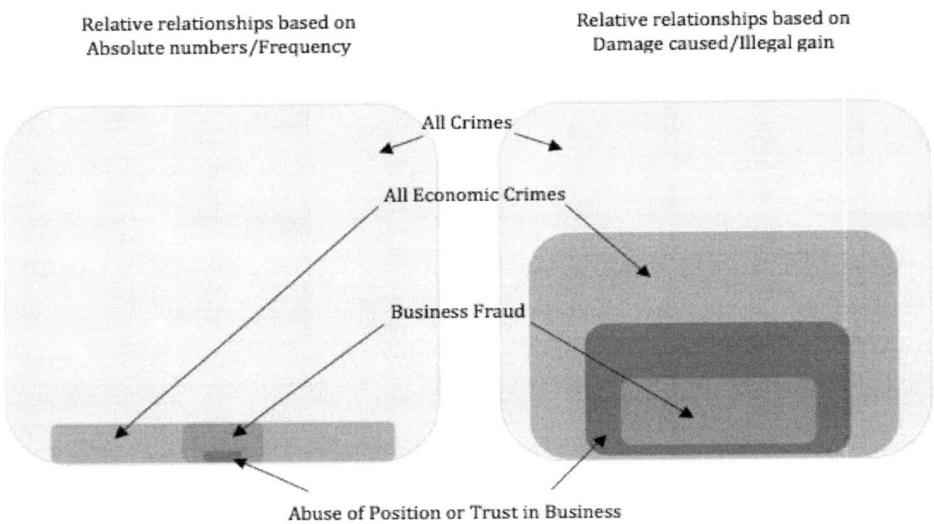

Different categories of serious crimes according to their frequency/numbers are shown on the left side of Figure 1. The sizes of individual rectangles preserve the relationships between frequencies/numbers of individual categories. This enables a quick visual conceptualization of the relationships. The biggest and the brightest rectangle represents the cumulative number of all serious crimes, a bit darker shade is used to represent the frequency/number of all economic crimes and inside that category the darker of the two shades represents APTB and the brighter BF. At a mere glance of the left side of Figure 1 one can quickly deduce that APTB, in terms of frequency/numbers represents a relatively small number both in terms of the share of economic crime and even more in the share of all recorded crime. However, the moment we look to the right side of Figure 1, we see a completely different picture.

The rectangles on the right side of Figure 1 demonstrate the estimated damage/illegal gain attributed to an individual category in terms of its overall share of damage attributed to each category cumulatively. The first thing we notice is that the category of economic crime causes more than half of the total damages/illegal gain despite the relatively lower number of recorded crimes from that category (on the left side). What is perhaps the most interesting thing is that the little speck representing APTB on the left side becomes disproportionally bigger when looking at the damage/illegal gain APTB causes. In terms of damages APTB overtakes BF despite the fact that we have a much higher recorded frequency of BF (on the left side). The reason for this is a higher "potential damage charge" of the serious crime of APTB. We calculated the "potential damage charges" of both categories as a coefficient between the estimated illegal damage or illegal gain and the frequency of recorded occurrence of individual categories.

As can be seen from Table 1, in the time span 1999-2011 the "potential damage charge" for APTB was on average € 221.079. This is 17 times more than the same calculation showed for BF (€ 12.939) and 90 times more than the same average for all criminal acts (2.461 EUR/per crime).

Figure 1 was made using aggregate average numbers from Table 1. The data was processed with an open source program called Sparklines.[10] We used the aggregate average numbers from Table 1. However, when one looks at the numbers in the table, one can quickly discern some rather conspicuous deviations from the general trend that undoubtedly had an effect on the average aggregates. We can thus observe extremely high estimates for damages caused by APTB in 2010 – this was the year that some of the so called 'tycoon cases' (*i.e.* 'privatisations' that had gone bad due to the economic crisis and the crumbling of established shady financial business networks) started being processed by the police and prosecutors.

We pointed out at the beginning that we will not dwell on the methodology of gathering data by MNZ – we accepted the numbers as given. The method which we described, together with the data from Table 1, makes it possible for anyone to reproduce the results with the desired corrections (e.g. valorization of the damages to a common denominator etc . . .). The main goal for us in this (sub)section was to provide a general orientation or rather build up a basic sense of the scale of the two serious crimes that will be analysed further in the following (sub)sections. With this basic sense of a wider quantitative context we can now turn to the statistical analysis of our field sample of raw prosecutorial case files at the District prosecutor's office in Ljubljana.

---

10 The method which we named 'Matryoshka analysis' in our application is generally referred to as 'tree mapping' in English. The open source program Sparklines is an add-on for Excel which adds the function of tree mapping to Excel spreadsheets.

b. A quantitative overview of our sample

The fieldwork was conducted *in situ* of the District prosecutor's office in Ljubljana [DPOL]. The head of the register office at DPOL prepared an electronic printed output of all criminal complaints that were filed at the DPOL for each year separately. For APTB the selection ranged from 1996 to 2010 and for BF from 1999 to 2010. The case files were brought from the archives in batches by year and type of cases and were returned back after analysis. I had virtually undisturbed access to all closed cases in the abovementioned period, including the unofficial work product of the prosecutors (*i.e.* their notes). More specifically, out of 879 cases of APTB received by DPOL, 693 cases were analysed, which is 79% of all the cases of APTB received by DPOL from 1996 to 2010. Furthermore, 562 cases out of 1873 cases of BF (30 % of all the cases of BF in that period that were processed by DPOL) were examined in detail. Some of the cases were still on-going or attached to other on-going cases for which reason they were not available. However, with regard to BF it was decided in an early phase that a more selective approach is adequate as most of the cases were repetitive *de minimis cases* bordering on civil infringements (i.e. mostly cases of simple non-payment for goods delivered). Therefore, I primarily focused on the initial period 1999-2003 when the BF incrimination first became part of SCC and the most recent cases from 2009 and 2010 that we could get our hands on.[11] A more comprehensive overview of the sample can be discerned from Table 2.

Table 2

An overview of the DPOL sample with data regarding the type of final decision*

Exemplar type – DPOL sample overview	Number
Abuse of position or trust in business *(sum of all cases in the sample)*	693
Business fraud *(sum of all cases in the sample)*	562
"Prima facie" **dismissals by the prosecutor's office**	810
for Abuse of position or trust in business	489
for Business fraud	321

11 We analysed the cases from the initial period and the most recent cases to make sure there was no significant shift in practice. We hoped that analysing both periods would alleviate the exclusion of (what we expected to be mostly repetitive) BF cases from the period 2004-2008.

End of procedure in the investigative phase	133
for Abuse of position or trust in business	68
for Business fraud	65
Indictments filed at the court by the prosecutor's office	312
for Abuse of position or trust in business	136 (56 convictions)
for Business fraud	176 (63 convictions)
"All in All" - Total sum	**1255**

* A methodological note: In the Excel table that was used to keep track of reviewed files there were 1264 entries; 575 for BF and 689 for APTB. We had to make some adjustments when we converted the data into the SPSS format for statistical analysis (e.g. missing values, double counting, manual mistakes at the input phase, etc.) Considering the number of entries the differences in numbers are small and statistically insignificant. In order to be consistent however, the numbers used are those that were used in the SPSS program for further processing.

Table 3

DPOL sample data about the duration of an active case file in months

	Entire sample *(duration in months)*	**APTB** *(duration in months)*	**BF** *(duration in months)*
Average	27	34	19
Standard deviation	28	31	22
Median	16	23	11
Minimum	1	1	1
Maximum	154	154	111

In this chapter only some of the more instructive findings of the statistical analysis of our sample will be singled out.[12] The quantitative findings fully confirmed our qualitative observations, namely that cases of APTB are *on average* more complex than cases of BF. For example, in terms of the number of suspects per case file, there was on average a bigger percentage of three or more suspects in cases of APTB. Furthermore, as can be discerned from Table 3 above, the average/median processing time of APTB cases was considerably longer than the average/median processing time of BF cases.

12 A much more detailed statistical analysis of the results regarding the number of suspects in a particular case (i), the length of the proceedings (ii), the final outcome (iii) and the amount of damages caused/illegal gain obtained (iv) is presented in Kersmanc (2013b).

Last but not least, the estimated amount of damage caused/illegal gain obtained also confirmed that cases of APTB are more 'dangerous' than cases of BF. For each of the analysed prosecutorial files official estimates from criminal complaints were noted down. Because the intent was to compare the numbers, we had to find a common denominator (1 EUR two years ago is not worth the same as 1 EUR today) or to use a metaphor, we had to translate them in the same language. This was achieved thus: the amount of estimated damage caused/illegal gain obtained was divided by the net salary for the month when the criminal complaint was made. All of the estimates were thus expressed in the units of average net salaries for the month when the complaint was made. The currency (EUR) in the equation cancelled itself out and the coefficient which we got out of the calculation enables us to make a direct comparison with the current period in terms of net salaries. In all respects this turned out to be a rather elegant and simplified valorization. The results are presented in Table 4.

Table 4
DPOL sample data regarding the amount of damage/illegal gain expressed in net monthly salaries

Damage expressed in multiplication of the average monthly net salaries	No. in whole sample	Total sample in %	No. of APTB	APTB in %	No. of BF	BF in %
From 0,1 to 1	123	*12,9*	33	7,7	90	16,9
1,1 to 5	201	*21,0*	39	9,2	162	30,5
5,1 to 10	94	*9,8*	27	6,3	67	12,6
10,1 to 20	116	*12,1*	49	11,5	67	12,6
20,1 to 50	139	*14,5*	77	18,1	62	11,7
50,1 to 100	87	*9,1*	52	12,3	35	6,6
100,1 to 200	61	*6,4*	40	9,4	21	4,0
200,1 to 500	60	*6,3*	41	9,6	19	3,6
500,1 to 1000	32	*3,4*	29	6,8	3	0,6
more than 1000	44	*4,6*	39	9,2	5	1,0
Total = 100%	957	100	426	100,1	531	100,1
Damage not recorded or = 0	297		267		31	
All in all - Total	1255		693		562	

In Table 4 we grouped the results in classes of unequal density/size based on the amount of damage/illegal gain obtained in terms of net salaries. The first two columns show the number of both APTB and BF which fall into a specific net salary class/range. The same is then repeated for APTB and BF separately. If we compare the percentages between the columns we can quickly observe that cases of APTB have a higher amount of damage/illegal gain obtained attributed to them on average than BF cases.

As can be observed a relatively large number of APTB cases were excluded from the calculation (267 out of 693). The reason was not that so many cases fell into the category of non-property damage[13] or that we omitted to record the data. There were simply a number of criminal complaints in which the person who put them forward was unable to provide a calculation or estimation of the damage. These cases were often dismissed *prima facie* by the prosecutor. Nonetheless they do offer some insight into the issues surrounding formulation of estimates in other cases where the person making the estimate ultimately decides not to be too conservative and rather gives a relatively high estimate. In the latter instance, for example, imagine a case concerning privatisation of a partially state owned company where an individual shareholder has to make an estimate of how the management team damaged his company's bottom line with a specific conversion or sale while conducting an MBO. This is being pointed out to relativise the value of estimates and inferences from statistical data about the amount of damages caused by fraud in general.[14]

There is, however, another point we would like to emphasise in connection to damage estimates. Policy makers should be wary of making decisions regarding prosecutorial priorities based solely on damage estimates, possibly in connection to the possibility of (non-conviction based) confiscation. We offer the following extreme example of APTB to substantiate our argument: imagine that a CEO of a company oversteps his rights and issues a guarantee to a bank in the name of the company he manages in order to secure a private loan of € 500 million for himself. He does this without the knowledge of his supervisory board. He plans to use the

---

13 According to the third paragraph of article 240 in SCC, APTB is also incriminated in cases of non-property illegal gain (such as for example a loan which was received by the CEO in violation of the procedural rules for obtaining a loan, even if such a loan was ultimately repaid with market interest rates).

14 For a more in depth analysis of this problem see Levi; Burrows, 2008. To illustrate, even in the UK, the estimates are generally unreliable and methodology dependent. From the 13,9 or rather £ 20 billion in 2007 (Levi et al. 2007), the National Fraud Authority [NFA] has published their Annual Fraud Indicator [AFI] in 2010 putting UK fraud damage estimates in 2008 at £ 30 billion, the corresponding AFI estimate in 2011 was 38,4 and in 2012 it was at a record 73 billion £, only to drop to £ 52 billion in the 2013 AFI (NFA, 2010-2013). The NFA openly admitted that it is still homing in its methodology which is changing constantly, meaning that existing AFIs are not comparable at all and offer nothing in terms of trend projections which is the only useful thing one can ever get from rough estimates. One cannot but wonder what is the point to this somewhat embarrassing exercise . . .

money received from the bank to finance a very lucrative investment which has a 50 % chance of materialising. In essence we are dealing with a flip of the coin. Now let us assume that he in fact makes more than enough money to repay the bank loan without the guarantee ever being cashed in by the bank. There was no actual damage/loss in this particular case for the company, however we are still dealing with a clear case of APTB (at least according to SCC). A crime was committed – the CEO abused the credit rating of the company that he managed for a purely personal gain. If we use a probability calculation, he exposed the company he manages (its shareholders) to damages/loss in the amount of € 250 million (which of course did not materialize, but nonetheless). Such concealed gambling is in our opinion substantially more dangerous (from a systemic point of view) and prosecution-worthy than most of the cases of *de minimis* BFs that we came across. While on the one hand the described cases of APTB usually go by unnoticed (especially if the investment pays out well), *de minimis* cases of BF on the other hand are usually prosecuted with full force of the law for a relatively negligible amount of damages/illegal gain obtained. A perfect example of what we are talking about is the case of "47 Teddy Bears". With this last example we have already begun to cross into the qualitative part of our analysis which will be at the centre of the next subsection.

A qualitative medley of exemplars – the bestiae in the flesh

As was pointed out earlier, our quantitative analysis only confirmed our qualitative observations stemming from case file analysis: the number of suspects, the length of the procedure and the "potential damage/illegal gain obtained charge" per case file all lead to a conclusion that in cases of APTB we are *on average* dealing with more complex cases compared to BFs. What remains is to fill up the statistics which are the bones of our analysis with some meat in terms of concrete exemplars. The following case selection is information-oriented.[15] While the "47 Teddy Bears" (a.) case is a paradigmatic exemplar of what was encountered most often in BF case file analysis, the rest of the exemplars were all uncovered in the analysis of APTB case files. The specific APTB cases were chosen because all of them have a meta-reflexive value in

15 As Flyvbjerg noted when describing various strategies for the selection of samples and cases this selection method is used "[t]o maximize the utility of information from small samples and single cases. Cases are selected on the basis of expectations about their information content" (Flyvbjerg, 2006: 230).

the sense that they transcend the narrower confines of criminal law and criminology. "The Compartmentalised Cesspit Case" (b.) goes back to the first wave of privatisation of state owned firms and demonstrates the creative imagination of the new capitalist elite on the one hand, and the overly formalistic thinking of the prosecutors in the early period of transition from socialism to capitalism on the other hand. "The Insurance Scheme Case" (c.) demonstrates how the teething capitalist system soon began to offer 'products' that enabled the management elites to 'legally' funnel money out of state owned companies to private pockets. Similarly the "Case of The Fictitious Third Breast?" (d.) demonstrates one of the many ways public money was/is being funnelled out of the state health-insurance scheme. And last but not least, "The Casino Case" (e.) is a perfect (paradigmatic) case reflecting the reality of the capitalist system in which we live in today.

a. The 47 Teddy Bears case(s)

Over-criminalisation is often criticised, however the criticism in academic discussions is mainly 'grounded' on the value based principle of criminal law as the *ultima ratio* or the last resort. The usual abstract or rather dogmatically-normative and value based top-down analysis will in this part of the chapter be complemented by shedding light on the problem at hand by analysing the case of the "47 Teddy Bears" in connection to BF; primarily from the bottom up.

The 'serious' crime of BF was introduced into the Slovenian Penal Code in 1999. While the classic definition of fraud requires *mens rea* from the outset of a (business/commercial) relationship, the *mens rea* requirement for BF is extended in the sense that the intent to defraud can come at a later point in a business relationship. This caused an additional blurring of the line between criminal and civil, that is non-criminal, cases. Since BF is one of the serious crimes under the regime of compulsory *(ex officio)* prosecution, some companies started using criminal complaints for BF against their debtors to shift the costs of collecting their debts to the state, effectively using the prosecutors and police as a 'free' (at least for the creditor) debt collection agency. We will briefly outline one of many such prosecutions we came across when analysing original prosecutorial files of BF.

The case or rather cases at issue involve a limited liability company "*Teddy Bear Ltd.*" (the company is real, but the name is made up) which filed (at least) 47 individual criminal complaints for the serious crime of business fraud against its debtors for non-payment of goods delivered. To sum up the complaints, the creditor wrote that he delivered goods to the defendant and received no payment. He usually added that the defendant did not respond to either telephone calls or letters and was avoiding the creditor. There is little doubt as to why the creditor decided for criminal prosecution and not civil enforcement. In one of the cases the prosecutor asked the creditor to be more concrete, whereupon he wrote this in reply:

> "*. . . our financial/civil law legislation does not give us an effective means to collect what is owed to us . . . We decided to file a criminal complaint because there is unfortunately an extremely long waiting period at the regular courts for the creditor to get processed. We hoped that by filing a criminal complaint we will scare the debtor/defendant into paying. Not paying your bills has become a national sport . . . the debtor has a lot more options to avoid paying the bills in a civil enforcement case than the creditor has of being paid. The debtor can manoeuvre out of paying what is owed for years and the creditor ultimately has nothing to show for it. . .*"

In another case Teddy Bear Ltd. was even more forthcoming:

> "*. . . we did not decide for civil law debt enforcement, because in similar cases the debtors had no movable or immovable property and they successfully play with the law – our company only had additional costs and was left with additional lawyer's fees. We also had 7 successful civil enforcement cases and despite the fact that we won them in court, we did not get repaid, because the debtors officially had no means, even though we have proof to the contrary. Based on the above we thus decided in most of the cases to file a criminal complaint and were successful – the debtor either paid his bills straight after a visit from the police or after being interrogated by the prosecutor or the investigative judge. . .*"

In essence criminal law was/is being used as the ultimate ratio in the wider sense of the term. This is not, however, according to the principle of criminal law as ultimate ratio in the narrow criminal law sense according to which criminal law should not be (ab)used as a substitute for an ineffective system of civil law enforcement.

Even though we are dealing with practically identical facts and formulaic wording of the criminal complaints in most of the 47 cases, they did not all end the same way. In 25 of the cases, the complaint was dismissed *prima facie*; in 9 cases the case was dropped at a later phase of the criminal procedure; 4 cases ended in acquittals or judicial rejection of the charges and there are even 8 cases where the debtors were ultimately convicted for BF. In the one remaining case, prosecution was conferred to Italy and there is no data on how the case ended. The thing to note is that even though the majority of cases did not end in convictions, most of them ended successfully for the creditor who got paid.

Figure 2
An overview of final outcomes in the 47 Teddy bear case(s)

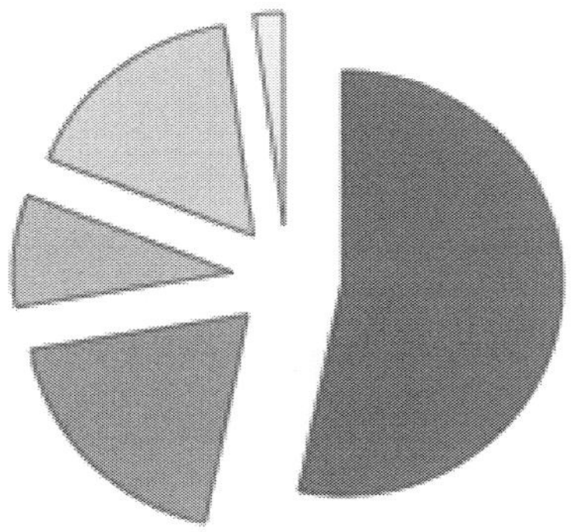

However, the variation of decisions, for what are essentially identical cases, opens up relevant questions regarding the principle of equality and legality as the central tenets of criminal law. Based on a larger sample of 562 cases of BF which were analysed, we concluded that the case of the "47 Teddy bears" is a paradigmatic case of how criminal law is (ab)used in practice by creditors who use it to transfer their private debt collection costs on the state, specifically by means of its criminal law system. The volume of such BF cases[16] has another negative effect in the sense that it 'steals' valuable resources from the criminal law system that could otherwise have been used to tackle more insidious and dangerous cases of economic crime. That is not to say that systematic non-paying is not a real problem, but merely that criminal law is not the way to go about fixing it. There are other ways for creditors to mitigate the risk of non-payment besides using criminal law.[17]

---

16 As we have demonstrated above, BF as defined in the SCC, is one of the most numerous economic serious crimes in Slovenia.

17 Let me give the following example as an illustration: in one of the '47 Teddy bear' cases the prosecutor dismissed the case after a very long (and costly) investigation with these words: "Considering the way in which both Teddy bear Ltd. as well as the manager of company X [the suspect] conducted their business, the prosecution cannot find sufficient grounds on which to base and build up the suspect's deceptive intent . . . Based on the way the debtor/suspect conducted his business . . . we can infer that Teddy bear Ltd. pursued a very risky business policy aimed only at optimising sales, while at the same time neglecting the realisation of sales in terms of actual income collected. It was in the interest of Teddy bear Ltd. to move as much product as possible, that is why they continued with the deliveries even to those business partners which did not settle their accounts for several months . . . The business policy of Teddy bear Ltd. was to tolerate non-payment even up to five or six months and only after that time, they stopped with the deliveries . . ." Other methods of mitigating

This is far from being a purely Slovenian problem. When analysing the situation in the US about twenty years ago, Coffee wrote that

> "*. . .[t]he dominant development in substantive federal criminal law over the last decade has been the disappearance of any clearly definable line between civil and criminal law. Second this blurring of the border between tort and crime predictably will result in injustice, and ultimately will weaken the efficacy of the criminal law as an instrument of social control.*" (Coffee, 1991: 193).

About forty years earlier, his compatriot Kadish argued that the use of criminal law is ineffective and/or counterproductive when it comes to: (1) using criminal law for declaring or enforcing public standards of private morality, (2) delegating jurisdiction to police enforcement via administrative (*e.g.* anti-social behaviour) sanctioning as a way to circumvent the safeguards of due process in the form of criminal procedure guarantees[18] and (3) using criminal law as a social service to specific needy segments of the society (Kadish, 1968/1969: 17,19).

As an example of the latter he put forward (among others) criminal law provisions that safeguard creditors in cases of cheque frauds. Kadish did not take issue with the prosecution of serious cheque frauds; his criticism was focused on those instances where one is dealing with so called '*de trifle*' cases. He argued that the legislator has given merchants criminal law as a means to mitigate their business risks in case of non-payment, even though they were fully aware beforehand that the use of a cheque as a means of payment is risky:

> "*When complaints are filed, the police, or sometimes the prosecutor, investigate to determine if there was a genuine intent to defraud or if the accused is an habitual bad-check writer. If not, the usual practice is to discourage prosecution and instead to assume the role of free collection agencies for the merchants. The cost to law enforcement is the diversion of resources from genuine threatening criminality*" (Kadish, 1968/1969: 29).

We came to the exact same conclusion after analysing the case(s) of the "47 Teddy Bears". A closer analysis of each of the 47 case(s)[19] showed that prosecutors and judges have at their disposal enough interpretative discretion to quickly clear *trifle*

---

risks for the creditor are for example various kinds of surety, advance payments, etc. The problem is that creditors in a competitive environment very often race to the bottom with their offers to keep their market share – this is a legitimate choice, but it comes at a price.

18 Or as he put it "as a disingenuous means of permitting police to do indirectly what the law forbids them to do directly" (Kadish, 1968/1969: 19).

19 For a much more detailed analysis of the 47 cases see Keršmanc, 2013a: 128-156, also Keršmanc 2013b. There each of the 47 cases is dissected in the search of those incidental factors that lead prosecutors or judges to decide one way or another.

cases *à la Teddy bear* of their dockets and thus curb over-criminalisation themselves, if they want to. When it comes to defining the limits of the zone of criminality they are far from being passive mouthpieces of the legislator(s). What can sometimes lead them astray is an overly simplified quantitative measure of their productivity in terms of quantitative output: 'solving' an x number of BFs does not always equal to solving an x number of more complex cases in terms of actual work done. Processing simple BF cases requires less actual work, that is why pure numbers can give the wrong idea or impression. This is something that any quantitative based incentive system should take into consideration.[20]

b. The Compartmentalised Cesspit case

This is a particularly interesting case of APTB going back to the early days of privatisation of state owned property in Slovenia in the mid 1990s. It involves the privatisation of a meat processing company. As in numerous other similar cases the management team in cahoots with the employees founded a by-pass company with the same business activity and started to divert business and profits to that company (*e.g.* the private daughter company 'rented' space from the mother company, the mother also provided the equipment and delivered the processed meat at a discounted price according to a very favourable franchising agreement to the daughter who sold it at a considerable higher price . . .). However this is not what made this case stand out. There was another method of funnelling the money out of the mother company that was much more intricate and interesting.

The management of the state owned mother company put in place very detailed "Rules on innovation, invention, stimulation and rewards for creative enhancements (Innovation Rules)". The Innovation Rules were no joke – all in all 19 pages of rules and 81 articles detailing the legal relationships in connection to inventions, technical

---

20 To illustrate why, let me give this quite telling example. In one of the BF cases that I got my hands on the police report was 195 pages long! The police categorised 388 unpaid bills of a certain businessman as individual criminal acts. Each one of the acts was described in a paragraph that was copy-pasted 388 times. The only difference being the date of the issuance of the bill. This was not an isolated case (it was probably the most extreme one). I can only assume that such creative deviations are the consequence of simplified quantitative indicators of productivity. The case described above is extreme for which reason it caught our attention – but imagine for a moment how many cases of this nature slip under the radar (e.g. cases that have 3 or 4 unpaid bills) that can give us a completely wrong picture of reality.– in my opinion there simply is no other way of knowing what is true than digging into case files themselves.

improvements, patents, intellectual property, . . . Article 2 of the Innovation Rules stated that they represent

> "*. . . the foundation for an innovative company. To be economically efficient, innovation has to be based on expertise and everyone should endeavour to achieve it. The purpose of the Innovation Rules is to stimulate every single employee and all other business associates to creativity, innovation and implementation of new solutions into the production, information and management processes with the aim to increase the quality, productivity, economic viability and reputation of the company while at the same time achieving the highest standards of safety at work.*"

The Innovation Rules required each employee to file or co-author at least one innovation suggestion per year. The sanction if he did not do so was designating the worker as "less useful" which meant that he would not participate in the profits. The Innovation Rules detailed individual categories of inventions and enhancements and prescribed the model for the calculation of rewards in the form of additional payments and variable salaries to the innovative workers. In theory, everything seems to be on the up and up.

Not long after the Innovation Rules came into effect, the first three suggestions were filed. Each of them had a leading author (for the first suggestion it was the CEO, the second was his CFO and the third the representative of the workers council – also the ex CEO) who was entitled to a larger piece of the pie and a number of co-authors (between 15-18). All in all every single employee that was also a shareholder in the daughter company was included on the list.

And what were the suggested innovations? The first suggestion was the construction of a "Compartmentalised cesspit and the installation of a centrifugal ventilation system (*i.e.* a propeller-fan)". The second suggestion was "replacing the old boiler in the basement with a new one" and the third suggestion put forward "new recipes for meat products including: treated domestic stomachs, sausages and salami" with the proviso that the recipes will be delivered at a later date . . .

For the abovementioned suggestions the co-actors received 171, 166 and 161 average net salaries or cumulatively (all 52 employees together) 498 average net salaries in September of 1992 (the rewards were not distributed equally, the leading author received approximately 200% of the rewards that the co-actors received).

When it came to prosecution, the prosecutor used a very formalistic approach which meant that she did not go into the absurd nature of the innovations (again we are talking about a hole in the ground with three compartments, a new boiler and recipes for sausages to be delivered at a later date . . .). The case was prosecuted on the grounds that the rewards that were paid out in net amounts and not gross amounts (*i.e.* the company paid all the taxes on top of the rewards themselves which was in contravention of the Innovation Rules). Because the monies were returned, the prosecutor dropped the charges.

If the prosecutor considered their actions in the context of what they were doing to the mother company she could have gone beyond the strictly formalistic approach, but she did not. The same happened in many other cases. It took a while before the prosecutors began to be more courageous in their prosecutions and started to look at the bigger picture.

This particular case might seem comic and obvious – we are dealing with a meat processing plant which means concrete meat products and processes that one can see, touch and taste. However, before one becomes too judgmental, consider for a moment the financial and banking sector – their innovations and inventions in the form of financial 'sausages' and 'salami' were up till recently far from being obvious. It was only the context that changed and brought them to light (*Cf.* Levi, 2012).

c. The Insurance Scheme case(s)

This is another classic example of an APTB. It was not long after the transition into the capitalist-market economy that a very interesting insurance product began to be marketed by insurance companies to the management elite of (primarily) state owned companies. Specifically, the so called 'endowment insurance'. It worked like this: the company as the owner of the insurance policy paid the premiums to the insurance company which were after a certain amount of time paid out to the CEO as the beneficiary of the policy together with possible profits that were made while the insurance company invested the sums.

The endowment insurance on its own would have been far too obvious, for which reason the insurance companies mixed the endowment elements into life insurance contracts that were covered by the company generally for all its employees. It was a legitimate product – at least it would have been if it were not for the fact that the company as the owner of the policy paying the premiums was not the beneficiary. It seemed as though insurance companies were targeting unscrupulous CEOs, giving them a legitimate way to funnel money out of the (primarily state owned) companies into their private pockets. These 'mixed' endowment policies were in effect 'concealed' bonuses.

In one case a state owned company was paying a premium in the amount of four average net salaries monthly for the CEO, the assistant to the CEO and their councillor. After a state supervisory agency (Agencija Republike Slovenije za plačilni promet, nadziranje in informiranje) got wind of the payouts, they were returned and the criminal charges were consequently dropped by the prosecutor on the basis that the amounts were returned and that: "There was no illegal gain obtained as the endowment was paid out according to the contracts."

The prosecutor was missing the point that the problem lied in the contracts themselves that should never have been put into place as there was no legal basis for them – at least not for the endowment insurance part. In another similar case one of the witnesses testified that:

> "*. . . such insurance contracts were completely normal and widespread at the time, the insurance companies themselves offered them as a product. That is why we considered them to be completely legal . . .*"

In the abovementioned cases, the internal supervisory mechanisms of the state owned companies failed to fulfil their task as it was not them who put an end to the harmful insurance scheme for their company. There was no internal discussion about the practice at all. To contrast that, we have another case dealing with a private company several years later. As was written down in the minutes of its supervisory board meeting, the following was stated on the topic:

> "*The opinion of the supervisory board is that the suggested method of incentives for the management is not suitable. If the results of the company are such that they merit additional rewards and bonuses for the management, it is preferable to find a way which is more suitable and is not contrary to the existing contracts and annexes.*"

What happened was that after the CEO received the note from the insurance company that the endowment insurance expired, he allegedly gave the order to transfer the funds to his personal account, even though in this particular case he was not listed as the beneficiary. Apparently the practice was so widespread that he considered himself to be entitled to the disbursement.[21] In the end the supervisory board consented to such a reward scheme – but not for the existing contract, only for future ones, however, in a very limited form.

To put it in perspective: in the first case we mentioned the monthly premium being 4 average net salaries, here, after a rather critical debate and scrutiny of the practice by the supervisory board, the monthly premium was set to 0,4 average net

21 This is consistent with the results from the so called 'Cookie experiment' in which the authors confirmed that those in position of authority, no matter how arbitrary it is, feel that they are entitled to more rights than others. In the experiment groups of 3, same sex individuals were chosen, and one of them was arbitrarily given the leading position. They were given a set of social issues to discuss. 30 minutes into the experiment, the experimenter came into the room with a plate with four cookies. It was established that the high power individual was more likely to take the second cookie. See Keltner et al., 2003: 277.

salaries. We cannot make any general claims based on the two examples, but just comparing the amount of the two premiums we see that a good supervisory board and oversight can mean the difference of a factor of 10.

d. The Fictitious Third Breast case; aka the "*Mamma accessoria fictiva*" case

This case came to light thanks to oversight in the public health care system. A criminal complaint was filed against a plastic surgeon for falsifying records and APTB. He wrote in the official medical documentation that he removed a congenital malformation from one of his patients – a third gland, that is a third breast (lat. diagnosis *mamma accessoria*).

His supervisor at the hospital apparently wanted to have a closer look and it turned out that in fact the accused plastic surgeon was not removing a third breast, but doing an augmentation mamma plastic on the other two breasts, i.e. a cosmetic surgery of breast enhancement (colloquially called a 'boob job'). He falsified the documents to pay for a correction of the breast enhancement operation from the public health care insurance scheme which does not cover cosmetic plastic surgeries, but it does cover removals of congenital malformations.

To sum up, the public health care insurance system paid 4,3 average net salaries for the removal of a fictitious third breast. When interrogated at the police, the accused had among others this to say in his defence:

> ". . . *As for the charge that patient X's correction of an aesthetic surgery was unjustly covered at the cost of the public health care system, I want to stress that doing corrections at the cost of the public health care system is the usual practice of a majority of the surgeons.* . "

Besides being particularly titillating, this case also has a metaphorical value to it. The cost of removing a *fictitious* third breast had a *real* effect - it symbolizes the basic method of depleting public finances via fictitious (or too expensive and unnecessary) services or goods.

e. The Casino case

Sometimes we can stumble over a case that offers particular insight and clarity. The Casino case is such a case, because it is a micro version of how the capitalist system works on a macro level.

In this particular case, the head of a casino when reviewing the business data came across an inconsistency, an abnormality with the payouts of one of the electronic roulettes. His statement is particularly noteworthy:

> "... *roulette is pure mathematics and it is all about statistics ... The profit percentage [on the roulette in question] always has to be around 2,7% with minute variations ... [S]tatistical data are consistent in the long run, you cannot analyse them for one or more games, you have to look at least a period of one month. A month is a long enough period when statistical data reveal their true worth. At the end of the month we look at all the sums received and paid out and the profit has to be within a margin of 18-22 % of what is expected. If that is so, everything is OK, if not, something has to be wrong, because there must not be any deviations. If there are, we take a closer look to see what went wrong. It was so in this case ... What became obvious was that the payouts were considerably higher on the days that the accused was working ... At first I tried to use video surveillance cameras, but then I found out that the accused had access to the video surveillance room and every time he cheated, he turned the cameras off ... It was more luck than anything else that led me to figure it out. The sums from the machines are collected at the end of the day when we close the casino and the payouts to the players are recorded when they happen. On the day in question there was an odd occurrence, because a guest of the casino, who was the accused's accomplice, left the casino soon after 12.00 with a very substantial sum. This was odd and unusual from the viewpoint of an ordinary game. That is why I went over electronic data for the roulette very carefully ... I inspected the individual games for every single game that was played and paid out more than € 1300 ...*"

His analysis ultimately showed that the accused who was in charge of an electronic American roulette table and at the same time also carried out maintenance of the machines removed the protective dome at the roulette table, put in a small amount of credit and then manually manipulated the roulette to increase the credit by putting the balls on the locations that he bet on. He simulated real game play to 'deceive' the machine and increase the electronic credit. When he was done, he put the dome back on. Straight at the opening hour of the casino his friend/accomplice was the first person to come through the door and sit at this particular table. After he 'played' for a while, he cashed in his profits and left the casino. Both of them were convicted for APTB, one as perpetrator and the other as his accomplice.

The case has great representative potential for describing how the capitalist system in which we live works. It is a microcosm, a fractal in which we can observe the laws of the capitalist system on a macro level. A possible application would be an analogy with how the parliaments function. In a perfect world, the parliaments should be systemic institutions free and independent of particular private interests. Parliaments should have as their aim a level of systemic profit that would guarantee a decent living for each individual, with minor deviations. At a superficial glance this does not seem to be so. "Partytocracy" opened the "parliamentary domes" to lobbyists. They have become such an indispensable fixture of modern capitalism that their activities and interactions became heavily regulated – at least on a nominal level – which somehow purified them (*Cf.* Silverstein and Taylor, 2004:262-274).

On a nominal level we also have independent supervisory institutions. But what good are they to us, if the keys to the surveillance rooms end up in the hands of those people who make sure that the cameras are turned off at the critical moment(s) (*Cf.* Dorn, 2010). It also seems that most of the payouts of the more sophisticated frauds are done under the radar and below the sums that raise supervisory eyebrows. When it comes to more sophisticated frauds something really off the charts has to happen from the view point of the "normal" game to make the issue a priority for the prosecutors and police. This can be nothing more than a lucky coincidence in a specific case that the media takes under its wing. It can also be the result of more profound systemic changes. The financial crisis in the 1930s accelerated the development of economic criminal law (*Cf.* Mulder, 1953). We are witnessing something similar since the onset of the financial crisis in 2008 not only at the normative level (*e.g.* non-conviction based confiscation), but also at the operative level (*Cf.* Levi, 2013: 205-207). The financial crisis has shattered some of the global and domestic financial networks that were covering each other's backs with various financial securities and transactions, prosecutions ensued. At least that was the impression that we got from our raw case file analysis at DPOL.

There is one more interesting detail from the Casino case. A witness in the case mentioned that the casino kept "a systematically archived collection of every irregular event that they recorded on tape". In essence they were collecting didactically interesting exemplars, something similar to what we aimed to do with our qualitative medley of economic crime exemplars.

Concluding remarks

The search for the balance between the golden rule of "nullum crimen nulla poena sine lege praevia et certa" on the one hand, and the relatively (un)defined criminal norms as an unavoidable characteristic of economic criminal law (as a subset of criminal law in general) on the other hand, is a tricky thing. What our analysis showed is that in practice the extra margin of interpretative discretion tends to lead to over-criminalization of trifle cases and de facto under-criminalisation or at least under-prosecution of complex economic crimes (*Cf.* Rakoff, 2014). The reason for this is quite banal – complex cases mean that there is more work for the person(s) who gets tasked with them. And who in his right mind, except for a possibly overzealous young prosecutor looking to make a name for himself, would not wish them away with a magic wand, if he had the chance to do so. As was demonstrated, the extra margin of interpretative discretion is often used as that magic wand, at least until trophy exemplars fix the standards.

We started the paper with a quantitative snapshot of the divergence within the concept of economic crime and continued by giving it colour and texture with some of the more interesting and picturesque examples. Same as with Medieval bestiaries, each one of the exemplar 'beasts' from the Slovene volume on economic crime that was chosen has a transcending quality to it.

The case of the 47 Teddy bears demonstrates that going too far with criminalising conduct in business can have a crippling effect on the entire criminal law system which becomes swamped[22] with work and costs that should be borne by the creditors and not the rest of the ordinary taxpayers. I would like to reiterate that this is not a local Slovenian problem, as the UK Crown Prosecution Service (CPS) warns: "*Prosecutors should guard against the criminal law being used as a debt collection agency or to protect the commercial interests of companies or organizations . . . The criminal law should not be used to protect private confidences.*" (CPS, n.d). So be warned, each jurisdiction probably has its own teddy bears . ..

The biggest threat of the teddy bear case(s)[23] is their threat to the system of criminal law on a systemic level. The teddy bears gnaw at limited resources of the prosecutors, police and courts, which could have been used tackling more serious crimes, such as some of those that were encountered during the APTB case file analysis.

The Compartmentalised cesspit case offers considerable insight into the wheeler dealings that went on during the initial phase of privatization. However, it also demonstrates the modus operandi that can be applied to the more recent cases in the banking sector with their bonuses. There is another moral to this case: if read carefully, one can see that in the initial privatization phase of state property, the smart elites made their employees complicit. At the beginning the workers were more than eager to participate in the scheme cooked up by the management. However this

22 This association might be lost on the reader not familiar with the original Star Trek series, but nonetheless – think of episode 44, entitled "The trouble with Tribbles" and substitute tribbles with massive numbers of stuffed teddy bears in the offices of the police, prosecution and the courts which represent the Enterprise in this analogy. What might seem as a cute fluffy thing, soon becomes a very troubling problem for the entire crew . . .

23 The capital letter is omitted intentionally, because the term is now being used as a generic name for all cases similar to the 47 Teddy bear case(s).

meant that in a way they lost their 'moral capital' by dirtying their own hands. For each consequent (criminal) act, the management elite could quickly quash any rebellion from the workers pointing out that they were themselves complicit in the original sin. Think of the subprime mortgage frauds for a more modern version of the same story.

The Insurance scheme case(s) shows how the deceptive nature of the capitalist system quickly evolved also in Slovenia. Here we have legitimate products offered by insurance companies that were "sold" to the management elites to legally funnel money out of shareholders' pockets (in most of the Slovenian cases, the shareholder was the state). This case also clearly demonstrated the importance of effective internal control mechanisms.

The latter are often lacking in the public system. Just try to imagine how many 'fictitious third breasts' are removed each year at the cost of the public health care system. As we saw in the Fictitious third breast aka the 'Mamma accessoria fictiva' case, the accused argued that what he was doing was the usual practice of most surgeons.

We have an excellent example of how an effective internal control system should work in the Casino case. However the case itself becomes troubling when one uses it as a metaphor for the modern capitalist system. Let me conclude by repeating the point that struck a particular cord in my head – the idea of giving the keys of the surveillance room to the wrong person. What we get is surveillance without security – does that sound familiar?

Žižek often uses the examples of "coffee without caffeine, cream without fat, beer without alcohol . . . And the list goes on . . ." as products deprived of their substance: "[they] provide reality itself deprived of its substance, of the hard resistant kernel of the Real" (Žižek, 2003). In a similar manner we could posit that economic criminal law without a criminal policy which effectively prioritises and incentivises prosecution of high-level complex economic crimes is like coffee without caffeine – a product deprived of its substance.

References

Coffee, J.C., Does "unlawful" mean "criminal". *Boston University Law Review*, 1991, 71

Crown Prosecution Service, n.d., Legal Guidance: The Fraud Act 2006. Retrieved November 2, 2013, from http://www.cps.gov.uk/legal/d_to_g/fraud_act/

Dorn, N., Ponzi finance and state capture: the crisis of the financial market regulation. In P. C. van Duyne *et al.* (eds.), *Cross-border crime inroads on integrity in Europe*. Nijmegen: Wolf Legal Publishers, 2010

Duyne, P.C. van, Serbian anti-corruption policy: Welcome to Potemkin village? In P. C. van Duyne, J. Harvey, G.A. Antonopoulos, K. von Lampe, A. Maljević, J. Spencer (eds.), *Human dimensions in organized crime, money laundering and corruption*. Nijmegen: Wolf Legal Publishers, 2013

Emily Runde, n.d., Books of Beasts in the British Library: The Medieval Bestiary and its context. Retrieved November 2, 2013, from www.bl.uk/catalogues/illuminatedmanuscripts/TourBestiaryGen.asp

Ferme, J. and J. Kebe, Kriminaliteta v Sloveniji v letu 2011. *Revija za kriminalistiko in kriminologijo*, 2012, *63*(2), 85–102

Flyvbjerg, B., Five misunderstandings about case-study research. *Qualitative Inquiry*, 2006, 12 (2), pp. 219-245

Kadish,S.H., The crisis of over-criminalization. *American Law Quarterly*, 1968/1969, 7

Kazenski zakonik (KZ-1). *Uradni list RS*, (55/2008, 91/2011, 50/2012

Keltner, D., D.H. Gruenfeld and C. Anderson, Power, approach and inhibition. *Psychological Review*, 2003, 110 (2), 265-284.

Keršmanc, C., *Preslepitve na meji in onkraj pregona [Deception at the Outskirts and Beyond Prosecution]* (Doctoral dissertation). Ljubljana: Pravna fakulteta, 2013a

Keršmanc, C., Glosa o "47 medotih" h kaznivemu dejanju poslovne goljufije in širjenju cone kriminalnosti v gospodarsko bagatelo. *Zbornik znanstvenih razprav*, 2013b, LXXIII

Keršmanc, C., Kvantitativna glosa o kompliciranosti in kompleksnosti gospodarskih kaznivih dejanj. *Revija za kriminalistiko in kriminologijo*, 2013c, *64*(2), 140–153

Kobe, P., Meje represije na področju gospodarskih deliktov. *Revija za kriminalistiko in kriminologijo*, 1973, 24(4), 275–285.

Levi M., Fraud vulnerabilities and the global financial crisis. *Trends and issues in crime and criminal justice*, 2011, p. 1-6

Levi M. and J. Burrows, Measuring the impact of fraud: a conceptual and empirical journey. *British Journal of Criminology*, 2008, 48 (3), p. 293–318

Levi M., J. Burrows, M. Fleming and M. Hopkins (with the assistance of K. Matthews) 2007. The nature, extent and economic impact of fraud in the UK. London: Association of Chief Police Officers. Available at: http://www.cardiff.ac.uk/socsi/resources/ACPO%20final%20nature%20extent%20and%20economic%20impact%20of%20fraud.pdf

Levi, M., Financial crimes and the global financial crisis. In P.C. van Duyne, J. Harvey, G.A. Antonopoulos, K. von Lampe, A. Maljević, J. Spencer (eds.),

Human dimensions in organized crime, money laundering and corruption. Nijmegen: Wolf Legal Publishers, 2013

Lukan, A. and T. Kolenc, Kriminaliteta v Sloveniji v letu 2009. *Revija za kriminalistiko in kriminologijo*, 2010, *61*(2), 117–140

Lukan, A., J. Kebe and A. Bukovnik, Kriminaliteta v Sloveniji v letu 2010. *Revija za kriminalistiko in kriminologijo*, 2011, *62*(2), 103–124

Lukan, A., Kriminaliteta v letu 2006. *Revija za kriminalistiko in kriminologijo,* 2007, *58*(2), 113–132

Lukan, A., Kriminaliteta v letu 2007. *Revija za kriminalistiko in kriminologijo*, 2008, 59(2), 99–113

Lukan, A., Kriminaliteta v letu 2008. *Revija za kriminalistiko in kriminologijo*, 2009, *60*(2), 77–90

Markovska, A. and A. Serdyuk, A dysfunctional system of data collection as an obstacle to tackle crime. In P.C. van Duyne, J. Harvey, G.A. Antonopoulos, K. von Lampe, A. Maljević, J. Spencer (eds.), *Human dimensions in organized crime, money laundering and corruption*. Nijmegen: Wolf Legal Publishers, 2013

Mulder, A., Le droit pénal social economique, *Revue international de droit pénal*, 1953, 1-2

NFA, *Annual fraud indicator*. London, National Fraud Authority, 2010. Available at: https://www.gov.uk/government/uploads/system/uploads/attachment_data/file/118536/afi-2010.pdf

NFA, *Annual fraud indicator*. London, National Fraud Authority, 2011. Available at: https://www.gov.uk/government/uploads/system/uploads/attachment_data/file/118532/annual-fraud-indicator-2011.pdf

NFA, *Annual fraud indicator*. London, National Fraud Authority, 2012. Available at: https://www.gov.uk/government/uploads/system/uploads/attachment_data/file/118530/annual-fraud-indicator-2012.pdf

NFA, *Annual fraud indicator*. London, National Fraud Authority, 2013. Available at: https://www.gov.uk/government/uploads/system/uploads/attachment_data/file/206552/nfa-annual-fraud-indicator-2013.pdf

Rakoff, J.S., The financial crisis: Why have no high level executives been prosecuted?, The New York Review of Books, 9-1-2014. Available at: http://www.nybooks.com/articles/archives/2014/jan/09/financial-crisis-why-no-executive-prosecutions/?pagination=false

Silverstein, K., J. Taylor, Profiting through influence. The Phramaceuticals and Lobbying Industries. In N. Passas and N. Goodwin (eds.), *It's legal, but it ain't right. Harmful social consequences of legal industries*. Ann Arbor: University of Michigan Press, 2004

Svetek, S., Kriminaliteta in kriminalistično delo v letu 1999. *Revija za kriminalistiko in kriminologijo*, 2000, *51*(2), 91–104

Svetek, S., Kriminaliteta in kriminalistično delo v letu 2000. *Revija za kriminalistiko in kriminologijo*, 2001, *52*(2), 95–108

Svetek, S., Kriminaliteta in kriminalistično delo v letu 2001. *Revija za kriminalistiko in kriminologijo*, 2002, *53*(2), 99–108

Svetek, S., Kriminaliteta in kriminalistično delo v letu 2002, *Revija za kriminalistiko in kriminologijo*, 2003, *54*(2), 115–124

Svetek, S., Kriminaliteta in kriminalistično delo v letu 2003. *Revija za kriminalistiko in kriminologijo*, 2004, *55*(2), 107–118

Svetek, S., Kriminaliteta v letu 2005. *Revija za kriminalistiko in kriminologijo*, 2006a, *57*(2), 95–109

Svetek, S., Ne(uspešnost) policije na področju kriminalitete. *Dignitas: revija za človekove pravice*, 2006b, 31/32, 124–155

Svetek, S., Značilnosti kriminalitete v Sloveniji. *Revija za kriminalistiko in kriminologijo*, 2005, *56*(2), 121–133

Zakon o državnem tožilstvu (ZDT-1), *Uradni list RS*, (58/2011)

Zakon o državnem tožilstvu (ZDT-UPB5). *Uradni list RS*, (94/2007, 77/2009)

Žižek, S., *The Puppet and the Dwarf: the Perverse Core of Christianity*. Cambridge: MIT Press, 2003

Boom and bust in financial and housing markets: re-readings through Schumpeter and Bourdieu

Nicholas Dorn[1]

Introduction

This chapter explores policy on and regulation of financial markets from the perspectives of rightist economist Joseph Schumpeter and leftist sociologist Pierre Bourdieu. Schumpeter's ideas – on crises and on disruption of incumbent interests – are important today because they have been taken up by policy makers, albeit in a selective manner. Troubled financial firms are bailed out, ideas about failure, disruption and reform being displaced onto public services. To explain why such actions appeal within policy circles, we turn to Bourdieu's work, focussing here on his studies of housing policy, this being one vehicle for the wider rise of neo-liberal thinking and a diminution of competing visions within policy circles. Today, there is considerable disillusionment with finance markets, yet 'reform' is being ever more strongly directed onto the public sphere – including disruption of the European welfare state and (ironically) of the architecture of financial market regulations.

Why these two theorists? Because one, Schumpeter – a critical friend of markets – well illustrates contemporary *economic thinking* on causes of market crises. He gets us half way to understanding why crises occur and why policy makers repeatedly do more to hasten than to lessen them. Schumpeter gives us the 'what happens' half of the sad story. The other, Bourdieu, represents the *sociological and cultural thinking* that remains so undeveloped in economic analysis. He has a nuanced, empirically-based account of the social sources of power, is sympathetic to non-market forms of social interaction, and is a fierce critic of neoliberalism and of what today has become known as market fundamentalism. Bourdieu gives us the cultural 'why and how' of the story.

Taken together – or rather alongside each other (for they offer complementary rather than similar stories) – these two permit us to better understand policy issues

[1] Formerly of Erasmus School of Law, The Netherlands

and regulatory failures vis-à-vis boom and bust in financial and housing markets. Also, taking these two together, as bearers of the split in knowledge between economics and the social sciences, provokes some thoughts about the inadequacy of the present knowledge base for policy making and about the intellectual challenge that this implies.

Markets: conflict zone

"Capitalism's biggest political enemies are not the firebrand trade unionists spewing vitriol against the system but the executives in pin-striped suits extolling the virtues of competitive markets with every breath while attempting to extinguish them with every action." (Raghuram and Zingales 2004: 276).

"In effect, the state – and those able to impose their views through it – contributes very substantially to producing the state of the housing market, doing this largely through all the forms of regulation and financial assistance [. . .] such as loans, tax exemptions, cheap credit, etc." (Bourdieu 2005: 15-16)

The financial market crisis and the associated housing boom and bust form now part of the heritage of a widely-shared European experience of hyped-up aspirations and sad dénouement. The two quotations above, between them, reflect commentary from a neoliberal standpoint and a critique thereof. Joseph Schumpeter, an Austrian economist, has become an intellectual landmark for true believers in the capitalist system who, rather like Tea Party people today in the United States, believe that government should not interfere with markets. The first quotation above, from Schumpeterian acolytes Raghuram and Zingales (2004), lambastes governments for listening to special economic interests, instead of facilitating the running of markets as truly competitive fora. From that position, governmental bail-out of international banking is an instance of favouring investors who have failed in the marketplace and should have been allowed to experience the full consequences – thus pedagogically inculcating greater discipline in future. Saving risk-takers from the consequences of their folly weakens the market system in the longer run, Schumpeter claimed. In this paper we explore the highly selective manner in which neo-liberal ideas are taken up today.

The second quotation above is from a compilation and analytical commentary by Pierre Bourdieu (2005) of studies done by him and his colleagues of French housing policy in the period from the 1960s to the 1980s, a turning point from social (public) housing to individual (private) housing. It is relevant that there is a *plural* in the title of Bourdieu's book: the social structures of the economy (Bourdieu, 2005). Bourdieu's team documented struggles within policy circles, the relations between finance and big and small builders, the seduction of families away from established communities and their dispersal in new housing estates, and the 'petit bourgeois suffering' incurred as they sought to match the dreams constructed by the above forces with the available realities. It would be several decades before this 'democratisation' of finance and of housing (see below) reached it apotheosis in the financial crisis of 2007 onwards, first in the United States, then spreading to Eurozone 'peripheral' countries and finally, in 2011, knocking on the doors of the treasuries of 'core' European states such as Italy and France.

This chapter proposes that Schumpeter gives us some tools for describing the dominant political tendencies in relation to the financial crisis, including 'light touch' regulation in the build-up to the crisis (Black 2011); then strong intervention in favour of the banks; followed by cutbacks and deliberately 'disruptive' reforms to public services (see below). In short, Schumpeter bequeaths to the ascendant political right the notion that 'creative destruction' is an integral and necessary part of the development of capitalism, as new and dynamic entrepreneurs arise out of the ruins of failed businesses. Yet some of his present-day followers apply that idea more readily to the public sector than to the market. Market rigour is selectively deployed – against the public sphere – whilst financial market elites are shielded from such harsh remedies, through deployment of such arguments as 'Too Big To Fail' (see below).

Economic theory (Schumpeter's or any others') cannot tell how and why such policies gain assent: why the financial sector, despite being discredited as a result of its crisis, has retained intellectual leadership, providing the knowledge base for the management of the crisis. To understand the ideas that are at the heart of power, we have to shift from economics to sociology. Bourdieu describes a long-term historical process of convergence of previously diverse cultural perspectives – a narrowing which the present paper articulates as a narrowing of the intellectual resources available to policy makers, regulators, market participants and publics and a consequent inability to think 'outside the box'.

It will be taken for granted here that readers have ideas about what the financial crisis is, about its origins in certain public policies and market practices, particularly in the United States (henceforth US) and about its recent transformation, from being a crisis of banks to being a crisis of countries. The Eurozone crisis is the latest in a series: banks and other finance firms make initially profitable but ultimately unsustainable loans, for which they seek public 'bailouts'. Throughout the first phase of the crisis, policy makers readily granted bailouts. Indeed there is evidence for the US that the authorities foisted money on banks that had not requested it (Silva, 2010). It is striking that, in a period widely regarded as characterised in terms of neoliberal policies (Prasad, 2006) – in which it might be expected that the public authorities would allow failures in the market to run their course – the opposite happened. This is now explored with reference first to Schumpeter's ideas, which have been taken up rather selectively by the governments, in such a manner that their critical implications are displaced from the private sector generally, and from banking in particular, onto public services. The following section focuses upon the UK, however the strategies and rigours described here have become familiar in other countries, notable 'peripheral' member states of the European Union (see *inter alia* Dorn 2014a).

Schumpeter in Whitehall

Joseph Schumpeter conceptualised crises as an integral aspect of the market society. He is therefore attractive for those policy makers, such as former Federal Reserve chairman Alan Greenspan, who might be vulnerable to blame for sleep-walking into the current crisis – the *non culpa* being that it is not anyone's fault, since the system itself is crisis-prone. Moreover, Schumpeter's ideas have been taken up as a template for remodelling public services. We refer here briefly to the latter agenda before going on to explore its rationale in Schumpeterian theory, its implications for policy towards and regulation of the financial sector and, in the second part of the chapter, a contrasting and yet complementary approach to understanding and responding to the current predicament.

Schumpeter is taken up today in relation to public services in the following manner. First, following popularisation of aspects of his work by the consulting firm, McKinsey, 'disruption' is equated with 'innovation' and out-performance of enterprises, be they in the private or public sectors (Foster and Kaplan 2001 and see below). Second, the logic is focussed upon the public sector – radical cuts in public expenditure being represented as an opportunity to transform services, so as to make them more cost effective, whilst also opening up room for the private sector to grow. Thus, in a publication entitled 'Schumpeter Comes to Whitehall', Bunt *et al.* (2010: 24) say that "Cuts should be made in a way that prompts the transformation of public services [which] requires a move away from 'best practice' towards a more diverse and potentially more disruptive approach". Whereas modest cuts to public budgets whilst leaving their modus operandi intact would only demoralise service providers, what is being attempted in the UK is a profoundly more 'disruptive' approach. It aims at fundamental change, with services being radically reconfigurated by those capable and willing of carrying through such innovation, whilst allowing inflexible incumbent and less dynamic public service-providers to fail in the public marketplace.

Thus, taking up Schumpeter's writings on entrepreneurship and innovation in the private sector – that "the function of entrepreneurs is to reform or revolutionize the pattern of production [so that] innovators can transform markets, with incumbent businesses being forced to adapt or fail" – Bunt *et al.* (2010: 32) apply this to the public sector, calling for "radical innovations". These will pay off "precisely because they create new rules by changing what kind of product or service is delivered, to what specification, at what cost, to meet a particular need" (ibid). The authors point out that this implies a move away from evidence-based planning (the pre-crisis policy mantra), since existing evidence refers to best practices, whilst what radical Schumpeterians seek is innovation which is, by definition, the enemy of all existing practices. Likewise, audit and indicators should be scaled down, so as to allow for the emergence of the new. Bunt *et al.* (2010: 55) cite Schumpeter: "The world of possible innovation cannot be mapped out [in advance]" (taken from Schumpeter 1939: 500).

Schumpeter on disruption (creative and otherwise)

'Creative destruction' is a key concept for Schumpeter. Induced at times of crisis, it is supposed to stimulate market innovations and re-configurations, which he regarded as being inevitable and desirable. Indeed, crisis is not exceptional, it is the essence of the market system, as indicated by his reference to a "perennial gale of creative destruction" (Schumpeter, 1950, p. 85). Thus for Schumpeter, the essence of capitalism is not the ordinary competition that goes on within an existing industry structure – incremental changes in prices, quality or products that leave the underlying marketplace unchanged. Rather, economic progress comes from revolutionary changes that subvert the "ancient regime." As Schumpeter put it: "the problem that is usually being visualized is how capitalism administers existing structures, whereas the relevant problem is how it creates and destroys them" (Gilson and Kraakman 2005: 1431).

Such a disruptive vision could not be further from the assumption, widely held prior to the financial crisis of 2007 onwards, that economic history had somehow been smoothed out, creating a 'great moderation' (Bernanke, 2004). The latter is a post-modern vista in which wealth and innovation sustain each other without hiccup or interruption, risk being contained within the statistically smooth curves described by the theories and *morbus mathematicus* (Bourdieu 2005: 13) of neoclassical economics (for a contemporary critique of which, see Acharya *et al.* 2010).

We may add that, powerful as Schumpeterian thinking might now appear as a critique of pre-crisis complacency (on which see Engelen *et al.* 2011), it does not follow that such thinking holds the germs of recovery (Macartney 2009). As Rajan and Zingales (2004: 25) put it, "Free financial markets are the elixir that fuels the process of creative destruction, continuously rejuvenating the capitalist system. As such, they are also the primary target of the powerful interests that fear change." Indeed, bankers, investors in banks and representatives of powerful interests prefer that capitalism's *creative destruction be applied to others*. Thus they mobilise political connections and knowledge claims – to the effect that that their activities and interests correspond to the public interest. We now explore some of these claims-making processes.

Some history: the 'democratisation' of finance

Many finance innovations from the 1990s onwards were indeed quite disruptive to established interests. A 'democratisation' of finance (Ertürt *et al.* 2007) evolved in several stages. First, through the creation of 'junk bonds' by Michael Milken at Drexel Lambert in the 1990s (Gilson and Kraakman 2005). Second, by a great expansion in the use of financial derivatives, used ostensibly to offset risks but, because of their complexity, equally having the capacity to hide risks (as become clear in 1998 with the collapse of Long Term Capital Management and in 2001 with the bankruptcies of Enron and Global Crossing, see Partnoy, 2002). Third, leverage was much extended in the 2000s, on the one hand to retail consumers, as unsustainable credit was granted to 'subprime' borrowers and, on the other hand, to sovereign borrowers such as Greece.

Thus the concept of the 'democratisation' of finance applies in an economic rather than political sense: financial innovation can disrupt established patterns of private ownership, allowing new social groups to make claims. There was little concern about any collective risks because, in all the above-mentioned cases (junk bonds, complex derivatives and subprime), the calculation made by the issuers and promoters of the debt was that, even though a proportion of the borrowers would get into difficulties and default, still the higher 'coupon' (rate of interest) payable on the remaining, honoured bonds would give rise to superior returns for the portfolio as a whole (*The Economist*, 2010). That proved correct in good times (a rising tide lifts all boats), however when conditions deteriorated to an extent that repayment by many borrowers became doubtful, there was a stampede by investors wishing to get out of such securities.

Schumpeter observed (1939, pp 116-117) that failures by bankers to discern the boundaries of such risks "account for most of the events which the majority of observers would call 'catastrophes'". As many contemporary interpreters of Schumpeter insist (Leathers and Raines 2004: 671), he was by no means agog over financial markets, nor was he hostile to regulation, lauding 'important reforms' following the onset of the 1930s crisis and recession, even going so far as to refer to such reforms as 'innovations' (high praise from Schumpeter: see Leathers and Raines 2004: 671).

Finance as hero and villain

What then is Schumpeter's basic paradigm, from which he derives his somewhat pessimistic conclusions that crises are inevitable, even necessary, yet might to some extent be managed? Drawing equally upon his work (Schumpeter 1939), Leathers and Raines (2004) and Swedberg (2002), we can summarise Schumpeter's model of the business cycle, with the financial sector being implicated differently in each phase.

- First, industrial entrepreneurs – Schumpeter's heroes – propose new ideas to investors and the best ideas (in the eyes of the investors) are funded. This investment leads to a general expansion of the economy, as jobs are created in supplier firms, workers have more money to spend, they put aside some savings (part of which circulate to become available to support new investments) and so on. In this phase, the financial sector is seen by Schumpeter as playing a valuable role.
- Second, the moment of danger arrives, as all kinds of 'wannabe' entrepreneurs and investors chase each other and, in a general atmosphere of overconfidence, make indiscriminative investments. As Leathers and Raines (2004: 672-3) put it, writing just after the bursting of the 'tech bubble' in 2001, but before the onset of the present crisis, "pure financial speculation occurs and may intensify into a speculative mania". In this phase many ordinary people get carried along, taking up debts that will become burdensome in any downturn. The finance sector, or large parts of it, feels unable to stand back when things are going so swimmingly: in the familiar and hackneyed words of a previous chairman of the financial conglomerate Citigroup, Chuck Prince: "When the music stops, in terms of liquidity, things will be complicated. But, as long as the music is playing, you've got to get up and dance. We're still dancing".
- Third, the *dénouement* duly arrives, as many investments fail to pay off, causing losses that banks and other investors compensate for by withdrawing or withholding credit from other, economically marginal firms – whereupon failures multiply and 'creative destruction' clears the decks for a resumption of the cycle.

Schumpeter's policy response was that intervention was merited *in the second phase*, in order to discourage 'speculative mania' and 'excesses', although that would be difficult, due to the manner in which all classes were 'led on' by 'haute finance' (Schumpeter 1939: 5, 248 and 437). Schumpeter's analysis is broadly similar to

Hyman Minsky's notion that finance moves from a careful and selective phase into a Ponzi-like phase, as late-comers to the party seek to invest in a broadly imitative or herd-like manner, leading to collective disappointment and withdrawal (Minsky 2003, McCauley et al 1999, Dorn 2010). Prince's tendency to dance was pervasive not only in the finance sector but amongst policy makers and regulators until the beginning of the crisis in 2007. Schumpeter would have seen such behaviour as being neither inevitable nor desirable. Even though he feared public control of financial markets as constituting the road to socialism, to which he was ill-disposed, he saw "powerful and intelligent government" as a means of mitigating the worst excesses of speculation and thus of the recessions that follow (Leathers and Raines 2004: 677). In his view, 'creative destruction' could still act as the motor of general improvement, indeed all the more so – with less damage during downturns – if some of the speculative froth could be avoided, by astute policy makers and regulators acting in a pre-emptive manner. Such advice might be regarded somewhat ruefully after the event, since it was not taken at the appropriate time. The present writer does not recall today's conservative advocates of Schumpeter warning governments in power during the bubble years that they should intervene and "take away the punch bowl" (a phrase attributed to William McChesney Martin, Chairman of the US Federal Reserve in the 1950s and 1960s). Such advice is by it nature unpopular, even if it might in Schumpeter's words constitute "intelligent government".

Concerning the third stage in Schumpeter's models – the recession after the bursting of the bubble – a practical problem is that there is little that can be done, other than to wait, according to Schumpeter. The emergence of new private sector entrepreneurs is a process with its own market logic, he believed, to which government action can contribute little (this is also a problem preoccupying Bunt *et al.* (2010) above, in relation to revitalisation of the public sector). Entrepreneurs will prove themselves by their innovative actions. Meanwhile, trying to 'cherry pick' them would risk degenerating into propping up failing (or at least inefficient) operators, which would be a misdirection and waste of resources (be they private or public). If applied consistently, Schumpeter's views imply allowing whole industries to fail (the policy followed in relation to industrial sectors, such as coal and steel, recalling previous UK conservative governments under Margaret Thatcher). Thus, financial firms would be allowed to fail, so as to hasten reorganisation of the sector. That however is exactly what has *not* happened.

'Too Big To Fail'

In the US and the EU, governments have done their utmost to retain financial firms, bailing them out with the aid of public money and relieving them of the worst of their troubled assets. Whilst there have been some conflicts around the policy of bailouts, they have become the norm (Lehman Brothers' demise being more a case of accident than design, as the US authorities expected it be bought by Barclays, who were prevented from doing so fast enough by UK rules requiring shareholders' consent). In the following quotation, the European Commission presents bailouts as necessary.

> "During the financial crisis, governments discovered that banks and other systemic financial institutions could not be allowed to fail. Put bluntly, there was no simple way for a bank to continue to provide essential banking functions whilst in insolvency, and in the case of a failure of a large bank, those functions could not be shut down without significant systemic damage." (European Commission 2010: 2)

Not to put too fine a point on it, this is poppycock. Of course no bank could continue to function in insolvency, however that is not the issue. Viable and socially-needed parts of banks can be selectively stripped out and utilised – given political will.

Unfortunately, the crisis has once again shown that governments, in the US, Europe and elsewhere "are very reluctant to let their large banks fail" or to radically restructure them, using methods that include haircuts for unsecured creditors (senior as well as subordinated) and the mandatory conversion of unsecured creditors into shareholders (Buiter *et al.*, 2011: 52).

Even before the crisis, there was legislation in place in the US that would have allowed the costs of failure to fall fully upon investors, whilst retaining the structures and services necessary for retail customers of banks. Similar legislation now also exists in the UK and many other jurisdictions (Brierley 2009; Silva 2010). It is deeply unfortunate that the European Union gives signs of putting off such legislation until well in the future (European Commission 2011). Nevertheless, even lacking standing legislation at EU level, national legislation could be utilised. What has been lacking – and remains lacking – is the political will to do as Buiter *et al.* (2011) prescribe. Instead, policy makers continue to act as if banks are Too Big To Fail (TBTF). This is despite the recognition that this carries many negative consequences:

> "First, such institutions exacerbate systemic risk by removing incentives to prudently manage risks and by creating a massive contingent liability for governments [. . .] Second, TBTF institutions distort competition [. . .] Third, the treatment of TBTF institutions lowers public trust in the fairness of the system [. . .] when it boils down to the privatisation of gains and socialisation of losses." (Goldstein and Véron, 2011, pp 2-3)

These issues are widely understood at policy level. As the House of Commons Treasury Committee has put it, "The assumption that certain firms cannot be allowed to fail results in market distortion, entrenches the market power of large incumbents and thereby stifles competition. That lack of market discipline may, over the long term, itself engender systemic instability" (House of Commons Treasury Committee 2011: 73). On that basis, one might expect policy to seek to dilute "the market power of large incumbents" in financial services and to invest public resources in other sectors of the economy, or indeed in public services. Quite the opposite is occurring in most European countries.

The difficulty of articulating alternatives

Clearly, Schumpeterian perspectives on the crisis, whilst being adopted in countries such as the UK as a rationale for public sector reform and as an aspiration for industrial regeneration generally, have not been applied to banking, which in political terms remains a zone of exception, to be ministered to in a manner enjoyed by no other sector. It is not surprising that incumbent but damaged firms in all sectors should intervene forcefully to garner public support for their endangered enterprises. What does however require explanation is the success enjoyed by the financial sector in this regard. Whilst particular individuals in senior management may lose their jobs, financial sector senior managers *as a community* find themselves in ever greater demand to assist the public authorities in managing the temporarily publicly-owned banks, turning them around so as hopefully to make them profitable again and eventually to re-privatise them. For example, they have found themselves much in demand as policy advisors and even as public servants by ministries such as the UK Treasury, within which UK Financial Investments Ltd (UKFI) applies pre-crisis business models to the now largely publicly-owned banks. Thus: "It is not clear is whether the banks have been nationalised or the Treasury has been privatised as a new kind of investment fund" (CRESC 2009: 14).

It might be asked, what alternative is there to continuing to run banks using the objectives, methods, senior staffing, culture and incentives inherited from before the crisis? Here we point briefly to a vision of what, the above commentators claim, could be a safer financial system. If, for understandable reasons, international and national elites find difficulty in tackling banks in ways that would be really 'radical', then local and regional social and economic forces should no longer look to existing policy regulatory leadership at national (or international) level (Ertürt et al 2011). Instead, they could look to a strategy of re-invention of regional and local banking, investing scarce capital in socially productive ways (ibid). Instead of continuing the hapless task of trying to transform international banks into safe entities, regional and local efforts could be made to support small and independent financial entities (be they private banks or collectively-owned Building Societies) that are dispersed in terms of ownership, are diverse in their business models, and are willing to invest locally and regionally (Ertürt *et al.*, op cit). Whilst those authors and strategists are by no means Schumpeterian in their views, nevertheless their proposal to reorientate away from international political elites and financial firms that have failed three times over – once in directing funds ways from productive industry, again in directing funds into a bubble and then again in propping up failed incumbents – would have been understood and possibly appreciated by Schumpeter. Other critical commentators also find it remarkable that (inter)national financial elites remain so entrenched after the onset of the crisis (Hall 2009, Tsingou 2010).

To sum up on Schumpeter, we can say that, intellectually, he has had a 'good crisis' in respect of his account of the genesis of the current situation. Previously broadly ignored by policy makers, for whom crises were in the past, his rediscovery and contemporary interpretation now support a conservative framework for political assessment and management of the crisis (Osborne 2010, Bacon and Eltis 1976, Smith 2010). Where contemporary political takers-on of his mantle part company with the master is in their reluctance to allow failure in the financial sector to run its 'natural' (in Schumpeterian terms) course. Instead they ever more firmly embed financiers in governance, at national European and international levels. Schumpeter would have been incredulous at the activities of London and Wall Street financial and political elites. However his own market-centric work does not identify an adequate counterbalance. For clues, we have to transpose his hints about the emotional dimension of finance into a more structural and historical perspective.

Culture and emotion in market regulation

Prior to the crisis, financial regulation not only had forms of knowledge – rational choice theory, modes of calculation, risk models – it also had a mood. Engelen *et al.*, (2011) characterised this in terms of a 'great complaisance', an ironic reference to the previously dominant notion that market stability or a 'great moderation' had been achieved (Bernanke 2004).

However, 'complaisance' may not go far enough in describing the pre-crisis mood. James Anderson has offered 'regulatory rapture' as a re-interpretation and *dépassement* of the well-established but contentious idea of regulatory capture (Anderson, 1982, cited in Dorn, 2010). In rapture, regulatory agencies are seen as not simply slipping under the influence of particular firms within the sector that they are supposed to regulate (as in capture). Rather, they are seen as being politically and emotionally committed to 'their' industry, so doing whatever could advance short-term opportunities for competitive advantage, profit and market positioning. In rapture, regulatory agencies are no longer 'conflicted' (in the American parlance), they are cheer leaders. Thus we come to the question of the resources – cultural and emotional as well as intellectual – available to policy makers and regulators.

Re-reading Bourdieu's studies of housing policy through today's crisis

"To break with the dominant paradigm, we must – taking note, within an expanded rationalist vision, of the historicity constitutive of agents and of their space of action – attempt to construct a realist definition of economic reason as an encounter between dispositions which are socially constructed (in relation to a field) and the structures, themselves socially constructed, of that field." (Bourdieu 2005: 193).

By this, Bourdieu simply meant that all modes of thinking – including thinking and calculating in market (rationalist) terms – are shaped by their historical and social contexts. Bourdieu was an anthropologist first and a sociologist second, whose research on post-Second World War France was itself shaped by his earlier work in Algeria, a province/colony in which the market was a strange, indeed alien and unsettling intrusion. His work on French housing and finance is energised by that feeling. The concepts at the heart of his work are forms of capital (meaning capabilities); habitus (taken-for-granted ways of thinking and feeling, derived from social backgrounds); fields (spaces or settings within which the above deployed); and reproduction (Bourdieu 1963, 1984, 1993, 1996, 2005). Economic capital and cultural capital are of particular interest here, when viewed from a historical perspective. We may summarise his views on the evolution of relations between economic and cultural capital thus:

i. constituting separate spheres in colonial societies (as studied by Bourdieu in his early years, see Bourdieu et al, 1963);
ii. partially overlapping, interacting and mutually contesting in modern, market societies, in which social groups and their mentalities remain differentiated;
iii. increasingly homogenous in late modern and increasingly global society, as cultural diversity is absorbed into the global market.

The argument made here is that the transition from (ii) to (iii) above impacts negatively upon the quality of thinking of policy makers and of financial market regulators. In his *The Social Structures of the Economy*, Bourdieu examines this transition in relation to the development of the housing markets in France, which he sees as a phenomenon at the intersection of politics, finance, and popular taste.

Schumpeterians might seek to appropriate this transition solely in terms of the business cycle in its first (expansionist) and second (bubble) phases. However, whereas Schumpeter identifies entrepreneurship and innovation as arising primarily in the private sector, Bourdieu is more even-handed, drawing attention to the state as a key site for innovation, and specifically for encouragement of innovation in housing and finance. His work traces the roles of many actors. Political elites, particularly those at national level, were much concerned with questions of legitimisation of the system: family policy, the modernisation of the economy, social integration and consent. Civil servants were variously entrenched defenders of the *status quo*, or high-status challengers and innovators holding new technical skills such as mathematical modelling (Bourdieu 2005: 116-118). The development of banking (especially personal loans) provided private finance for lower and intermediate social classes. Expansion of and competition within the building sector resulted in new market offerings, including prefabricated 'catalogue' housing, which was quicker and cheaper than traditional building techniques (even if it was less 'tasteful'). Advertisers and marketers spun a vision drawing upon a historical sense of community and the convenience and affordability of a modern home, stoking buyers' aspirations for home ownership and social status. Public finance, which previously had been directed to encouraging low-cost rental social housing, via subsidies to house builders and purchasers (Bourdieu 2005: 94), was scaled back, and private mortgages for home ownership were encouraged..

Bourdieu's analysis concerned transitions in state policies in one particular modern society (1960s-1980s). Nevertheless, by applying his key concepts to the present, late modern period – in which the ascendency of economic over cultural capital has become complete and the financial sector has broken the bounds of national markets and jurisdictions – we can re-read recent US, British and other European housing bubbles. The market forms that were encouraged by policy elites eventually took charge of their thinking, overwhelming critical reflection. Indeed, Bourdieu's (sociologically strong) analysis of the rise of neoliberalism usefully fills in the cultural and political detail in Schumpeter's (sociologically weak) analysis of finance in its pre-Ponzi phase. Starting in the US from the 1980s onwards, as related by Anderson (op cit) and proceeding internationally, as described by Moran (2006), Picciotto and Haines (1999), Tsingou (2010), policy makers and regulators no longer acted as innovators in favour of financial markets; rather they became swept along on the latter. As cultural differences disappear – at least within elites – so does the potential for diversity in regulatory knowledge and mood (since knowledge and mood are seated in culture).

Reconfiguring – disrupting? – the regulatory agencies today

In principle, significant changes in regulation can occur *without there being much change in the structures or architectures of the state and its agencies*. Bourdieu's (2005) analysis shows how key individuals within elites – often scions of high class families and graduates of prestigious universities – made existing state machinery serve new private-public sector objectives. In the US, strongly networked members of a 'revolving door' culture in business and politics managed change (Hellwig 2008: 55): states do not have to restructure themselves in order to facilitate market innovations. Nor did states have to restructure themselves or their regulatory agencies in order to react to the crisis from 2007 onward. After 2007, the US and UK both moved fast: the US Federal Reserve used an obscure and previously politically unnoticed clause in the new legislation for the TARP (Troubled Assets Recovery Programme) to recapitalise the banking system, whilst the UK government stemmed an incipient bank run by passing a bill through parliament on an emergency basis (later legislation generalised and deepened these powers, see Lastra 2008). Leaving aside a normative assessment of the above actions, the point is that the key to them all was political determination, not reorganisation.

What then of a situation in which the position is taken that the architecture of government or of its agencies must be changed, in order to enable the delivery of new policy objectives, or to enable existing objectives to be pursued more effectively than hitherto? That is the position taken in the UK in relation to financial regulation. Despite scholarly protests (Ferran 2011) that the inherited regulatory structure could deliver a more robust safeguarding of financial market stability, if only policy makers would let it do so, the government embarked on a reform of structures. The public arguments for reorganisation were twofold. First, the regulators had failed to anticipate the crisis: thus there was a sense of popular justice in changing structures – quite absurd in practical terms, since more or less the same people might be expected to emerge in the reorganisation, as indeed has been the case. Second, and more substantially, the previous structures embodied ambiguity over which arm of government was responsible for key aspects of financial stability. That point is a fair one, however it could easily have been addressed by more clearly allocating responsibility, rather than re-organising the whole structure.

Here we briefly examine the process and the argument whereby the need for functional change was reformulated as organisational change in the UK. After the Northern Rock Building Society got into difficulties in 2007 (related to its activities in the wholesale financial markets, rather than with its retail customers), the then Labour government effectively took it into public ownership. A subsequent parliamentary committee found that the 'regulatory engagement' with Northern Rock had "failed to tackle the fundamental weakness in [Northern Rock's] funding model and did nothing to prevent the problems that came to the fore" (House of Commons Treasury Committee 2008a: 24). The committee recommended a series of policy changes, including powers for US-style "prompt corrective action" by government when a financial firm experienced difficulties (*ibid* 151), however the committee was not in favour of radical regulatory reorganisation. (*ibid*: 156). The report – an interesting example of parliamentary investigation made within a short time – was broadly accepted by the then Labour government (House of Commons Treasury Committee 2008b: 18).

However, following the general election in 2010, there was a change of government and the incoming Conservative-Liberal collation decided to redraw the regulatory map. In public consultations on the architecture and objectives for financial market regulators, the new government favoured multiple regulators, each having quite simple, unitary objectives, which would give each one "a clear mandate and focus" (HM Treasury 2010). The general argument was that separation of functions might permit each regulator to focus on its stated task(s). As a result (HM Treasury 2011), there is now a hierarchy in financial regulation in the UK. At the 'apex' (ibid. p10) there sits a 'macro-prudential regulator', the Financial Policy Committee (FPC) within the Bank of England, responsible for identifying and monitoring systemic risks, taking action to address them and giving directions to the two following regulators. There is a 'micro-prudential regulator', the Prudential Regulation Authority (PRA), to keep an eye on large firms whose activities might have destabilising effects or might be destabilised by events elsewhere. Finally, a Financial Conduct Authority (FCA) is concerned with consumer choice, efficiency, integrity and fairness (HM Treasury 2011).

We might observe that multiple actors necessarily create a complex regulatory space, raising questions of overlap, communication, coordination and 'pecking order'. Complexity further increases when the multiple national regulators talk with their counterparts in other jurisdictions. With the proliferation of international networks, coordination forums, EU Authorities and national actors, there remains much scope for negotiation, not to mention procrastination. Regulatory agencies have to negotiate 'ownership' of issues that arise and there have to be trade-offs between the many interested parties, leading to blurring of responsibilities in practice, if not on paper. On the one hand, the three main objectives for UK financial regulation – macro-stability, dealing with large firms, and fairness in market – are now distributed between formally different regulators. On the other hand, these objectives will have to be pursued in a coherent manner (if they are not then the regulatees will complain and the regulators will look silly). So there is scope for regulatory conversations to become interminable.

To make these observations is not to argue one way or the other on the detail of regulatory structures. As Ferran (2011: 455) puts it, "all institutional models for financial market supervision have pros and cons". Political will is more relevant than organisational structure. That said, the amount of time and energy absorbed in *changing* structures – first negotiating the new structures and responsibilities and then operationalising them – must be considerable and it cannot but distract energies from the task of regulating the market.

It is not the purpose here to make the claim that policy makers explicitly seek to apply Schumpeterian disruption to the regulatory system – undoubtedly, the forces in play have been multiple and the dynamics too complex for any such reductive logic. However, it remains the case that policy makers have been prepared to tolerate any disruption to regulation that might be caused by its reorganisation. Likewise, in reform of the UK welfare state discussed at the onset of this paper: that too is a policy arena in which shock therapy is presented as being beneficial. The general picture is that creative destruction is taken out of its intellection 'home', the private sector, and is installed in the public sector.

Synthesis and prognosis

In this chapter we apply frameworks from Schumpeter and Bourdieu to contemporary developments in policy and regulation regarding the financial markets. Whilst the two traditions of thought are antagonistic on many grounds, the tensions created between them usefully highlight issues of market culture, innovation, private and public interests, regulation and reorganisation. Also it is possible to point to some communalities in thinking and some implications for policy debate.

Following Schumpeter in his analysis of the over-optimism that is characteristic of the inflation of a bubble, and with the benefit of hindsight after the subprime phenomenon in the US and similar housing and financial bubbles and collapses in parts of the EU (Ireland, Spain, Portugal, Greece, even the Netherlands), readers will have no problem in identifying the typical stages of capitalist boom and bust. Whilst Schumpeter himself might admire the entrepreneurial spirit and the inventiveness of the financial industry in terms of its power to disrupt incumbent interests – after all, entrepreneurs were his heroes – he might however share contemporary concerns that the financial sector has become the master instead of the servant of economic life. Perhaps the most significant part of his legacy is his lament over the repeated failure of policy makers and regulators to take action to prick bubbles before they expand so dangerously. Schumpeter acknowledged the political difficulties of trying to "take away the punch bowl" – however he believed that failure to intervene in the boom years resulted in crashes being deeper, longer-lasting and more dangerous than they need be. More dangerous partly in the political sense, because recessions might lead to socialism, he believed (recalling that Schumpeter lived in an era when socialism was a real political competitor, which seems no longer to be the case). Schumpeter also believed that, once a crash has occurred, propping up failed firms does nothing to re-ignite economic health: to the contrary, it misdirects resources and so prolongs the recession. This part of his critique is today echoed in the observation that politicians' and central bankers' labelling of banks as Too Big To Fail (or Too Connected To Fail), and bailing them out, has created 'zombie banks': hollow shells, which absorb public funds but do little to invest in the real economy. These views are quite mainstream today, particularly on the political right (notably in US Republican Party and Tea Party circles), also in the political centre – which however seems to have difficulty in detaching itself from the pre-crisis phantasy that the financial sector is a Golden Goose, whose working constitute some kind of alchemy, turning base metals into gold. Interestingly, then, the politically right wing (anti-socialist) Schumpeter may have more of interest to tell us about the crisis than the political centre has.

What then about the leftist Bourdieu? He would have been impatient with questions about the optimal management of financial markets, given his views on neo-liberalism in general. Such management would be of concern only for those political forces advocating markets as the lynchpin of society, which Bourdieu certainly did not. He would also have been impatient with debates over what are and what are not acceptable trading practices: the Bernard Madoff fraud; subprime mortgage mis-selling; the Spanish cajas' desperate tactic of selling bonds to its small customers; Goldman Sachs' provision of financial services to Greece that allowed it to misrepresent its financial health in order to enter the Eurozone; the LIBOR manipulations of currencies and interest rates, etc. Over-emphasising the deviant nature of such acts might run the risk of suggesting that, if cleaned up, big finance (and capital in general) might function in the collective and public interest.

Bourdieu's general concern was that dynamic markets and corresponding forms of thinking (economic capital) tend to overwhelm and colonise pre-existing social forms (cultural capital) and potential future alternatives. Rather than engaging with centrist and reformist forces, Bourdieu in his day engaged in debates with those offering (what then appeared to be) fundamental challenges, such as squatters, Maoists and prisoners. Oddly, if around today he might have found himself engaged in debate with Tea Party people, given the paucity of interlocutors on the left. Indeed there might also be others who would prefer possibly prefer a rightist rabble to a clutch of technocrats, who bail out financial services whilst 'restructuring' public budgets and services.

However, recovering Bourdieu's analytical toolbox, we have sought to use him to make some more analytical and less angry points, bringing him and Schumpeter closer together. There are several points of convergence.

- Markets are not technical or mechanical bodies, they are socially constructed, having cycles of boom and bust that are driven by collective sentiment (so say Schumpeterians and indeed many other economists, whilst those influenced by Bourdieu or by sociology more generally might agree, given the view that apparently 'rationalist', calculative thinking is always culturally constructed).
- Such sentiments may initially be shaped by strategic actions by public and private actors, deploying technical knowledge and mobilising strong emotions, however, these create dynamics that then escape formal political control and can be very damaging (drawing on both Schumpeter and Bourdieu, although followers of the latter would emphasise that not only the bust part of the cycle but also its commencement impose significant harms).
- The crucial and most effective moment for policy design and intervention is not the crash and resulting recession (too late) but the period in which risks are building up.
- A diversity of cultural and economic practices would be preferable to a single form of market society: preferable from a normative point of view, because a society that nurtures a variety of ways of life is less alienating (Bourdieu); preferable from an economic point of view, because undifferentiated collective sentiments lack checks and balances, provoking herding and other excesses (Schumpeter, but see also Dorn 2014b).

We now come to 'so what, right now?' part of this chapter, which unfortunately is rather short, albeit for good reason. As an old Irish saying has it, when asked for best route forward, the reply may be given: "Well I would not start from here". Nevertheless, some remarks can be addressed to the policy and academic spheres.

As for policy action in the period when crisis has manifested itself, two main points can be made. First, vigorous support should be given to important policy initiatives aiming at an end to TBTF – Too Big To Fail, the doctrine that the international, regional and national financial infrastructures are so vital that they must be preserved at whatever cost to other interests. In principle, all policy actors (even banks, curiously) today declare themselves in favour of an end to TBTF, and legislation to that effect exists in many countries and is being developed for the EU. However there remain doubts as to whether, in practice, regulators might veer on the side of continuing to prop up broken banks, using public money (Dorn 2012). The most notorious example of this occurred in Ireland, where the authorities used money from the public pension fund, following pressure from both the US authorities and the European Central Bank (*ibid*). Only if faced with a real prospect of financial wipe-out will investors in and managers of banks rein in risk in the boom years. Any vacillation by policy makers in the coming months and years would signal doubt and room for manoeuvre by financial entities that can get themselves accepted as being 'systemically important' – a status that might get them to be more closely scrutinised by regulators but, equally, implies that regulators would be all the more reluctant to see them fold. After all, failure of a more closely regulated financial entity would imply regulatory fault.

This brings us to the second closing policy point, the regulators. Recent and contemporary restructuring of financial market regulators in the EU and in the UK might turn out to be worse than a diversion, if the resulting bodies are drawn more closely to the market and away from other interests (Dorn 2014a and b). Whilst this chapter has not been a review of the literature on the development of financial market regulation during the period of the housing bubble, the author can offer the opinion that, whatever the merits of that literature (e.g., Black 2011), in terms of analytical scope and empirical depth, it pales beside the work of Bourdieu. The former merely describes, whilst latter really contextualises regulatory change. To begin to approach tomorrows' policy issues, we need an equivalent rigour.

As for the academy, future work on financial market policy, risk-taking and regulation should continue to bring together disparate thinkers and disciplines. The separation of economics and sociology is part and parcel of the problem of governance of markets. The socio-cultural disciplines that might have supplied policy makers and regulators with cognitive and emotional checks, balances, critiques and alternative agendas have been pushed to the margins. That process must be reversed or transcended, drawing on and attempting to re-unite social and economic thinking.

References

Acharya, V., T. Cooley, M. Richardson, I Walter, Manufacturing tail risk: A perspective on the financial crisis of 2007-09. *Foundations and Trends in Finance*, 2010, *4*: 249-325.

Anderson, J., The Public Utility Commission of Texas: A case of capture or rapture? *Policy Studies Review*, 1982., *1*(3): 484-490.

Bacon, R. and W. Eltis, *Britain's economic problem: Too few producers*, Macmillan, 1976

Bernanke, B. 2004, *The Great moderation. Remarks by Governor Ben S. Bernanke at the meeting of the Eastern Economic Association*, 20 February, Washington DC: Federal Reserve.
http://www.federalreserve.gov/BOARDDOCS/SPEECHES/2004/20040220/default.htm

Black, J., The rise, fall and fate of principles based regulation. In K. Alexander and N. Moloney (eds), *Law reform and financial markets*. Cheltenham, Elgar, 2011

Bourdieu, P., *The social structures of the economy*. Cambridge, Polity, 2005

Bourdieu, P. and L. Wacquant, L. 1999, On the cunning of imperialist reason. *Theory, Culture & Society*, 1999, *16*(1): 41-58

Bourdieu, P., *Distinction: A social critique of the judgment of taste*. London, Routledge, 1984

Bourdieu, P., Cultural reproduction and social reproduction. In R. Brown (ed.), *Knowledge, education and cultural change*. London, Tavistock, 1993

Bourdieu, P., *The state nobility: Elite schools in the field of power*. Translated by Clough, L, Stanford: Stanford University Press, 1996

Bourdieu, P., *The social structures of the economy*. Cambridge, Polity Press, 2005

Bourdieu, P., A. Darbel, J-P River and C. Seibel, *Travail et travaileurs en Algérie*. Pasis, Mouton & Co, 1963

Brierley, P., *The UK Special Resolution Regime for failing banks in an international context*, Financial Stability Paper 5. London, Bank of England, 2009

Buiter, W., E. Rahbari, J. Michels, J.G. Giani, *Global Economics View*, 7 January, London, Citi Investment Research & Analysis, 2011
http://www.nber.org/~wbuiter/DoN.pdf

Bunt, L., M. Harris and S. Westlake, *Schumpeter comes to Whitehall: Cuts and innovation in public services*. Discussion paper, July. London, National Endowment for Science Technology and the Arts, 2010
http://www.nesta.org.uk/library/documents/Schumpeter.pdf

CRESC. 2009, *An alternative report on UK banking reform*. Manchester: Centre for Research on Socio Cultural Change. www.cresc.ac.uk/

Dorn, N., The governance of securities: Ponzi finance, regulatory convergence, credit crunch', *British Journal of Criminology*, 2010, *50*(1): 23-45

Dorn, N. 2012, 'Lehman – lemon: "Too Connected To Fail" as a policy construct'. *Law and Financial Markets Review*, volume 6(4), 2012, pp 271-283

Dorn, N., Connectedness, crisis and the challenge to European democracy: from rapture, through fear, to banalisation of financial markets. In J. Cruz, C. Cardoso, A. Leite and R. Faria, (eds.), *Infrações Económicas e Financeiras: estudos de criminologia e de direito*. Coimbra: Coimbra Editora, February 2014a

Dorn, N., *Democracy and diversity in financial market regulation.* Abingdon, Routledge (GlassHouse Books) 2014b

Economist, The. 2010, Drexel Burnham Lambert's legacy: Stars of the junkyard, 21 October. http://www.economist.com/node/17306419

Engelen, E., I. Ertürk, J. Froud, S. Johal, M. Moran, A. Nilsson and K. Williams, *After the great complaisance.* Oxford University Press, Oxford, 2011

Ertürt, I., J. Froud, S. Johal, A. Leaver, M. Moran and K. Williams, *City state against national settlement: UK economic policy and politics after the financial crisis.* CRESC working paper number 101. Manchester: Centre for Research on Socio-Cultural Change, 2011

Ertürt, I., J. Froud, S. Johal, A. Leaver and K. Williams, 2007, The democratization of finance? Promises, outcomes and conditions. *Review of International Political Economy*, 2007, *14*(4): 553-575

European Commission, *Communication from the Commission to the European Parliament, the Council, the European Economic and Social Committee, the Committee of the Regions and the European Central Bank: an EU Framework for Crisis Management in the Financial Sector*, Brussels, European Commission, 2010 http://ec.europa.eu/internal_market/bank/docs/crisis-management/framework/com2010_579_en.pdf

European Commission, *Technical Details of a Possible EU Framework for Bank Recovery and Resolution: DG Internal Market and Services Working Document*, Brussels, European Commission, 2011 http://ec.europa.eu/internal_market/consultations/docs/2011/crisis_management/consultation_paper_en.pdf

Ferran, E., The break-up of the financial services authority. *Oxford Journal of Legal Studies*, 2011, *31*(3): 455-480

Financial Times, 25 September 2013, Financial stability watchdog alert to risk posed by UK housing bubble. http://www.ft.com/cms/s/0/7a867732-25c3-11e3-aee8-00144feab7de.html

Foster, R. and S. Kaplan, *Creative disruption.* New York, Knopf Doubleday, 2001

Gilson, R. and R. Kraakman, Takeovers in the boardroom: Burke versus Schumpeter', *Business Lawyer*, 2005, *60*(4): 1419-1434

Goldstein, M. and N. Véron, *Too big to fail: the transatlantic debate: working paper 11-2*, January 2011. Peterson Institute for International Economics, Washington. http://www.iie.com/publications/wp/wp11-2.pdf

Hall, S., Financialised elites and the changing nature of finance capitalism: Investment bankers in London's financial district. *Competition and Change*, 2009, *13*(2): 173-189

Hellwig, M., *Systemic risk in the financial sector: An analysis of the subprime-mortgage financial crisis*. MPI Collective Goods Preprint Number 2008/43. Bonn, Max Planck Institute for Research on Collective Goods, 2008 http://www.coll.mpg.de/pdf_dat/2008_43online.pdf

HM Treasury, *A new approach to financial regulation: Summary of consultation responses*. Document PU1100, November: 29 2010, HM Treasury. London. http://www.hm-treasury.gov.uk/d/summaryofcondocresponses241110.pdf

HM Treasury, *A new approach to financial regulation: the blueprint for reform* (413 pages including draft legislation), Cm 8083, June 2011. London, HM Treasury. http://www.hm-treasury.gov.uk/d/consult_finreg__new_approach_blueprint.pdf

House of Commons Treasury Committee, *The run on the Rock, Fifth Report of Session 2007-08*, volume I (report, together with formal minutes), HC 56-I, 24 January. London, The Stationery Office, 2008a. http://www.publications.parliament.uk/pa/cm200708/cmselect/cmtreasy/56/56i.pdf

House of Commons Treasury Committee, *The Run on the Rock: Government Response to the Committee's Fifth Report of Session 2007–08*, HC 918. London, The Stationery Office, 2008b http://www.publications.parliament.uk/pa/cm200708/cmselect/cmtreasy/918/918.pdf

House of Commons Treasury Committee. 2011, *Financial Regulation: a preliminary consideration of the Government's proposals*, Seventh Report of Session 2010–11, HC 430–I, 3 February. London, Stationary Office. http://www.publications.parliament.uk/pa/cm201011/cmselect/cmtreasy/430/430i.pdf

Macartney, H., Disagreeing to agree: Financial crisis management within the "Logic of No Alternative", *Politics*, 2009, 29(2): 111–120

Lastra, R.. Northern Rock, UK bank insolvency and cross-border bank insolvency. *Journal of Banking Regulation*, 2008, *9*, 165-186

Leathers, C. and P. Raines, The Schumpeterian role of financial innovations in the New Economy's business cycle. *Cambridge Journal of Economics*, 2004, *38*(5): 667-681

Minsky, H., The financial instability hypothesis. In F. Stilwell and G. Argyrous, (eds.), *Economics as a social science: readings in political economy*: 201-203. North Melbourne, Pluto Press, 2003

Moran, M., The company of strangers: Defending the power of business in Britain, 1975-2005. *New Political Economy*, 2006, *11*(4): 453-477

Osborne, G., *Budget statement by the Chancellor of the Exchequer, the Rt Hon George Osborne MP*. London, HM Treasury, 2010
http://www.hm-treasury.gov.uk/junebudget_speech.htm

Partnoy, F., *Enron and the Use of Derivatives: Testimony before the Senate Committee on Governmental Affairs*, Testimony 02-3, March 2002. Washington DC: AEI-Brookings Joint Center for Regulatory Studies
http://regulation2point0.org/wp-content/uploads/downloads/2010/04/testimony_02_03.pdf

Picciotto, S. and J. Haines, Regulating global financial markets. *Journal of Law & Society*, 1999, *26*: 351–68

Prasad, M., *The politics of free markets: The rise of Neoliberal Economic Policies in Britain, France, Germany, and the United States*. Chicago, University of Chicago Press, 2006

Raghuram G. and L. Zingales, *Saving capitalism from the capitalists: Unleashing the power of financial markets to create wealth and spread opportunity*. Princeton, Princeton University Press, 2004

Schumpeter, J., *Business cycles: A theoretical, historical, and statistical analysis of the capitalist process*. 1st edition. New York and London, McGraw-Hill, 1939

Schumpeter, J., *Capitalism, socialism and democracy*. New York: Harper Torchbooks, 1950

Silva, Y., The credit crisis of 2008, section XII: the "Too Big to Fail" doctrine and the credit crisis. *Developments In Banking and Financial Law*, 2010, *28*: 115-131

Smith, M., From big government to big society: Changing the state-society balance. *Parliamentary Affairs*, 2010, *63*(4): 818-833

Swedberg, R. 2002, The economic sociology of capitalism: Weber and Schumpeter', *Journal of Classical Sociology*, 2(3): 227-255.

Tsingou, E., Regulatory reactions to the credit crisis: Analysing a policy community under stress. In: E. Helleiner, S. Pagliari and H. Zimmermann (eds.), *Global finance in crisis: The politics of international regulatory change*: 21-36. London, Routledge, 2010

14W37264/ T12/ 9789462401280